Fäther,
   MERRY XMAS!
   love Always,
yr oldest daughter
  - ☆ MARY LOVENE ☆ -

Live Albom IV

BY MITCH ALBOM

Detroit Free Press

CREDITS

Editor: Bob Ellis

Art direction: Wayne Kamidoi

Copy editing: Ken Kraemer, Tom Panzenhagen and the Free Press sports copy desk.

Cover photography: Steven R. Nickerson

Cover illustration: Marty Westman

Chapter illustrations and back cover: Jef Mallett

Technical assistance: Andrew J. Hartley

Coordinators: Dave Robinson and Gene Myers

Printed in USA on recycled paper

Detroit Free Press Inc. 1995
321 W. Lafayette Blvd.
Detroit, Michigan 48226

ISBN 0-937247-66-9

The columns in this book would not be possible without the exceptional help of the Detroit Free Press sports staff. Each person, at one point or another, has had to put up with something annoying about me. I thank them collectively for their patience, good humor and support.

I also wish to especially thank:

Bob Ellis, Wayne Kamidoi, Ken Kraemer, A.J. Hartley, Tom Panzenhagen and Christie Innes Attard.

Also, Jef Mallett for his brilliant cartoons and designing mind.

Steve Nickerson, whose amazing photography is exceeded only by his warped sense of humor.

Gene Myers, Dave Robinson, Bob McGruder, Heath Meriwether and Neal Shine, the chain of command that makes my job possible.

Chris Kucharski, and everyone in the library.

Terry Hamlin, for the typewriter.

Kerri Alexander, for everything.

Ken Droz, Mike Stone.

Janine.

And Elvis, who says, "Woof."

*"To Morrie Schwartz,
who in the days before his death,
opened my eyes to life."*

FOREWORD

I MET MITCH ALBOM at the 1994 Winter Olympics in Lillehammer, Norway. Mitch was writing columns for the Detroit Free Press; I was competing in the luge event.

No, really, I was also writing columns, and so Mitch and I quickly formed the kind of bond that forms between two guys who are writing columns in a country that has the same basic climate as Pluto. We spent many hours sharing journalistic insights, such as: "It's cold." And: "It is really cold."

But it was not his journalistic insights — although they are, of course, extremely insightful — that drew me to Mitch Albom. What drew me to Mitch was something that happened one night when I returned to the press center after watching an Olympic event, which as I recall was the finals of the Large Men Wearing Skates Throwing Tiny Women Wearing Skates As Far As Possible. It was around midnight, and Mitch was in the lounge area, tinkling on a small upright piano.* I immediately noticed that he was playing rock songs from the '50s and '60s, what some people call "classic oldies," and what my son calls "dead people music."

I happen to love classic oldies, so I grabbed a beer and strolled over to the piano, and I discovered, to my great happiness, that Mitch could play every song I could think of. He could even play and sing harmony, which meant we were able to perform a semi-flawless version of "What's Your Name?" by Don and Juan. I don't remember which one of us was Don and which one was Juan; all I knew was, it felt good belting it out.

And here's the amazing part: When we started singing, there were only a few journalists in the lounge; but by 1 a.m., after we'd been at it for more than an hour, I looked around and saw that there were no journalists in the lounge. They had elected to go outside and risk death by freezing, rather than listen to us.

But journalists were not the only people who occupied the press center. There were also Norwegian staff people, and they liked us. They liked us a lot.

---

* Insert your own "tinkling on a piano" joke here.

Norway is not, historically, a hotbed of homegrown rock talent. It is more of a hotbed of reindeer. So to the Norwegians, Mitch and I actually sounded like the real thing, a pair of get-down, get-funky, happening dudes. We were by far the hottest rock act in the entire press center.

And so the Norwegians gathered around us, clapping their hands as rhythmically as they could, calling out requests, and actually applauding us at the end of songs. The high point for me came near the very end, when we performed "Land of 1,000 Dances," and, on the chorus, we shouted out, "Come on, Norwegians! Join in!" and the Norwegians — I will never forget this — raised their voices with ours, a multicultural chorus screaming:

> I said a na, na na na na
> Na na na na na na na na na na
> Na na na na

Talk about your great moments in international understanding.

A few months after that, I asked Mitch to sit in with a rock band I belong to, called the Rock Bottom Remainders, consisting mostly of authors, including Roy Blount Jr., Matt Groening, Stephen King, Dave Marsh, Ridley Pearson, Joel Selvin and Amy Tan. Musically, we suck. But we have a lot of fun, and Mitch has become a regular with us, astounding crowds with his Elvis impersonation.

My point is that when you read this book, you're not just reading the work of an award-winning, nationally acclaimed sports columnist. You're also reading the words of a guy who knows all the chords to "Cool Jerk" and is willing to get up in front of a crowd and sing "Blue Suede Shoes" with approximately three pounds of Dippity-Do in his hair.

You know that a guy like that is going to write a good book, right?

Dave Barry
Miami, September 1995

TABLE OF CONTENTS

1995

SECRET WORLD SERIES

COMMENT

Smiley face is taken from us

August 20, 1992

S HE WAS A MEMBER of the supporting cast, one of those special people who keeps the stars in the sky, yet still gets tagged with a two-word introduction: "His brother, Sam." Or, "His daughter, Janice." Or, "His wife, Millie."

It shouldn't take her death to bring Millie Schembechler, wife of Bo, to the front of the sentence. But so be it. She was never interested in top billing. She was more concerned with how your family was doing, or if the couch was comfortable and the food was OK. She could invite you in with a smile, she could lecture you in motherly tones even though she was not your mother. She could do something few mortals can do: tell her husband he was wrong.

Try that sometime.

She died yesterday of cancer on a beautiful summer afternoon, the kind of day she would have loved. And while it didn't stir the headlines of a Rose Bowl win, or a Tigers sale, it did send a ripple of pain through those who knew her.

It sent a ripple through me. If today be the day for telling stories about Millie Schembechler, here is the best one I know: I was working on a book with her famous husband, and the time came for him to read the first-draft chapters. As I watched anxiously, he looked them over, grunting "umm … umm-hmm." Finally, he nodded approval. Then he lowered his reading glasses and looked me dead on.

"Of course, we have to see what Millie thinks."

Thus did Millie Schembechler become my "editor." And although the book was in Bo's words, each chapter came back with these suggestions:

On the top left side, in red pencil, she drew a frowning face. In this category went the "naughty" words Bo had used.

Atop the right side, she drew a smiling face. And under it, she wrote her substitutions:

"Damn" became "darn." "Son of a bitch" became "son of a gun."

Frowning face to smiley face.

I was being edited by cartoon.

A ND YET, IF YOU KNEW Millie, you had to laugh, because if she could have slapped a happy face over every sad one in the world, she would have done it. Cover asphalt with daffodils. Fill silence with music. Make things better.

People who have seen both sides can do that. Millie saw both sides. She was born poor, in rural Mississippi, part of a large family that, according to a family friend, "lived in a run-down place with a dirt floor." Millie never forgot that. She never looked down at people. Once, working as a nurse in Buffalo in the early '60s, a black man entered the hospital, needing emergency treatment. He was ignored because of his color. Millie informed the doctors. She, too, was ignored.

So she walked out and tended to the man herself. It was the right thing to do.

That was her way. Those of you who knew her only as the first lady of Michigan football for 20 years really didn't know her. Millie was a healer, an organizer, a charity addict, and, above all, a mother. She had been raising three sons on her own before Bo arrived on a blind date in the summer of 1968. Before she would marry him, she asked their OK.

Even in her last sickly days, she retained that indomitable knack of motherhood. A friend, hoping to cheer her up, sent videotapes of happier times, when Millie was healthy, attending functions with famous people, beaming that perfect smile.

Not long after, the friend received a note. The handwriting was scratchy: "Thank you for the videos. They will be precious mementos for the kids should this ugly cancer do me in."

IT DID HER IN, FINALLY. No one will ever know the long battle Millie, 63, fought with this disease, or the hours her husband spent urging her back to health, searching for doctors, fighting the inevitable the way he once fought a fourth-quarter clock.

Bo would leave Tiger Stadium early, go home and tend to his wife, week after week, month after month. When she seemed to have the strength, he would cajole her downstairs, and get her on the stationary bicycle.

"I got her to go five minutes today," he told me once. "Tomorrow, we start with the weights."

It broke your heart. Here was this ex-football coach, trying to keep his wife alive by doing the one thing he knew best: work out, get in shape, get stronger than your opponent.

But cancer is not sports; when it wants you, it takes you. And so, a few weeks ago, on the day he was fired as Tigers president, Bo passed his 24th wedding anniversary alone with his ailing wife. They had take-out food.

And today, no one can feel the emptiness inside the Schembechler house. No one can hurt the way her four sons, Chip, Geoff, Matt and Shemy, are hurting. No one can console the old coach.

The Academy Awards have something called Best Supporting Actress, and if life gave out such statuettes, Millie would have a few. But to those who knew her, she deserved marquee billing. So, in the last mention, maybe we should skip the two-word intro and move her to the front of the sentence:

Millie Schembechler, whose husband and children loved her dearly, said good-bye yesterday, leaving us in the sunshine, a happy face over the clouds, one last edit on the way to heaven. She will be missed. She will be missed.

Final word on Salley: Good-bye
September 9, 1992

JOHN SALLEY WILL BE MISSED most by people like me, that is, people who talked to him for a living. Salley could talk. From his car, from a phone in his coat pocket, after a loss, after a playoff elimination, in the mornings, in the shower, in the middle of the night. Didn't matter. You could call him — his phone number, considering his status in this town, was as easy to get as a lottery ticket — and when you said hello and he recognized you, his voice would jump an octave — "YO! WHASSSUP!" — and he was on his way, the words tumbling out of him, your fingers straining to keep up.

So words were never a problem for Salley in Detroit. Basketball was. Money was. Swallowing his pride under the Isiah Thomas-run, Chuck Daly-dictated Pistons, that was a problem. He never really found his place in that Palace locker room. He was drafted high out of college — a full round ahead of Dennis Rodman — but his development in six seasons here was stunted, like a tree that grows branches but no leaves. Was he a starter? Was he a bench player? Was he a success? Was he a disappointment? Did the Pistons need him? Could they do without him?

I guess they answered that last one.

"I told my girlfriend I'm scared, and she said, 'What are you scared for — you got everything you wanted,' " Salley said after news of the trade sending him to Miami for a first-round draft pick and rookie forward Isaiah Morris was released Tuesday night. "And she's right. I get to be a real NBA player now. I get to be a leader. I get to be recognized as a starter, not just someone who was once on a championship team."

And we get a championship team that we barely recognize anymore.

This trade makes sense if you understand the big picture: That it's not over yet. I don't believe the Pistons dealt Salley to wind up with a draft pick and Morris, whom they really don't need. No. I think more moves are coming, for Dennis Rodman to get his walking papers, and maybe an effort to bring in Stanley Roberts from Orlando.

WHY THE WHOLESALE CHANGES? Well, first of all, if we're talking Pistons, we're talking Isiah Thomas, the General, and I can only assume he wants all of this and gave it his blessing, otherwise, nothing gets done with this team. I half-expect he was on the phone with Miami people, helping close the deal. Also, remember, you have a new coach in town, Ron Rothstein, who wants his own guys, guys who won't moan in the middle of January about how

"Chuck Daly never made us do that." Rodman has already said he misses Daly so much he doesn't want to play here. He all but wrote his boarding pass with that one.

Salley, meanwhile, was becoming an expensive burden. A free agent at the end of this season, he wanted to renegotiate a still-wet-ink contract. And some felt it was already too generous. Critics question Salley's toughness, say he can't finish the break, or box out, that he spends more time on party life than basketball. Salley is nonplussed. He looks at his age, 28, his height, about 7-feet, and says, "Pay me."

And Miami will.

I do not know how great a ballplayer Salley could have been if he only had a mind for the court. You accept Salley as a whole package, a Brooklyn kid who used to go door-to-door for Jehovah's Witnesses and learned early that unless you want that door slammed, you'd better make 'em smile. "I'm an entertainer who happens to play basketball," he will tell you.

He was always honest.

And funny. I once saw him take the stage in a New York City comedy club and crack up the room:

SALLEY: "You hear Michael Jordan's getting married? (Girl moans.) Oh, yeah, like you had a chance."

I HAVE SEEN HIM ENTERTAIN a row full of hockey fans at Joe Louis Arena just by asking questions about the game. ("Those guys jump off the bench and don't have to check in or nothing?") I have seen him hold little kids spellbound, and secretaries and auto mechanics. I have seen him do more charity work than pretty much anybody else in this town and, best of all, he didn't insist on sticking his name on it, like some athletes. With his departure, the DETROIT Pistons lose the only player they have who actually lives in the city. That says something.

"Hey, I'm not moving," Salley said. "I'll be back in the summers. And my music studio is going good here, and so's the record company. ... "

Same old Salley. Still juggling. In a way, I'm gonna miss that. He is not the first championship player to leave Detroit. Rick Mahorn, James Edwards, Vinnie Johnson, all gone, to name a few. But Salley was drafted into this franchise, he grew up as the team grew up, and he became its emotional release: first to laugh, first to cry.

He won't be the last to go. You look at what's left of the "old" Pistons: Thomas, who wants to be king; Rodman, who wants out; Mark Aguirre, whom they would like to ship out; Joe Dumars, who keeps quiet; Bill Laimbeer, who creaks when he walks.

And there goes John Salley, with his worldful of words. About the only noise in Pistonland now is the sound of the roster being snipped apart, and our whispered prayers that these people know what they're doing.

Funny Girl, Funny Guy

September 10, 1992

NEW YORK — You know what I always say.
People. People who need people. They're the luckiest people in the world.

So I had to come to the Big Apple to check out this rumor about two lucky people who have been — and you're not going to believe this — romantically linked at the U.S. Open.

Andre Agassi and . . . Barbra Streisand.

Go ahead, take a Maalox. I'll wait.

It was last weekend that Barbra was first spotted in the stands during one of Andre's matches. Just a coincidence? I thought so. Then she showed up for his match Monday night and was seen cheering wildly on Andre's manly ground strokes. Then a USA Network camera found her seat, and the 50-year-old Streisand, who almost never gives interviews, began to gush. On cable, no less.

"Andre called me after he saw 'Prince of Tides.' He's very sweet, and he was moved by the movie. And we stayed on the phone for two hours — and found we had a lot in common."

I'm thinking, what, hair dye?

"He's very, very intelligent — very, very sensitive — very evolved, more than his linear years. He's an extraordinary human being."

Are we talking about the same guy here? Andre Agassi and Barbra Streisand? What's next? Michael Chang and Bea Arthur?

Also: What is a linear year?

NOW, WE SHOULD MENTION that the Open has been an odd matchmaker before. Remember last year, when Monica Seles — who was what, 9 years old? — rushed out to sit with actor Alec Baldwin? And a few years ago, teen queen Jennifer Capriati shared box seats with Mr. Tom Cruise.

So there is something about this stadium. Maybe it's the romantic rumble of those low-flying planes coming into LaGuardia. But still. Andre Agassi and … Barbra Streisand?

"What moves you about Andre?" Babs was asked.

"He plays like a Zen Master. It's very in the moment. And in fact, very concentrated, very focused, but very much aware of what's happening."

You get the feeling Barbra has been shopping in those New Age bookstores again?

I have heard Andre described with many words over the years. Those words include "petulant," "spoiled" and "phony." Lately they include "calmer," "nicer" and "still phony." I have never heard "Zen Master." That's a new one.

Even Agassi said, "I'll have to talk to Barbra about that."

Barbra wasn't around for last night's 6-3, 6-7 (6-8), 6-1, 6-4 loss to Jim Courier, which might be why the Zen Master blew a gasket. After flopping a point, Andre threw his racket and the umpire gave Agassi a warning. Andre responded by glaring, covering his mouth with a towel and screaming, "Bleep you!" into it three times.

The Zen Master speaks.

But back to Funny Girl and Funny Guy. Andre admits he and Barbra enjoy each other's company, although he says, "She is her own woman." That's nice. Respect. You should show that to someone older than your mother.

Now, I admit, it is hard to imagine these two sharing many activities together, except blow-drying. But maybe Barbra is teaching him some of her songs from "Funny Girl." Like: *I'm the greatest star, I am by far ...*

And Andre can play the Omar Sharif role. True, Omar had more hair. And no earring. But it might work. Or maybe Streisand is helping Andre with his acting. After all, when he won Wimbledon this summer, he fell to the grass, kissed it, then began to get up — until he saw his coach (or Zen Master) Nick Bollettieri, waving at him to "Stay down!" so the cameras could capture the moment longer.

Hey. Image is everything. "Andre is kind," Streisand said. "He's a kind human being ... and that just amazes me."

Amazes me, too. I always thought he was a ditz.

NOW. I WANT TO THINK THIS is all very innocent, just an aging singer with a fond interest in tennis. Agassi has a girlfriend, who attended his match last night. I want to believe in that. I don't want to believe these stories of Andre sneaking over to Streisand's apartment late at night. I thought her falling for Kris Kristofferson was bad, and that was just a movie.

But you know how it is in New York. They just got done chewing up Woody Allen. They need new material. So it's Barbra and Andre. Her voice, his ponytail. Her fingernails, his belly button. Think of the possibilities.

"(Barbra) obviously has a lot of respect for me on a personal level," Andre admitted, "and now it is overflowing into the professional level. That is the ultimate compliment."

And I thought the ultimate compliment was, "Hey, you lose weight?"

But what do I know? I came to see some tennis. I got the National Enquirer. Either Barbra-Andre shows the power of sports, or the power of movies. Or the boredom that is setting into New York.

Whatever. It is hard to believe all this began with the simple viewing of a film. I mean, imagine if Andre had watched "Yentl" instead of "Prince of Tides?"

He might be a rabbi by now.

Real life, which passed Rodman by
November 11, 1992

THERE ARE NO BASKETBALLS here, no cheering fans, only the hard, cold smell of factory life. Instead of applause we have the whirring of air tools. Instead of mink coats we have drab cotton overalls. The light is by fluorescent bulb, the color is concrete gray. Wherever you walk, you hear the chug and clang of the assembly line.

They are making trucks here. This is a local Ford assembly plant. Dennis Rodman always calls himself "a regular guy, like everyone else," so I figured I'd go to where regular guys work for a living and see how they felt about Dennis' behavior lately.

Meet Louis. He is a spray painter. Like Rodman, he went through a divorce a little while ago. One night, he learned his ex-wife had taken off with some guy for a quick fling in New Orleans — and left his kids with a friend.

The kids phoned Louis. "We want you, Daddy!" They were crying. Louis was distraught. Under the court ruling, he couldn't get them, even though they were staying with a woman he didn't know.

He took their tears to bed that night.

And at 4 a.m., he got up and went to work.

"You think I felt like working that day?" Louis says. "Hell, no. It was damn hard to concentrate, but I had to. If I didn't, I couldn't pay their child support."

Wouldn't your employer let you take a few days or weeks off, like Rodman's did?

"Are you kidding?"

Hmm.

MEET BRIAN. HE'S A UAW committeeman. Been with Ford more than 20 years. Like Rodman, he suffered through a divorce. Like Rodman, he was unable to see his young daughter. Unlike Rodman, Brian didn't make $2.35 million a year.

Instead, he would come home some weeks with a paycheck of less than $20, after child support and bills. Never mind that his ex-wife was living in his old house with a new man. Never mind that she slammed the door on Brian when he went to visit the kids, and that he suffered a year and a half without seeing his daughter before a court intervened.

Never mind that Brian had to fix cars at night just to make enough money to eat. Using his far-too-extended credit cards, he bought Christmas presents for his little girl one year, but her mother made her call and say she didn't want them.

"That was the lowest moment," Brian says.

But next day, 6 a.m., he went to work.

"I had no choice. Hey, I love basketball, but Dennis Rodman doesn't know what problems are until he comes home with a $20 paycheck."

Wouldn't your company understand if you put out half an effort or walked out after a few minutes as Rodman has done with the Pistons?

"Yeah, right."

Hmm.

Meet another Louis, 46. He's in the sealer deck. As we speak, he is applying sealant with a gun, running it along the interior of a truck frame. He can't stop to talk, so he speaks while he works.

"Not too long ago, I lost my brother. He died of cancer. They only gave me two days off. Two days. I thought I had at least three coming to me. I had to fly to California to get my mother, bring her in. I wound up taking extra days off with no pay because it wasn't enough time, you know? Two days, man."

Like Rodman — who misses coach Chuck Daly — Louis misses his brother. He misses the trips they would take, the talks they would have.

For nearly 10 months, Louis would finish his shift at the Ford plant and go directly to a hospital. One day, Louis watched in horror as they hooked his brother to a machine to help him breathe. He knew it was the end. He felt helpless. He felt terrible.

Next day, 4 a.m., he went to work. "By the way," Louis adds, "I'm divorced, too. Never missed a day for it. But I'll tell you what: Every day I had to go to court, they didn't pay me a dime. I lost all my wages."

RODMAN SPENT MOST OF THE summer thinking about his life. Most of the fall now, too. He missed nearly all of Pistons training camp without as much as a phone call to explain, yet he was only lightly fined and welcomed back when he returned.

In the two games he has played, he seems to drift in and out of concentration. On Monday, he showed up late for practice, stretched, put some ice on his knees, then abruptly walked out. He says basketball "isn't fun anymore" and that his mind is on his daughter and ex-wife. Some reports say he is only acting this way to get himself traded.

He still has his job today. Dave would not be so lucky. He is an inspector at the plant. One day he came home to find his entire home emptied out, his kids gone, his clothes thrown in the middle of the floor. Where was his wife? Where were the kids? His world was upside down. Next day, 6 a.m. ...

You get the picture. Everyone has problems. Everyone has distractions. But there's an expression here on the assembly line: "If you can't hack it, grab your jacket." It is harsh. It is cold. And for 99 percent of the world, it is very, very real.

Dennis Rodman — the regular guy — might keep it in mind.

Amid scum, Holyfield's dignity

November 15, 1992

H E SAT AGAINST A DRESSING-ROOM WALL, his eyes puffed, his scar tissue soft and swollen. His legs were elevated, and his head was slumped, and it seemed as if lifting his arms was out of the question. This is often the way boxers look in the drained moments after losing it all, their title, their championship, their belts, their fame. Like you could leave them there to rot. This was Evander Holyfield two nights ago.

A shame. I long ago stopped caring about boxing. Too much slime. Too many pretenders. And yet, I felt empty and sad when Holyfield lost to young loudmouth Riddick Bowe in that 12-round heavyweight championship in Las Vegas, a fight that pushed both men to the front porch of hell. Holyfield, three inches smaller and 30 pounds lighter, took an enormous beating, especially in a 10th round that ranks with the most furious in recent memory. He should have hit the canvas several times, taking hooks and uppercuts from Bowe's powerful, lineman-like form. At one point, the champ was so dazed by punches that he half-turned his back to the challenger, who quickly lowered the boom to the backside of his head. Holyfield wobbled, hung on the ropes, he was over, finished.

But he would not go down.

There are moments that define a boxer, and in that moment, Holyfield, woozy and blurred, yet still commanding his legs to move, his arms to box, somehow returning from the singing of angels to throw his own punches, not only throw them but land them, and stun the kid one last time — where was he getting the strength to do this? — in that moment we learned Holyfield was indeed a champion, with a champion's heart.

We may never have known this in the two years and 19 days he held the title.

We had three minutes to appreciate it.

And his reign was over.

T HERE GOES THE GENTLEMAN CHAMPION. People complained about Holyfield being "too boring," but these people think boxing should be one promoter with electrified hair yelling at another promoter wearing a sports coat with no shirt underneath — or one boxer with a neck full of gold chains taunting another boxer in a sequined jumpsuit.

You want that? You can have it. I liked Holyfield. I never heard him swear at anyone. Never heard him harass a challenger by saying, "I'm gonna make you kiss me like a woman," as Mike Tyson once did. I never read about Holyfield arrested with his car wrapped around a telephone pole. Never saw him leap across a craps table to throw a punch.

He didn't smoke. He didn't do drugs. He never insulted a former champion by saying, "He couldn't carry my jockstrap." (Do you remember when Larry Holmes said that about Rocky Marciano?)

Holyfield never got fat. He looked like an athlete should, ready to go, all the time. He talked about family and God. He was in church every Sunday, even in Reno, Nev., and I didn't know that was possible. He shrugged and looked away when others tried to taunt him. And while his list of opponents during his championship reign wasn't exactly a who's who of great heavyweights (hey, Tyson was in jail), they were pretty much all he had. He fought them, he never came out of shape, flabby or disinterested. He gave you a performance. He took the sport seriously.

Aren't those the things you want in a champion? Or do you want this: Bowe, just minutes after winning the crown, grabbing the microphone and screaming at his critics, "YOU NEVER SHOULDA DOUBTED ME!" Then challenging the next contender, Lennox Lewis, to "knock me down right now, come on, knock me down!"

Some folks think this is great stuff. They probably like Wrestlemania. Others say this hearkens the tradition of Muhammad Ali. Come on. When will boxers stop trying to imitate the man? Ali was a black champion at a time of racial upheaval. When he shouted, he shook our consciousness.

These guys today just make noise.

SO MAYBE WITH BOWE we have poems and boasts and sound bites. And maybe the soap-opera lovers can get back into the heavyweight scene.

Me? I'm gonna miss Holyfield. He gave an honest glaze to a slab of a sport that one day, when we come to our senses, will be abolished. In the meantime, he treated it with respect. And when he was dethroned — and, he says, retired — he said only this of his challenger: "I wanted it, but he wanted it more. He fought a great fight. I take off my hat to him."

He said this without the strength to take a hat off a shelf. He said this with his eyes puffed to the point of closing. He said this with his shoulders dead, his head aching and his gutsiest fight, the fight that proved his mettle, just minutes behind him.

You know what he showed us? Honor. I, for one, am going to miss that from the loser, and no longer champion, Evander Holyfield.

A song in their hearts
December 20, 1992

I LOOK OUT MY DOOR. Here they are again. Those Christmas carolers, from the sports world, making their own kind of music …

Baseball owners (to "Frosty, The Snowman"):
Marge Schott, the owner,
got in trouble with her mouth
'cause she made these cracks
'bout Jews and blacks.
She's not even from the South!

Marge Schott, the owner,
now she's hiding with her pups,
and as she sits, eating Kibbles'N Bits,
boy are we glad it's not us.

It must have been those racial slurs
that sent her to her doom.
Lord knows we'd never say such things
… with a microphone in the room.

Marge Schott, the owner,
was a bossy, loud, old twit.
But with dogs in charge, we all knew Marge
would one day step in …

Wayne Fontes (to "The Christmas Song"):
Chestnuts roasting on an open fire,
Linemen dropping every dawn.
Quarterback woes, and Jerry is mad
and Willie says his helmet's gone.
Fans think we're a yawn,
I'm offering this simple phrase,
For a team that's missing what it needs.
As we go on, losing east, losing west,
Glad my contract's … guaranteed.

Riddick Bowe (to "Jingle Bells"):
Jingle Bells, this belt smells,
throw it in the trash.
Who needs golden waistbands
when I can have the cash?

Jingle Bells, Foreman sells,
He'll be my next foe.
I'd fight Katherine Hepburn
if I could make some dough.

**Rodney Peete, Erik Kramer, Andre Ware
(to "The Little Drummer Boy"):**
I am the quarterback, yes, I am the one.
No, Rodney, you're a hack, and I am the one.
Oh, Andre, take a nap, I, Erik, have come.
You both are maniacs, I, Rodney, can run.
Andre's the one! Erik's the one!
We are all quarterbacks and when it is done,
I-I-I am the one.

Mike Ditka (to "Santa Claus is Coming to Town"):
You better watch out, you better not pry.
You better not ask, I'll chew on your eye.
Iron Mike is coming to town.

I'll swallow your camcorder,
I'll bite my quarterback's head.
And if you ask me why, I think
I may kill you instead, so,

You better watch out, you better unload,
any sec now, I'm bound to explode.
Iron Mike is coming to town.

Andre Agassi & Barbra Streisand (to "I'll be Home for Christmas"):
I'll be home for Christmas,
You can touch my hair.
Oh, Andre, the things you say,
They really show you care.

Blow me dry for Christmas,
Use mousse, Babs, it never fails.
Coming, my Zen Master!
Just let me dry my nails.

Eric Lindros (to "Winter Wonderland"):
Goalie's scared, see him shakin'?
Watch me check, now you're achin',
I'm 19 years old, my sink's made of gold,
skating in a hockey wonderland.

See me score, on the Rooskies,
Or in the bar, spittin' brewskies,
It's so much more fun
than my junior prom,
Skating in a hockey wonderland.

Barry Bonds (to "Sleigh Ride"):
Just hear my bank vault jingling,
ring-ting-tingling, too.
Come on it's lovely weather
to blow a million or two.

Will I hit, will I hit, will I hit?
Who cares? Just look at those stares,
I'm raking in mega-dough that's rare.

Will we win, will we win, will we win?
Who knows? It's only a show.
And if we lose, here's my excuse,
It's the manager's fault, you know —
My cheeks are nice and rosy and comfy-cozy am I,
Inside my own Jacuzzi with my new Uzi, I-I.

Let Willie keep his number,
and tell the Pirates: Screw you.
Come on it's lovely weather
to blow a million or two.

Michael Jordan (to "Silent Night"):
Silent Night, Nike night,
I am King, I am Flight.

Won two championships, rings in the box.
Won the Olympics, did not wear Reeboks.

Life would really be fine,
'cept I'm bored and I'm 29.

One bullet at a time

December 24, 1992

T HE INSTRUCTIONS ARE TAPED to the wall above his bed. They show diagrams of hands and feet, with arrows pointing left and right. His mother pulls on his limp right arm, forward and backward, forward and backward, as if rowing a boat.

"He couldn't move nothing at first," she says. "Now he can do some on his own. Show him, Damon."

The young man in the blue pajamas turns his head and squints. He is nearly blind now. The room is dark, the air stale, the one window closed. The rails along his single bed keep him from falling out. On the wall above him are small cut-out magazine photos of basketball players, including Steve Smith, his favorite. Once, he took a green T-shirt and drew Smith's number on it with a pen and wore that shirt to the courts. This was back when he could still see the ball and a small ray of hope inside it.

Now he looks at his arm and concentrates. It does nothing at first. Then, finally, it jerks in the air as if yanked by a puppeteer's string. It stays up for one second, two seconds. Damon Bailes, the most tragic currency in the city of Detroit, a young black male with a bullet hole in his head, smiles briefly, then lets go.

His arm drops, dead as air.

W E GOT NEXT!" It was a warm May night and the basketball game was moving up and down the asphalt.

"We got next!" The kids were sweating as they waited. They dribbled in place. Damon, whose nickname was "Smooth," looked around. He had never been to this court before, outside old Bentley High in Livonia. He and four friends, Lawrence Poole, Torrin Cottrell, Kevin Franklin and Terrill Malone, had started the afternoon in the city, but they lost their first game, and the line was too long to wait for another. There are not enough playable courts in Detroit. And far too many kids with time on their hands.

Poole said he knew a place in the suburbs where the competition was pretty good. So they got in the car and drove to Livonia. Five black kids in a Ford Escort. They were not there long before a police car stopped them.

"Your plates are expired," the officer said. When he ran their names through the computer, one of them, Kevin Franklin, was shown as delinquent on child-support payments. He was arrested and taken to jail.

"Let's just go home," Torrin said.

They almost did. But Damon wanted to play ball, and Poole did, too. So now they stood under the floodlights at Bentley, four city kids, waiting for the suburban rims.

"Check the guy in the red shorts," Poole said to Damon as they watched the game.

"Uh-huh."

"There go the shorts we want, the long kind."

"Yeah, they nice. We should buy some of those."

That was it, they claim. Nothing more. The guy in the red shorts, Tyrone Swint, also from Detroit, might have seen them looking and pointing. He would later tell police he thought Damon was "a guy who jumped me" at a Detroit nightclub. Whatever. Something set him off.

And he had a gun.

"Bring the car around," he told a friend.

"What for?"

"We might have a fight."

The suburbs were about to meet the city.

L ET'S PLAY," TORRIN SAID, and he bounced an inbounds pass. They ran up and down the court several times. Damon, a 6-foot-2, baby-faced guard who had dropped out of high school but starred in church leagues and was hoping to get to a small college if he could pass his equivalency exams, tossed in a couple of baskets. Now he dribbled the ball upcourt. He loved this part of the game, when everything was open, everyone was moving, and he was in control. He felt special. Maybe this was the only place he ever felt special.

He was about to make a pass to his best friend, Poole. Suddenly, witnesses say, Tyrone Swint, the guy in the red shorts, came up behind Damon and pulled out a gun. He shot Damon in the back of the head. This was before anyone had the chance to yell, "Look out!" This was while Damon was dribbling a basketball. The bullet went through Damon's brain and lodged between the skull and the skin. He went down. The ball rolled away.

"Everyone started running," Torrin Cottrell says. "I saw the guy shoot Damon, and then he shot again at someone else. As I was running, I saw him go jumping into the window of this black car, and they drove away."

The black car was the escape horse, and Tyrone and his buddy were cowboys heading out of town. They drove down Five Mile Road and turned onto Middlebelt. Tyrone threw his gun out the window. It landed in the dirt. Later, Tyrone jumped out of the car and ran through the streets alone.

Back on the court, under the suburban floodlights, Damon Bailes was lying in blood. One of the players was trying to take his pulse. Poole was yelling at the oncoming EMS workers: "My boy's lying here shot! He's shot!"

Torrin was crying. He had known Damon since they were kids. They played in church leagues together. The summer before, they had gone to Saginaw for an all-day tournament, and they won the whole thing, and everyone got trophies. On the bus ride home, Damon was laughing and talking about how good they were. He had scored all these points. They waved their trophies at each other.

Now Damon was flat, not moving, his head was swollen and bloody, and there was a big knot on his forehead where he had hit the pavement. Torrin and Poole couldn't stop crying. They were still kids, really. They had never been in trouble like this. They ran to the school and found a pay phone. They called Damon's aunt.

"Damon been shot!" Poole said. "Damon been shot!"

INSIDE THE QUIET A-FRAME HOUSE on Greenlawn in Detroit there is a small, white, plastic Christmas tree. Velma Bailes, Damon's mother, a woman who looks too young for nine children, no husband and an ominous pile of hospital bills, bought the tree last year, at Shoppers World, for $25.99. She walks around its needles and says Damon wants a small TV for Christmas, so he can watch programs from his bed.

"Will he get what he wants?"

"He'll get what he needs."

"What does he need?

"He needs boots for the snow."

It has been seven months since the bullet, which was taken from Damon's brain and given to the police. Damon was in a coma for the first five weeks. Velma would try to talk to him in the hospital, as the doctors had suggested.

"Damon, we need you to come back," she would say. She would hold his hand and look at the tubes in his throat, nose and arms. She would go home.

One night, a nurse called and said to come down quickly. The patient next to Damon was saying, "Damon can't see."

"How do you know?"

"He woke up yellin', 'I can't see! I can't see!' "

The bullet had hit the lobe that controls vision. It also had left Damon paralyzed on the right side. In the months that followed, he would regain a slurred speech, partial vision and some feeling in his otherwise dead right leg and arm. The vision bothered him most. He would cry for hours over his near-blindness.

"He was always saying, 'How can I play basketball if I can't see?' " recalls Mary Roy, who manages the brain-injury program at the Rehabilitation Institute of Michigan. "We tried to tell him, 'Damon, there are other things you can do that are more important than basketball.' "

This, of course, is wishful thinking. The truth is, for a kid like Damon, there was only basketball. He was never college material. He couldn't get through two high schools. He never held a job. He lived at home, he had a baby with his girlfriend. Maybe he foolishly figured that little leather ball would someday lift him up above all this, the welfare checks, the food stamps, the porch that is falling apart.

If he was stupid, so be it. He is not the first. But he did no wrong. He committed no crimes. The tendency in well-to-do circles is to dismiss a kid such as Damon as hopeless, destined to a bad finish, as if this were some kind of birthright as an urban baby. But if we think like that, we cut the veins out of our city, and, don't kid yourself, our suburbs, too. Young black males. Wounded by gunshot. Young black males. Killed by gunshot. This is all our story. This is where we live. Detroit. A place where, this year alone, 266 children under the age of 17 have been shot.

We are dying, one bullet at a time.

"I don't know what parents are thinking when they let kids have them, guns," Velma Bailes sighs. "If one of my children had a gun in the house, they got to go. I don't care. All they ever do is get you killed."

Damon, lying in bed, is looking at the ceiling. He is asked whether he ever fired a gun. He snorts a breath and closes his eyes.

"Nuh-uh," he whispers.

IT DIDN'T TAKE POLICE LONG to find Tyrone Swint. They found the gun. They found the car. He still was wearing the red shorts when they pulled up several hours later in Detroit. Swint admitted to the shooting. He claimed self-defense, although how you do that and shoot someone in the back of the head is still a mystery. Why did he do it? Did he even know Damon? Is it true, as Damon's friends claim, that the two had never met? The trial, already postponed once, is now scheduled for February.

Meanwhile, the basketball courts at Bentley have been closed since that night. The gates are padlocked, the rims removed. Signs reading "NO TRESPASSING" are posted. This is a quick suburban reaction: You have trouble, cut off its food supply.

"It's a real shame," says Sgt. Lawrence Little, who works in Livonia and made the arrest. "They had a nice setup at that school, nice courts and all. But you can't have bullets flying near a subdivision.

"We asked those kids why they came up from Detroit to play basketball. You know what they said? They said, 'You can't play down in Detroit. You get shot.' "

Damon Bailes is still waiting for Medicaid to approve his much-needed physical therapy. It could take weeks, even months, the rehab center says. Meanwhile, he sits in bed, and his mother and brothers must bathe him, exercise him, walk him down the hallway and help him to the bathroom. He is 21 years old.

Tyrone Swint, who is 20, sits in the Wayne County jail. When a verification call is made, a worker there is intrigued.

"Swint? What'd he do?"

"He shot someone on a basketball court."

"Yeah? He shoot one of the Pistons?"

"No, nobody famous."

"Oh. Well. Yep, he's in here."

"Thank you."

"Merry Christmas."

W HAT CAN YOU REMEMBER?" Damon is asked. He looks at his arm. He speaks in a whisper. "Can't ... remember nothing."

"What do you see when you close your eyes?"

He closes his eyes. He tries.

"Don't ... see ... nothin'."

"What do you see when you dream?"

He sniffs. He slowly smiles.

"I see ... me ... playing ball ... "

Damon Bailes can be easily ignored. He can be ignored in a backlog of police reports. He can be ignored in a backlog of Medicaid requests. He can be ignored because he lives in the lowest strata of our city, and, at times, he might as well live in a cave.

But he counts. He may not be William Kennedy Smith, but he counts. On the wall of his tiny bedroom is a note from Poole: "Damon, you are a precious part of my life and I won't ever forget you." Underneath the word "precious" Poole wrote, in parentheses, "Don't think I'm gay."

He counts. And we cannot solve his problem with a padlock and a sign. We are linked to the city, whether we work there, live there, or even go in for a meal. There is no moat around Eight Mile Road. Their problems are our problems. They bleed, we all bleed.

"All we were doing was playing basketball," says Torrin Cottrell, almost pleading. "You don't expect someone to run up and shoot you. It's like, if basketball is doing something wrong, then what are we supposed to do?"

What are we supposed to do? The future of our city is being taken down, gangland style, one ambulance after another. We have to do something. Tonight is Christmas Eve, they are talking flurries, and that should make our suburbs pretty and white. But try to remember, while you open your presents, that somewhere, not far away, Damon Bailes is struggling to see the drawings on the wall, the ones teaching him how to walk again. For what, you keep asking yourself? For what? For what? For what?

For nothing.

And the snow falls.

1993

In a classified by himself
January 6, 1993

WELL, NOW WE'VE SEEN IT ALL. Mike Ditka, the howling wind of Chicago, fired as coach of the Bears? Axed? Dusted? As if he were just another Ray Perkins?

Yep. There he was yesterday, fighting back tears at his farewell press conference.

"All things must pass," Ditka said, obviously not referring to Jim Harbaugh on the audible.

"I'll be all right," he said.

"Regrets, just a few, too few to remember."

Uh, Mike? It's "Regrets, I've had a few, but then again, too few to mention … "

But OK. You're not Sinatra.

Which brings us to the most important question: What next for Mike Ditka? Let's face it. The man who always said he identified with the average, blue-jeaned, beer-bellied fans, is now, truly, like many of them: out of work.

And despite the fact that Ditka won a Super Bowl, six NFC Central titles and scares the snot out of most everyone he deals with, well, this is still a tough economy. A man wants work, he's got to be aggressive.

I have an idea. The want ads.

SITUATION WANTED: Experienced football coach, with Hall of Fame credentials, seeks NFL team with winning record or lots of high draft picks. Eager to mold, shape and even strangle young players until they listen to me and I make them winners. Call 1-800-IRNMIKE.

Snappy? Direct? Sure. Ditka could place it in the Denver Post, the New York Times and any other market where coaching jobs are available.

Of course, there are outlets besides newspapers for Ditka. For example, magazines. Not Time or Newsweek. Something like Muscle and Fitness — where his ad can have attitude:

HEY. YOU. NFL OWNER. A heart attack couldn't kill me. Hip surgery couldn't kill me. Jim McMahon couldn't kill me. What the hell is so tough about your football team? You want help? Leave a message. I'll think about it.

Or Popular Mechanics:

Build your own coach: All pieces included. Gum. Mustache. Needs minor assembly and occasional mouth-to-mouth resuscitation. P.O. Box 12, Chicago.

Of course, Ditka might try the personals.

Married White Male, 53, into physical contact and gang-tackling. Virile, sensitive, often misunderstood just because smoke is coming from my ears and I have a piece of someone's nose between my teeth. Can you love me better than my last significant other, the jerk, who ditched me? Heal me. Please. I want. I need. Am into leather and lace. Actually, leather and laces. Also, in private, I like to wear pads. Call 1-800-MIKEY.

That should get some response. But why stop with print? There's always radio, which, come to think of it, Ditka covered pretty well this season, particularly on call-in talk shows. He could do it again, right?

NOW YOU LISTEN TO ME, YOU WEAK LITTLE NFL OWNER. IF YOU'RE MAN ENOUGH TO SHOW UP AND HIRE ME, COME ON DOWN, BIG BOY. MY ADDRESS IS 250 NORTH WASHINGTON ROAD. ANYTIME, ANYPLACE, ANYWHERE …

Maybe one of those Dewar's profiles:

Name: Mike Ditka.

Age: 53.

Occupation: Deposed Football Legend.

Favorite book: Bears Playbook, 1985.

Favorite philosopher: Nietzsche, Ray.

Motto: "Why, you son of a bitch!"

Scotch: Dewar's.

There's also the MTV route, which Ditka's Bears once embraced. Remember the Super Bowl shuffle?

My name is Mike, Da Bear you like

I'm screamin' and I'm schemin' cause

they said to take a hike,

Here I sit, my bags all a-duffel.

I'm just here to do the outta-work shuffle.

Wait. Doesn't Ditka have his own restaurant? Why, he could drop a line at the end of each menu.

No substitutions. Gratuity not included. Take-out available. Owner for hire.

He could even list himself as an item:

THE IRON MIKE — Beefy, well-aged dish served with hot sauce and fiery temperament. Hard-boiled potato. No string beans. May be difficult to digest, could trigger cholesterol. Market price. See owner.

So, you see, as Ditka might say, the world is full of possibilities. Nice guy like Mike? No problem finding work.

Of course, if he does go to the classifieds, he should watch out for similar ads, some of which have been running for a while. Such as:

FOOTBALL COACH. SITUATION WANTED. Remember me? I got famous in the Super Bowl in the '85 season and have been living off it ever since! Hire me! Please! Call Buddy Ryan, 1-800-WHA-HAPPN?

Golf on cable: Fore!

February 28, 1993

N EWS ITEM: THE GOLF CHANNEL, a 24-hour cable network devoted entirely to the sport of golf, was announced recently. Programming is yet to be determined, but creators promise "a nonstop feast" of shows dealing with the nation's new No. 1 pastime.

TV GUIDE ...

6:00 a.m. GolfCenter.

6:30 Good FORE-ning, America!

6:55 Masters Update. Live coverage of sunrise at Augusta National.

7:00 The 700 Club. World's worst golfers share their misery.

7:45 Body by Jake. Golfer Peter Jacobsen demonstrates slouching, slumping and how to pick a nice white belt.

8:30 GolfCenter.

8:45 Golf! Live! Practice-round action from the Nabisco Federal Express Mr. Coffee Hertz Prudential Jamie Farr Classic in Toledo, Ohio.

9:00 Regis & Kathie & Lee. Lee Trevino joins famous morning talkers and does what many have wanted to do for years: clubs them over the head with a pitching wedge.

10:00 Geraldo! Golfers who cross-dress.

10:30 Oprah! Men who sleep with putters.

11:00 All In The Family. The Bunkers.

11:30 M*A*S*H. Amateur golf swings.

11:55 Masters Update. Live coverage of grass growing at Augusta National.

Noon GolfCenter.

12:15 p.m. Golf! Live! (Rerun) Second-round action from the Wal-Mart Amoco Sunkist Xerox Merrill Lynch Junior Amateur Rainbow Classic at Maui, Hawaii.

12:30 At the Links With Siskel & Ebert. The famous critics give thumbs-up or down on golfers' styles and personalities. This week, Gene and Roger disagree on whether Fred Couples is actually dead or really that dull.

1:00 The Young and the Restless. With John Daly.

1:30 One Stroke To Live.

2:00 All My Titlists.

2:30 GolfCenter.

2:45 Golf! Live! Rainout action from the Buick Kraft PaineWebber General Electric Mobil Weed Eater Senior Golf Classic from Sleepy Hollow, Wash.

3:00 Film: "Driving, Miss Daisy." Aging chauffeur teaches widow how to hit tee shot.

4:00 News At Fore!

4:30 Sea Hunt. Craig Stadler (The Walrus) leads scenic tour of the world's best water traps.

5:00 Bogey Film Festival.

5:55 Masters Update. Live coverage of hedge trimming at Augusta National.

6:00 GolfCenter.

6:15 Golf! Live! Greens-keeping action from the Pebble Beach General Mills Turtle Wax Smith Barney Coca-Cola Invitational Junior Women's Championships at Montego Bay, Jamaica.

7:00 Murder, She Wrote. Golfers' wives discuss plans for the future.

7:30 Rescue 911. Medics perform Heimlich maneuver on Greg Norman, who's been choking for years.

8:00 Film: "Hook." Dustin Hoffman and Robin Williams star as pirates who can't hit the green.

9:00 The Wonder Years. Narrator (Daniel Stern) reflects on good old days, when hardest part of life was getting ball to go through windmill.

10:00 America's Funniest Golf Videos.

10:30 Knotts Landing. Don Knotts goes looking for the ball he hit in 1965.

10:55 Masters Update. Live coverage of night watchman making rounds at Augusta National.

11:00 GolfCenter.

11:15 Golf! Live! Sprinkler action from the Mountain Dew Minolta Virginia Slims British Petroleum Northwest Airlines Invitational Lefties-Only Championship at Walnut Creek, Calif.

11:30 In Living Color. Fashion designers discuss golf pants and how to put them out in case of fire.

Midnight Nightline. Golf in the Persian Gulf. Should you play through?

1:00 a.m. Film: "The Bells of St. Andrews." Santa Claus visits Scotland with his three-iron.

2:00 GolfCenter.

2:15 Golf! Live! Final-round action from Honda Goodyear Wendy's Nutter-Butter H&R Block Senior Women's Invitational Classic at Miami Beach.

2:30 Film: "The Sands of Iwo Jima." John Wayne stars as man caught in world's largest bunker.

3:55 Masters Update. Live coverage of groundhog running across fairway at Augusta National.

4:00 Deep Thoughts. By Jack Nicklaus.

4:15 Morning benediction. Handicappers.

4:20 Morning benediction. Non-handicappers.

The shot heard 'round U-M

March 21, 1993

TUCSON, ARIZ. — He didn't want much. Just one basket. That's not a lot to ask from a college career, is it? One basket? For this, he would work. For this, he would sacrifice. For this, he would sit at the end of the bench, night after night, year after year. Without a scholarship. Without fame. He would travel to cities, dress in the uniform, go through warm-ups. Then take off the uniform, travel back home, go to class. Year after year. Night after night.

One basket.

Sean Dobbins is the other side of the Fab Five. The far side. He was a good little high school basketball player who chose Michigan, like most kids, to get an education. He paid his own tuition. No one recruited him.

One day, early in his freshman year, Dobbins got an idea. He took his high school scrapbook to the basketball office and asked to see Steve Fisher.

"Coach, I'd like to play for your team," he said. "These are some articles about me in high school."

Fisher, who had just won a national championship, was amused. Big-time college basketball schools begin recruiting players when they are in eighth or ninth grade. They follow them — hound them, sometimes — until they sign. Only the best get taken.

Now here was a kid with a scrapbook.

"I'll take a look," Fisher said.

FIVE WEEKS LATER — to everyone's surprise — Dobbins was on the team. A walk-on. True, he still had to pay his own tuition. True, he was mostly there to help practice. But the kid with the scrapbook was in the club, dressing next to stars like Rumeal Robinson and Terry Mills.

He went through drills. He sweated every scrimmage. He dressed for the games, but almost never got in. To be honest, it was a big deal if he unzipped his sweat suit.

Sophomore year, he made a free throw.

That was the highlight of his season. "I still dreamed about making a basket," he says. "I figured I had two years left."

Then, a setback. Michigan recruited five star freshmen — the Fab Five — and there was no room on the team for Dobbins. He spent his junior year practicing in the gym with other students. When the NCAA tournament came around, he drove to Atlanta, on his own. And he drove to Lexington. And he drove to Minneapolis. He sat behind the team, in the stands, longing to be part of it again, to wear the uniform, to maybe get a shot at that one basket he'd been dreaming about since freshman year.

Suddenly, he was a senior.

T HE GUYS ON THE TEAM were really pulling for me now," he says. Given his old spot back — and the fact that because U-M was so talented, there should be plenty of "garbage time" — Dobbins was optimistic. He practiced hard, as usual. He dressed and undressed, as usual.

But the games slipped away. Pretty soon, it was the regular-season finale against Northwestern, and Dobbins still hadn't scored a hoop. Fisher put him in, and he quickly took a shot — which clanked off the rim. The crowd moaned. In the final seconds he got the ball again, spun toward the basket and — AHNNNNNNN!

The buzzer sounded. The season was gone. And so, Dobbins figured, was his chance.

Which is what made two nights ago so special. It was the first game of the NCAA tournament, the most serious basketball of the year. Michigan found itself ahead by 30 points late against Coastal Carolina. Fisher looked down the bench, saw the kid with the scrapbook, and said, "Get in there."

This time, the whole U-M team, which has come to love Dobbins for his never-quit spirit, was ready. With four seconds left and a free throw about to be shot at the opposite end, the Wolverines called Dobbins over and hid him in their midst. "Don't move," they whispered, "just wait."

The other team didn't even see him.

So when the free throw was made, Rob Pelinka grabbed the ball and heaved it downcourt to Dobbins, who stepped out of the camouflage and was suddenly all alone.

"All I could think of was, 'Catch it! Catch it!' " Dobbins said.

He caught it. He dribbled toward the basket. Three seconds. Two seconds. He laid it up … and in!

Score! The buzzer sounded. And the Wolverines mobbed Dobbins as if he'd just won a championship. "You shoulda dunked it!" Chris Webber laughed. "DOBBS! DOBBS!" yelled Juwan Howard, grabbing him in a headlock and carrying him to the locker room.

We watch so much college basketball, we forget that they are kids out there. Kids with dreams. Some dream of winning it all. Some just dream of scoring two points. "It was the greatest moment of my life," Dobbins said. "If I never scored, the experience would still have been worthwhile. But now, it feels … great."

Mission accomplished.

Unless any NBA teams are interested …

When time stopped for Webber

April 6, 1993

NEW ORLEANS — It ended with Chris Webber looking desperately for something he didn't have — time, hope, help. He grabbed a rebound, his team trailing by two points, and he called for time, he screamed for it. The ref stared at him blankly. Confused, Webber muscled his way up court, panic in his eyes, he traveled, but this one-man-against-everything journey seemed to have everyone's tongues tied, including the referee's. And so here was Webber, clock ticking down, still running, still dribbling, pounding the ball with his giant hands, going past his bench, wanting help, wanting a time-out, no one able to make clear to him that Chris, we don't have any time-outs left. Finally, he pulled up, stopped, like a man who realizes he is cornered by police. He made the "T" sign, looked at the ref, who made the "T" sign right back.

Technical foul.

Disaster.

"We were screaming, 'No time-outs! No time-outs!' " James Voskuil said in the dejected Michigan locker room after the Wolverines fell for the second straight time in the NCAA championship game, losing to North Carolina, 77-71. "But with all that noise and all those people screaming, 'No time-out!' who knows? Maybe all you hear is 'Time-out!' and he called for one."

And with that, the run on destiny that these Wolverines had made, against their own legend, against amazing odds, all the way to the very end of the college basketball rainbow, was over. North Carolina, which won a national championship 11 years earlier in this same building, on another freakish play, a pass from the opposition, won it again, same way.

And instead of a U-M celebration, Wolverines cutting down nets, the sad final picture of this 1993 season will be this: The Fab Five standing on the half-court line, watching helplessly as North Carolina sank the two technical free throws that would put this game out of reach. Ray Jackson was on one knee, as if praying. Juwan Howard looked like he had lost a friend. Jimmy King had his hands on his hips, Jalen Rose had his head lowered, and Webber, well, he was stunned. All he had done, all the slams, the monster rebounds, the steals, the baskets he made falling down, his 23 points, his 11 boards, his 33 minutes — all that, gone in a simple, desperate mistake.

"I cost us the game," he mumbled afterward.

A few minutes later: "I cost us the game."

He left the postgame podium and shut himself inside a staff room, and he didn't emerge for almost an hour. He walked quickly toward the bus, eyes forward, fighting everything inside him, ignoring reporters, ignoring the lights, ignoring everything until one of his younger brothers came up and hugged him, and Chris Webber could hold it no more. He began to cry. His father stepped up and hugged him, too, and now Chris began to sob. He was, at that moment, in the hallway of a stadium 1,000 miles from home, what we always forget that all these college basketball players are:

A kid.

"I cost us the game."

IN THE SADNESS OF THAT MOMENT, you almost don't want to analyze it. A basketball game is 40 minutes long, and every bad play counts the same. You only remember the last ones.

But OK. The truth is, they'll be talking about it forever, so for what it's worth, here is the responsibility chain: The coach is supposed to make sure the players know the time-out situation. The coach is supposed to get the players' eyes when he is in doubt. According to most of the players, Steve Fisher did tell his players they were out of time-outs in their last huddle. "But whether everyone heard it," Rose said, "well, you know, there's a lot goin' on ... "

Fisher said, "We thought we said it, but apparently we didn't get specific enough."

Later, Fisher was near tears in his sorrow and his sympathy for Webber. "It's hard," he whispered, when asked how he could make a player feel better after that. "I don't know what you do ... except try to hug him."

Yes. And tell him that without his courage, his excellence, getting off the floor with a bad eye poke and coming back in to score a basket, stealing the ball and dribbling the length of the floor for a slam, without that, this isn't even a close game. In fact, Michigan seemed all but finished before Webber came down with that rebound.

"When he got it, I said to myself: 'It's Michigan's ballgame,' " Rose said later. "But you know, the whole night was unusual. It was like I looked up and there were two minutes left and I was like, where did the game go?"

Indeed, the whole game took less than two hours to play, including all the TV interruptions. The first half was a tug-of-war, Michigan opening tightly, then exploding for a 10-point lead, then falling back to a six-point halftime deficit.

And the second half? What can you say? It was quick and seemed like forever. At times it was so brutal, so intense, force on force, defense vs. defense, that it felt like someone trying to push a refrigerator up the stairs. Minutes would pass without a good shot. The defenses were like soggy blankets. It was less a game than a slugfest, one in which the referee just lets them go at each other, to the body, to the head, the body, the head, last one standing wins. "It was," Fisher said afterward, "what I expected. A game that went down to the wire."

But the ending he didn't expect. So many times Michigan had pulled off this type of miracle. The Wolverines don't lose overtime games in postseason play. They don't lose in crunch time. Isn't that their reputation?

And when Pat Sullivan missed the second free throw with 19 seconds left, the Wolverines were perched on another great finish. How terribly sad, then, that the game slipped out of Webber's hands, even as he cradled the ball. Last year's loss to Duke, he had said, "was the lowest moment of my life."

You can only imagine how he feels this morning.

AND NOW, THE MORNING AFTER. The Wolverines had plenty of critics, but only a truly hard-boiled person would delight in their defeat Monday night. Like them or not, they fought the good fight this year with the enormous burden of being one half shy of a national championship last year. From the first day of practice, way back in November, they had one Monday night circled on the calendar, and it wasn't the Oscars.

But don't kill the season just because it ended badly. Michigan won 31 games, a school record, it beat teams it wasn't supposed to beat and, I think I can say this safely, it provided the most entertainment in college basketball, hands down. It just didn't win the whole thing. That joy went to Carolina, a well-schooled team with a very deliberate game plan. Yes, the Tar Heels are dull compared to Michigan, lacking in color and quotes. But they got the job done. They executed a swing-around offense when they had to, got the ball inside to Eric Montross, their 7-foot center, and got 25 points out of Donald Williams, many of them on crucial three-pointers. Michigan knew it had to stop Williams to win. It didn't.

"They seemed to get a basket whenever they had to," Rose sighed.

Isn't that what they usually say about Michigan?

BUT OK. IT'S OVER. It's done. The questions will arise now about Webber and a possible pro career, and you will hear all kinds of theories, ranging from 1) "He'll never leave now, he can't live with that being his last college play" to 2) "He'll leave because sticking around all year will be too painful."

You know what?

It's not important right now.

What is important is a salute to effort. The Wolverines didn't lose this game because of trash talking or a bad attitude. They turned the ball over too often and they had a few disastrous plays at the end. King throwing up an air ball. Rose losing a pass inside that was stolen away. Any of those things happen in the final seconds, and we're feeling sorry for another Wolverine instead of Webber.

The point is, you win and lose as a team. And if you can't forget that last bungled play, then try not to forget this either: The celebration when U-M beat Kentucky the game before, a win that was never supposed to happen. Or the comeback from the 19-point deficit to beat UCLA, which was never supposed to happen. Remember Webber slamming and Rose making his faces and Jackson coming out of nowhere for a basket and Howard squaring for a pretty jump shot and King monster-jamming that fast break Monday night. Remember seniors Rob Pelinka and Voskuil and Eric Riley and Michael Talley in happier poses. They are still kids. It is still a game. Sometimes you make mistakes. Sometimes your dreams have to wait.

The Fab Five will be upperclassmen next time you see them, but that is not a curse. That, in fact, gives them hope and time, two things they simply ran out of on a very sad Monday night in April.

Coffey's timepiece: Winning
April 19, 1993

IN THE MOVIES, DIRECTORS USE a trick called "timepieces." A dog, for example, will enter the film as a puppy. Next time you see it, its legs and ears are longer. Next time you see it, it's shaggy and full grown. This lets you know that years are passing, quietly, quickly.

Paul Coffey, who has been in hockey long enough to do a movie and a sequel, has a timepiece of his own: his nephew, who came into the world about a dozen years ago, when Coffey was just starting his NHL career as an Edmonton Oiler. Coffey remembers holding the child in his arms. And he remembers walking him as a 2-year-old on Maple Leaf Gardens ice. He remembers the schoolboy visiting him in Pittsburgh. And he remembers the budding teenager who came to Detroit recently and laced 'em up, and they hit the ice and the kid tried to skate past his Uncle Paul, to outshoot him, to steal the puck.

"They grow up so fast," Coffey sighs, like a grandmother looking out her porch window. Then, as if to remind himself, he adds, "Hey, I can't wait to have kids of my own."

Such is the curious blend of Paul Coffey, old enough to be nostalgic, young enough to be optimistic, savvy enough to combine the two on the eve of the playoffs and feel as if he is doing the same thing for the first time. How many 31-year-old bachelors are at the top of their game, can hang with Wayne Gretzky, can say they've won four Stanley Cups with two teams and are about to try to lead a new favorite to another one?

Coffey can.

Get it? Coffey can?

That was a joke. A bad one. Coffey is bad at jokes, too. "Can't tell 'em to save my life," he says. Because of this, and because of his heavy whiskers, soulful stare and tendency to listen first, talk second, people sometimes accuse him of being too serious. They say, "Lighten up, Paul!" or, "Why aren't you smiling, Paul?"

Here's the secret of Coffey: Beneath all the years, the trades and the whiskers, this guy is having the time of his life.

YOU KNOW, WHEN YOU'RE 20 or 21, I don't care what they say, you want to make a name for yourself," Coffey says, slouching deep in a couch in a back room at Joe Louis Arena. His black hair is mussed, his whiskers thick as usual. He wears a gray T-shirt and shorts and an ice bag. He looks as if he just came from a grad school pickup game.

"At that age, you want to reach this certain plateau so you can make some money.

"If you do that, then you want to join a great team, a great organization.

"And if you do that, then you want to win it all."

Well, I say. You've done all three.

"Yeah," he says.

So what's left?

"Win."

But you've already won.

"Keep winning."

He grins when he says this. Grinning, he can do. Smiling just won't come naturally. Sometimes, he says, he thinks he's smiling, and he checks a mirror and he isn't. "I don't have one of those faces, I guess," he says. "I'm smiling inside." And he does have a fine sense of humor. He also has a raging passion for his sport. He says his only plans for life after hockey are — and this is a direct quote — "hockey."

"I just can't imagine doing anything else," he admits. Thirteen years, four teams and more than 1,000 games have not soured him on the pro game. Neither has the fact that, despite his All-Star credentials, his five seasons of more than 100 points — and he's a defenseman, don't forget — Coffey has been let go by several successful teams.

"You know what I do the moment I find out I've been traded?" asks the man who was sent from Edmonton to Pittsburgh, Pittsburgh to LA, and LA to Detroit. "I immediately think of all the bad things about the place that traded me and all the good things about the place I'm going to. I put all the negative on the past and all the positive on the future."

Smart.

Age has its wisdom, you know.

COFFEY GREW UP IN ONTARIO, the son of an airplane-factory worker who would take his boy to work, show him the hard life, and say, "I want better than this for you." The father had a compact philosophy: "Work hard, have fun." Living up to the former was more difficult than the latter. Now and then, when the Coffeys drove to see Paul play in a tournament, and the boy didn't give his full effort, the usually laid-back father would let his kid have it.

"You think we drove all the way up here just to watch you not try?"

The words stuck in Coffey's head. And so, even today, with all those photos of him holding the Stanley Cup somewhere in his closet, he still pushes his body to the limit, showering himself in sweaty workouts, doing extra repetitions on the StairMaster or the bike, driving in practice, pushing, pushing. Even during the summer, when he escapes to a cottage on Lake Joseph, he hangs out with lumber workers and forest types. These people scale trees. They live off barges. Coffey admires that type of existence, he enjoys the draining pleasure of pushing your body. "Relaxing" means playing baseball, golf or waterskiing. Not surprisingly, his favorite singer is workmanlike Bruce Springsteen, he of the four-hour concerts.

"If I could trade places with anyone for a day, that's who I'd pick," Coffey says.

Springsteen?

"Yeah. I love that guy."

You'd be him during a concert?

"Oh, yeah. That's the only time to do it."

AND REMEMBER, IT'S NOT AS IF Coffey is lacking for big-name friends. Until last season, he was chumming around with Mario Lemieux. And his best buddy is Gretzky, with whom he shared the ice for several years in Edmonton and a season-and-a-half in LA. They were so close, Coffey woke Gretzky at 7 a.m. when he learned of the trade to Detroit, just so Gretzky wouldn't hear it from someone else. Gretzky was devastated.

"That's the hardest part of this business, making friends and then leaving," Coffey admits. "But I think of it this way: If they're really your friends, they're your friends forever, right?"

Coffey has added an unusual best buddy in his brief time with the Wings: Bob Probert. The unlikely pairing of the savvy, veteran defenseman and the once-wild, still-feared forward is one of those sports relationships that makes you shake your head. At a recent radio broadcast, Probert asked to introduce Coffey, then moved over when he was brought onstage, deferring to him, saying Paul should talk, and Probert would listen. That was about respect.

Other times, it's about laughs.

"We were golfing down in Tampa and we laughed our heads off," Coffey says. "We bet on anything. Sergei (Fedorov) was in a sand trap and Probie said, 'Ten bucks it takes him three shots to get out!' We bet. It did. And he won.

"I dunno. Stuff like that just cracks us up."

NOW MAYBE YOU FIGURE COFFEY, having been around, should be taking life more seriously, thinking about the future, clucking his tongue at childish antics. But wait a second. Weren't we just telling him to "lighten up" a few minutes ago?

Such is Coffey's touch. A little young, a little old. It is not just those thread-the-needle passes he gets to his teammates for all those assists; Coffey is also deft in handling humans. Bryan Murray, the Wings' coach, says in addition to Coffey's obvious skills on the ice, his presence in the locker room "has made a huge difference in team chemistry. It could be the thing we've needed."

Coffey says he is just following an example by Gretzky, who despite his status as a living legend, always had time for the kid who just arrived from the minors. Gretzky even organized team get-togethers every day on the road, for a beer or a quick bite, to keep camaraderie high.

"That was great," Coffey says. "I never forget it. That was one of the ways Wayne led.

"You know, when I first got here, Stevie (Yzerman) asked me about Gretzky, about his leadership, what he was like. I told him, 'Steve, he's just like you. He does his job. He works hard. And he's very approachable.' "

Yzerman's inquiry was one of the few times in Coffey's 10 weeks with the Wings that anyone has pumped him for stories. Contrary to popular belief, hockey players don't sit at a veteran's knee, their eyes all aflutter, as he waxes on about the good old days.

Or, as Coffey puts it, "Nobody wants to hear that bleep."

But if they did ask about Gretzky and Lemieux, he'd tell them nobody works harder. And if they did ask about championships, he'd say there's no feeling like it. And if they did ask about winning, he'd say that once you get a Stanley Cup, you feel like you should have it every year, and every year you don't there's something wrong.

"When you win the first one, you're not sure what to do. It's like someone's been telling you about this great movie, over and over, so when you finally see it, you're like, 'That wasn't that great.'

"All the buildup to the Cup, when you win it, it's like, 'Now what? Do I do a cartwheel? Do I stand on my head? What?' Only after a couple weeks, when you sit down with your teammates and talk about it, do you realize what you've done.

"And it's bleeping great."

That's what Coffey is looking for now. That's what he wants. One more kiss on the Cup. One more notch on the tree. He doesn't think about age and he doesn't think about uniforms and he doesn't think about what used to be. He thinks about winning, he thinks about a final victorious buzzer. He thinks about one more notch on his timepiece, and another smile you can't see.

Webber boards his star

May 6, 1993

HOW FAST THE TIME GOES, Doris Webber thought, as she watched her son step to the podium. She heard the lenses click. Saw the TV lights flick on. Not long ago, it seemed, her firstborn was just starting to talk. Now the cameras whirred and the tape decks rolled and he was telling the world, in his deep, mumbly voice, that he was done with college basketball — after only two years — and his next step would be a pro career, at age 20.

She folded her hands. She tried to look hopeful. Her daughter, Rachel, Chris' younger sister, leaned on her shoulder, as if ready to cry. Chris' kid brothers were half-excited, half-depressed. His father crossed his legs, uncrossed them, crossed them again.

Anyone who thinks this was automatic, a no-brainer, anyone who figures, "Hey, you throw $15 million in the water, any fish will bite" doesn't know Chris Webber. Unlike many athletes, he thinks first, acts second. Maybe he thinks too much. But he has this unshakable belief in fate, and from the moment his last game ended, that Monday night in April, when Michigan lost the national championship to North Carolina and his Fab Five group again fell hard off the rainbow, he had been waiting for a sign. A thunderclap. A burning bush. Anything that would shake these clouds, make him say, "Of course! It's so clear! I should (stay, leave, stay, leave) … "

He called friends. He called relatives. He flew to visit famous people — athletes, rap artists — to seek their counsel. Experts were predicting he'd be an easy top three draft pick, multimillion-dollar contract, and almost all the NBA players he asked said, "You're ready, come out." Shaquille O'Neal told him and Joe Dumars told him and Magic Johnson told him.

Other people, including his younger sister, said "stay."

For a moment, over the weekend, he decided she was right. He would come back one more year, play with Jalen, Juwan, Ray, Jimmy, come out next season. Then, on Monday, a woman in a Cadillac stopped her car to ask for his autograph — and something snapped. Understand that Webber, an inner-city kid, has long had this dream of buying a big home for his family. Of telling his mother, "You don't have to work at that school anymore" and his father, "Can you manage my career, instead of your GM assembly-line job?"

Most often, he dreamt of cars, Cadillacs, presenting his parents with a matching pair, shiny and new, then standing back and seeing their tears flow. Kids have these dreams. It makes them feel paid up.

So Webber saw this woman in her Cadillac, asking for his signature, and a voice inside said, "This isn't fair." It was a voice he had heard a million times. But here, in the heat of Decision Time — and with his belief that he could play with those NBA guys — the voice was especially clear.

He had his sign.

Not long after, Webber went home to Detroit and took his mother around in a hug. "It may not be your first choice," he told her, "but it's my choice. It'll be good."

Say good-bye to Fabulous.

W E HAD HIM FOR TWO YEARS," said his coach, now his ex-coach, Steve Fisher, who, despite his worried expression, seemed determined to put a positive spin on this loss, "and that's two years more than anyone else. He's ready to compete in the NBA. I can't say he's not. If he stayed another year, he'd be able to come out and dominate, but … " He stopped himself.

No point in buts.

Say good-bye to Fabulous.

"I think I'm ready," Webber said. "If I came back, it would only be for one game (the national championship), and if we didn't get to that …

"I'm still part of the Fab Five. The only thing is we won't be playing on the same court anymore."

That's a big "only thing." Webber leaves a legacy in Ann Arbor as arresting and curious as the team he played for. Perhaps the most dominating player to ever wear a Michigan uniform, he will never be first on any all-time list. And in some ways, the Fab Five Wolverines will now be known as the Greatest Team To Never Win A Title. No Big Ten ring. No national championship.

Yet there is no denying their impact: They shook up college sports; they made everybody watch. With their baggy shorts and shaved heads and black shoes and black socks they played basketball and played with the basketball. They flew and dunked and yelled trash and slapped fists and inspired fan mail and inspired hate mail and drew more TV close-ups than any other college team in history.

They will not be the same without Webber. It's like the Beatles without McCartney. Webber was the one who commanded the most attention. He was The Face. The Force. In two years' time, he had become internationally famous, he was mobbed when the team went to Europe, and that was last summer. As the nation's top high school player his senior year, he arrived at Ann Arbor with the brightest pedigree and started every game in his brief career. While he often made overeager mistakes — passes too high, shots too hard — he also made backboard-rattling dunks and vacuum rebounds. He held the ball the way a longshoreman holds an orange, and he showed the most expressive faces, hanging on the rim after a slam, charging downcourt after a basket, running out of the tunnel, waving a fist and urging on his teammates.

"THEY DON'T BELIEVE IN US! THEY SAID WE'RE UNDERDOGS!"
he yelled before the Final Four game against Kentucky, pointing at reporters as
the team raced through the press area. And those same reporters leapt to their feet
and ran alongside him, jotting down his words, hoping for more.

Webber had that kind of charisma. He is fascinating to listen to — he can
ponder race relations, jump shots and TV announcers in a single sentence — and
because of that, he inspired emotion, from resentment to sympathy, especially
after what is now the final play of his college career: the ill-fated dribble upcourt
in the last minute against North Carolina, when he froze, then called a time-out
the Wolverines didn't have. He watched, slack-jawed, as the ball, the game and
the dream were grabbed away by the referee.

Someone asked whether that play was the reason he would not return.

"No," he said. "At first I thought, 'No way I can end my college career on
that.' But nobody died from it. Nobody lost their job from it. And I just have to
go on."

Time passes. Wounds heal.

Say good-bye to Fabulous.

NOW, THERE ARE MANY out there who feel burned by this, as if Webber just
reneged on a loan, or took training here and got a job somewhere else. And
maybe, once upon a time, you could say that about college athletes. After all,
they get a free scholarship, free coaching, and in return, they are expected to give
the school their best years, which are usually their last two.

But let's be candid here. Michigan has already made a zillion dollars off
these kids. Count the ticket sales, the TV revenue, the extra money for twice
reaching the Final Four, the publicity, the merchandising, the uniforms with
Webber's number on them — take all that, and then figure that not only don't the
athletes see any of that money, but they are not even allowed to work during the
season, and you quickly stop objecting.

The system is outdated. It clanks with hypocrisy. These kids will keep
leaving, younger and younger, until college sports wakes up and comes into
the '90s.

And I don't mean the 1890s.

"I don't feel Michigan owes me anything, and I don't think I owe them
anything either," Webber said. "Coach Fisher kept all his promises. I made some
great friendships. I played on a once-in-a-lifetime team."

And he's gone. Outta here. Will he make it in the NBA? No question. As
quickly as if he stayed another year? Maybe not. Is he ready for a life where
money is the bottom line, where teammates can be traded, where nobody watches
to make sure you're OK, going to class, getting a degree, staying out of trouble?

He thinks so.

They always do.

Maybe this one is. Chris Webber is a unique young man, with a broad view of life and an undying devotion to his parents and siblings. He used to hold his sister's and brothers' hands when they walked across the street. He slept with them in their beds when he came home from college. They cried when he told them he was going pro, mostly because they felt they wouldn't see him anymore.

Because he aspires to taking care of them all, because the fame is there, the money is there, the confidence is there, and the path is open, he is stepping through the looking glass. Whether we like it or not, his era ends today.

So be it. Just an hour before the press conference, he was in the gym, shooting baskets with his buddies. And during the announcement, the lights grew so hot, he began to sweat. His mother quickly sent up a tissue so he could wipe his forehead, because your children are still your children, even the ones about to make a boatload of money.

Sunrise, sunset, says the song. Quickly go the years. Right or wrong, Chris Webber has found his sign, his star light, star bright, and we can only wish him luck as he tries to follow it through the sky.

Picking a Softball Team II

May 12, 1993

S ANY SPORTS FAN CAN tell you, there is more to softball than wearing a uniform. There is also drinking beer. And the burping contest. But, shucks, all that comes after the game, and we haven't even picked our team yet. Wait. Our team. Is it time to pick our team?

It is. Five years ago, I wrote a primer on how to select a company softball team. The response was incredible. Millions, or at least dozens, of grateful readers wrote to say they clipped that column and hung it on the bulletin board at work, where, no doubt, it was quickly covered by an ad for kittens.

Nonetheless, many forward-thinking companies did follow my suggestions — including "Never pick your boss" and "Always take Vinnie from the stockroom" — and they quickly discovered that, thanks to my advice, their teams did not perform any better.

In fact, some of them wrote and said, "Yo, we did what you told us — and we still stink! What gives?"To which I respond: "Hey. How much did you pay for the newspaper? A quarter? Whadya expect? The '27 Yankees?"

Besides, I did not write that column to help the few. I wrote it because millions of American workers endure softball leagues every summer, and because the Tigers were out of town and I needed a subject.

Guess what? The Tigers are out of town again.

Picking a Company Softball Team: Part Deux

Now, last time, perhaps, I failed to raise an important question: Are we really interested in winning? Are we that shallow? Do we yearn for the trophy at the end of the season, or do we seek a higher, more spiritual purpose, such as learning how to slide while holding a sandwich?

People who want the trophy, well, they're not reading this. It's 7 a.m. and they're already down at the field, taking laps. Their uniforms are crisp, their chatter is lively, and the best we can hope for is that, in search of excellence, they drive off a cliff.

Meanwhile, those of you still here, gulping a third cup of coffee, must decide whether your team is going for the glory or, as we like to say around the water cooler, going for the long lunch.

Let's assume you want to win. Here's how you pick a squad:

1. Go to the shipping department. 2. Find anyone with a tattoo.

3. Ask him what he'd do to his boss if he got the chance, and as you do this, hand him a bat.

4. Observe his swing. 5. You just found your cleanup hitter.

6. Check the rest of the building. Avoid those who say, "I'll play! Can I

design the uniforms?"

7. Anyone named Rocco is in.

8. Same goes for Vito.

9. Always take at least one person from the legal department. They're hungry, aggressive and, we assume, they know how to cheat.

10. You got spikes? You're in.

11. A backstop in your garage? You're in.

12. Anyone who says, "Does it have to be a glove or can I use mittens?" is out. 13. Brenda, the red-headed receptionist, is in.

14. (If you are female, the above sentence reads, "Wayne, the hunk from the mail room, is in.")

15. I don't think we need to explain that.

16. Who has a van? 17. There's our first baseman.

18. Avoid players driving Jaguars and Mercedes 450SLs. They are either too rich to break up a double play or too nicely dressed.

19. Wait a minute. They're driving a Jaguar and working at your office? What gives? Let's get 'em! 20. Mmph %$ #@$ %$!

21. NEVER PICK YOUR BOSS! Never pick your boss' boss or your boss' boss' boss. Those people are all in it together. Trust me.

22. If someone shows up for tryouts in a leisure suit, be kind, and send him to the hospital.

23. Any woman who swings with a cigarette in her mouth is trouble.

24. Sign her up.

25. Check dogs. Anyone with a golden retriever, a bloodhound or a beagle is OK. A Chihuahua? Let 'em play polo.

26. No Walkmen. Even in rightfield.

27. NEVER PICK YOUR BOSS! Did I say this?

28. All candidates must at least be able to cover their stomachs with an extra-large T-shirt. Otherwise, they play catcher.

29. Take anyone named "Spike."

30. Whoever brings the cooler, pitches.

31. In case of two coolers, pick whoever's cooler.

32. Ask for team-song ideas. Anyone who suggests Barry Manilow, let 'em play polo.

33. See if Vinnie from the stockroom, who is now president of the company, has any nephews.

34. Take someone with a boom box. 35. Take someone with a barbecue.

36. Take someone with ice.

37. If they can slide while holding a sandwich, they get to be captain.

There you have it. Follow these rules and I personally guarantee that your softball team will take the field. After that, you're on your own. Be sure to look for my next column, five years from now, in which we go over the most important thing: how to win the burping contest.

Lions lay their burden down
September 6, 1993

CHRIS SPIELMAN DROPPED INTO HIS stance, set his jaw and snorted. He waited for the snap. Then he sprang forward — and threw a block. A block? For the running Barry Sanders? Chris Spielman? Fullback?

This was all you needed to know about the stunning event called the season opener at the Silverdome: the Lions' defense was everywhere — including its own backfield.

"Aw, you just get out there and hit somebody," Spielman, normally a linebacker, said of his brief stint on offense late in the Lions' 30-13 crushing of Atlanta. "I can do that. I can hit anyone they want me to hit."

Who's left? They're all dead, aren't they? This was the game that blue-collar, beer-toasting fans have been waiting for around here since, what, the dawn of time? Lions on the quarterback. Lions on the running back. Lions charging into the opposing backfield as if coming through an open door.

Six sacks? SIX SACKS? The last time the words "six," "sacks" and "Lions" were used in the same sentence, that sentence was: "The sad sacks on the Lions were deep-sixed again … "

"That's probably the most defensive pressure I've encountered since I've been here," Chris Miller, the bruised Atlanta quarterback, lamented after the defeat. "Their pass rush took away almost everything."

The Lions' pass rush? Did I go to the right stadium?

WELL, THE LIONS CAN Pat themselves on the back for this one. As in Pat Swilling, the new, pass-rushing specialist who carries such a reputation in the NFL, you can hear the opposing team's teeth chattering from up in the stands. With Swilling charging from the outside, the Falcons curled in to protect themselves and — boom! They got crushed by Dan Owens and Robert Porcher. And if they stepped out to avoid the inside charge of those guys — boom! They ran into the crunching arms of Swilling and George Jamison.

You know what they say in football: Hit 'em high, hit 'em low. Hit 'em early, hit 'em often. Hit 'em where they ain't. No, wait, that's baseball.

"Watching the defense play today was a thing of beauty," admitted Rodney Peete, the Lions' quarterback. And he's not supposed to be watching!

But who can blame him? The Silver Storm — when a defense is good, you have to give it a nickname, so I just made this one up — was arresting. In the first half, The Blue Blitzkrieg — like that one better? — gave up just 12 yards rushing, had four sacks, forced two fumbles and intercepted a pass.

Best of all, when it counted, the Motown Menace — how's that? —

surrendered only two field goals before a meaningless touchdown with six minutes left in garbage time.

"That's the best defensive effort I've seen since I've been here," said coach Wayne Fontes, who has seen his share of the other kind, believe me.

New? Improved? Here were several things Sunday that haven't been witnessed at the Silverdome in some time:

1) A defensive line of six linebackers, all standing up, ready to charge.

2) Spielman staying in on all downs.

3) No Jerry Ball, and his Body By Nestle.

"If you notice, we're all a lot lighter now," said Owens, who had his best game as a Lion. "Instead of a 285-pound guy trying to blitz in from outside, we have a 245-pound guy, and even the guys up front are lighter, so we're faster."

This, you may recall, is one way the Dallas Cowboys built the best defense in the NFL and won the Super Bowl. Speed over size.

So the Lions, if nothing else, are hip.

ALL THIS FROM NEW DEFENSIVE coordinator Hank Bullough, who was supposedly too old to be hip, or even effective. The game had passed him by, they said, he'd been out of it for several years.

Obviously, he was busy devising schemes.

"Hank has known more football then I forgot," Spielman said, fumbling with the words. "I mean, he's forgotten more football than I've known. Than I know. Then he … aw, you know the cliche I'm trying to say."

I know it, I just haven't had to use it much with the Lions. But the evidence was convincing. Not once on Sunday did you see that terribly common sight from years past, where the opposing quarterback stands back in the pocket, untouched, humming a tune, deciding what restaurant to visit tonight before picking out a receiver.

Nu-uh. Even when Miller completed his passes, he was moving or under attack. Atlanta was completely befuddled.

"Could you see their confusion?" Swilling was asked.

"Oh yes. I think they knew Pat Swilling was coming. But they didn't expect me to bring my four or five friends."

Hey, Pat. If they can tackle, bring your whole family.

Now, true, the Lions' offense had some shaky moments. And yes, Sunday was just the opener, and any team coached by Jerry Glanville is, at best, unpredictable.

But a win is a win, a good start is a good start, and a linebacker is … a fullback — at least when it comes to Spielman.

"Why didn't you carry the ball and try to score?" Spielman was asked.

"If I told you that, I'd have to kill you," he said.

I think he was joking.

But the way they played Sunday, I'm not taking any chances.

Good call: Harwells safe at home

October 1, 1993

S HE CAN PUT THE CHAIR away now. The one she jams under the bedroom doorknob whenever her husband is away. She feels safer when that chair is wedged in. She reads. She sews. She watches TV. Now and then she'll run the vacuum because the whirring noise gives a buffer against the loneliness. And, of course, she has the radio. She can turn on the radio and have her husband nearby, or as near as a man can be when his life is broadcasting baseball.

Lulu Harwell gets her husband home for good after 46 years of waiting through road trips, 46 years of driving him to airports, 46 years of working the garden, paying the bills, being the one adult they run to when the kids fall off their bikes, or come home scratching with poison ivy.

Once, when they were living in Baltimore, the Harwells kept a horse in the farmhouse garage. Lulu was tending her babies one night when the horse broke free. It pranced through a nearby college for a couple of hours before the police lassoed it and brought it back. Lulu saw the flashing lights, went rushing outside and heard the door slam behind her. Then she realized she had locked herself out of the house, and the babies were inside crying. While she held the horse, the police busted in.

The next morning, when Ernie called and said, "What's new?" she said, "Pick up a newspaper. The AP wrote all about it."

The Women Who Wait. You often hear about the athlete's wife, the coach's wife. They never mention announcers' wives. Why? After all, the athlete usually comes home to roost by age 35, and often with enough money to last a lifetime.

The announcer stays out till he's old and gray, until his back hurts when he squeezes into the booth and everyone he interviews is young enough to call him Grandpa.

Forty-six years. Time to come home.

I KNOW SOME ANNOUNCERS' WIVES have a difficult time with this life," Lulu Harwell says, sitting in a chair in the Harwells' tidy Farmington Hills home. "But I knew Ernie would be doing this from the day I married him. We used to walk in the parks in Atlanta — we didn't own a car then — and he would say, 'What do you want to hear? Baseball? Tennis? Golf?' And I would pick and he would start announcing, right there, a make-believe game."

She smiles. "Mostly, I picked baseball."

Which, of course, is where her husband was destined to star. His warm, rich voice, with the trace of Georgia accent, became an enjoyment and later a comfort to baseball fans in Michigan. Season after season. Decade after decade. Hearing that voice meant the snow really was going to melt, and the coats really would be put in the closet, and summer really would come again.

For everyone but Harwell — and his family. Summer was work time in their world. The Fourth of July, Memorial Day, Labor Day — these were traditionally doubleheader baseball days.

Lulu remembers watching neighbors barbecuing all day, while her family ate inside. It's not the same, barbecuing without your father.

Harwell, 75, broadcast the Brooklyn Dodgers, the Giants, the Orioles, and of course, the Tigers. In 33 years, he missed just two Detroit games.

But he missed other things. When one of the Harwell boys smashed his hand with a hammer, Ernie was on the road. When his two girls got the chicken pox and mumps — simultaneously — Ernie was on the road. When the horse ran away, Ernie was, well, you get the idea.

This is the life of a baseball voice. The Harwells have lived in countless houses and apartments in Michigan, Baltimore, Atlanta, New York. For 16 years they came north from Florida when Tigers seasons began, lived wherever they could. Ernie would pack, Lulu would drive him to the airport. Ernie would come home, Lulu would pick him up. She knew he was home when she came downstairs "and saw a pile of newspapers on the floor by his chair."

Her eyes are bad now. She can't drive him anymore. The lawn of their home, bare when they moved here, is covered with her beautiful rosebushes, asters, lilacs, baby's breath.

It is harvest time. For the plants and the planters.

S O ERNIE ENDS HIS RICH CAREER, and — as in the false end once before — the feelings are dipped in nostalgia. Fans would love to see Harwell broadcast until the day he dies, but how fair would that be for the others in his life? This farewell is much more subdued, and better this way, because Ernie prefers it quiet. It's more elegant. And as much as a baseball man can be that word, he is.

If it had any sense, WJR would have him broadcast the whole game Sunday, his Tigers finale, because you should not hear anyone else's voice after Harwell's. Just silence. Let it sink in.

And then let him go. His new job with the Tigers will be in a promotional/goodwill capacity, and the Tigers are richer for having him there.

Lulu and the family are richer for having him home. She can put away the chair. Stop wedging her loneliness under the doorknob. The world they always dreamed of — together — can begin.

Funny, isn't it, how art imitates us? For all his baseball expertise, Harwell's most notable broadcast expression is the one that actually best describes his personal life: "Lonnng gone!"

Long home now. May it be the best of stays.

Michael will be back

October 7, 1993

H E WILL BE BACK. History tells us that. So does the man who guarded him better than anyone in the NBA, who looked into his eyes night after night, feeling the heat of his competitive furnace. Three hundred miles from Chicago, where Michael Jordan was dropping a bomb on the sports world by telling the NBA good-bye, Joe Dumars was driving up I-75, on his way to see the team physician. His nose was stuffy. He had a slight fever. It was the day before the start of Pistons training camp, and that was the last place on Earth he felt like going.

"Right now," Dumars said, fighting a cold, "I can definitely understand what Jordan is going through. Believe me. Yesterday and today, even I felt like retiring."

This is the time of year that NBA players get the blues. They ask themselves, "Do I really want to go through this again? The training camp? The questions from reporters? The sweat, the pain, the pounding? Months of travel? Months of spotlight?" If you're weary of the game, the week before preseason starts is a seductive time to quit. The NBA seems like the world's biggest mountain.

And if you've been to the top of that mountain three times in a row …

Jordan, king of the mountain until yesterday, when he retired at age 30, stunning the world, will be back. He will be back. I say that from the gut. I say that from everything I've learned about the best athletes in the world. They almost always come back if they retire early because their whole lives have been about sports, the rush of victory, the anger of defeat, and they find the rest of the world isn't as challenging, or, frankly, as easy.

So Jordan will be back because he's only 30, with a body from the planet Krypton. He can disappear for two years and be a better player when he returns. Jordan himself even admitted this when he told the packed news conference in Deerfield, Ill., "Will I ever unretire? The word retire means I can do anything I want to do, right?"

He'll be back.

A ND YET, RIGHT NOW, coming back is the furthest thing from his mind. And no one can blame him. He is a kid who has climbed every tree in the backyard. A teenager who has listened to every record in his collection. When Jordan asked his own coach, Phil Jackson — whose vested interest in Jordan playing is like a farmer's vested interest in rain — "Phil, do I have anything left to prove in the game?" even Jackson had to pause and think.

"That's when I knew it was the right move," Jordan said.

Remember, this is not O.J. Simpson, who shone brightly but for dull teams. This is not Nolan Ryan, whose statistics far outspeak his championships. No. This is the greatest athlete to ever play the sport of basketball realizing he has every toy he can collect from it. Not only does he have three championship rings, he has them in three straights years. He has more MVP awards than mantel space. He has as many scoring titles as days of the week. And he has more money than you can store in a vault — most of it from endorsement deals, not basketball. He also has two Olympic gold medals from two different Games eight years apart. Even Mark Spitz can't say that.

Spitz, by the way, tried to come back.

And so will Jordan.

I say this despite his words of good-bye to an incredibly large media gathering, despite the fact that the story was played higher in newspapers and TV stations than Moscow, Mogadishu or other places in the world where people are actually losing their lives. You wouldn't figure a story this huge might have to be rescinded one day, but one day, it will be.

One day.

"I thought about what George Brett said when he retired," Jordan, wearing a tidy tan suit, white shirt and striped tie, told the media throng. "Brett said, 'If you ride a roller coaster for nine years, don't you want to ride something else?' ...

"There's nothing left for me to prove. I can't step out on the court and know it's for no reason. It's not worth it for me. It's not worth it for my teammates."

He is right.

But the condition is temporary.

This is not a fire that has been extinguished. This is more like a coal that has momentarily lost its flame. Jordan has been slapped by the death of his father, whacked by the spotlight on his gambling habits and hounded into an Elvis-like seclusion. His desire for a breath of air is completely understandable.

But Magic Johnson quit, then wanted to come back and play. Kareem Abdul-Jabbar quit, then wanted to come back and play. Every boxer under the sun has come back after he's retired. Kirk Gibson, Sugar Ray Leonard, smart athletes, accomplished athletes, rich athletes. It is a pattern. And at the risk of playing armchair psychiatrist, this would be the way I envision things might unfold for Jordan:

He will wake up today and for many days to come feeling lighter, relieved. He may even sleep in. For a while, doing business will be interesting. He will travel. He will speak to enraptured corporate executives. He'll enjoy visiting family, having conversations that don't have to end because the plane is waiting. He will make up for the emptiness he feels due to his father's death. He will breathe easier.

And time will pass. And maybe he'll make a quick ton of money in some venture overseas — be it playing basketball or teaching a Nike clinic or just cutting endorsement deals — but he will do it because the money will be too lucrative.

And time will pass. He will watch a few Bulls games, and have his number retired, and maybe do some TV analysis, and he will go to the gym, keep himself in shape, and eventually, after many rounds of golf and tennis and other distractions, he will pick up a basketball.

And time will pass. He will wonder whether it's still there. He will scrimmage against some old friends, maybe some current players. He will dominate because at 30 or 31 or 32 you not only still have skill, you have smarts. The joy of playing will begin to stir again.

And time will pass. He will wait until he hears the voices that have always moved him in life, the ones that say: "You can't do it. You can't come back and win again."

And that's when he will make his move.

I NEVER WANTED TO LEAVE the game when my skills started to diminish," Jordan said, "because that's when you feel the foot in your back."

And yet, anyone who knows Jordan knows when you stick a foot in his back, he pushes back harder. Tell him no, he tells you yes. Tell him he can't win two rings, he wins three. John Starks says he will shut him down in the playoffs? John Starks is buried. The media say he shouldn't gamble, he says, "Mind your own business" and heads for a casino. The Olympic committee says he has to wear a Reebok logo during the Barcelona Games, he says, "I'm Michael Jordan" and throws a flag over the emblem.

He is the greatest competitor of his time and his game. You don't just lose that. Sorry. You can't.

"Right now, he's looking at a season where he has nothing to gain," Dumars, who knows him as both friend and competitor, said while riding up I-75. "He's had three short summers. He had the tragedy with his father. He's had all that attention for the gambling stuff.

"He's done everything. And now he's looking at a season and saying, 'I have to do this again?' ...

"You know, Michael always told me when he left, he wanted to surprise everybody. And I'll tell you this, if he comes back, he'll want to do it the same way."

Count on it. One day. As sure as his jump shot.

We'll be waiting.

Fun

October 19, 1993

PHILADELPHIA — I needed the money. It was that simple. When you're 11 years old, your allowance is gone, and there are all these great comic books to buy, well, what choice does a kid have? I went to work. I took my first job. I got on the subway, rode down Broad Street and got off at my personal field of dreams. It was new at the time, round, with different colored seats, and a machine that shot fireworks out beyond centerfield.

They called it Veterans Stadium.

"Don't say anything dumb," my friend warned me. He already was working there, selling programs, and he said he could "get me in." He dragged me to this dank room beneath a concrete ramp on the stadium's lowest level. It smelled of cigar smoke. On the gray walls hung dozens of red-and-white-striped uniforms. I was a small kid. They looked awfully big.

"How old are you?" barked a man. I spun around. He had a cigar between his teeth and thinning gray hair. The boss.

"Thirteen," I said, glancing at my friend. I lied. Should I have picked a higher number? Thirteen seems pretty old when you're 11.

"Thirteen? Can you handle one of these?"

He hoisted a canvas bag containing 20 Philadelphia Phillies programs and five Philadelphia Phillies yearbooks. I tightened my shoulders as he draped it over me. "Yeah, no problem," I said, gritting my teeth.

"Good." He stuffed another 30 programs into the bag. Suddenly it felt like two bowling balls hanging around my neck.

"You get a nickel for every program and 15 cents for every yearbook," he said. "Get out and sell them and don't come back until they're gone."

He turned. He never asked my name. Others were now filing in, bigger kids, grown men, grabbing the bags wordlessly, taking a uniform off the hook. It was another day on the job for them. But it was a whole new world for me. Someone was paying me to do something. I grabbed a striped shirt and slipped it on. Too big. I scampered out before anyone saw me, looking like I was wearing a dress.

THAT I CAN REMEMBER ALL THAT, I think, is due to what came next. I walked through the opening and was hit with the most startling visual burst of my life. A major league baseball field. Such a view! A huge stadium full of colored seats, a round blue sky, green turf, brown dirt and the steady plunking sound of ball meeting bat as the players took early practice.

I was knocked out. There was Steve Carlton and Tommy Hutton and Greg

(Bull) Luzinski, real live players, just a few feet away. And suddenly I bonded with them. We had all come to work. This is what Disney calls an E-ticket sensation.

"Get moving," my friend said, breaking my trance. He and the others were fanning out across the stadium, claiming ground, holding positions. As the fans began to file in, it seemed all my colleagues were right where they needed to be, selling programs like jugglers moving balls.

And there I was, always a second too late, missing a sale, losing to someone else, my bag drooping. I ran foolishly to the upper deck. My shoulders ached. The sweat poured down my face and soaked me under my uniform. I yelled what the others yelled. "Programs! Yearbooks! Scorecards! Lineups!"

I saw a man waving at me from the last row of the stadium. I trudged up, my bag bumping me with every step. Breathless when I finally got there, I stammered, "Program, sir?"

"Nah," he said. "Send the hot dog guy up, OK?"

EVENTUALLY I LEARNED THE TRICKS of the trade — although, admittedly, the most I ever made was $43 the night of a July doubleheader against the Cincinnati Reds. Usually I went home with about $9 for five hours' work. And I never complained. Because as long as I had that red-and-white uniform, I could sit and watch the games when I was done.

And I did. I watched. I learned every player. We would get there early and catch the balls they hit out during batting practice. Once or twice, the Phillies let us come onto the field and throw to them. It was the most incredible summer, night after night of hawking programs, then "relaxing" in the seats, sharing hot dogs, guessing what song the organist would play. We cheered, we argued, we booed bad calls. The summer wind blew.

This is how boys fall in love with baseball.

I quit the job when I was 14. I left for college a few years later. I grew into one of those men who would rather leave his roots than nurture them. Eventually, sports became my work, and on nights off, going to a ballpark held no magic.

Until tonight. Tonight, Game 3 of the World Series, will be my first baseball game at the Vet since I walked out the employees' exit as a teen. And for some reason, I am excited. Why? I seem to have reached that midpoint in life, where glimpses of our youth become vitally important. We want to remember how it smelled, how it felt, how it tasted. Why is this?

Maybe because it was fun. These Phils are fun, and I'm glad they inhabit my old stomping grounds. For me they carry on tradition. They even look a little like we did in the early '70s, long hair and all.

Fun. There was no finer backyard for a boy than that stadium. I'm not sure I ever appreciated it until now. But tonight, just before game time, I know what I'm going to do. I'm going to find the youngest-looking vendor, and I'm going to buy up all his programs, just to see the look on his face.

Next time? God only knows

November 7, 1993

MAYBE YOU SEE GOD. Maybe that's the sensation football players whisper about after a crunching hit coughs the life from their bodies and they collapse like puppets into the turf. Maybe it's a religious thing, the gates of heaven swinging open, your maker taking a fleeting look, ready to call you home.

But only for a moment. Then, there is nothing. You say, "Fingers, move" but your fingers will not move. You say, "Legs, rise" but your legs are stiff as wood. The gates have swung closed and you are still on the field, and macho is replaced by fear, tears, a cry for help. "Oh, please," you pray, "not me, please … " You lay there, weak as paper, as the paramedics rush out with the stretcher.

Lions defensive back Tim McKyer was facedown on the AstroTurf of the Minneapolis Metrodome last Sunday, going through all of this. No legs. No toes. No feeling. The doctors were poking him up and down his calves and thighs.

"Tim, can you feel this? … "

He thought about his mother, watching in Port Arthur, Texas, where football is religion and they avoid talk of moments like this. He thought about his wife, Fontella, whom he married several years ago. They had no kids. We should have had kids, he thought.

"Don't move him!" the doctors kept saying. "Everybody back!" McKyer, a cornerback, was still flat, just the way he'd landed after the Vikings' Robert Smith smacked a knee into his head. The impact was so great that Smith flipped over. But Smith got up. McKyer, crumpled, could see only dark green carpet now. A distant buzz of stadium noise seeped into his helmet. How strange. All these doctors, unstrapping the spine board, barking orders, "Get ready to roll him … one … two … " And meanwhile, to fill the break, cheerleaders danced and rock music blasted from loudspeakers, like a carnival.

THE GAME GOES ON. No surprise. This is not grade school, where you walk the injured kid back to his house and his mother comes running out the door. Before the ambulance doors were closed, football had resumed at the Metrodome. At the hospital, McKyer asked to see the final minute on a TV set. They rolled him around, and when the Lions scored the winning touchdown he mumbled, "They did it. All right." He was immobile at the time.

No surprise. Neither is the fact that McKyer, who thankfully regained all feeling in his body — bad concussion, they said — still stayed at that

Minneapolis hospital two days, for tests on his spine and brain.

Here is the surprise: On Wednesday, McKyer was back in Detroit, at practice. On Thursday, he was there as well. And while he did not take part in drills, if he feels up to it, he may play against Tampa Bay.

And this is unbelievable.

If one of us — a nonprofessional athlete — took a blow that left us temporarily disconnected from our body, we would not be back next week for more. We might not be back next year.

"I'm ready if they let me," McKyer said Thursday, stretching gingerly in the Silverdome. "The doctors said I'm OK."

"Aren't you worried?" he was asked.

"You can't think about getting hurt. That's when you get hurt."

That is a very brave sports cliche.

It's a lie.

MIKE UTLEY WAS NOT THINKING ABOUT getting hurt when he landed on his head that day against the Rams. Neither was Dennis Byrd when he broke his neck last year. Chucky Mullins, from Mississippi, was not thinking hurt when he made the brutal hit that left him paralyzed for life. Darryl Stingley was not thinking hurt when he flew across the middle and landed in a wheelchair.

Football is like dropping bodies from a second-floor window and hoping they land on a mattress. You needn't think about injury; it will happen. Knees will be destroyed. Shoulders will be ripped from sockets. Perfectly healthy young men will ensure, each week, their need for canes and crutches when they reach their 50s.

Tim McKyer — or the coaching staff — even thinking about his playing today, despite the encouraging tests, is insane. A week ago he couldn't move. Isn't that some kind of sign? The doctors say they're still not sure why he lost feeling. On Thursday, as he spoke, McKyer winced occasionally, bent over, and said, "I don't know, man, my legs feel weird." Then, in the next breath, "I'm ready to play."

He should not play. It's on the Lions' conscience if he does. In a normal world, he would not even attend today's game. But in a normal world, you don't tackle moving objects. The truth is, Sunday comes around, and for all the noise we make, Utley, Byrd, Mullins, Stingley, they're just names to shake your head over before kickoff.

This is pro football. You bandage your wounds, get back in line. Next time, maybe you see God for real.

Hail! to the student valiant
November 19, 1993

WHEN THE TRUMPETS BLARE, he will not be there. When they clomp through the tunnel, he will not be among them. When the roar of the crowd, 100,000 strong, lifts the Michigan players to a state of violent euphoria before the big game Saturday, banging helmets, slamming pads, howling as they leap into a bouncing pile, he will be quietly here on Earth, watching from the stands. A college student. No more, no less.

Shawn Collins quit football. He just quit. No injuries. No run-ins with the coaches. He was once rated America's best high school linebacker. He belonged to one of the world's most famous college teams. He is only a sophomore, he has years to go. Against Penn State last month, he got to start, and it turned out to be the biggest victory of the year.

Two days later, he walked into Gary Moeller's office.

"I've thought about it, Coach," he said, "and I just don't want to play football anymore."

Moeller, who bleeds the sport, was stunned. "Shawn, I don't get it. You just started a game. Why?"

Why? It was a mystery that buzzed around campus. A rumor that brushfired across the nation's sports machine. A stud recruit, and he quit the Wolverines? A sophomore? There must be something wrong, people figured. Must be a hidden problem. A discipline thing. He's unhappy with their record. He just quit? Gave up his scholarship? Just like that? You can do almost anything in football — vomit, weep, get dizzy drunk, beat someone senseless, lie in the middle of traffic, sing your fight song naked on the 50-yard line — but you can't just quit. That's the one thing football doesn't comprehend.

Maybe Shawn Collins will show them all something before he's through.

IT REALLY HIT ME DURING an accounting exam," he says, sitting on the bed in his small dorm room in South Quad. The late-fall sun comes in through the single window. Collins, a polite, thoughtful student, still carries the athlete's tightly muscled frame, even though he hasn't done hard workouts in weeks. "I knew I was falling behind in my academics, but I thought I could get by. Then they handed me this exam, and I looked at it, and I had no idea what was going on. No idea."

He raises his shoulders, then lets them droop. It is mid-afternoon, and were he still on the team, he would not be sitting here now. He never just sat in his room while he was on the team. There was no time. He was getting up at 6:30

a.m. to go to Schembechler Hall and watch film. Then back to the dorm for a fast breakfast and a brief nap. Then off to class from 10 until noon. Then back for a fast lunch and a faster nap, because he was already sleepy again, then off to the football building by 1:15 for taping and prep. Then three hours of practice. Then training table. Then study table.

By 9:30 p.m., he was trudging back to the dorm. He had a bit of conversation with whomever was around, then fell off to sleep, exhausted.

And the next morning he started again.

This is a typical football player schedule in any major-college program. There is little time for studying besides study table — which can often be a distraction itself — and there is almost no time for going-out socializing during the week, unless you get by on three hours' sleep. Which is damn hard when you're banging your body and pounding weights six days a week.

Many make up for the limited study time by taking fewer classes during the season, or taking incomplete grades, or, quite simply, taking easier classes and skating by. As for fatigue and the lack of a non-sports life? Most endure it, because for them, football is either worth it, or it's all they have.

For Shawn Collins, it was neither.

"THERE WAS THIS DAY, EARLIER IN the season, where Coach gave us off because we had a bye week," he says. "I'll never forget it. It was a Monday, and a lot of the players didn't know how to act. Honest. They did not know how to act! They were like, 'What are we gonna do?' We weren't used to that kind of freedom."

And you? Did you like it?

"Oh, yes. I loved it."

Maybe it started then, the voice in his head. Maybe it started when he saw the other students relaxing under trees, or playing volleyball, or just sitting in coffee shops in no apparent rush.

Or maybe it started long before, when Collins was a high school star in New Jersey. He liked football, but it came naturally to him, as did most sports. At 6-feet-2 and a strong 215 pounds, Collins excelled in pretty much everything. He played linebacker, fullback, he even won a state title in the hurdles. He had tremendous speed, and speed was very fashionable in college football, thanks to teams like Florida State.

So Collins was a blue-chip recruit. Several services rated him the best linebacker in the country. And all the while, he never got caught up in the ratings or recruiting as much as the fun he anticipated having at college. He enjoyed high school. He was a good student and a great athlete. Now he heard people say, "College will be the best four years of your life." He was looking forward to it.

When it started, however, he felt a certain emptiness. He was part of this huge football machine, where things were done for you, tutors, schedules, meals.

Some kids love this. Some expect it. Collins, 19, found it constraining, like a jacket that was too tight. He still liked the game of football, but he didn't love it the way everyone around him seemed to love it. There would be times during practice, especially toward the end, where his heart wasn't in it, he was thinking about his grades and his future and meanwhile he was trying to tackle players who were trying to clobber him. He thought about getting injured. He thought about his slim odds of ever making the NFL. The voice in his head said, "If you're not in this to get to the next level, why are you in it?"

Meanwhile, wherever he went, he was treated as a player first, because that's what happens when you're a stud recruit at a big-time football school. The questions were: "How's the team doing? ... How will the team play this week? ... What's the latest with the team? ... "

"I never got the feeling they cared about me," Collins says, "as much as the fact that I was a player."

STILL, HE MIGHT HAVE ENDURED all that, had his academics stayed strong. But when his grades started to slip, he felt he was sacrificing the wrong thing. "I've always been taught to value education. Both my parents are teachers. And I want to go into business one day.

"It seemed like, whenever I thought about my life without football, I had this fascinated feeling. And whenever I thought about my life with football, it was like this ugly feeling. Like everything was already predictable."

One day, when it got to be too much, he put his head down, and focused on the two worlds, a member of the team, a regular college student, member of the team, regular college student. When he lifted his head, he had his conclusion.

He sat outside Moeller's office, on that Monday after the Penn State game, "for the longest 15 minutes of my life." He imagined Moeller's booming voice trying to talk him out of his decision. He focused on his opening sentence.

"I thought of it like a thesis statement," he says. "You know, state your purpose right up front."

How do you like that? An athlete making an academic metaphor.

When the deed was done, he went down to where the players dressed. It was after two o'clock, and when his teammates saw him, they said, "Hurry up, get dressed, man. You'll be late."

"I'm not on the team anymore," he said.

"WHAT? Come on. Stop joking."

"I'm serious."

"Come on, man."

He tried to explain in the brief and rushed moments, but the meetings were starting, you can't be late, and next thing Shawn Collins knew, he was alone, a man without a team, looking at a whole new world that had to be paid for and negotiated without a safety net.

How could he explain it?

He felt … great.

UNDERSTAND THAT COLLINS HAS absolutely nothing against U-M football. He says he loves his ex-teammates, considers them like family, he has no problem with Moeller, his staff, or this year's mediocre record. He respects everyone who plays football. He just wanted a more normal college life, with a focus on being a student planning for a future.

Why is that so strange, he wonders?

"It's funny, but I get a chance to do my own laundry now, and clean the room, and go and meet with professors and people. If I want to come back to the dorm and study, I can. If I want to just hang around, visit with friends, I can do that, too. I feel like I'm learning to be responsible …

"The day I left the team, I remember walking outside. It was beautiful. The sun was out, and all these people were on campus, all these people at three o'clock that I'd never seen before. I liked it."

It will be a costly enjoyment. Michigan, for an out-of-state kid like Collins, can cost upwards of $21,000 a year when you total everything. Collins' parents are school teachers. They don't make that kind of money. Collins says he's trying desperately to line up financial aid, loans, grants.

He says he wants to stay at U-M, not transfer to some cheaper school, but he admits he may be forced to do that.

You see him turn his back on a scholarship, a free ride, and there's a part of you that wants to say, "Go back, it's a good deal, never mind if you don't want to be there."

But how can you tell that to a young man?

So here he goes, into Michigan-Ohio State weekend, a student, rooting for his college team. His grades have improved, he says he feels "relaxed," and he still enjoys wearing his letter jacket from his freshman season because, he says, "I earned that."

There have been whispers about Collins. Some have questioned his heart, as if not wanting to pummel a football opponent makes you less of a man. And some, of course, simply whisper the word "quitter," a label that always will shadow him.

It is unfair. When Collins made his decision, the last words Gary Moeller said to him when he left his office were these: "Good luck." It brings to mind the old sports quote that football coaches often recite: "I'd rather be lucky than good."

Collins was already lucky. Now he's trying to be good, on his own, the hard way. That doesn't deserve to be labeled anything, except admirable.

Good-bye, and good riddance
December 1, 1993

MAYBE NOW THAT HE'S RETIRING, Bill Laimbeer expects gratitude. A suspended sentence. A shrug, a grin, an "aw, heck, you weren't so bad." Maybe he figures, now that he's hanging up 14 long, bumpy years, the spotlight will fall on the good parts of his story — like his statistics — and not the bad parts — like his elbows.

Well. He should know better. Not long ago, I asked Laimbeer whether he thought he'd ever make the Hall of Fame. He snorted a laugh and said, "No."

Why not?

"Because the powers that be don't want me in there."

He said this with little emotion, like a mechanic tallying a bill. He was always good at that. Tallying the bill. Keeping track. Remembering his statistics during a game. Being realistic. He was good at being realistic.

So on the day that he is expected to say good-bye to the NBA, a league that he roused, bumped, aggravated, incited, angered, amused and financially supported through the biggest collection of fines this side of a New York City parking violations office, it is only fair that we do the same.

Be realistic.

START WITH THE THINGS he did admirably. He showed up for work. He played with pain. He had a tiger's eyes during a game, unwavering, locked on the enemy; he had the fiercest mood; he dripped competition, and if that meant shoving, pushing, elbowing, flopping, arguing calls, threatening opponents, he did it. In a league in which winning is the goal, you can only fault that so much.

He also had a pride in workmanship. He was like a good mechanic with an ugly car. He made it go. Never mind that he ran like a crippled antelope, or jumped like a refrigerator during an earthquake. He showed up. He pushed himself. He rebounded like a madman and amassed admirable numbers in his 14 years (becoming the 19th player with 10,000 points and 10,000 rebounds). And he didn't complain about money, not in public, anyhow.

He was a rich kid, and if he learned anything from his privileged youth, it was not to bitch about being a millionaire.

He was kind to his own children, and most everyone else's. And he has the world's most patient wife (although she deserves the credit for this, not Bill). Now and then, he had a sense of humor, when it wasn't directed at a victim. And he never bragged about his talent. That would have been stupid, seeing how limited it was.

Laimbeer was never stupid. Quite the contrary.

WHICH BRINGS US TO THE REST. Although smart enough to be anything he wanted to be, this is what he chose: to be boorish, haughty and rude. He behaved, much of the time, as if he expected his nanny to show up after he left and apologize for his childish behavior. I have seen him completely belittle the most innocent of visitors. I have seen him snarl, "What paper are you from?" to an obviously young reporter, and when the answer came meekly, he'd bark, "I'm not answering any of your dumb questions. Your paper stinks."

I have seen him ignore fans. Seen him rip on teammates. Seen him sneer at someone's ignorance, and yell insults across the room at people who weren't even talking to him. If you barked back at Bill Laimbeer, he usually backed down. But you shouldn't have to bark back. He was old enough to know better. He was smart enough to have patience and manners. He simply chose not to.

He bent the rules of the game, and, let's face it, he used every cheap trick in the book — on everyone from Robert Parish to Karl Malone. Maybe it was to help the Pistons win. Maybe you wanted the Pistons to win. That doesn't make what he did right or admirable. Only effective.

Laimbeer, 36, is arguably the most hated man in the game, by both players and fans. In his time, he has stiffed the biggest names in the league. He says he never congratulated anyone besides Kareem Abdul-Jabbar. He didn't love the NBA or its members.

I've heard him say on more than one occasion, "I have no plans to stay friendly with NBA players after I retire. I have my world. They have theirs."

As they say in the Sufi religion, "He will not be missed."

HIS DEPARTURE COMES AT AN odd time, and yet, when you think about it, a logical one. He always joked that he was staying in the game "because I can't find a job that pays like this." But he leaves it now not because of wages, but because of woes.

There is no fun left for Laimbeer. Also, no status. He looks around the locker room and sees a struggling team with mostly new faces. Macon? Liberty? Elliott? Wood? These are Detroit Pistons? What do they know of the building years? What do they know of the Bad Boys legacy? What do they know of "the speech" that Laimbeer and Isiah Thomas used to give all new players, scaring the hell out of them, telling them this is Detroit, we have our way of playing here and you better get into it?

They know nothing of this — and have no reason to listen to Laimbeer talk about it. He was once the second-most powerful person on team, behind Thomas; now he is a backup. One of the ironic reasons he and Thomas got into a fistfight recently is that Laimbeer is now practicing with the B squad while Isiah remains on the A.

The team is mediocre, going nowhere; he's in pain, and he's a sub. Where is the fun in this?

Besides, although he will not admit it, I believe Laimbeer is hesitant about continuing the season when Thomas returns to the lineup. All those questions on every trip about "the fight." Have you made up? Is all forgiven? What was that all about?

Who needs that?

NOT LAIMBEER. HE CAN have more fun fishing, and he will. Today the TV stations no doubt will clip together highlight footage, fond memories, his defensive rebounds, his long, flick-wrist jumpers, his almost charmingly awkward celebrations after victories. Maybe they'll put sentimental music behind it. Maybe they'll run it in slow motion. Maybe you'll feel sorry for the guy, like he was misunderstood all these years.

Don't be fooled. Life is not a highlight reel. You are who you are not by how you look in the warm and cozy lights of a farewell, but by the final tally of every day you lived your life. Most days, to most people, Laimbeer behaved like a jerk. That doesn't wash off. It stains him even today.

No More Mr. Nice Guy. How's that for a farewell headline? Bill Laimbeer, fine player, fierce competitor, two-time NBA champion, nonetheless collected his mountain of dislike the old-fashioned way: He earned it.

He gets to take it with him, as he walks out the door.

Peplowski to the rescue
December 15, 1993

H E RAN BACK TO THE TRUCK for his hunting jacket because you're supposed to keep injured people warm, right? He rumbled down the embankment, and his feet squashed in the water of the drainage ditch. So much mud. He kneeled, wrapped the jacket around Bobby Hurley's shoulders and tugged it tightly.

Hurley looked up. "Pep ... what happened?" His voice was weak, almost dream-like. His eyes were glassy, and blood dripped from his ear. "Pep? ... "

"You're gonna be all right," Mike Peplowski said.

He cradled him, breathing hard. Peplowski had no idea if Hurley would be all right. He had never been this close to a seriously wounded man; he knew he shouldn't move him — they say that in the movies — but he also knew this was no minor accident. Hurley was soaked in blood and dirty water, his hair and face a slimy mess.

The impact of the crash had sent him hurtling through the air, like an apple core tossed from a speeding car, and dropped him in a ditch. He was facedown in water when a witness found him, rolled him over and saved him from drowning. Peplowski arrived minutes later, and now he held his teammate, waiting for the paramedics, and wondered how on Earth something this terrible could happen this fast.

"My back ... it hurts," Hurley groaned.

"We'll take care of it," Peplowski said. That was a good sign, wasn't it? That he could feel his back? Wasn't it?

"Pep ... what happened?" Hurley asked again.

Peplowski hugged him. How could he explain? He saw more blood over Hurley's eye and a gash on the side of his head. Hurley was gasping, and Peplowski thought he might choke. He kept asking him questions, trying to keep him conscious because conscious meant he was alive, right?

"Do you know where you are?" he asked.

"Do you remember the game?"

"Do you know what day it is?"

The night was cold, but Peplowski was sweating heavily. His heart was pounding like a frightened deer's. They were both wet now, and they were both helpless. It was dark. It was eerily quiet.

"Pep ... am I gonna die?" Bobby Hurley asked.

Peplowski shivered. "Don't be ridiculous," he whispered, and he looked to the road, praying the ambulance would get there already.

D ON'T STOP, HE HAD TOLD HIMSELF. He had seen the overturned vehicle on Del Paso Road, a lightly traveled route some Sacramento players take home from Arco Arena. The Kings had lost yet another game, this time to the Clippers. Peplowski had friends visiting from out of town and he was in a hurry to get home. Don't stop.

He stopped. He had to. He has always been that kind of person. Back in college at Michigan State, he was riding his motorcycle when a car drove off the highway, went straight across the grassy median, then suddenly straightened and stopped. The driver had fallen asleep. Peplowski drove to the window, made sure everything was OK.

This is the kind of kid he is. His friends call him "a big softie."

On Del Paso Road, he killed his engine and stared at the gold-colored truck that seemed to be sliced in two. He saw another vehicle, a station wagon, that looked like balled-up aluminum foil. A man was trapped inside that vehicle, and someone was tending to him. "Man, this is really bad," Peplowski thought. He heard someone yell: "Look for bodies on that side!"

He ran across the road. He saw nothing. He crossed back and, in the weak glow of the streetlight, he saw the figure down the embankment. "So far from the wreck?" Peplowski wondered. Then he realized whoever it was had been ejected like a rag-doll astronaut. He looked down, and he felt a horrible shiver.

In the grass, along the road, was a pair of basketball sneakers.

The crash had separated Bobby Hurley from his shoes.

H ANG ON, BOB, HANG ON," Peplowski said now, still hugging his bleeding teammate as the paramedics raced down the hill, the lights flashing, people screaming directions …

How strange this was. Almost surreal. Just a few hours earlier, Hurley and Peplowski had been in the Kings' locker room, comparing notes about their rookie seasons. They were both starters, Hurley, the intense, buck-toothed point guard from Jersey City, Peplowski, the hulking, easygoing center from Michigan. An odd pair. Sort of Mutt and Jeff. Rookie teammates.

"Man, I'm just not happy with the way things are going," Hurley had said. The Kings were 5-14, and coming from Duke, where Hurley had won two national titles, this was most abnormal.

"Relax," Peplowski said, laughing. "You're playing great. Don't be so hard on yourself. It'll get better."

They were just starting to be friends. They played cards together. They ate together on the road. Now this — Peplowski holding Hurley's hand as the medics strapped Hurley to a board. Peplowski looked in Hurley's eyes, so dazed, the mud and blood covering his face.

They were just starting to be friends.

"Don't worry, Bob, I'll take care of everything."

And, man of his word, he did.

USING THE POLICE CAR RADIO, Peplowski called the Kings' trainer, so that a team doctor would be there for his teammate. Then he called the Kings' coach, Garry St. Jean, who kept asking, "What happened? What happened?" Then he called Hurley's girlfriend. He didn't know her name. He had to ask if it was she. When she said it was, he cleared his throat and said, as calmly as he could, "Listen, Bob has been in a serious car accident. I think he'll be OK. I'm coming to pick you up. We'll go to the hospital. Do you understand?"

She began to cry, but Peplowski calmed her and said he'd be right over. Less than an hour earlier, he was thinking about his buddies and the fun they'd have. Now he got into his truck and headed for the home of a guy he was just getting to know, to pick up a crying woman whom he had never met, to drive to a hospital and hope that death didn't follow.

Peplowski, who is only 23, keeps a rosary on his rearview mirror. He grabbed it as he drove off, and he said every prayer he knew.

HURLEY'S LUNGS HAD COLLAPSED. His ribs were broken. He suffered cuts and bruises, but remarkably — considering he wasn't wearing his seat belt when the station wagon, which police said didn't have its headlights on, smashed his truck at 50-60 m.p.h. — he didn't suffer any head or heart injuries. He was in serious but stable condition. With luck, eventually, he should be OK.

With luck — and friends. Hurley never knew what kind of friend he had in Peplowski. He may not even remember what Peplowski did. The TV cameras found the big guy and peppered him with questions, and he answered a few, but he really didn't feel like telling the whole story because every time he closes his eyes, he sees it all over. The blood. The shoes. Hurley's asking: "Pep ... am I going to die?"

"I never want to see anything like that again," Peplowski said. "It was the most horrible thing." That night he stuffed the rosary in his pants pocket. It is still there. He keeps transferring it from one pair of pants to another, as if anticipating another catastrophe. Still, his thoughts are with Hurley.

"I feel so bad for Bob's family," he said.

We live in a time in which getting involved is a hazard. We put on blinders. We drive past. In the world of high-priced sports, this is even more true because famous people often feel they are above cleaning up anyone else's mess. Often, they don't clean their own.

But when Mike Peplowski was 14 years old, his family took a trip to Northern Michigan, a cabin they had there. Late at night, someone knocked on the door. Peplowski and his uncle answered. A man's car had broken down. His family was scared. He asked for help. Without another word, Peplowski's uncle took his nephew, got in his car, picked up the stranger's family and drove them all to the nearest lodging.

"How can we thank you?" the man said. "Can we pay you?"

"No," the uncle answered, "just remember this the next time someone asks you for help, and do the same thing. That'll be thanks enough."

Peplowski never forgot that night. Which is partly why he stopped his truck and, who knows, might have even saved Hurley's life. This is what Peplowski knows that too many of us have forgotten: Life is with people. You have to be involved.

You think about what happened on Del Paso Road. You think about this big kid with a rosary in his pocket. And you realize we throw around the word "hero" far too cheaply in the sports world. We should save it for when it really counts. Like now.

Even in sports, life stops
December 29, 1993

B ECAUSE I COULD NOT STOP FOR DEATH,
He kindly stopped for me,
He held his darkened carriage low,
And waited patiently.
A chill across these pages blew
A blanket ripping free,
As we journeyed to the fallen souls
Of 1993.

AT first we passed the tennis courts
Of Arthur Ashe's grace,
And grief began anew again,
Just watching Arthur's face.
The image of him at the net
Or sharing his life's story,
Could fate so cruel as tainted blood
Steal all his hard-earned glory?

BEFORE I asked, Death's wooden carriage
Rolled upon a lake,
The bodies of two baseball pitchers
Caused my hands to shake.
A picnic day, a pleasure boat
Now turned to widows' sighs.
"But this is sports" I asked the ghost
"How is it death applies?"

HE answered not, but pulled the reins
His horses brayed in chorus,
And suddenly, a Final Four scene
Filled the air before us.
Jim Valvano ran the floor
In search of players' hugs,
But later, choked back cancer
In toasting those he loved.

HE looked so young, I wanted to
Scream out in haughty anguish,
After all, what place is sports
For all this death to languish?
But as I opened lips to speak
The specter waved a finger,
Valvano gone, and now inside
An empty gym we lingered.

A smiling man, with quiet ways,
And long arms made for flying
Collapsed, playing the game he loved
Was Reggie Lewis dying?
And even as he came our way
A man just one year older,
Who wore the jersey "Petrovic"
Joined in, a fallen soldier.

I wanted then to shut my eyes,
And ask for my release.
But Death drove on with silent wheels
Into the tragic crease.
And suddenly the air was filled with
Planes and crashes burning,
And families named Allison and
Kulwicki were left yearning.

ON this went, our woeful ride
Through tears and sighs and speeches.
Heather Farr, a withered star,
Chris Street — how far this reaches.
In Zambia, the mounds of dirt,
Are graves for soccer players.
In Houston, off a highway pass,
For Jeff Alm, they say prayers.

SOON the carriage struggled with
The weight Death brought to bear,
And surely we were finished with
His horror and despair.

"What brings you here?"
I asked again, "Why must we pay your wages?
"Have you no more noble task
"Than haunting our sports pages?"

HE made no sound, but steered the carriage
Onward without bother,
Until he reached the flowered grave
Of Michael Jordan's father.
The photo of the face they shared
Was withered now in two,
The famous son was crying,
Death seemed to nod, "Him, too."

BEHIND that scene, I heard the noise
A click and then a fire,
Guns and bullets, sirens, broken
Glass and drunken tires.
I shut my ears and wished for sports
To hush these baying hounds,
A football cheer, a golfer's swing,
A baseball organ's sounds …

"ENOUGH!" I screamed unto my guide
"This never was my choosing
Wasn't I to write about the
Winning and the losing?
Send me back to innocence,
Of baseball and March Madness.
Return to us the sports page
Minus all this sadness!"

BECAUSE I could not stop for Death
He kindly stopped for me.
He pointed once at glory
And once at agony,
He crossed the fingers, then he spoke
"One world, one fate, one plea"
And we have learned that all too well
In 1993.

Godspeed, Golden Boy
December 30, 1993

CHELSEA — The trophy stands near a plate of Christmas cookies in the middle of the kitchen table. On the black plastic base is a fading inscription, "Member, 1959 World Champions." Above the base is the gold-colored statuette, a little boy in baseball knickers and a small billed cap. He is poised, shoulders high, waiting for the pitch.

His hands are empty.

The bat is missing.

"It fell off," Marlene Piasecki says. "Joe wanted to get it fixed, but we never found anyone to do it."

She crosses her hands on her lap, and looks at her son, and her daughter, and Joe's sister, and Joe's mother. The coffee cups are full, snow is falling outside, and the Christmas tree is still in the living room. It could be any holiday table conversation. Except, of course, for one empty chair.

"None of us could ever see this coming," whispers Pat, Joe's sister. "I mean, how do you see it coming?"

This is the story of a good man in a good town who nine days before Christmas told his wife to meet him after school and they'd finish the shopping. He never came home. Marlene was waiting when she flicked on the TV and saw the special news report — "Two school administrators shot by a teacher in Chelsea High." She didn't wait for names. She ran to the car, sped to the school, passed the ambulance going the other way. She ran inside the building and yelled, "Was it Joe?"

Moments later she, too, was racing to the hospital, thinking only that you can be shot and not die, it happens all the time, right? As she prayed, the word was spreading, up and down Main Street, and through the Jiffy Mix factory. Chelsea, population 3,800, which hadn't seen a murder in two decades, began to shiver. It was small-town America, late afternoon, and school was out ...

SMALL-TOWN AMERICA, late afternoon, school was out. That meant one thing in Hamtramck in the summer of 1959: baseball practice. In the shadow of the factories that kept the town alive, a group of 12-year-old players was about to climb a rainbow. They were on their way to Williamsport, Pa., for the Little League World Series. All those drills, all those practices, all those night games and day games and chasing fly balls and working double plays — it was all paying off.

The Little League World Series! More than 5,000 teams began the competition. But Hamtramck, then a town of extraordinary pride in youth, sports and dirt-under-the-fingernails spirit, well, Hamtramck had hitters and Hamtramck had fielders and Hamtramck had a pitcher named Art (Pinky) Deras, a hulking 5-foot-8 kid with thick black hair and a man's grin who threw something like 10 no-hitters in a row. This was some team. Everybody knew it. With crew cuts and high sneakers, they boarded the bus to their destiny.

"Remember what's written on the front of your uniforms," the coaches urged. "Hamtramck."

In 1959, that was enough.

Joe Piasecki was the backup catcher on that team. The son of a tavern owner, he was an altar boy in a Catholic church, and his face indeed seemed blessed by light: reddish hair, freckles, a smile that jumped out at you like that of John F. Kennedy, the young Democrat who soon would run for president.

Those were the final days of American innocence, a time when kids like Joe and Pinky and Greg Pniewski, the starting catcher, and Mark Modich, the second baseman, hung around Cunningham's Drug Store after practice and ordered cherry Cokes and spun on the stools and sang the words to "Stand By Me" and "Under The Boardwalk." On the bus to Williamsport, they wore their caps and slapped their gloves and passed the time chanting call-and-responds like:

Oh, you can't get to heaven!

(Oh, you can't get to heaven!)

In Joe P's socks!

(In Joe P's socks!)

Because Joe P's socks!

(Because Joe P's socks!)

Stink for 48 blocks!

(Stink for 48 blocks!)

When they reached Williamsport, they marveled at the foothills — "Where we came from, everything was flat," one would later say — and they cooed at the stadium, which seemed like the biggest place on Earth. During games, fans would crowd on blankets on the slopes above the field until you couldn't even see the grass beneath them.

Maybe they should have been nervous, these Hamtramck kids. Maybe they should have been overwhelmed. Instead, they were invincible. In their red, white and blue uniforms, they beat Puerto Rico, 5-0 (Deras struck out 17 of the 19 batters he faced); they beat Hawaii, 7-1, and in the title game, they clobbered California behind another Deras shutout, 12-0. They raced to the mound in a happy, youthful rush as photographers snapped the first — and still the only — Midwestern team to win the Little League title.

"You did it!" yelled "Shy" Piasecki, Joe's father, as he hugged his son with the pride of a million small-town dreams. "You did it!" ...

W HO DID IT? WHILE Marlene Piasecki agonized in the hospital waiting
room, the questions burned through Chelsea like fire burns through thatch.
What had happened between 3 p.m. and 4 p.m. in Joe's office on Thursday, Dec.
16? The story that emerged was this:

Stephen Leith, a 39-year-old chemistry teacher who wore a ponytail,
sometimes let his students blast rock music, and took unkindly to supervisory
criticism, had met with Piasecki, 47, the superintendent of schools, over a
grievance Leith had filed. Something about access to a file. They talked, things
got heated and, eventually, Leith stormed out, slamming the door behind him.

Maybe 15 minutes later, Leith's wife, Alice, who also teaches at the school,
called a teachers union representative to say she was worried that her husband
might "do harm." That representative immediately called Piasecki, and urged him
and everyone else to "get out of the building."

For whatever reason, Joe Piasecki, who always looked for the good in
people, played down the warning. Maybe he figured nobody gets that mad.
Maybe, being the honest and direct person he had been through more than 20
years in education, he felt whatever Leith had to say, he would listen and answer.

But Leith was done talking. Police say he came back with a gun, a 9-mm
semiautomatic — one of many guns he owns — and entered Piasecki's office. He
pulled the trigger, again and again.

Four shots hit Piasecki in the chest. Another hit school principal Ron Mead in
the leg, and another hit Phil Jones, a teacher and union representative, grazing his
abdomen. Out in the hall, someone pulled a fire alarm. A secretary dived under
her desk, grabbed a phone and called 911. Amid the hysteria, Leith's wife, who
had called in the warning, suddenly appeared in the doorway. Her husband,
allegedly, pointed the gun at her, too. She pleaded with him, he lowered his aim,
and she ran to Piasecki and tried to revive him.

When the police came, they found Leith alone in his chemistry classroom,
sitting quietly at a desk. He did not resist arrest. In the days that followed, his
profile would slip out: He was using Prozac. He was seeing a psychiatrist. He has
a strange history of flirting with female students.

It was all too late. You need that kind of information before the guy reaches
for the gun. At the hospital, Marlene Piasecki waited breathlessly for the doctor,
hoping against hope. Funny. She and Joe had begun to fall in love at a hospital,
back in college, on a winter night, when a group of students went tobogganing
down the hills near Central Michigan's campus. It was cold, and, for some
reason, Marlene began to hyperventilate. They took her to the hospital. Joe, who
barely knew her, stayed right next to her. At one point, her palms began to curl
from lack of oxygen.

"Shouldn't we do something?" one of Marlene's friends asked.

And Joe Piasecki, former Little League hero, former altar boy, a kid who told
his mother as a teenager "I want to be a priest," did what came naturally to him:
He put his hand inside Marlene's hand and held it tight.

Now someone else was holding her hand, a doctor, a stranger, a man she didn't know, sitting down in front of her. "Why is he sitting down?" Marlene thought. "If he's sitting down, he can't be saving Joe."

The doctor looked at her. He couldn't say the words. Marlene said them for him.

Joe's dead.

She cried so hard, "I heard sounds from my body I had never heard before."

WHEN MARK MODICH SAW THE NEWS on the TV, he felt a jolt inside, as if a spirit had touched him from a previous life. Although he hadn't really kept up with Joe or the other guys from the team, he made a few calls, and pretty soon, he was on his way to the funeral home in Chelsea. When he walked in, one of the first things he saw was a photo of the 1959 Little League champions. In it, he was standing next to Joe.

"Look," he says now, pointing at the same photo in the tidy kitchen of his home in Royal Oak, where he works as a sixth-grade teacher. "We always seemed to stand next to each other. You see that smile? That's the way Joe looked. Always smiling."

He holds a photo of the team with Lawrence Welk. As celebration for their title, Hamtramck flew the boys to California for an all-expenses-paid extravaganza, which included Disneyland and an appearance on Welk's show. In fact, Welk met the team at the airport in a long Chrysler convertible. In one black-and-white picture, the kids are stuffed inside that car, and Joe Piasecki, age 12, is on top of them all, arms lifted to the sky.

"I felt so old when I heard about his death," Modich says now. "The last time I saw him was at a reunion banquet a few years ago. He got up and made this great speech, really funny, great speaker. I remember looking at a guy we both knew and saying, 'Is this quiet Joe Piasecki, the backup catcher?' "

Modich shakes his head and closes the scrapbook. Later, he is asked whether he still has the trophy from Williamsport. He rummages through the basement. When he brings it upstairs, he finds, to his surprise, that the bat is broken.

A FEW HOURS LATER, IN A small house in east side Detroit, Greg Pniewski is also talking about Joe.

"We were in Catholic school together. The teachers loved Joe. Me, they kept locked in the closet. I ended up stealing other kids' lunch money from their coat pockets."

Pniewski laughs. He no longer resembles the scrawny kid in the old photos. He has shaggy gray hair, a mustache and swelling midsection beneath his "Carolina Panthers" sweatshirt. He makes his living going from place to place, hawking stuff like this from tables.

Pniewski was the starting catcher on the 1959 team, the guy who played ahead of Joe Piasecki. "It never bothered Joe. He worked just as hard as everyone else.

"When I read the story about him in the paper, I went, 'Damn.' He would never provoke nobody. Not Joe. He was a clean-cut kid."

Pniewski led a different life. He went to prison when he was 18. Forgery. Did nearly two years. He says there were inmates there who told him, "I remember you. That Little League team. Look at you now, you're a bum."

Everyone knew about Pniewski's troubles. But when the team got together for its reunion in 1989, nobody judged him, least of all Joe Piasecki. "He treated me like he always did. He was a great kid. I can't believe he's dead."

Pniewski is asked whether he keeps any souvenirs from the old team. He says, "I dunno. My mom has 'em somewhere. …

"I do have this."

He lifts the golden boy statue from behind some photos on his mother's fireplace. It is dirty, and slightly rusting.

The bat is missing.

B ACK IN CHELSEA, THE PIASECKI family sits together in the kitchen, glancing now and then at the falling snow. "There were so many people at the funeral," says Joe's mother, Margie.

"There were lines outside," says Pat, his sister.

"The girls swim team came, and the boys swim team, and the wrestling team," says Nicki, his teenage daughter.

Nicki is a student at Chelsea High. Stephen Leith, charged as her father's killer, was her chemistry teacher. In fact, she thought, he was "one of the best teachers I ever had." Leith's wife, Alice, is also Nicki's English teacher. They met last week, at a neutral site, to talk, and Nicki encouraged Alice to come back and teach her class, hard as it will be, because she didn't blame Alice for what happened. This is the kind of child Joe Piasecki raised.

And these are the kind of issues that now face a family that did nothing to deserve this. A trial, publicity, a rehashing of the worst hour of their lives, over and over. Marlene Piasecki says, "We do nothing these days but cry, remember, cry, not sleep. I don't want to go out, I don't want to read a paper, I don't want to watch TV. Everything else seems insignificant."

And the reminders never stop. On Christmas morning, last week, there were presents under the Piasecki tree. The cards read "From Dad," who died nine days earlier, but not before he had done his shopping.

The family hugs, and tries to go on. These are remarkable people. In two hours of conversation, Marlene Piasecki cries only once. Not when she talks about all the good her husband did for the school systems, not when she talks about the trips he took with students to Washington, D.C., or all the charities he worked for. Not when she talks about his endless support for Chelsea's sports teams, or his bellowing laugh, or how his 1959 team jacket now hangs in the Little League museum in Williamsport.

Not even when she mentions the sign on his desk at school that read "Do What's Right," or how that desk had to be "chopped up" because of the bullet holes, or how her daughter asked the other day, "Does Mr. Leith know how badly he has hurt us forever?"

No. The only time she cries is when she tells of a letter that came after Joe's death, a letter from an old female high school friend.

"She said there was this time when she had a party, and about 20 girls came but only four boys showed up. And she didn't know what to do. So she called this pool hall where she knew the guys hung out in Hamtramck, and she asked who was there. And when she heard Joe was there, she said to 'put him on the phone.'

"She hardly even knew Joe, but she thought he was nice, and she asked if he could help. And he didn't even know her ... and ... but ... he got all the guys from the place to go to her party ... you know, to help her out ... "

You ask yourself for a moral in these stories. There is no moral. This is the world we live in now. The snow falls, summer is a distant memory, and even golden boys of Little League have the bats taken out of their hands.

1994

I get Troy; he keeps country

January 28, 1994

ATLANTA — Troy Aikman wants to be a regular guy. I have decided to help him out. All week at the Super Bowl, I have heard his plea. "I just want to be a regular guy," Troy laments, while surrounded by reporters and security guards. His friends — some of whom like to chew tobacco and spit — back him up. "Hell, Troy's just a regular guy. Leave 'im 'lone. (Ptew!)"

Of course, being a regular guy is tough when you're the highest-paid player in the NFL and the star quarterback of the Dallas Cowboys, the most popular football team on the planet. But not to worry. You want regular? I am bringing my stuff. Meet me tomorrow, Troy, at sunrise, outside the hotel.

We'll make the switch. I will be you, and you will be me. You get my press pass, my shoulder bag and my weary — but regular — body.

I get to be 6-feet-4, blond, blue-eyed, handsome, 27, single and loaded.

No need to thank me. As you cowfolk say, "Jus' tryin' to help."

Readers may recall I did this once before, back in 1986, with Ron Darling, the New York Mets pitcher who was raised in Hawaii, spoke three languages, looked like Elvis, graduated from Yale, and was pitching in the World Series. He also had a gorgeous wife. This, clearly, was too great a burden for one man, so I dashed to his aid. And he appreciated it. Sent me a nice note, in French. Or was it Italian? I think he wanted his wife back.

Anyhow, if I can do it for a man named Darling, I can do it for a man named Troy. Tomorrow morning, the day before the Super Bowl, we switch:

My notebook for your playbook. My hotel key for your house key. My bar tab for your eight-year, $50-million contract. Jus' tryin' to help.

WAIT. I KNOW WHAT you readers are thinking. What about Lorrie Morgan, the stunning blond country music star Troy's been dating?

Come on! He keeps her, of course. What kind of man do you think I am? I hate country music.

The other women, naturally, I'll have to deal with. The ones who mob Troy when he enters a hotel and blow kisses and sigh, "Ain't he dreamy?" — they will be my burden. Every last one of them. I know. It's tough. But I want to help. I really do.

Same goes for the major corporations throwing money like confetti to get Troy to be their spokesman. Not to worry, kid. Regular guys shouldn't tolerate such nonsense. I'll do their silly commercials and shoo them off, as quickly as I can, once I cash their checks.

Meanwhile, you can change the oil in my car, and shovel the snow from my driveway. It's regular work, and I believe you'll like it.

Your homestead? I'll take good care of it. Your huge house, your pool, your private blackjack table and your big-screen TVs. Consider it done.

You let my dog out, OK? As for the woman you hired to cook your meals — don't worry. My home also comes with female cuisine. Her name is Mrs. Paul. She makes a mean fish stick. Enjoy.

"Sometimes we go to hockey games in Dallas, but it's no fun for Troy," says his buddy, Cowboys lineman Dale Hellestrae. "He gets bothered from the minute we sit down."

Never fear. In my body, Troy, you can go to hockey games, sit in the press box, and nobody, but nobody, will bother you. Except maybe my boss, who likes to call every 15 minutes. And Troy. Listen. You have my permission to tell him anything you want. Really. You want to call him an obsessive, annoying, mealy-mouthed, yellow-bellied sapsucker, go right ahead. It's OK with me.

Is it OK with you if I tell your owner, Jerry Jones — who likes to blow kisses to the crowd — to stop acting like such a dork? I mean, someone has to.

Get back to me on that, will you?

A S FOR THE SUPER BOWL, well, don't you worry. I have watched you play enough to know what to do with your amazing arm and impervious body. I just point at Michael Irvin, and if he's covered I point at Alvin Harper, and if he's covered I look for Emmitt Smith, right? Cock my arm and throw it?

By the way, if Emmitt starts complaining about how easily you got your contract, I tell him to shut up and run off-tackle, right?

Oh. I forgot. You don't do that. You're a great guy. Everybody says so. They call you the sweetest, most normal, unaffected, Californian-turned-Oklahoman-turned-Texan they've ever met. Question about the body: those lips. Are you wearing sun block, or does it just look that way?

Also, the country music thing. I know you love it, and I know you said you got to the hotel here and they didn't have the Country Music Television channel on TV, so you "went out and bought a stereo and some CDs to have some music with me in the room." Well. Be careful of that stuff in my body, OK? First of all, my credit card doesn't go that high. Secondly, if you play too much country music, my dog has an accident on the carpet.

Question: Is it Disneyland or Disney World I'm going to? I always get that confused. Whatever. I'll be sure to do you proud in Super Bowl XXVIII, and I'm sure you — we — the Cowboys, will win. I'll do the whole dirty party thing, the music, the women, the beer. You just relax.

The Pro Bowl — that's in Hawaii, right? Never mind, I'll figure it out. You have a grand old time in my regular old life, being a regular guy again. I'm happy to oblige. Of course, regular guys don't play in the Super Bowl. But they do sit in the press box and write about it. I do your job, you do mine, right? Deadline is 10:45 p.m., Troy.

Don't blow it.

Four of a kind for Bills

January 31, 1994

ATLANTA — Bruce Smith, the symbol of Buffalo power, was on his knees in the end zone, the posture of surrender. All around him, Cowboys were dancing, doing high steps, mugging for the crowd. Half of them had their helmets off so the TV cameras could catch their faces. They mobbed Emmitt Smith, who had just scored a touchdown on fourth-and-one, a muscle test, yours versus ours, late in the game, the championship on the line; Smith had gone in standing up. Touchdown. Now flashbulbs exploded and rolls of toilet paper came flying from the stands.

Bruce Smith watched all this, still on his knees, looking from player to player, as if trying to find someone to blame. In the end, he stopped watching Cowboys and turned to Bills, his own bench.

And the truth is, that's where the fault lies.

Four on the floor. Stomped once more. The Bills couldn't beat Dallas in the Super Bowl last year because they made too many mistakes, and they couldn't beat them this year because they made too many mistakes. The past will come back to haunt you if you don't lear- …

Aw, hell, you don't need to tell that to Buffalo, do you?

"We're all wondering, what do we have to do to win one of these?" Jim Kelly said glumly after the Cowboys beat the Bills, 30-13, to claim back-to-back Super Bowl victories — over the same victim, the Bills, who have now lost a record four straight Super Sundays. "What does it take?"

What does it take? Well, stop fumbling, for one thing. Stop throwing crushing interceptions. And stop playing the Dallas Cowboys. That would help.

The Bills could have won this game — they probably should have. But their history seems to creep up on them now the longer they play these Super Bowls, like a shadow that grows as the day goes on. They self-destructed. Thurman Thomas coughed up two fumbles, Kelly threw an interception, and the coaching staff kept calling plays that got dumped in the backfield. This all happened in the second half.

In the end, here were Bruce Smith and Kelly and Thomas and the rest, an hour after the game, dressed in street clothes, the same long faces, the same postgame sighs, trying to explain their failure, even as the opposing team could be heard whooping it up down the corridor.

Four on the floor.

"DOES THIS ONE HURT MORE than the rest?" Smith was asked. "It does," he said. "Because this is still in the present. Those others are history."

Well, let history show that Buffalo did win something Sunday: the first half. It was clearly theirs, in points (13-6), in yardage and in emotion. The Bills came out smooth and focused, as if they'd never been here before.

In some ways, so did Dallas. The Cowboys committed a dumb penalty on a punt that gave the ball back to the Bills and led to their only touchdown. And Troy Aikman threw an uncharacteristic interception toward the end of the second quarter, killing a drive.

By the time the country music singers came out for their halftime extravaganza "Rockin' Country Sunday" — the first halftime in NFL history to feature four acts and three chords — the Cowboys were losing for real.

But here's the thing about the Cowboys that makes them so great: If it's not one thing, it's another. Last year, Aikman was a razor, the MVP, slicing apart the Buffalo defense. This year, Aikman was a little hazy, so up steps a kid named James Washington, a kid the lowly LA Rams let loose — a Plan B free agent, for heaven's sake! — and he makes three huge plays that change the game completely.

Washington was Thurman Thomas' nightmare — not that Thomas needed any help in that department. Washington knocked the ball loose from Thomas early in the game, and in the third quarter he scooped up Thomas' second fumble and proceeded to gain more yards on that play than Thomas would all night. Washington ran, darted, cut back, waited for blockers, cut back again, broke free, and finally dashed into the end zone for a 46-yard touchdown that tied the game.

His first career touchdown? In the Super Bowl? A Plan B guy?

Where does Jimmy Johnson come up with these kids?

"I look for playmakers," Johnson said, espousing the essence of the Cowboys' roster. "Everybody on this team is capable of making a big play, causing a turnover or a touchdown. That's what I look for. Turnovers and touchdowns. And we have guys like that on this team — even our backups."

Turnovers and touchdowns. Not coincidentally, in a prayer huddle before the game, Washington and Emmitt Smith said those same words to each other: "Turnovers and touchdowns."

Must have been some prayer. Washington got the turnovers — and Smith got the touchdowns. Two of them. His wind-sucking effort on the go-ahead drive in the third quarter was the reason he — and not Barry Sanders, sorry, folks — is the most reliable running back in football. Smith simply bulled through the Bills, leaving them grasping, cursing, looking at his back. He carried on seven of the eight plays in that drive for 64 yards. And when he sliced into the end zone, voters began filling out their MVP ballots.

"At the start of that drive, I was asking (offensive coordinator) Norv Turner for the ball," Smith laughed, after winning the MVP trophy and gaining 132 yards. "By the end of that drive, I was saying, 'OK. Give it to somebody else.' "

Fat chance. Smith is the pump that keeps the Dallas machine running — and the monkey wrench that ruins the Bills. On that remarkable drive alone, Bruce Smith went out with a rib injury trying to slow Emmitt down. Darryl Talley went out with a shoulder injury trying to do the same. Phil Hansen was injured on the touchdown play.

All these Buffalo bodies, limping to the sidelines, while Smith cruised to the end zone like a fine roadster. Says it all, doesn't it?

Four on the floor.

DID YOU EARN YOUR PAY TODAY?" someone asked Smith after the game. "Earn my pay?" he mocked. "I'm kinda shortchanged right now, if you ask me."

No, Emmitt. That adjective belongs to the Bills. No one should laugh at what they've accomplished. But history will. Not next week. Not next year. But five years from now, and 10 years, and 20 years — when nobody remembers the efforts, only the results. Four straight trips to the Super Bowl, four straight defeats? You thought the Minnesota Vikings took a bad rap? The Bills made history Sunday, the wrong way. Has there ever been a team that has so raised our sympathy and our eyebrows — at the same time?

"It is kind of weird," sighed Thomas, whose two fumbles, meager output (37 yards) and inability to play much of the game with leg cramps made him the goat yet again. "Why did it have to happen today? I fumbled twice, and it's 10 points. If that doesn't happen, we can win the game. …

"I had one of the best games of my career last week, and now here I have one of my worst."

How do you explain it? You don't. Toward the end of the game, Thomas was all alone on the Bills' bench, and the TV cameras zoomed in on his face, two sad eyes, wide open. All that was missing was the paw over his head and the whimpering.

But then, that's a picture for all the Bills and their weary fans. Maybe it's something about this game. Maybe it's something about the opponent. Or maybe it's something about the Bills themselves. Perhaps they need a change — a shakeup, a new philosophy, something. They clearly are not learning from mistakes, including the ones they should know the best:

Their own.

Four on the floor.

And you know what? They're talking about coming back next year!

Carrying this torch too far
February 12, 1994

L ILLEHAMMER, NORWAY — As this might be the last column I ever
write, I want to get everything down. I have been chosen for a dangerous
task. I am a heartbeat away from the riskiest job in the Olympics.
I am the backup-backup torchbearer.

Hey. I saw it on the job board. It paid five bucks an hour. Easy money, I
figured, they'll never use me. Maybe, maybe, the first guy gets the chicken pox
(see: Michigan basketball team), and they have to go to the backup. But the odds
of getting to the backup-backup? Zero, right?

Yeah, except in Norway (translation: "frozen brains"), where they decided to
spice up the opening ceremonies by making the torchbearer carry the torch —
and I'm not kidding here — down a ski jump! Yes. He is to soar through the air,
land in the snow and hand the torch to a Norwegian prince. It is "the crowning
spectacle" of the opening ceremonies.

Assuming the jumper survives.

The first choice, someone named Ole Gunnar Fidjestol — who I believe is a
distant relative of that guy on the "Wide World of Sports" opening — is already
gone. The other day, during a practice run — practice, mind you! — Ole came
flying off the jump and went splat! (Translation: splat!)

His picture, showing him lying sideways in the snow, unconscious, as a
crowd of curious Norwegians stood over him ("Look, Sven, a dead ski jumper,
how precious"), was beamed over the international wires, with the headline,
"PASSING THE TORCH."

It should have read: "Next?"

W ITH NO. 1 GONE, THEY TURNED to No. 2, Stein Gruben, a 26-year-old
Norwegian who vows to do what Ole Gunnar Fidjestol (translation: "too
much wax") could not do: Survive the jump and light the torch. As I am No. 3, I
am rooting hard for No. 2. I am rooting for him like I root for my heart to keep
pumping.

Says the confident Gruben: "I will succeed. Ski jumping is not as difficult as
it looks."

Especially if you drink as much cough syrup as Stein does.

(By the way, jumper No. 1, Ole Gunnar Fidjestol, is resting comfortably in
the hospital, where he was visited by International Olympic Committee president
Juan Antonio Samaranch. The sympathetic president grasped Ole's hand, leaned
over and whispered, "You're fired.")

Anyhow, I think we should all put our hands together and say a big prayer for Stein Gruben, especially since, if he goes down, they're coming after me. In the meantime, I will bring you up to date on the latest news here in Lillehammer, as quickly as I can, from inside this closet:

NEW NATION ADDED: Thailand has joined the Winter Games, just in time for the opening ceremonies. Its late entry was blamed on the time it took to translate the word "Winter," which Thailand does not actually have. Thailand joins fellow Olympic nations Bermuda, Fiji, Cyprus and the Virgin Islands, whose official team slogan is "Cripes! It's freezing!"

FOOD UPDATE: The Norwegian version of the hamburger is the oxburger, made from, surprise, ox. Interestingly, the sandwich was not named after the American equivalent, but rather after John Candy's character in the movie "Stripes," Dewey Oxburger, who mud-wrestles women in a bar. Candy is a hero in Norway because, as one local said, "He is all man, ja?"

Sure. Let's see him do the ski jump.

THIS BRINGS ME BACK TO my "job" — I can't get this out of my mind — and as I lay here, in this closet, under the carpet, I must comment on the dangerous precedent being set by these Olympic opening ceremonies.

Once upon a time, all they did was get some famous ex-athlete, usually around 60 years old, and have him climb about 900 stairs and pass out. Then some kid took the torch and lit the flame, the president said, "Let the Games begin!" and they carried the ex-Olympian away in an ambulance.

This was a fine tradition. But lately, the Olympics have gotten into a "Can You Top This?" thing with the flame. You recall the Barcelona Games of 1992, where an archer shot a flaming arrow into the torch? This was a huge success because the torch lit, and no deaths were reported.

We later found out, however, that the archer had overshot by 30 feet. I'm not making this up. Fortunately, there was a secret backup ignition for the torch. Probably some man in a room with a button marked "Flame: on/off."

Meanwhile, the actual arrow, I believe, landed in a Spanish cornfield and destroyed next year's crop. This went widely unreported. So I am concerned that — should Stein Gruben go down and I must make the jump — the same fate will await me. Unreported. Unrepentant.

And I probably won't get my five bucks.

So as I await the opening ceremonies, down here, in the closet, under the carpet, in this locked wine cellar, I must say that Norway seems well prepared for these Games, and my personal prayers go out to all the athletes, and especially Mr. Stein Gruben. May the wind be at his feet.

May he soar like an eagle. May h—

Ka-plump!

Uh-oh.

Pouring shame on his wound
February 13, 1994

L ILLEHAMMER, NORWAY — Although the Winter Olympics have barely
begun, we've already had our first major clash. It took place a few days
ago, in a packed auditorium, during a press conference. It was not a clash
of skis or hockey sticks, but a clash of cultures. In many ways, it set the stage for
these Olympics.

The focus of that press conference was Norway's Vegard Ulvang, a top cross-
country skier and a national hero. Cross-country is to Norway what basketball is
to America. Ulvang is hugely famous. When he speaks, people listen.

He addressed the news media on various subjects, including his role as
Olympic oath-taker, and of course, skiing.

During most of this, the American reporters sat motionless, their eyes glazing
over. Few seemed interested in Ulvang's thoughts on snow conditions. Even
fewer would have known who he was if not for a recent Sports Illustrated profile,
which detailed the disappearance of his brother Ketil, who vanished while
jogging four months ago. Ketil is feared dead.

This, naturally, piqued the curiosity of the U.S. media looking for a feature
story. Near the end of the press conference, an American reporter rose and asked
Ulvang: "Has the loss of your brother affected your training, and is it true that
after the Olympics you will go back to look for him?"

A hush fell over the room.

U LVANG WAS SILENT FOR A MOMENT. Then, in broken English, he replied,
"It was a big tragedy for me and my family …

"We will miss (Ketil) a lot … "

He was shaking, his voice trembling.

"I will return in the springtime … "

He was crying now.

" … As soon as the snow is gone, I will try and find him … "

He put his head in his hands and began to sob. The press conference
quickly ended.

What happened next was most interesting. A crowd of Norwegian journalists
surrounded the American questioner and began shouting at him for lack of
sensitivity.

"Why did you ask him that?" they demanded. "Why did you upset him?
Were you trying to hurt him?"

The reporter, a man from Baltimore, was taken aback. He defended his actions by saying that in America, such questions are not out of line. He noted that when Michael Jordan lost his father, reporters asked him about that.

Although many American journalists would agree with him — and that crying clip would be replayed a million times on TV — the Norwegians were unmoved. The issue created a public debate. And the consensus in Norway was that the American reporter was insensitive and wrong, and, to coin a motherly phrase, he should be ashamed of himself.

IN MANY WAYS, THIS IS A classic joust between how America sees the Olympics and how the rest of the planet sees them. We look for stories. They look for results. We look for teardrops. They look for split times. We want Nancy-Tonya, a TV Movie of the Week. They want to know who wins the biathlon.

We can dismiss this as their way, our way. And yet the anger of those Norwegian reporters recalls something we have nearly forgotten in American journalism: the concept of shame.

Surely the Norwegian reporters wondered the same thing as our man from Baltimore, but they were too polite to ask such a question before a large group. Can you imagine their reaction to the questions on a Phil Donahue show? Or Howard Stern? (Somehow, I don't think Stern translates into Norwegian.)

By the same token, Norwegian heroes exhibit modesty of their own. There are no publicity vampires here like Roseanne Arnold and Drew Barrymore, who run to People magazine with every scarring childhood memory. Norway does not produce a Madonna, or Geraldo Rivera, who will do anything for more publicity.

Shame limits action here on both sides of the media line. To our way of thinking, this makes Norwegians dull.

Maybe they are. But maybe there's a lesson. The American media — me included — is trained to hunt down every sob story, every athlete with a sick mother, a dying sister or a missing brother. We think nothing of going for the open wound — in the interest of "probing journalism." And, of course, these Olympic Games are already overshadowed by the Nancy Kerrigan-Tonya Harding drama because drama sells, and what sells is always of peak importance in the United States.

Yet it plays on the brain, that scene between the Norwegians and the man from Baltimore. Shame on you, they seemed to say. Did you really have to ask that? It's a question worth repeating — ideally, we should ask it first of ourselves. Something tells me we'll have plenty of chances here in Lillehammer. Plenty of chances indeed.

Jansen: Love-hate relationship

February 19, 1994

LILLEHAMMER, NORWAY — You hate the Olympics. The worst moments of your life have been wrapped up inside them. At the starting line, you hear a drumroll over the loudspeakers, you dig your skate blade into ice, and the only comforting thought in your windless universe is the one you had last night: No matter what, when this race is over, 73 seconds from now, that's it for the Olympic experience. No more five-ring circus. Good-bye. Good riddance.

And there's the gun …

You hate the Olympics. Your name is Dan Jansen, and it seems as if the world has been nagging you for the last 10 years, and it always, always, has to do with the Olympics. "Too bad about the Olympics." "Sorry about the Olympics." You just missed getting a medal at Sarajevo in 1984; you came in fourth. Too bad about the Olympics. Then, in Calgary, 1988, your sister died the morning of your race, you raced anyhow, you slipped, you fell. They said you were "tragic." Too bad about the Olympics.

In Albertville, 1992, you should have won, you were tentative, the ice was soft, you finished fourth in the 500, and you bombed out in the 1,000. They said you choked. Too bad about the Olympics.

Then you get here, Lillehammer, two years later. You're the world-record holder in the 500, they say this is your time — and damn it, again you slip in the next-to-last curve. You cross the line in disbelief, almost a second slower than your ability. There's your family in the stands, looking heartbroken, your wife, Robin, wanting to cry. The press is scribbling notes. God almighty. You're a walking catastrophe.

Ten years? Seven races? No medals? And now, all you have left is this 1,000 meters, four Olympics scraped down to a final crumb. It is not your best event. The only good thing is that you won't be back for more. After this, you're going home, live with your wife, raise your daughter, a simple life in Wisconsin.

One more race.

You hate the Olympics.

THE GUN SENDS YOU DIGGING, your arms pull like hacksaws, back, forth, back, forth. You are speeding, but relaxed. For some reason, more relaxed than you figured. Your strides are long and you bend in aerodynamic position, back, forth, back, forth. You've been speed skating since you were 4 — you are

28 now — and you still don't feel good on this track. "Don't push," you tell yourself. "You'll slip."

That's just what you need, right? Another slip? Bad enough, that fiasco in '88. Your sister Jane. Remember that? They put you on the phone that morning. Jane was in the hospital, dying of cancer. You heard the hum of her respirator. She couldn't speak. You said good-bye. Four hours later she was gone. "Race, Dan," your family said. "That's what she'd want." You tried. You failed. Ten seconds in, you were crashing on the mats. Hell on Earth began.

You hate the Olympics. Anyone who knows speed skating knows that slipping happens, it's not that unusual. But how many of the millions watching TV that night even knew that? How many knew that the same year as "the fall" you were also the world sprint champion? Did they see you win that?

Of course not. They were watching basketball or football. Did they know that in '92 — the year you bombed in Albertville — you were still the best in the world in the 500 meters? Where were they when you took that trophy?

Where are they now, when you win in Ikaho, Japan, or Sundstrom, Sweden, or Butte, Montana? Where are they when you take those medals around your neck, when you hoist those plaques, when you breathe cold smoke on all those winter nights — "Ladies and gentlemen, again the winner, Dan Jansen, the champion, Dan Jansen, the record holder. Dan Jansen, the king, Dan Jansen … " Norway knows you. Finland knows you. Germany knows you.

America? They know Eric Heiden because he hung five Olympic gold medals around his neck, and they know Carl Lewis because he did the same. Don't they realize you've been to more Olympics than both those guys, set more world records, collected 20 — count 'em, 20 — medals in your world championships?

No. How could they? Your home country does this quadrennial inspection of your life, they see you lose, they cluck their tongues, they go away.

The hell with them.

You hate the Olympics.

BUT ALL RIGHT. ALMOST over now. The world is in fast-forward, you can hear cowbells and whistles, and as you make the turn, you see these flags waving. You churn, churn, the announcer calls your final split time, but you miss it. The crowd roars. "Must be good," you tell yourself. "Just keep going." You are breathing hard. Less than 30 seconds and your Olympic service is over. You'll be free.

As you come out of the next-to-last curve, you feel a sudden wobble — no, no! — you almost slip, but you steady yourself quickly, you're still standing, you're still going, the long strides, the crowd getting louder. If that was your disaster, it drew no blood. Last curve now. Down the straightaway, the homestretch, sucking air, you lean, you streak past, it's done! The Olympics are behind you, no disasters, no catastrophes, the clock, check the clock —

"A NEW WORLD RECORD FOR DAN JANSEN!" the announcer screams.

For a moment you are stunned, and suddenly, the strangest feeling, a full-body exhale, an unlocking of the soul. You hold your head in disbelief. You grab your hair. It's like stepping under this massive waterfall, washing everything away. A world record? Is that scoreboard correct?

American flags are waving. Norwegian flags are waving. Other skaters still compete, but somehow you know this is the end of your story. Your disasters have always been by your own hand. This time, this one last time, you did everything right.

No one will beat you now.

You find Robin, your wife, with a USA flag painted on her cheek. She is weeping like a child, she grabs you, pulls you close, and what she says, again and again, is: "It's over. ... It's over. ... It's over."

And you know what she means. It's over, '84, '88, '92, it's over. You can finally let go, those shadows that danced in your sleep, these strangers who run their fingernails on your personal chalkboard. It's over. All you hear now are cheers, and roars, and reporters pushing to ask questions.

"I would have been happy no matter what," you hear yourself say, "but this just makes it ... happier."

You laugh at yourself. You want to say, "See?" You want to say you knew it all along. You should have five of these. You want to say, "Are you satisfied now? Is this what you wanted? Does this make it better?"

You do not do that. You don't have it in you. Instead, you take your 9-month-old daughter for a victory skate, holding her close as she waves a little flag. And you point to the fans like a rock star, and hear them explode.

And in the end, as your Olympic life disappears, you are where you always dreamed after all, on the podium, and you lean over, and there it is, that little chunk of hardware that has snubbed you all these years.

It kisses you now. It fits like destiny. You stand up straight, the music begins, and you give a tiny salute to your sister, who is watching somewhere above the Norwegian sky. All the heartbreak, all the anger, all the nights spent alone, wondering what you did to have this hole in your heart, it pushes up now, from the deepest part of you, through the lungs, the throat, and out, finally, through the corner of your right eye, a single teardrop, falling down your cheek.

"Finally," you hear yourself say. "Finally."

You love the Olympics.

And "finally" is the perfect farewell.

Baiul, Kerrigan: Perfect ending

February 26, 1994

L ILLEHAMMER, NORWAY — One at a time, the medalists peeked out from behind the stage, like children looking for their mothers after the school play. First the teenager from China, who waved and smiled. Then the woman from America, who made a bored motion like, "Come on already." Where was the gold medalist? The crowd buzzed impatiently. In the back, a 16-year-old Ukrainian, who was still feeling pain from an injection in her back, was weeping, half in agony, half in joy, while the people who run the medal ceremonies were scampering around in a desperate search.

"We found it!" someone said, finally.

Her national anthem.

Good ending. Maybe the best. Oh, not for Americans, but you have to take a global view of these things. After all, these are the Olympics. The world at play, remember?

And as world stories go, the best one, Oksana Baiul, was up there at the end, with the gold medal around her neck. Sure, Nancy Kerrigan skated beautifully. Sure, she hit all her jumps — although she simplified one in midair. Sure, she has been dubbed America's Victim, due her share of glory.

And sure, the Olympic Amphitheater was packed with Americans, who made it sound as if there were no other skaters, only Nancy. Our Nancy! These were the same people bitching on the way out that "some judge had it in for her," that's why she got the silver. Once again, we show the world our best face.

Nancy got robbed? Please. Let's not dare start talking about lutzes and salchows and a tenth of a point here and artistic merit there. What are we, experts all of a sudden? The sum total of what anyone who isn't in this sport can tell you about figure skating is this: Someone always gets screwed. That's because it's not a sport but a graded exhibition. There are no finish lines. Only what the judges see, think and score. You accept that going in. Otherwise, run track.

"Did you think the medals were awarded correctly?" someone asked Chen Lu, the bronze medalist.

"The judges don't award marks casually," she said. "Yes, I think they were correct."

This was an honorable answer, but no one listened to it, not in the crowded press conference room late Friday night, where U.S. reporters were busy interviewing Nancy's coach, Nancy's agent, Nancy's buddy, Paul Wylie, all of whom echoed Wylie's sentiment that "the decision was wrong."

Prove it. The difference between Kerrigan and Baiul was so thin, you couldn't fit a skate blade between them. But instead of griping about the results, take a look at the big picture here.

Trust me. It's a perfect ending.

START WITH KERRIGAN, WHO SEVEN weeks ago took a club to the right knee from an assailant in Detroit. Her life has been upside down ever since.

"I don't think I'll ever be able to go through what I did these last two months," she admitted Friday after skating. No one should have to. She handled herself, for the most part, with dignity and silence, much of it well-choreographed by her agents, who are with her all the time now.

But let's be honest. Because of what happened to her, she also came to these Olympics more financially secure than maybe any other skater in American history. She had a million-dollar deal with Disney for a movie, a book, an ice show. That was all waiting for her — even if she fell on her butt. There were pros and cons for Kerrigan in this mess. That was a pro.

So was this: She found a champion's toughness. For the first time in her career, she finished a long program in a major competition with no mistakes. Skating to Neil Diamond music — we'll overlook that — she landed eight jumps, five of them triples. She looked good. She smiled.

More important: She discovered that, when pushed, she has the grit of a winner. Long after these Games are over, that will serve her most well.

And in a funny way, she might never have learned it had that attack not happened. Life is strange.

Nancy Kerrigan will be just fine.

Now let's take the winner, Oksana Baiul. You think Kerrigan has a movie? Disney ought to negotiate this one right now.

Go back just a few years on Baiul's life chart and you'll find a skinny orphaned girl with rusting skate blades in a Ukrainian rink. Her mother died of cancer. Her grandmother died, too. Her father ran away. And, thanks to the crumbling of the Soviet Union, her coach bolted, in search of a better life. Oksana was 14, and didn't have a soul. Of all the skaters in Friday's competition — Kerrigan included — she had the right to yell, "Why me?"

She didn't because life is hard all over Eastern Europe, you deal with it, like Northerners deal with snowstorms. Baiul was "found" by Viktor Petrenko, the 1992 gold medalist in Albertville, who saw something not only in her skating, but in the way she lit up when he said she could have some of his fabric to sew an actual uniform. Ukraine, at the time, was a brand-new country, maybe four ice rinks. Sometimes they were open, sometimes not.

From that, to this: Friday night, the Olympics. Just an hour before she went on, a doctor was sticking a needle in Baiul's skinny back. The day before, she had collided with a German skater during practice, wrenching her back and slicing open her leg with a skate blade. Now, before the biggest stage in the world, the doctor was injecting her and restitching her wounds?

"Can I skate?" she asked.

Her coach said she wasn't sure.

That she came out there anyhow, took center ice and dug into her happy little program, well, folks, that's a hell of a performance. If she were American, she would have her own TV show by now.

Baiul played coy, cute, showy, even a little sexy, as she skated to a medley of American show tunes. She hit all but one of her jumps cleanly, like Kerrigan, but toward the end, she changed one, a triple to a double. "In my mind, I thought I lost the gold medal," she would say. But rather than give up easily, she threw in an extra jump at the end, hoping to compensate.

She got technical marks from the judges ranging from 5.6 (Canadian) to 5.9 (Chinese) and all 5.8s and 5.9s for artistic merit.

Kerrigan, by contrast, scored no lower than 5.7 in technical, but no higher than 5.8, while earning basically identical marks as Baiul for artistry.

The difference between the two, if you added it up, was one judge. Five had Baiul first, four had Kerrigan.

Now. You want me to explain to you why Baiul got a 5.9 from someone and Kerrigan got a 5.8? For artistic? I can't. You can't. CBS can't. How do you compare Neil Diamond to Marvin Hamlisch? Kerrigan's marks counted. Baiul's counted. So be it. The world has seen enough bad American losers.

There's no shame in a silver medal.

TONYA HARDING WOULD HAVE taken it. Oh, yes, we can't leave her out. In the evening's weirdest moment, she emerged with six seconds to go on the clock, started skating, floated through her first jump and began to cry. She stopped, went to the judges and said she had ripped a lace. Could she do her Olympics again?

At this moment, with her music still playing, the crowd hooting and tears coming down her face, she was as pathetic as possible: a screwy, mixed-up trailer kid who may or may not have conned her way into these Olympics, and who suddenly realized she was as unprepared as a student without homework.

That she returned, four skaters later, and did a complete but rather uninspired program was almost after-the-fact. Her skating off the ice, yelling, "Open that door!" then telling her confused coaches, "It's no good" and stalking back into the tunnel was so odd, so jolting and so sad, it could only be Tonya Harding.

She finished eighth, and slinks off the page now, back to America, where the courts await. What will become of her is anyone's guess. Oddly, she seemed most defined here by her skating music. On Wednesday, it was "Much Ado About Nothing." On Friday, she did "Jurassic Park" — a movie about dinosaurs.

Perhaps she sensed her own extinction.

Bring down the curtain. So ends the most prolonged and ludicrous soap opera ever to prelude a Winter Games. Years from now, we might be ashamed at the attention we gave this story. Perhaps we won't believe we did it. But more people watched this skating competition than watched almost anything else in the history of television.

How fitting then, that it wound down with this scene: the American press noisily interviewing each other, convincing themselves of Kerrigan's victimization, while the few Ukrainian reporters — whose national anthem was so new it was hard to find — struggled to hear their gold medalist speak.

"Oksana, is there anything that you want now that you've won the gold medal?"

The question was translated, and she smiled from the heart, the smile of a child, the smile that, in the end, might have won her the Olympics.

"Yes," she answered, barely audible over the noise. "A Snickers bar."

Perfect. Absolutely perfect.

The lines of a lion

March 25, 1994

DALLAS — Steve Fisher is aging like a president. The crow's-feet seem to multiply each year, the jowls seem to droop as if a world war was tugging them down. The hair is thinning, the eyes seem more tired. You look at pictures of Fisher when he first got this head-coaching job five years ago. Compared to now, he looks like a kid.

Thursday, Fisher turned 49 years old. One year shy of half-century. There are those who say that coaching Jalen Rose will age you that much by itself. Not to mention Chris Webber — just trying to keep him safe from his adoring public could kill you — and Jimmy King and Ray Jackson, whose bad judgment concerning free beer gave Fisher sleepless nights this season. And Sean Higgins, a few years ago, he was a piece of work. And Michael Talley, who moped and complained his last two seasons. That'll age you. And the travel. And the stress. And the media, can't forget the media. Has there ever been a college team as covered as this one? Whenever Fisher looks at a TV or a newspaper he sees his players, often wrapped around the word "controversial."

"I won't lie to you," Fisher says, "when they (the Fab Five kids) are all gone, I won't miss the noise. I probably prefer it a bit more quiet."

But that's Fab Five noise he's talking about. There'll be new noise. It never ends in college basketball. This week, even as he was preparing for tonight's tournament showdown with Maryland, a crucial game, a game that could end the whole season, Fisher dashed off to a high school gym to see a recruit play ball. That is the job. The well goes dry. You replenish or die. More players! More players! More players!

No wonder he has those presidential creases in his forehead.

But at least Bill Clinton — who, by the way, is here to root for his favorite team, Arkansas — still gets to be president when the buzzer sounds. What does Fisher get? For all his labor, for all the whistles, the practices, the fast-food meals, the prop planes to jerkwater towns, meetings with academic advisers, boxes of game film, packs of hotel keys, alumni letters, media teleconferences, NCAA paperwork, phone calls in the middle of the night, parents complaining that their sons aren't getting enough playing time — for all that, if Michigan loses to Maryland, Fisher's "reward" will be people debating his job. They'll wonder if he blew it.

Nice job, huh? Sure, sometimes it's glory, a Sports Illustrated cover. And sometimes it's this: Last week, in Wichita, Fisher emerged from a team meeting.

He looked at freshman Bobby Crawford and rolled his eyes.

"Bobby," Fisher said, exasperated, "pull your pants up."

Bobby, pull your pants up?

Sometimes it's that.

I HAVE A THEORY AS TO why Steve Fisher faces such an uphill battle for national respect. It's in two parts.

The first is how he began. He inherited the Michigan job, won a championship in six games, and was given the position full time. Quadrupled his paycheck. I think a lot of people — particularly in the coaching community — resented that. Michigan is a plum job, and had there been an open search, the line would have been longer than the one for Streisand tickets.

Instead, Fisher got it. And he got it with a Rumeal Robinson and a Terry Mills. Had he taken over a down program, turned it around, then led it to a national championship, he would no doubt be hailed as a miracle worker today, a roll-up-the-shirtsleeves guy who could go anywhere and be great, a Rick Pitino — who, by the way, has never won a championship of any kind.

But because he inherited both team and talent, there is this vague notion that all of Fisher's successes — the NCAA championship, the runner-up finishes the last two years — have been done with mirrors. That if you gave him straw, Steve Fisher couldn't weave it into gold.

This is unfair, and untrue, because people forget that Fisher actually had a straw situation only three years ago, when his team lost more than it won, and its star player was a guard named Demetrius Calip.

Back then, people whispered that maybe Fisher was the wrong guy for the job, a mistaken hire made in the euphoria of winning the 1989 title.

That he bounced back, that he recruited a team for the ages, should be proof enough he can build from scratch. But before he could glean any credit, he was getting hosed for the bald-headed mayhem of the Fab Five.

Which brings us to Part Two.

D ID YOU EVER HEAR THE STORY about how Fisher and his wife, Angie, decided to get married? He was at her apartment on New Year's Day, 1974, watching the Rose Bowl. They had been going out for a while, and Angie wanted some answers. She slipped a piece of paper in front of Fisher, which read:

If we don't get married this summer,

I am leaving you.

Check a box

X—Yes, I will marry you

X—No, I won't marry you.

Fisher checked the "yes," they kissed and Angie went off to call her family, while Fisher continued watching the game.

Besides being a cute story, this tells you a little something about Steve Fisher. He will go with the flow. He will take the path of least resistance. He is not the blabbermouth on an airplane, he is not the town speed demon, gunning his engine at a red light. When an assistant tells him the players would really like to wear big shorts, Fisher shrugs and figures, how's it gonna hurt? When he gets together with other coaches, Fisher stands with a Diet Coke and listens to their stories and laughs like a spectator, never steering the conversation to himself.

He is passive on things he feels aren't really important — but this creates an image that he's passive on everything. That is not true. But because he's not out there tooting his horn, making convention speeches, getting himself elected the head of this or that coaches committee and jockeying for a chair on ESPN or CBS, there is a tendency to, well, overlook him. At least as far as the good stuff goes.

"Do you think if your team had lost to Boston College in the second round (as North Carolina, the defending national champion, did earlier this week), that people would be as understanding as they're being to Dean Smith?" Fisher is asked.

"If I had won 800 games and been around 30 years, I would hope they would," he says. "Dean Smith is a great coach, and will go down as one of the best in the business."

You see? Right there, he had a chance to attack, and he opted for praise.

This gets you points in church, but not in the temple of public perception.

IN THE MIDDLE OF AN interview Thursday, Fisher glances up and says, "Can you excuse me for a second?" He is looking toward the door, where his youngest son Jonathan has just entered and is running his way, arms open.

"Hey, big fella!" Fisher says, lifting the boy. Both their faces light up, and the father's crow's-feet and fatigue fairly melt away. If there is salvation for Steve Fisher, it lies in moments like these, the smiles of his towheaded sons, for whom Fisher is a father that Papa Walton would envy. He still reads them stories. Still lies down in their beds for nightly chats. While some coaches send their families as far away as possible during tournament time, Fisher doesn't feel right if the clan isn't around when the game is over.

And yet, even within his own family, Steve Fisher is not a dictator. When he talks to Mark, his teenage son, he listens as much as commands. There are these prolonged silences sometimes between asking Fisher a question and getting an answer. He stares off. He looks at his feet. He lives in these silences, and few people understand what he is doing.

I believe he is thinking.

"Can you still see yourself doing this coaching stuff on your 59th birthday?" he is asked.

He laughs. "I don't know. At 39, you say, 'No way.' At 49, you say, 'Probably no.' At 52, you may say, 'Why not?' "

"Can you see changing a whole lot in the next 10 years?"

"No, I'm probably done changing. I'm pretty much who I am and who I'm gonna be. I'm happy. I like what I do. I'm not suffering from middle-aged crazy or anything like that. ...

"People sometimes misunderstand me. They think I never dreamed I would have a job like this, or go through what we've gone through. But I've always been quietly ambitious. I always felt I would find a way to get what I wanted, and I've been fortunate, when I most needed something to happen, it seemed to happen."

HE ADMITS THAT THERE IS SOME jealousy in the coaching community for what he has done, and how he got to do it. He shrugs it off. He also says if he knew then what he knows now, he would have done some things differently with the Fab Five. Maybe sheltered the players a little more. Maybe controlled their free-form statements. Maybe nixed the shorts.

But he doesn't look back because that can really make you feel old, and the way things are going, who needs that?

"You know, I don't feel any older," he says of his birthday. "But I look in the mirror, and I know something's happening."

He laughs. Every day, before practice, Fisher tries to give his players one quote or slogan. He writes it down and discusses it before they start. One of these recently was a Winston Churchill line: "I may not be the lion, but I have been given the lion's voice."

It's a good summation of Fisher's unique position. He has never been a natural lion. But he was given the fur, the mane, the claws and the voice, and in his own quiet way, he has taken command.

"What did your players think of that quote?"

"To be honest," he says, smiling, "they didn't get it."

And you wonder why he's aging?

Seeing is believing
April 4, 1994

CHARLOTTE, N.C. — The big lie began every morning, with the book bag he carried and the clothes he wore. He would eat breakfast, kiss his mother good-bye, make like he was going to school, then not go to school at all. He would go to a gym and play ball. All day. When one gym closed, he would go to another. In between, he'd sit in parks and stare at the sky.

When he got home, his parents would ask, "How was school?" He lied. Then, one day, his mother asked to see a report card. He hadn't thought about that. He hemmed. And she knew. She knew, the way mothers know, and she pleaded with him to return, not to drop out. He was stubborn. He refused.

A year passed. Then another. Soon, he was a man in his 20s, and all he did was play ball, work odd jobs and watch the hope die in his parents' eyes.

You can call him Al. His last name is Dillard. He comes from Alabama, plays for Arkansas, and is not the most famous story at this Final Four. But he is the most important — because he answers the question, "What is this hoop madness all about?"

In the case of Dillard, who is 25 years old and playing his first year of college basketball, it's about saving a life. His own.

"I figured I'd end up in the military, or in the steel mills like my father," he admits. "I even got an application to be a steelworker once. I filled it out. But for some reason, I never turned it in."

He shrugs and fixes his Final Four cap. His face is soft and fleshy, without teenage pimples or sprouting whiskers. His fellow Razorbacks, many of them six or seven years younger, teasingly call him "Father Time." When he doesn't hear something, they roll their eyes in mock aggravation.

"You can still see, can't you?" they ask.

HE CAN SEE JUST FINE. It's believing that trips him. After all, just a few years back, the closest he came to college was the players he faced in summer pickup games. Thanks to years of killing time with a basketball, Dillard was a gym-rat legend, banging jump shots from zip-code distance. But every fall, the college kids went back, and Dillard stayed where he was, going nowhere.

Until he met a woman. "She is the reason I'm here," he says proudly, "she" being Jean Wiser, his girlfriend and a former college player herself. Every night and every day she told him the same thing. "You must get a high school diploma. You should be in the college game. Your time is running out."

Wiser sat with Dillard and helped him read. She tutored him. She looked up words in the dictionary. "I hadn't read a book in four years," Dillard says. "It was so frustrating. It was like starting school all over again."

At times he felt like giving up, and he looked at Wiser and asked why she was so stubborn. "Because," she said simply, "I love you."

The lessons continued. When a junior-college coach saw Dillard play — saw him bury jump shots from way past three-point range — he was so impressed that he promised a scholarship if Dillard could pass his GED exam. For the first time since dropping out, Dillard had a glimmer of a future.

He studied. He took the test. When he passed, he was so excited he jumped in the car and drove two hours straight to the junior college, "because I didn't want the coach giving away my scholarship."

T HE REST YOU CAN READ in a media guide. Dillard lit up the junior college scoreboards — he once scored 40 points in the second half of a game, and Arkansas, one of the best teams in the country, gave him a scholarship once he met transfer requirements. He arrived for his first college practice already older than the graduated seniors.

No matter. Dillard was pointed in the right direction, and he wasn't turning back. He is now a Razorback weapon off the bench, averaging nine points a game and the longest shots on the team.

Of course, he's a bit of a long shot himself.

"When I was playing pickup, there were guys 27, 28 years old. They were so good, they could have been in the NBA. But they never even finished high school. They always had an excuse — I got screwed; this or that happened. …

"I didn't want to be that way. My girlfriend says you can have a below-average life, an average life, or an above-average life."

He pauses. "I want an above-average life."

He is getting his wish. Tonight, he plays in the national championship game, before a worldwide TV audience. And recently, President Bill Clinton, a Razorbacks fan, declared Dillard his favorite player. Not long ago, Dillard's younger brother Harold started talking about quitting high school. Al took him aside and, he says unashamedly, "beat him until he came to his senses."

Harold stayed in school and graduated.

You see the fuss over March Madness, the money, the hype. And perhaps you say, "What for? Isn't college basketball just spoiled jocks winning games for someone's alma mater?"

Sometimes. And sometimes not. If a kid can go from quitting high school to being the president's favorite college player, then something worthwhile must still tick inside this sport.

You can call him Al. He says he wants one thing more. You expect to hear the words "national championship," but instead, he opens his mouth and says "a diploma." And you realize, with a smile, that the dropout has become, quite remarkably, a teacher.

Whine leaves a sour taste

April 6, 1994

CHARLOTTE, N.C. — The sweat was still dripping from the national championship victory when Arkansas decided it was time to use the r-word.

"We didn't get any respect all year," Corliss Williamson said, holding the trophy.

"Nobody respected us," echoed Scotty Thurman.

"I hope this gets us the respect we deserve," said Nolan Richardson, before launching into yet another lecture about why he, more than any other college coach, deserves it.

Time out for a reality check. Who invented this new sports slogan? You can't find a winner anymore — let alone a loser — who doesn't blurt out during the celebration, "Everyone was against us!" or "Nobody gave us credit."

In the Final Four this past weekend, it could have been the banner at the team hotels. "THE HYATT WELCOMES THE TEAM NOBODY RESPECTS."

Arizona claimed it had been dissed for years, and coach Lute Olson made it his theme. Florida built its underdog image around being "ignored."

Duke — with two national championships in the last four years — noted that there weren't as many articles about the Blue Devils as usual, and maybe people were taking them for granted. No respect, they suggested.

Richardson was on the biggest soapbox of all, using "lack of respect" like a political platform — despite his team's being voted No. 1 much of the season, and Richardson's being voted national coach of the year.

Coach of the year? No respect?

After a while, this complaining, like the clanging of a broken school bell, fades into an annoying background. After all, weren't these teams playing before worldwide TV audiences? Didn't they have their pictures in newspapers around the nation? Weren't they being cheered by thousands of strangers, besieged for autographs, slapped on the back wherever they went?

If that's disrespect, I know a few people who want some sent their way.

NOW, IT'S INSULTING ENOUGH when a professional athlete complains about lack of recognition. He's making millions of dollars for a talent that, despite entertainment value, does nothing to better society. And he still beefs?

Well, he's beyond saving. But when college athletes, some 18 and 19 years old, are allowed to make "no respect" a team chant, then the people guiding them must be taken to task. What are we teaching our young people if everything is about being overlooked? What is the meaning of respect, anyhow? That everyone fawns over you? That not a single critical remark is made? That you deserve universal adulation, from the man on the street to Dick Vitale? Sorry. That's not real life.

Yet the whining goes on. And, as we saw last weekend, it gets even more sensitive when race is introduced — and Richardson made race a constant focal point.

Now, let's be clear: Nolan Richardson is a remarkable man with remarkable achievements. He worked his way up from a time and place of discrimination to become a leader in his field — a smart, inspirational coach, as good as any — and he has built a wonderful program that everyone knows about.

But Arkansas is no overlooked, backwater school. It's a major college sports program. The Razorbacks were favored to win throughout the tournament, and they had the biggest international spotlight of any team, thanks partly to superfan President Bill Clinton, who attended their last three games.

You wouldn't know it by Richardson. He took every opportunity to rail against perceived oversights, to claim that he, as a black coach, was "one step from the outhouse." He ripped TV announcers who give nicknames to Bobby Knight but not him. He acted as if no one knew who he was, or ever gave him a modicum of respect — all because he was black.

Though I know many people suffer this description, Nolan Richardson is not one of them. He hasn't been for a while.

THE DANGER IN THIS IS THAT, if you scream when screaming isn't required, people may not listen when screaming really is. College basketball is no nirvana, racially speaking, but it is no longer on the critical list. Coaches such as Richardson, John Thompson, John Chaney, Stu Jackson, Todd Bozeman and Randy Ayers are recognized as leaders in their field. The game itself, dominated by black athletes, is at an all-time high in popularity. With his NCAA championship — his first — Richardson has earned the right to have his accomplishments speak for themselves: He should exercise it.

Meanwhile, the issue of clamoring for respect has become a national epidemic. From the Buffalo Bills to the Atlanta Braves to the U.S. Olympic bobsled team. Somewhere, somehow, athletes have made this us-against-the-world thing part of their training. It's ugly. And, quite frankly, it is not a lesson we should be teaching college students.

Someone once said you command respect, you don't demand it. That's correct. If athletes really want to talk "no respect," they should talk to a schoolteacher who's earning $11,000 a year, or an immigrant who is turned away from a job because of his accent.

But playing a sport and thinking someone's not cheering loudly enough? That's not lack of respect. That's called being spoiled rotten. And the world is too serious a place to be bothered by that.

Born in Russia, blooms in America

April 18, 1994

YOU CAN'T TELL ANYMORE BY the way he looks. With that stringy blond hair that he flicks out of his eyes, he could be any Generation X-er with high cheekbones and pouting lips.

Nor can you tell by the way he talks. Most of the time, it's awfully American — although, now and then, he sews together a foreign malaprop, like when he describes the location of his northern Russian home: "It is way upstairs," he says.

But forget such peripheral things. Here is how you know Sergei Fedorov is still getting used to this country: Have him tell you a "first time" story. Like the first time he got a speeding ticket. There he was, coming to work on a winter night, driving 60 m.p.h. in a 40-m.p.h. zone, and a cop pulls him over. The lights are flashing. The cop steps out, starts coming his way.

"Were you scared?" Fedorov is asked.

"No," he says. "I didn't know this would be bad for my license. It was dark, the flashing lights, it was like, wow, a detective thing! Like in the movies! I was excited!"

Excited.

About a speeding ticket?

Well. New experience, you understand. He felt the same way the first time he entered an American record store. Or the first time someone told him he could get money from a machine. A machine? He stuck his card in, pushed the buttons, watched the money come out.

"I went, 'Wow!' In Russia, with money like it is today, maybe 1,700 rubles for one dollar, sometimes you have to carry around a bag of money just to buy a meal. Back there, we did not have credit cards. And here I am, getting money from a machine …

"It's so different. I have to tell myself not to get excited about each thing because I'd spend all day" — he spins his head quickly, left, right, left — "going, 'Wow! … Wow! … Wow!' "

Which, coincidentally, is sort of how the hockey world is reacting to Sergei Fedorov these days. Spinning head. Wow! Wow! Wow! It is astounding, when you think about it, to go from one country to another, one culture to another, yet keep your hockey career in a straight and glorious line, right to the top. Never mind that Fedorov is all of 24 years old.

"I'm not sure," he says, when asked about this rise, "that people can imagine what has happened to my life since coming to this country. It has been so different. Every day there is something new to learn."

And that's just speeding tickets and cash machines. How about the fact that here, in the starting gate of the NHL playoffs, Sergei Fedorov might be the best player in the league?

Where do they teach that in the immigration manual?

NOWHERE, OF COURSE. FEDOROV teaches himself. Which is fine. He has been doing so, much of his life — from his childhood days skating on frozen soccer fields near his birthplace of Pskov, outside Leningrad, to the rinks of the distant northern town of Apatiti, above the Arctic Circle, where Fedorov fell in love with the cold. This is how remote his family was: If they had wanted to attend the Lillehammer Olympics, they would have headed south.

"We had big winters there," Fedorov recalls, "big" presumably meaning long and severe and not a place where you'd find George Hamilton. But it was here that a young Sergei played wing on an adult hockey team — and his father, Viktor, played center. It was here that Fedorov learned the discipline of the game, passing to men twice his age and hoping they would pass back. It was here that he fell in love with the glistening of hockey ice, the smooth surface left by a small truck with a large basket of water, pipes, tubes, and a blanket trailing behind like a tail.

"Russian Zamboni," he says.

In the morning, Fedorov would skate, and in the evening he would skate again. Later, when chosen for a special sports school outside Minsk — nearly 1,000 miles from his parents — he would practice by himself for hours, lying on the ice, then jumping up and racing to the blue line, kneeling on the ice, jumping up, racing to the blue line, going flat on his back, jumping up, racing to the blue line.

"Training secret," he says, grinning impishly. "My father told me the first five steps are the most important."

Which might explain his acceleration today. When people talk about Sergei Fedorov, they talk first about the way he skates. All from Steve Yzerman to the kid selling pizzas at Joe Louis Arena seem to think Fedorov is the best skater they have ever seen. That's on top of his excellent defensive skills, and completely ignoring his stellar 56 goals and 120 points this season. He was a focal point of this year's All-Star Game, and Wayne Gretzky, upon breaking Gordie Howe's all-time goal mark last month, said the guy most likely to surpass him someday would be … Fedorov.

Hard to believe the Red Wings acquired this guy with the 74th pick of the 1989 draft.

I mean, who were the other 73?

And where are they now?

SOME, OF COURSE, ARE PLAYING. Some are out of the game. Few, if any, had to surrender a culture, a passport and a way of life. And few had to endure the cooing temptations of America-for-the-suddenly-rich-immigrant.

Many is the foreign athlete who drowns in the waters of Fun City, USA. Remember Petr Klima? He was whisked out of Czechoslovakia, landed in Detroit, got behind the wheel of a sports car and never hit the brakes. Several arrests later, he was shipped out, his bright promise turning into just another dull reflection.

Fedorov began with a sports car, too. Not long after he defected in 1990 — walked off the Soviet team at the Goodwill Games in Seattle and flew in Mike Ilitch's private jet to Detroit — he was at a local Corvette dealership.

"Pick one," they told him, courtesy of the Red Wings. "Pick a Corvette."

He did. A nice burgundy model. That he didn't drive straight from that showroom to Doomsville, that he watched his money and respected his luck, is testament to his strong family ethic and upbringing. Not surprisingly, Fedorov has since brought his mother, father and younger brother over from Russia. They all live together in Sergei's house in Farmington Hills.

"It's great," he says of the arrangement. "I get to speak Russian again, and I get meals cooked just like I was back home."

And maybe this is the secret. No, not the borscht and sour cream and meat, rice and caviar that Fedorov calls his favorite home-cooked dinner — but the reminders of where you came from. The memories. The lessons. The perspective you get only from looking at your present through the prism of your past.

"My grandmother," Fedorov says, "she died not too long ago. But when she was alive, I called her a few times from here. She couldn't get it. She didn't know from America. She would say, 'When are you coming home?' like I was away for the weekend.

"I would say, 'I don't know, Grandma, I think I'll stay with my friends tonight. Maybe I'll come over next week.'

"If I really explained to her where I was … "

He shakes his head. "If I really explained to her where I was, she would think I'm on the moon."

FEDOROV — WHO NOW USES PHRASES such as "It's cool" and "Yeah, sure" — has proved himself good at transformations. The Red Wings will be looking for another starting tonight, the playoffs, first round, against the San Jose Sharks. Great players step up their games at money time.

It's money time.

But the odds are with Fedorov. This season, when Yzerman went down with a neck injury, Fedorov increased his role as team leader and had his best year. At the All-Star Game, despite a career that had previously been media-shy, Fedorov transformed himself again, into a willing conversationalist who stood patiently through wave after wave of interviews and left NHL reporters smiling as they walked away.

Now he stands as a legitimate MVP candidate of the world's finest hockey league.

"Did you know you would be this good a player when you came here?" he is asked.

"No," he says, "I took a chance. I had played against some NHL teams, and I thought I could be a good player. But I was 20 years old. I just took a chance, and said to myself, 'You have to adjust, whatever happens, you have to adjust.' "

He has.

It's a long way from Pskov. And yet Fedorov, in the middle of the conversation, remembers a detail that might be lost on many of his North American teammates. "Every year, when I was a kid, we skated on a river, and there was a plant that would freeze in the middle of the water. It was a green plant with a white flower, I can still see it because part of it would stick up above the ice. We used to skate around this plant, looking at it, skating around it. It was good exercise."

His eyes get a faraway look. It's the type of detail that makes Fedorov's memory special, and reflects the uniqueness of his story. After all, in a certain way, his talent is very much like that plant: born in a Russian winter, frozen in place, above the ice then, as it is today, sticking out, as the world skates around him, spinning its head and going wow, wow, wow.

All right, Juwan
April 19, 1994

W HAT MAKES A MAN? Strong hands, to bend destiny in his direction. Strong shoulders, to bear the weight of his actions. Strong heart, to weather the ups and downs of life, the grins, the headaches, the tears.

The tears. There were plenty of those in Steve Fisher's car last week, the night he and Juwan Howard went for a ride and talked about the future and came to a decision. The coach cried. The athlete cried. They were like family members parting at a train station, whistle blowing, steam rising.

And yet, for all the tears, can there be any doubt that Juwan Howard is a man? That he has the shoulders, hands and heart for the step he took Monday afternoon in the wood-paneled room of Crisler Arena?

"My dream has come true," said Howard, 21, announcing he would turn professional, skipping his senior year at Michigan to enter the NBA draft. He is projected as a lottery pick; with one contract, he can be set for life. But, although the words were familiar — how many athletes pay lip service about returning for a degree — yesterday, the difference was, everyone believed.

And all seemed to nod OK. The room was filled not only with reporters, but with players, assistant coaches, their wives, their children, other students. It was different from the frenzied crowd at Chris Webber's dramatic press conference last year, and different, no doubt, from what we'll see today, at Jalen Rose's press conference, when he'll likely become the third Fab Five player to leave early.

Howard's liftoff was, well, pleasant. Calm. Most attendees wore the satisfied expressions of uncles and aunts, watching the kids drive away. More than anything else, it seemed, they wanted one last look.

A H, THE LOOKS OF JUWAN HOWARD: the scowl of determination as he ripped down a rebound, the glare of concentration as he fired a trademark turnaround jumper, the wink he would sneak you while bent over at the free throw line, the innocent smile and deep, hearty laugh he saved for sick kids in hospitals, visits he refused to be publicized.

I have seen all these looks. I have been with Howard as he drove through his neighborhoods on Chicago's south side, pointing to a condemned building with boarded-up windows and saying, "See that? That's my old house."

I have witnessed his confidence, as he pranced around a Lexington, Kentucky, arena after Michigan beat Ohio State to reach the Final Four, shouting: "DO YOU BELIEVE US NOW?" And I have seen his manners, as he alone, in a group of his teammates, stood in a restaurant and said to an elderly woman,

"Would you like this seat, ma'am?"

The first time I interviewed him, his freshman year, I wore a leather coat and sunglasses. He looked at me and said, "So you're like a rock-star writer?" I laughed, and he quickly apologized. "I didn't mean nothing, I was just teasing."

That was Juwan. Curious, funny, but acutely aware of his effect on others, never wanting to hurt anyone, not with a fist, not with a word. In three years at Michigan he did nothing but honor his school, in the classroom, in public, and, of course, with his workmanlike excellence on the court.

"I've been here since '82," said Fisher, whose face was so red with emotion Monday he looked as if he would burst, "and we've never, ever had anyone better."

Little wonder that Fisher, who once talked Juwan into being the first of the Fab Five to choose U-M, tried to talk him out of leaving — something he didn't try with Webber. "Maybe it was for selfish reasons," the coach admitted, forcing a smile. "We all just want Juwan around."

HOWARD BEGAN HIS ANNOUNCEMENT THIS WAY: "I've made the decision — and I stress the word I ... "

Understand the significance of this. Juwan Howard is not Chris Webber, with two loving and influential parents. He is not Jalen Rose, with a savvy mother to advise him. Since the day he declared he was coming to Michigan, Juwan Howard basically has been on his own. That day, the woman who raised him, his grandmother, Jannie Mae Howard, died of a heart attack at the kitchen table.

Juwan has been a grown-up ever since.

So when time came to make this decision, he went inside himself, where Jannie Mae's memory lives, and he asked what she thought. And satisfied, he consulted himself. And satisfied, he told his coaches, and his teammates. He didn't ask. He told. The only victim is memories. There will be fewer with the big fellow gone.

What makes a man? The last time Howard called his own press conference, commitment day in high school, it was the worst day of his life, the day his grandmother died. He cried then for what he'd lost. He cried yesterday for what he'd found.

And in between, he developed what he needs, hands to pull himself to another level, shoulders to bear responsibility, and a heart that can handle pain and not grow cynical or impolite.

In general, you hate to see athletes leave early. In reality, there are times. When the interviews ended, a crowd of friends pushed Howard toward the door. Suddenly, as if forgetting something, he broke free and went back, found Fisher, and shook his hand gratefully.

"All right, Coach," he said with that smile, "all right." And the funny thing is, it was.

C, for character

April 30, 1994

S TEVE YZERMAN LOOKS LIKE HELL. Or as much as a heartthrob can look like hell. The left side of his face has a red mark from forehead to chin — "a glove cut," he says — and his pouty upper lip still has the vertical scar from 30 stitches, turning it purple and slightly swollen. His knees are both in the danger zone, one from an old injury and one from the newest injury, suffered two weeks ago — the one the Wings are so hush-hush about, but which, I can tell you, is the medial ligament of what used to be his "good" knee — and, given its severity, most people wouldn't even think jogging, let alone ice hockey.

Yzerman is not most people. He has spare tanks of courage and a shrinking supply of patience. He been playing this game professionally for 10 years, has been one of its superstars, certainly as much as a Charles Barkley or Patrick Ewing has been an NBA superstar, and yet, every spring, here he is, in a fight for his playoff life — just to get out of the first round.

"I was thinking the other day about 1987, when we went to the semifinals against Edmonton," Yzerman says, sitting in a sweatshirt and a baseball cap after Friday's practice. "I look around this room and there are so few guys left. There's Shawn Burr, Probie (Bob Probert), Steve Chiasson and me.

"But the thing I remember most is that we were playing one night, and we were the only game you could watch on TV. America or Canada. Only four teams were left in the playoffs, and that night was our game. All of hockey was watching us. That was such a great feeling."

He looks down, perhaps realizing that the highlight of his career was a semifinal that ended in defeat. And any sports fan has to feel for the guy.

S TEVE YZERMAN DOESN'T NEED my sympathy, yours either, but talk to him for a while and you find yourself wanting to help, the way you help a bright kid who needs a college scholarship or an innocent motorist broken down on the highway.

Yzerman, too, seems stranded on the highway. For much of his career, he was lumped with Wayne Gretzky and Mario Lemieux as the league's top three players. But Gretzky and Lemieux have tasted champagne from the Stanley Cup, more than once, and now Gretzky is about finished, and Lemieux is talking retirement. Meanwhile, Yzerman, who turns 29 soon, says, "They can retire because they've already accomplished what they want. I'm still chasing my dream."

Then, as if self-conscious about that last sentence, he adds, "Besides, I've got nothing else to do."

That's a lie. He has plenty else to do. For one thing, Steve Yzerman is now a father. He became one about nine weeks ago. He and his wife, Lisa, have discovered all the joys of parenthood, the crying, the middle-of-the-night feedings, but also the extra pair of eyes that now await them. Yzerman admits he thinks "about going home all the time now, just to see my daughter." It's the kind of statement you expect from the man.

And not the kind he wants printed. I'm sure Yzerman would prefer a column about his still-sharp hockey skills, or better yet, something about the team. Talk hockey, he'll say.

But the simple fact is, a lot of people can skate and shoot. What Yzerman has done — play at All-Star caliber, season after season, drag himself through countless injuries, lead the team through quiet example, never bitch about money, never hear a teammate knock him, throw himself into every night of icy warfare and still have to stand there, after the last game of the year, explaining in that muted voice what went wrong, why they lost — well, it shows something more than skill. It shows character.

Detroit knows this. The shame is, most of the nation does not.

IN 1983, WHEN YZERMAN FIRST joined the Red Wings, "the older guys were Ron Duguay, Brad Park, Johnny Ogrodnick, they were 27, 28, they had families, I remember being really intimidated.

"Now I'm that age. I have a family. I'm like the old man. But the funny thing is, I don't feel any different."

Here's my theory: Your dreams keep you young. Yzerman's dreams remain unfulfilled, hockey-wise, so he keeps pushing back the end of his rainbow.

And he keeps fighting to get there. You knew the guy would drag himself back from this most-recent injury, the way he's dragged himself back so many times before. And he'll be out there tonight, with the "C" on his sweater, trying yet again to push Detroit hockey into May.

Still, all these early exits during his prime years have torn away at his insides. Last summer, after the first-round loss to Toronto and the return of the nagging trade rumors, something snapped.

"I just decided the hell with all this worrying that I'll never get my chance. I can't do it anymore. It's so tiring.

"I decided I'll try to be a good player, a good person, and good things should happen. I tell myself I have lots of hockey left. That's how I live with it."

As a sports writer, you don't root. Rules of the job. Still, there is one scene I would like to see before I'm done. That scene is Steve Yzerman, after the last game of the season, his mouth open wide in euphoria, instead of explanation as to what went wrong.

It's every hockey player's dream, I know, and few get to see it. But when you try it out on Yzerman, after all those years and all these scars, it doesn't seem that much to ask. It really doesn't.

Isiah, we never knew ye
May 12, 1994

H E MADE NICE. WENT OUT LIKE a diplomat. He smiled, laughed loudly, and anyone he could possibly thank, he thanked. He thanked family, friends, children, teammates, his owner, his coaches, the ball boys, the water boys, reporters, trainers, the guys who cooked the food, the guys who laid out his uniform and socks, the guys who made plastic splints for his injured feet. Thirteen years in the National Basketball Association, two years in college, four years of high school ball — he went through all of it. At one point during the news conference, a cynical radio host leaned over and whispered: "Let me get this straight. Did he get the bicycle on his 12th birthday or his 13th?"

Ah, well. Such is the curious reaction to Isiah Thomas, who was always more inspiring on court than off. You can't blame him for a long good-bye. How else do you sum up a life? And that is what basketball is to the player Julius Erving calls "the greatest little man in NBA history" — not a career, not a job. A life.

"How do you let go of a thing that has shaped you?" Thomas, 33, said, holding up an imaginary ball and gazing like a child. "If not for this basketball … I wouldn't even have met my wife."

And he wouldn't have wound up here, Detroit, a city he once had no desire to see and now has no desire to leave. Thomas, the Pistons' all-time leader in points, steals and assists, was a lot of things during his storied career, some great, some not so great, some championship-caliber, some straight off the streets. He did good things and he did ugly things and he made some enemies and he probably didn't get the credit he deserved and he definitely didn't get the praise, the endorsements or the Olympic gold medals that peers such as Magic Johnson, Michael Jordan and Larry Bird carried off into their sunsets. But through it all, the one thing Thomas had that they never could was this city.

Detroit.

He owned it. He defined it. He represented it.

So funny, isn't it, that as he hobbled to the stage with his Achilles tendon injury — a walking contradiction, a basketball player on crutches, a kid from Chicago's streets now wearing silk suits and $100 ties — funny, isn't it, how this thought occurs:

Everybody here knows his name.

And so few know who he is.

Of all the questions a sports writer gets asked in this town, the most frequent is: "What is Isiah Thomas really like?" Or, "Is Isiah really the guy he pretends to be?" Or, "What's the deal with Isiah?"

How can you answer? There is no denying Thomas is a complex man, a powerful, intelligent, image-conscious entertainer who can flash a smile and use a smile in the same minute. Maybe because he came here so young — he was only 19 when he was drafted — and grew up before our eyes, we have so many conflicting pictures.

For example:

We see the childlike Isiah of the early 1980s, who seemed to laugh from jump ball to buzzer; and we see the spiteful Isiah of 1991, who led his teammates in a deliberate snub of Jordan and the Chicago Bulls.

We see the heroic Isiah who scored 25 points in a single championship quarter against the Los Angeles Lakers — while playing on a gimpy ankle — and the bully Isiah, who sucker-punched his own teammate, Bill Laimbeer, during practice.

We see the role model Isiah, so loved by our city's youth, and the unpopular Isiah, whom players from Adrian Dantley to Charles Barkley have privately — and publicly — lambasted.

We see the businessman Isiah who, just a few months ago, called his own news conference to announce a lucrative arrangement that would secure his future in the Pistons' front office. "I will be a Piston for life," Thomas crowed.

Yet yesterday, in that very same room, he said this: "I won't have any future role in the Pistons organization."

Huh?

"It just didn't work out," Thomas said. And later, "All the jobs were full."

Meanwhile, Bill Davidson, with whom Isiah supposedly had the original arrangement, only added to the confusion.

Was ownership the issue?

Davidson: "No comment on that."

Was there ever a deal like the one reported in the media?

"There was never such a deal."

Would you like Isiah to stay in the organization?

"Absolutely."

But he just said he has no role with the Pistons.

"That's what he's saying now."

Hmm. These two should take their act on the road.

But you know what? Stuff like this follows Thomas around. Misinformation. Coy responses. Rumors. Sometimes he's the victim. Sometimes he's the culprit. And you know what else?

It doesn't matter. Not anymore.

What will be, will be.

BETTER, ON THIS MORNING AFTER his good-bye, to remember Thomas for the show he put on, because ultimately, that's what entertainers are remembered for, isn't it? The show? And Thomas — at his best on center stage

— was impossible to ignore.

You can still see him screaming into the teeth of a defense, gliding, pumping and somehow dropping the ball in the basket while taller men swatted awkwardly at him, like a camel's tail swats at flies.

You can still see him dancing at center court, arms behind his back, holding the basketball and spinning in a delirious circle.

You can still see him jumping into Mark Aguirre's arms, Rick Mahorn's arms, John Salley's arms, you can still see that night he scored 16 points in 94 seconds in a playoff game against the New York Knicks, or the night he made 13 shots in a row, or that heroic twilight against the Lakers at the Forum, when he could feel his ankle going south and threw in 25 unbelievable points in the third quarter in a desperate attempt to win the championship before his leg went useless.

"Some guys know how to play," said Vinnie Johnson, his longtime backcourt mate, "and some guys know how to win. Isiah knew how to win."

And win he did. He won two championships, was Most Valuable Player of one, selected to 12 All-Star games, was MVP of two, he set all kinds of assists records, rewrote the Pistons' stats book and — perhaps most remarkably — never had anyone describe him as "short," even though, for his game, he is.

"I recently watched my highlight reel," Thomas, 6-feet-1, said in his unique way, "and I looked at a list of all the things I've done. And if someone said. 'You've got to do it all again,' I wouldn't even attempt it … "

A FEW NIGHTS AGO, THOMAS, Vinnie Johnson and Joe Dumars jumped into a private plane and flew to Springfield, Massachusetts, to see Chuck Daly's Hall of Fame induction. What a nostalgic journey, when you think about it. Here was Daly, now working in New Jersey, yet being immortalized for what he did in Detroit. And here were Johnson, now retired and doing radio commentary, and Dumars, the truly active player in the group, left to captain a ship that barely resembles the Bad Boys vessel of the late 1980s.

And Thomas, on the cusp that night, going from player to ex-player at 30,000 feet. What must he have been thinking during that trip?

"I'll never get on a court again," he said yesterday, almost wistfully. "The toughest thing of my life is to let it go."

He took questions. He spoke of memories. He denied rumors and deflected criticism. He was, in the course of the afternoon, charming, overbearing, sincere and a spin doctor. All those things. Give him credit for versatility.

Toward the end of the news conference, Thomas compared leaving the game to a poster he had on his wall at college, a picture of a dove above the phrase, "If you love something, set it free. If it was yours, it will come back to you."

"I love basketball," Thomas said, "but I know it will never come back to me."

And yet, Thomas will come back to basketball, in highlight reels and videos, in photos and media guides, in books and newspapers and stories told from father to son and mother to daughter, about hot nights in the Palace when Bad Boys flags flew from the stands and you couldn't go anywhere in this city and not talk basketball.

Who was Isiah Thomas? We never really knew. A mixed bag, seems the fairest way to put it. But here is the wonder of memory: all the rumors, the ugliness, the fisticuffs, the off-court shenanigans, all those things that were indeed a part of Thomas' career will ultimately sink like leaves on an autumn lake, leaving only this picture: Isiah streaking down a basketball floor, scissoring the ball through his legs, then pulling up and launching a rainbow jumper, backpedaling as it kisses through the net, licking his lips, a tiger with a taste, ready for more.

That's the snapshot you take of Thomas. In uniform. In action. It's the magic of the stage, the beauty of time. And, for a fellow who both delighted and confused, it's the nicest way to say good-bye.

The rise and fall of JenJen

May 20, 1994

IN GENERAL, TENNIS STARS ARE a miserable, pampered lot, and you can have 'em all, every one. It's hard to work up sympathy for people whose idea of a "problem" is no ice in the limo.

So let's be frank. Jennifer Capriati is not the first person, tennis or otherwise, to be found with drugs in a motel room. Nor is she the first to check into a rehab clinic. What happened this week — police booking her on marijuana possession, stories emerging that she may have been doing heroin and crack cocaine, her friends arrested on charges involving those drugs, Capriati's checking into a Miami treatment center — while it may have prompted a storm of conversation — doesn't necessarily make her sympathetic. She could be just another pampered teen who figures she's invincible, and some people will bail her out. Don't they always?

I might accept this explanation and speak no more about the story, except that using the words "Jennifer Capriati" and "just another" in the same sentence is inappropriate — unless it reads "Jennifer Capriati is just another victim of an uncontrollable father, blood-sucking agents, corporate smiley faces and a sport gone mad."

So maybe she warrants a closer look.

FROM HER ENTRY INTO THE pro tennis world at the ridiculous age of 13, to her first pro victory at 14, to her semifinal appearance at Wimbledon at 15, to her Olympic gold medal at 16, Jennifer Capriati has been the fascination of tennis watchers, a human petri dish slid under the microscope every few months, usually with this conclusion: "She's a regular kid!"

This was based on her giggling now and then, making a reference to rock music, or giving a quote in France describing Napoleon as "that little dead dude." I can't tell you how many articles, from People magazine ("she enjoys taking in a trip to the movies") to the Saturday Evening Post ("she seems totally unfazed by all the money"), bought into this "regular kid" angle. I can't tell you how many TV shows and radio programs broadcast it as gospel — an average kid! — when common sense screams there is no such thing.

You are not an average kid when your father starts pushing you through sit-ups while you are still drinking from a bottle. You are not an average kid when hundreds of reporters watch you play tennis before your 14th birthday. You are not an average kid when you fax in your homework from Paris or leave class to fly to Europe to endorse moisturizers.

You are not an average kid when you buy your parents their luxury home, move out to an apartment, quit your sport to concentrate on high school, then quit high school. Anyone who ever bought this normalcy bit about Capriati was sucking on a line that tennis, its sponsors, its agents and, mostly, the girl's parents desperately wanted the world to believe.

Because they knew it was a lie.

I remember doing a big story on female tennis players once. I visited and interviewed several dozen ex-teen sensations. From the famous — Tracy Austin, Andrea Jaeger — to the unknown, their tales were the same: pressure, worries, burnout, depression, early retirement. One told me how she vomited on her racket during her last match.

It's a pattern so familiar, an anthropologist would categorize it. Steal a girl from her childhood, tell the world "she loves the sport," push her into the pro life, milk as much money and fame as you can, then watch it unravel.

Even the successful female players today seem worse for it. Steffi Graf, who turned pro at 13, grows more melancholy each year. Monica Seles, a pro at 15, was in the middle of a rebellion before she was stabbed. And Gabriela Sabatini, a pro at 14? The next time she smiles will be the first.

Did anyone think Capriati would be different?

HER HERO WAS CHRIS EVERT. They both came from Florida, and Chris' father, Jimmy, was one of Jennifer's first coaches. But the elder Evert kept his daughter from turning pro until her 18th birthday. She had a childhood. She had high school. She played until she was 35. It is almost too ironic that Capriati was reportedly at that motel in Coral Gables because there were parties scheduled in the area.

Prom parties.

Now understand: I do not excuse Capriati's actions because she had a weird upbringing. Plenty of kids have weird upbringings — without $6 million in endorsement contracts — and don't wind up in motel rooms with drug users.

But compassion should always find its way to a child, and, to be fair, Capriati, tossed to the wolves by her parents, agents and tennis mavens, probably didn't know what was happening to her until it was too late. All you needed was to read her arrest story — a quote from her lawyer, a quote from her agent, a quote from her agent's publicist — to see the cocoon that has both shielded and suffocated her.

Tennis should have learned its lesson long ago: Make them pros as children, they'll be gone by adulthood. As for Capriati's parents, the big lie they told the world and maybe themselves has come home to roost.

Her lawyer, in explaining Capriati's arrest, said this: "She has a problem with good judgment."

At least she picked up something from her elders.

Jammin' with the Boss

June 1, 1994

WELL, THE TRUTH IS, I DIDN'T know if I should write this story. It's not really sports. But this morning, when I came into work, the first guy I saw chanted, "BRUCE! BRUCE!" and a woman asked if she could, and I'm not making this up, touch me.

So I guess the news is out.

OK. A little history. It's true, before becoming a sports writer, I roamed the streets of New York as a starving musician. Piano was my instrument. I took any job offered. I worked in clubs so disgusting, the Board of Health hung signs outside that read "You must be joking."

In those days, the most famous person I shared the stage with was a trumpet player named Phil, who used to wander into the bar after midnight. Phil was OK, but he often showed up to play, and this is hard to understand, without his trumpet. And it didn't stop him. He would just stand there, in front of the microphone, drooling.

So you can appreciate when I tell you that 15 years later, in a club on a street they call Sunset Boulevard, I shared a stage with — shucks, I hate dropping names — BRUCE SPRINGSTEEN. Maybe you missed that. BRUCE SPRINGSTEEN.

You know? The Boss? And I don't mean my executive sports editor.

We jammed. We double-jammed. We hit a stone groove, hooked a crazy riff, bopped till we dropped, and other musical phrases.

Actually, my favorite part was when Dave Barry, the humor writer, yelled to Springsteen: "Key of E!"

Like he needed help.

I mean, the song had only one chord.

WHICH BRINGS ME TO the other folks on stage, many of whom find one chord musically challenging, and, in some cases, overwhelming. These people included — oh, shucks, I doubt you know any of them — STEPHEN KING, AMY TAN, RIDLEY PEARSON, ROY BLOUNT JR. and other famous writers.

They compose the hot new sensation the Rock Bottom Remainders, a merry band of authors who all share the following: 1) a love of old rock and roll, 2) working knowledge of the "E" chord, 3) enough book sales to keep from being laughed at too loudly, at least by publishing types.

When I think of this band's special qualities, I think of Rob Reiner's tribute to the group Spinal Tap: "I was impressed by their volume — and their punctuality."

BRUCE! BRUCE! BRUCE!

I know. I'm getting to that.

OK. How I got into the group.

It began at the Lillehammer Olympics when, one night, with nothing to do but lie around counting salmon, Dave Barry and I wound up at a coffee bar piano, singing songs. They were classical songs, by which I mean they were classics to me, by which I mean, for example, "Wild Thing."

And, although we sounded like the Everly Brothers on codeine, the Norwegians considered Dave and me great entertainment, mostly because we weren't salmon.

"You're good," Dave told me. "You should play with this band I'm in."

He then described the Rock Bottom Remainders. They had been together for two years, playing book conventions and occasional nightclubs. Dave called the band "a chance of a lifetime," meaning the chance for respected writers to flush their hard-earned reputations down the toilet for a verse of "Louie Louie."

Naturally, I said yes.

And there I was, last week in LA, at my first practice for their show at the American Booksellers Convention. The band members, which also included rock critics Dave Marsh and Joel Selvin, and Matt Groening, creator of "The Simpsons," were extremely friendly. Kathi Goldmark, a real singer who started the band, welcomed me like an old friend.

Stephen King? Well. Stephen King greeted me for the first time by walking over and saying — and these are the first words he ever spoke to me — "Mitch. Who am I?"

He then made a "T" sign and yelled, "TIME OUT! TIME OUT!"

"Chris Webber," he cackled. "Get it? HAHAHAHAHAHAHA!"

And he walked away.

I did not mess with Stephen King.

BRUCE! BRUCE! BRUCE!

OK. OK. I'm getting to it.

DAY AFTER DAY, WE PRACTICED until our songs were perfect, by which I mean we were all in the same key. These songs ranged from "Leader of the Pack" by the Shangri-Las to "Midnight Hour" by Wilson Pickett — not that you could tell the difference. The Remainders operate on the age-old principle, first practiced by the Troggs, that the best audience is a deaf audience. So after cranking the amplifiers to levels loud enough to bring down aircraft, we were ready for the performance of a lifetime. I'm thinking a tadpole's lifetime.

Did I mention the roadies? One of the great benefits of this band is that, even if you can't sing within six notes of the actual melody, you still get treated like a rock star. Roadies carry your equipment. They set up keyboards, guitars, mikes. There is food and drink available upon request.

(I'm not sure why the band members are treated so well. I guess because they pay the help. Maybe Stephen King threatened them.)

Anyhow, the venue was the Hollywood Paladium, a great old nightclub with a huge dance floor. It was nearly sold out, maybe 3,000 people — the ticket money went to charity — and when we took the stage, baby, baby, lemme tell ya, that crowd was roaring. I think it was roaring, "LET US OUT!" Too late. We paid off the security people.

We rocked. We rolled. My part, in addition to playing keyboards, was to sing two Elvis songs in full costume, which meant a gold lame jacket, greased-back hair and shades. I think it's safe to say I thought LA was a lot farther from Detroit than it is.

BRUCE! BRUCE!

OK. When we finished our set, we ran off to thunderous applause from the crowd — "THEY'RE FINISHED! HALLELUJAH!" — and in the wing, stage left, was this bearded guy in grungy jeans and baseball cap. I swear, I thought he was a stagehand.

Then someone yelled, "ENCORE!" — I think it was a band member, throwing his voice — and we charged back out, and this guy with the cap runs out with us. And he picks up a guitar. And I'm thinking, "Great. Now the stagehand is gonna play better than we do."

And he looked at me and grinned, and I recognized that face from my college record albums and the cover of Time and the Academy Awards.

"Ladies and gentlemen," Dave Barry said, "we have a guy who isn't up to our musical standards, but we'll let him play anyhow. Bruce Springsteen."

The audience seemed to gasp. Turns out Bruce is friends with a band member, who invited him. And BANG! We launched into the only song we had left, a one-chord number named "Gloria," which I believe they use in "Hooked on Phonics."

G-L-O-R-I-A ... GLORIA!

B RUCE PLAYED. HE SANG. HE growled into the microphone the way he does — and the place came unglued. Fans were pushing toward the stage in a frenzied sea of hellish emotion. Suddenly, we were the greatest band on the planet. And when we hit that last note — same as the first note — and ran off stage, Springsteen cradled in our midst, that's how we were remembered.

Bruce hung around afterward. He talked, cracked jokes, told us we were good. He said he liked my Elvis, and I responded by drooling on his leg. I think

Stephen King best summed up the band's reaction. King said, "You can kill me now."

And that's how it happened. Jammin' with the Boss. I guess I'm still reeling. All I can say is, if you ever get the chance to play in a band where everyone else is famous, the amps go as loud as you want, and all the songs are in "E," you should grab it.

Especially you, Phil.

Rain-jah night in New York
June 15, 1994

NEW YORK — A bead of sweat was dripping down Jon's forehead, from his thick, sprayed hair toward his makeup-covered cheekbone. He tried to ignore it and hold his microphone straight, but man, it was hot, damn hot. The heat seemed to burst from the subway grates and the exhaust pipes of buses that rolled past Madison Square Garden, past rows of blue-uniformed riot police, hundreds of them, just waiting, leaning on their blue barricades, wiping sweat from their foreheads. It was June 14, almost summer, the latest day in hockey history, and the fever was all over 33rd Street.

"What TV station is this guy on?" a fan asked, pointing at Jon, even as he tried to slide in behind him.

"I have no bleepin' idea," said his buddy.

"Let's get in his shot."

There were already at least 50 people in Jon's shot, hoisting their Rangers jerseys, waving their caps. Up and down the block they marched, TV camera to TV camera, screaming, "This is the year!" — trying, in that very New York way, to steal a moment of fame and slip it on like a costume. One guy held a miniature Stanley Cup and pretended to guzzle beer.

"Yo, TV guy! Yo! Here's what da Rain-jahs gonna do tonight aftah they win. Yo, TV guy!"

The Rain-jahs. It was all about the Rain-jahs, now. There are Yankees nights in New York City, and Mets nights, Knicks nights, baseball nights, basketball nights, but now, finally, here was a hockey night, The Night of The Rain-jahs, a night for all the guys named Sal, Nick, Lenny, Duke, the lunatics who have been coming to the Garden forever, sitting in the high blue seats, raining down their noise in the many, many years this team didn't have a chance, and worse, in the few years it did and still couldn't win a title.

Five-and-a-half decades the Rangers had gone without a Stanley Cup, longest in the NHL. This was bad for the Apple. It was bad for hockey. All U.S. sports leagues need New York teams to win now and then, if only to ignite hatred — and thus, interest — across the rest of the country.

THE LONG WAIT WAS SUPPOSED to end with Game 7, Rangers against the upstart Vancouver Canucks, on the biggest single night the NHL has ever seen. The press coverage was massive. The TV audience was worldwide, North America, Europe, Russia. They were all gawkers, however. This was a New York party.

"Well, the players aren't the only ones who have waited a long time for a Stanley Cup ... " Jon began, TV camera humming, the bead of sweat dripping now to his collar. The crowd surged and began to scream.

"LET'S GO, RAIN-JAHS! LET'S GO, RAIN-JAHS!"

A few feet away, two middle-aged guys watched the bedlam, half-dazed.

"They don't win tonight, I'm gonna kill myself," one of them, a guy called Wolf, said. "They lose tonight, I kill myself and die."

His friend, taller, with glasses, looked at him blankly.

"Good," he said.

It was that kind of New York night, the heat, the noise, the police, the attitude, all whipped into this hurricane that touched down on the opening face-off at 8:08 p.m. So bright was the spotlight, you expected the ice to melt, until the players were left skating in a big pond.

Not that it mattered. The Rangers could have walked on water. Oh, they made their fans suffer. Put them through 60 minutes of nail-biting hell, in which a 2-0 lead was cut to 2-1, and a 3-1 lead cut to 3-2, and in the final, grueling period, they had to survive more close calls than a "Die Hard" movie. With 6:36 left, Martin Gelinas fired a shot that slapped off goalie Mike Richter's glove and skipped toward an open net, and the entire Garden held its breath as Kevin Lowe swooped in and plucked the puck just before disaster. Three minutes later, Nathan La Fayette banged another would-be tie game off the post. Another exhale.

"That final period," Brian Leetch, the eventual MVP, would say, "was like time stood still. To be on the verge of the greatest moment of your life, well, it doesn't come quickly."

Like he needs to tell Rangers fans that. Time standing still? Not a single player on this year's roster was alive the last time the Cup came to the Apple. Some of their fathers weren't alive. The curse! The 54-year curse! That's all they talked about.

Until Tuesday. When the horn sounded, and fireworks exploded in the Garden, the players threw their gloves and sticks in the air, as if graduating from the hardest college of their lives.

"The pressure we were under was incredible," said Mark Messier, the captain, whose arrival really put this franchise over the top. Fittingly, Messier scored the winning goal, and he was first to hoist Lord Stanley's Cup. Messier had done this five times before, all in Edmonton. None was as hard as this one.

"The microscope of that 1940 curse," Messier said, "it's tougher than anything you can imagine."

Curses, foiled.

Yet, it would have been fitting had this championship been won by Vancouver — a seventh seed that was one game over .500 this season — because this was the year San Jose knocked out the Red Wings, and Washington beat Pittsburgh.

The truth is, the Canucks gave the NHL the best show of any team in the playoffs, seven overtime games, six victories and a comeback in the final that defied logic.

B UT COMEBACKS ARE A MATTER of perspective. Just ask the Rangers. With that final horn, they came back from the ghosts of the 1950 final, and the 1972 final, and the 1979 final, all defeats. If there's a broken heart for every light on Broadway, then this team shut off the lights and started over.

Inside the press room of Madison Square Garden, Leetch was told the president was on the phone. They spoke for a moment.

"America's proud of you," Bill Clinton said.

"Thank you," Leetch said.

"Tell the team congratulations."

The line was disconnected. Leetch, the first American to win the playoff MVP award, immediately turned and said, "Was that Dana Carvey?"

Only in New York. Ah, well. The truth is, hockey needed this. The last time a Stanley Cup final went to a seventh game, 1987, it was won by Edmonton, which meant the celebration took place in a city most Americans couldn't find with a map and directions. The sad truth is, for the NHL to reach the next level of popularity, it needs a champion in a major TV market: New York, LA.

It has one now — and this will enlarge the game. Once they clean this place up.

The basketball nights will return, the baseball nights never go away, but the longest wait of any team and any season ended with this country's biggest metropolis finally giving itself to hockey. The Rain-jahs! The Rain-jahs! What an interesting picture. New York City, in the heat of summer, covered in ice.

O.J.'s last run
June 18, 1994

A T THE MOMENT OF TRUTH, he ran away, avoided the tackle, as if there were some end zone he could reach and be safe — safe from the handcuffs, the police, the cameras, the courts, the blood of the victims they say he killed, maybe even safe from the death penalty. The police were right behind him, 11 squad cars, like an opposing football team, and they chased patiently along the Southern California highway, even as spectators stopped their cars, some waving signs saying "GO JUICE." This is what the man who dashed through airports had become. O.J. Simpson was a fugitive, a murder suspect on the loose.

He left a suicide note and was running for home.

Nobody knows nobody. That's the lesson of this hero business. You buy into a smile, a style, a haircut, a commercial, a nickname, but you never really know the person. You don't know him because you watched him play, or because you shook his hand, or because he calls to you at an airport and you talk about golf. One "friend" of Simpson's figured this alone was proof of his innocence. That they flew together Sunday night and talked about golf. How could Simpson, just hours earlier, have done the unthinkable, killed his ex-wife and another man, stabbed them and left their bodies bloodied and crumpled by her condominium in LA, and be on this flight to Chicago talking about putts and tee shots? Murderers don't do that, right?

Says who? Nobody knows nobody. Until now, you wouldn't have said O.J. Simpson was the suicidal type either, not the type to be rolling down a highway with a gun pointed to his head, even as friends went to radio stations to tearfully beg him to surrender. It was a night the world went crazy, right before our eyes.

Simpson was finally arrested in the driveway of his Brentwood home in the murders of Nicole Brown Simpson, 35, and Ronald Goldman, 25, by an LA police force that, if anything, went out of its way to try to avoid doing so. They found blood on O.J.'s truck and blood in his driveway and a bloodied glove near his house — and they still took four days to decide to book him. When they did, they made an arrangement with his lawyer to have him surrender — a final nod to his celebrity status — and that special treatment could have led to his suicide.

It might not have led to justice, however. And that is supposedly the business a police force is in.

W HILE THE INCLINATION IS to feel sorry for Simpson — because we always gravitate to the more famous face, that is the American way —

let's consider the breaks O.J. was given here. His well-known lawyer, Robert Shapiro, was told by police at 8:30 a.m. that they were ready to arrest Simpson and charge him with double murder, special circumstances, which is a crime that could result in the death penalty.

Now. Under normal circumstances, in a double murder, police don't call ahead to make an arrest; they bust down the door. But Simpson was high-profile, Shapiro was high-profile, and the LA police — who will catch hell over this, you can count on that — made an exception, something they have done before with this lawyer, and gave him time, hours, to get things together.

So here were Simpson, Shapiro, two doctors, two forensic specialists, and Simpson's close friend, Al Cowlings, all at a large private home in the San Fernando Valley, with the clock ticking, but Shapiro calling the shots.

And somehow, with all those people there, just before the police were given the address, Cowlings and Simpson managed to be alone downstairs while the others were upstairs.

By the time the cops got there, the two men were gone.

"I had no reason to suspect" he would flee, Shapiro said, in the saddest and most bizarre press conference to ever hit the sports world. "It never entered our minds that he might run."

Nobody knows nobody.

I CAN'T GO ON," SIMPSON wrote, in an apparent suicide note that a friend read at the press conference, a touching tribute to his buddies, a plea for the media to leave his children alone, and an insistence that he had a happy marriage with his ex, despite reports to the contrary. He even included a message to his first wife: "Thanks for the early years, we had fun." But the most important issue, the one that they care about in the homes of two people who are dead but didn't want to be, Simpson barely addressed.

Did he do it?

"I had nothing to do with Nicole's death," he wrote.

Obviously the police felt differently.

"Mr. Simpson is a wanted murder suspect, two counts of murder, a terrible crime," said David Gascon, LAPD commander, in appealing for help in Simpson's apprehension.

What about his alibi?

"Obviously, we didn't believe it."

Gascon spoke about evidence. Blood types. He said that fleeing an arrest could also be considered a suggestion of guilt. Meanwhile, in his note, Simpson cryptically suggested he would kill himself because, "I can't go on. ... No matter what the outcome, people would look and point. ... I can't take that."

This, from a man who played professional football, who is looked at and pointed at every day of his life? The question is simple: If he didn't do it, why run away? Why threaten suicide?

Is it the suggestion that he did something wrong or the guilt that he did that he didn't want to live with?

These are terribly hard questions. No one knows the answer. The whole scene was bizarre, surreal, as if Hollywood had finally turned real life into a movie.

But the reaction across the nation was, in some ways, more bizarre. "We can't believe it," people said, "it's not possible."

Believe it. Nobody knows nobody.

And anything is possible.

DID YOU NOTICE HOW MANY people rushed to Simpson's defense when it was first suggested he committed this crime? "No way," they said. "He's the nicest guy we've ever met." And these were friends and coworkers, not fans. Few seemed willing to admit that Simpson had already once been charged with beating his wife, in 1989 — allegedly yelling "I'll kill you" — a charge to which he pleaded no contest.

Nor did anyone mention that Simpson's "punishment" for that crime included counseling, which he was able to take over the telephone.

"It seems he received special treatment," the LA district attorney, Gil Garcetti, admitted.

Nor did anyone speak of how the police were called for further incidents of violence between the Simpson couple before their divorce in 1992. And when a therapist admitted that the ex-Mrs. Simpson had told her of abuse by her husband, medical authorities criticized the therapist's "breach of confidentiality." Confidentiality? The woman was murdered!

Few things are as sad as the apathy we show athletes who beat, abuse and sexually assault women. And heaven help your blindness if you haven't noticed the pattern by now.

Consider: The one-time heavyweight champion of the world, Mike Tyson, is in prison for rape. The man he took the title from, Trevor Berbick, was convicted of rape less than a month later. Jim Brown, whom many consider the only running back in history better than O.J. Simpson, has a trail of abuse and violence toward women as long as one of his touchdown runs. A flight attendant last year charged the Boston Bruins hockey team with sexual assault, claiming one player fondled her while another took a picture.

The sad truth is, many big-time athletes — not all — believe women are there to serve them. And for boxers and football players, taking violence from the arena to the home, against women they really don't respect, is not a great leap.

Put this in a world where domestic violence is already beyond control, and where, as Garcetti points out, "we have a domestic-violence death in this city once every nine days," and nothing seems out of the ordinary.

Yet here we are, somehow incredulous that a beloved O.J. could possibly commit this crime? Why? Because we knew him so well?

CONSIDER WHAT THE AVERAGE PERSON knows of O.J. Simpson. 1) He was once a great football player. 2) He did some cute Hertz commercials. 3) He does football analysis on NBC. 4) He appears in those kooky "Naked Gun" movies, usually in slapstick situations, falling down a chute or being dragged by a car.

That's not a lot to go on. The real O.J.? You have no idea. I have no idea. All these reporters writing now about his rough childhood near the shipyards of San Francisco, his flirting with gangs in high school, his salvation through football — you know what? None of those people know him, either. They're just repeating stories.

What goes on inside the human mind — the rage, the fantasy, the torment, the delusion — well, you don't get that through interviews, or living next door to a guy, or sitting on a set with him a few days a week. Sometimes you don't even know when you marry him.

But you can say this. Two murders are the story here — not a high-drama chase. And our sympathies should first be with the murder victims. They didn't get a good-bye note read on television. They didn't get to rework their wills. They didn't get to call their mothers, children and friends — as Simpson did in his "gift" hours from police.

Nicole Simpson and Ronald Goldman are simply gone, their families left with grief. If Simpson — and this is a huge if — did indeed commit the murders, there is no sympathy for him. Even suicide would have been an act of cowardice.

At the very least, this was the strangest night on Earth, a man in a truck, who used to be a hero, talking about killing himself, as fans cheered his name just a block away. Then, finally, being walked off in the evening darkness, put in a police car, taken away.

A terrible odyssey. In his note, Simpson wrote, "Please remember the real O.J." — but who on Earth can say who that is? This proves only one thing: Commercials, football games, smiles and interviews don't bring anyone closer to the secrets inside the human mind. Nobody knows nobody.

Maybe nobody ever will.

Navratilova's choice, our fear

July 1, 1994

WIMBLEDON, ENGLAND — If she weren't gay, this would be such a big story. Cameras would be following her all week, and TV and radio would be updating her progress. But here is the dirty little secret about Martina Navratilova. Not that she's a lesbian. We've known that for years. She admits it. Talks about it. Doesn't try to hide it. The dirty little secret is that she keeps paying for it.

Name one athlete who has won the biggest championship in his or her field not once but nine times — and is on the verge of a 10th? Name me one athlete who is 37 years old and still beats challengers half that age? Name me one athlete who is the all-time money leader in his or her profession, has captured every important title and has never been arrested, investigated or rumored to be linked with drugs or gambling — yet still can't get a major endorsement deal outside of shoes or equipment?

We are what we fear. It turns us around. What is taking place on the hallowed grass of Wimbledon this week is one for the ages, the last lap of a great champion. And — thanks to her victory over Gigi Fernandez — Navratilova is in the finals! Could there be a better story?

No. So where is the overkill? Where is the media blitz that usually accompanies historic championship efforts? This isn't some minor event, Wimbledon. And it's not as if Navratilova caught us off guard. She announced long ago that this would be her last year as a singles player. Arnold Palmer's farewell to the U.S. Open was well-documented. Mario Andretti gets a yearlong "Arrivederci Mario" tour.

Martina? She came off Centre Court yesterday to the same old faces.

And the same old one-armed embrace.

I DON'T HAVE A PROBLEM with my being gay," Navratilova said, matter-of-factly, this week. "You guys seem to have the problem."

And the words sting, but consider them. For one thing, what athlete besides Martina gets asked questions about his or her sexuality, or has the guts to answer them? Imagine if Navratilova were married, with a nice husband and two darling kids sitting near Centre Court, waving at the cameras. Wouldn't this story be all over America?

It's not Martina's foreign roots; we embraced Olga Korbut and Oksana Baiul. It's not her muscled athleticism; we loved Florence Griffith-Joyner.

Face it. It's the homosexual thing. Back of our minds. Under a layer of political correctness. But there. Martina has come to Wimbledon, over the years, with Rita Mae Brown, Nancy Leiberman and Judy Nelson, the Texas-based mother of two. She never kissed them in public, but they were there, in the stands. And while TV announcers avoided the subject, the hero makers of America — the media, advertising and Hollywood — said, "Hold it. We can only go so far with this one."

We are willing to admit Martina's talent, maybe even admit she is the best female athlete ever.

But those are just words. How often do you hear people gush, "I love Martina, I hope she wins!" the way they did for Chris Evert or Jennifer Capriati?

Why? This has nothing to do with whether you approve or disapprove of a life-style. We are not electing school boards here. We're talking sports. And when Navratilova pulls out her racket, she is all the good things about sports, dedicated, magnificently gifted — and also polite, a fair player. And emotional. She has cried and laughed far more than Evert ever did. It's not as if Martina plays in combat boots or dresses in drag, so why do we hesitate, ever so slightly, to give her the hero's hug?

FOR 22 YEARS NAVRATILOVA HAS been coming here. If she wins again, she will own nearly 10 percent of all Wimbledon women's titles ever. She is synonymous with these courts and their history. Unlike other players, who demand the pampering of five-star hotels, Navratilova stays just off the grounds, in the same rented house, year after year. Now and then you can spot her riding a bike to practice. She likes it. From the time she was a child in Czechoslovakia and a coach told her of this wonderfully green place called Wimbledon — "I always imagined the grass was three inches high," she once said — she has loved this tournament and has painted her best tennis pictures here.

They call that honoring an event.

It would be fair if the favor were returned.

Navratilova has not had a great farewell season. She bombed at Eastbourne and the French Open. At times she seemed slow and privately wondered whether she stayed on stage one song too long.

And yet, this week, there have been flashes of the old form, and cunning and patience. And history. No one has ever threatened to win 10 Wimbledon titles. So where are the bands? Where is the media circus?

What a strange business this hero worship. Time after time, athlete after athlete, we seem willing to overlook drugs, violence, greed — yet we can't forgive whom Navratilova chooses to love.

She pays the price, the dirty little secret, and, admit it or not, it's the reason Navratilova is not being swarmed wherever she goes this week. A pity. For when she leaves, the gap in tennis will be huge.

Take a good look now at a real champion. The best there ever was. Maybe somewhere down the line, a generation, smarter than ours, will give the woman her due.

Nothing for nothing equals Probert

July 21, 1994

NOTHING FOR NOTHING. THAT'S THE bottom line of the Bob Probert equation. You watch him walk out the door now, motorcycle helmet under his arm, off to make big cash and who knows what trouble someplace else, and all you can do is shake your head and say what a mess, what a waste, what an ending. For all the stupid sympathy the Red Wings gave this guy, all the excuses, the lying, the coddling, the protection, the rehab — not to mention the money — in the end, he gives them his worst season and walks freely out the door, thanks mostly to their mistake. Nothing for nothing.

And no surprise. Probert has been a hot potato to management for years; why be shocked that they mishandled him now? And they did. Oh, you can listen to the claims that "Bob's no longer contributing" or that somehow, right now, in the third week of July, when they're not even playing hockey, he's hurting the club and he has to go. But come on. A little common sense here. Drinking, swerving on highways and late-night calls from police never caused the Red Wings to release Bob Probert before.

They do it now because they screwed up the paperwork, and they feared a judge would soon rule Probert an unrestricted free agent anyhow. It was math. Simple math. Probert's salary was one amount. His deferred salary was another. The Wings — just weeks after firing Bryan Murray, who would have handled this — made a qualifying contract offer before the July 1 deadline based on the first figure; it may be they were supposed to include the second. If the offer isn't high enough, the player becomes a free agent.

And if you think this sounds like a trite way to lose an employee, remember Mike Keenan just broke his Rangers contract because his bonus check came one day late. What's trite when it comes to money?

THE WINGS DON'T WANT TO look foolish — which, when it comes to dealing with Bob Probert, is often unavoidable. How can you help it?

But rather than have a judge free Probert, the Wings make what in war is called a "preemptive strike." They cluck their tongues and say, "We didn't want him anyhow, he's become an embarrassment" and, ta-da, Probert's a free agent. You never get the ruling — why bother? — it's a folded poker hand, the cards are reshuffled and everyone can claim he won. Or lost. How can you tell with Probert?

"I drafted him 11 years ago, and we've never spent more time on one player and his problems," said Jimmy Devellano, the Wings' senior vice president. "It's in his and our best interests to part company."

This, of course, is what you expect Devellano to say. But forget words; follow the action. The whole reason the Wings put up with Probert all these years — the drinking, the drugs, the broken promises, the often uninspired play — is that it was good business. They thought he could win games. They thought he put people in the seats.

Now, all of a sudden, they just let him go for nothing? When all they had to do was keep him until another team made an offer, then give him up and get two or three first-round draft picks in return? Whoa. If that's how the Ilitches are now doing business, I expect to get four pizzas for the price of one.

No. Much as I like Mike Ilitch and the Wings, it's pretty obvious someone is playing "cover your rear end" here. But Probert fans should know that — draft picks aside — he probably wasn't staying anyhow. I'm told the Wings made him an offer in excess of $1 million a year for three years — and there was still another team out there willing to pay more.

This, to me, is more incredible than his sudden departure. I figure the only smart business the Wings did here was to bow out of a bidding war for Probert. He's not worth it. Not with Scotty Bowman coaching this team.

BOWMAN DIDN'T CARE FOR Probert, and, more important, didn't use him much. When a guy like Probert doesn't feel effective, he plays ineffectively. And that's before his off-ice problems. If there's another team out there willing to use him more — I'm told the Rangers were ready to pay big for him, but that might have been when Keenan was there — then maybe he can get back to some kind of form.

Then again, he is 29 years old. He has fought a lot of fights. I don't think he has the same zest for it — he certainly doesn't have the same offensive skills that once made him an irresistible package — and contrary to popular belief, there are other goons out there with big fists. Quite frankly, the way Probert was coddled, lionized and given special treatment over the years was embarrassing to both the club and the community.

Yes, I know his boozy faithful at Joe Louis Arena will mourn. They're probably dressed in black this morning. But so what? Are the Wings being run by these people? Like I said, he was probably gone anyhow.

The most ironic thing is that, as a result of this fiasco, Probert — who had a total of seven goals last season — might get mega-rich. Teams now can bid freely for him, giving up only money, not draft picks. Whatever personal problems he's having — with alcohol, with driving, with conditioning — chances are he'll soon sign his most lucrative contract yet.

Crazy? That's sports. So, the last mistake the Wings make with Probert gives him his freedom. Nothing for nothing. Lousy ending. Then again, for those of us who have followed this story for years, it's typical. Almost fitting.

Dudin' the Lake Michigan wave

July 26, 1994

I AM A HANDSOME YOUNG PIRATE, adrift in a world of action adventure. I write, I surf. I do a column, I climb a mountain. Sometimes, when I finish a story, I'm so excited, I jump my horse and ride into the sunset. Other times, feeling mellow, I parachute.

This is my life. I am that kind of guy. My courage is mighty, my muscles are tight, I race with the wind, the sun burns my face …

And then I wake up.

And the dog is snoring.

Like most of us, I have one world in my imagination, and another world that takes attendance daily.

"Albom?" it asks, morning after morning.

"Here," I answer, meekly.

My job, which is fine, demands I get close to exciting things — then write about other people doing them. This is not the same as doing them yourself.

Which is why, when my boss came to me recently and said, "I want a series on fantasy adventure sports; go try them and report back," I looked to the heavens, clasped my hands, and said, "Lord, it has finally happened. My boss has gone insane."

I called the paramedics and had him taken away.

Just for fun, as they threw him in the truck, I grabbed his memo, copied it and submitted it to the big shots of this newspaper, who, in their normal, highly professional manner, sent it back with a note saying, "Can't read your handwriting. Whatever it is, go ahead."

I'm outta here.

Adventure! What would you try if you could try anything? Armed with an expense account, an atlas and a week before the boss gets back and fires me, I did what any free-spirited fellow would do under those circumstances:

I headed for the coast.

Cowabunga, dude.

Yes, my first dream was surfing, something I'd never done as a kid. Where I grew up, if you came home with a board under your arm, it meant you failed shop class again.

Like most Americans, I got my surfing knowledge from Beach Boys records:
They'll all be wearin' their baggies,
huarache sandals, too
a bushy, bushy blond hairdo,
Surfin' USA.

Oh, how I yearn to surf. True, I thought baggies came with Ziploc tops. But never mind. I dreamed of waves. I dreamed of sun. I dreamed of hanging ten, shooting the curl and going tubular.

I did not dream of getting knocked unconscious.

"This guy, not too long ago, he got conked on the head with a board, and he was, like, dead, you know?"

"Dead?"

This was my surf guide, Ned, and I, talking. I was shivering in the waters of Lake Michigan, in a wet suit, on a board the size of a Buick.

"Dead?" I said.

"Kinda. He never saw this other guy coming and ... bang!"

"Bang?"

"The board hit him. They dragged him out of the water."

"What happened?"

"Oh, he was back surfing two days later. Said he didn't remember a thing."

I SHOULD EXPLAIN. NED IS Ned Silverman, a happy-go-lucky fellow who owns a great surf shop called Chapter 11 Sports in Spring Lake, Michigan, just a mile or so from the shore. That's right! You can surf on the Great Lakes! Who knew! I was heading for the West Coast in California and discovered the west coast of Michigan. People have been surfing here for years, in Grand Haven, Ludington, Port Sheldon.

I'll bet you didn't know the original "Surfer Girl" was supposed to go like this:

Little surfer, little one,
met you down in Muskegon.

Anyhow, I discovered Ned when I was calling around for information about surfing. "Why go to California, dude?" he said. "They call Grand Haven the Malibu of the Midwest."

The Malibu of the Midwest?

"Come on out. We'll give you a board and throw you in the water."

Who could resist that?

Of course, he never mentioned getting conked in the head.

So there I was, in the lake, with Ned, who has an Ollie North haircut, a squat frame and a habit of giggling as he talks, so he sounds like this: "The other day, we were blastin' off the waves, hyee, hyee, it was rad, we almost killed ourselves, hyee-hyee."

With him were Dean Williams, a 43-year-old Michigander who has lived and surfed in Hawaii, California, Florida and Mexico, but keeps coming back here, and Dave Sypniewski, a young, blond athletic type who teaches at Ned's place and is, among other things, he says, "a bona fide, professional snowboarder."

Huh?

Also with us were Steve Nickerson, the fine photographer (and the only one willing to take pictures with water in his shorts) and Eric Sharp, our brilliant outdoors writer, who could, I believe, if a flood came, build his own ark.

These men had come to the big water with a single mission: to get me surfing. They took it so seriously, that as soon as we hit the beach, poof, they were gone.

It was me and the board.

The board grinned.

WHAT THEY TELL YOU TO DO IN SURFING: Paddle out, wait for a good wave, turn your board toward shore, paddle again, rise to your knees, rise to your feet, keep your balance, surf it in.

WHAT YOU REALLY DO: Fall off.

Trust me. You fall off. Not just when you stand up. I fell off trying to stand up. I fell off trying to get on. This might seem impossible, but surfboards are not the easiest things to control. Especially when, just as you get a good grip, a wave crashes on your head.

Also, you are exhausted from paddling.

I'm not kidding here. You paddle and paddle. You paddle more than you breathe. You begin by paddling out to deeper water, away from the beach crowd, paddle, paddle, paddle, paddle …

"Now look for a good wave," they say.

OK. I looked. Finally, I thought I spotted one. I turned the board toward shore — and knocked over a kid with a bucket.

I was back in the shallow water again. The riptide took me in.

Paddle, paddle, paddle. Out to deeper water. Wait for a wave. Here it comes. I tried to stand up, fell off — and landed on someone's sand castle.

Back in the shallow water again.

The riptide took me in. Tide is powerful. Maybe this is why real surfers call the sea "Big Mama" and people like myself "kooks." A "kook" sounds like a cute word meaning a likable eccentric, but in surf talk, a kook is someone who would rob your house and steal your dog. He is lower than low. He is a beginner. He should be killed.

I paddled out again. Paddle, paddle, paddle. My arms felt like rubber. I waited, a wave came, I turned, and amazingly, I stood up on the board …

It was stuck in the sand.

Back in the shallow water.

"How's it goin', bud?" Dave, the young instructor, asked me. Naturally, he'd been surfing nicely for an hour. His hair was a blond mop, his shorts were halfway down his waist, he looked "buff, rad and stoked," surf terms which mean, as near as I can tell, "something sports writers will never be."

"How's it going?" I answered. "Oh, I'm —"

WHHSHHSHHSHH!

A wave crashed on my head.

Call me kooky.

Did I mention the leash?

You are attached to your board by a leash, which goes around your ankle. Really. They call it a leash, I suppose, because, on a good day, you can take your board for a walk and it can play with the other boards.

"Nah, it keeps you from losing it," Ned explained. "And it keeps other boards from hitting you in the head."

I like that. Unfortunately, the leash also jerks you wherever your board goes. Mine insisted on getting as far away as possible. Each time I slipped off, my board immediately headed for Bermuda, hoping to lose me, but here I came, right behind it, yanked by the ankle, like a can on a wedding car.

"Hey, I grlrglr! ... can't grgrlgrgl! ... get uprrgrrgrl!"

B Y NOW, IT'S OBVIOUS THAT you swallow a lot of water while surfing. This is why the Great Lakes are an excellent place to begin. After all, if you have to gulp down 17 gallons, better go with the no-salt version, right?

Score one for fresh water.

But how did this tradition get started?

"The story goes that a guy came to Lake Michigan after World War II," Dean, the older surfer, told me during a break. "He had started surfing in Hawaii and wanted to try it in these waters. He began the whole thing."

That makes sense. Most historians credit the spread of surfing to the Hawaiians. True, Captain James Cook reported seeing surfers in Tahiti in 1777 — the same year the Beach Boys released their first album — but soon, surfing was discouraged by missionaries who visited the islands. They thought it was shameful.

They never saw me try.

Surfing grew again in the late 1800s, when they used boards made from redwoods, as big as 18 feet and 150 pounds. Over the years, the boards have shrunk, and the material has lightened: from heavy wood to balsa to foam to fiberglass. Today's smaller boards may only weigh five pounds and be six feet long. And you don't need 20-foot ocean waves to surf.

Not that you would want 20-foot waves.

"The waves around here are fine for most people," Dean said. "You just have to know where to find them."

Dean paused. He seemed more mature than the average surfer. And he'd done it for so long. I asked him what the attraction of the sport was.

"When you finally get a wave," he said, almost mystically, "there's no feeling like it."

I nodded. I felt his karma. I shared his vibe.

Of course, his board said "EAT ME" underneath it, so we can only take this serious stuff so far.

Anyhow, after flailing in the water for a good two hours, the time had come ... to cheat. Holding the board at the back end, my team of instructors — who really were good teachers — said, "Just look straight ahead, and when we say 'go,' paddle twice, then stand up."

And this is what we did. Naturally, I fell off about 14 more times. But then, in what can only be described as God running out of patience, the perfect wave arrived. My boys pushed the board forward, yelled "GO!" and I felt a jolt beneath my body, as if riding on the back of a shark. I squatted, I stood and, for a brief and shining moment, I was up, tall and proud, moving into the summer breeze, propelled by the thrust of these fabled waters, forward, forward, on the oldest source of energy on the planet. Catch a wave, and you're sitting on top of the world. It was stokaboka, amped, way cool, rad, I was aggro, primo, a big moke, I was Mooooondoggie —

I was down.

WHSHHSHSHSHH!

A wave buried me.

God had seen enough.

No matter. I had experienced the thrill. I can only compare a first surf ride to the first time you wobble along on a bicycle and realize you are no longer attached to the earth. It's that kind of rush.

Later, the surf dudes and I sat outside at a Mexican place, scarfing burritos in our shorts and T-shirts. Nickerson, the photographer, was hoping film still could be developed if it was waterlogged. Sharp, our outdoors genius, was already designing his own board for production in 1996.

"You should come out here more often," Ned said. "We can hook you up with some surfer shorts, a cool board, you'd be killer."

I smiled. This was cool, way cool, but the wanderlust was already kicking in. I had four days left, and was sensing another adventure, alone, on a rock, in a far-off place. It was like a vision. Without realizing it, I began to shape my burritos in the form of a mountain.

"What are you doing?" they asked.

I had no idea. I layered on the cheese, the guacamole, bigger and bigger. I heard these notes. Like alien music. I pushed up the beans and scraped them with a fork, making slits in the side of the sculpture.

"It's calling," I whispered, getting up to go. "It's calling."

The surfers looked at each other.

"Dude," Ned said, "if it's calling, just put on the answering machine."

Cliff-hanger gets down

July 27, 1994

D EVILS TOWER, WYO. — It was not a good time — with my fingers trembling, my feet slipping, my heart pumping and my body pressed like flypaper against the cold, hard rock — to look down.

It looked down anyhow.

This is what I saw: trees. The tops of trees. And pigeons. The tops of pigeons.

It is never good to be above pigeons. Especially when this is the first rock you have ever climbed, and the air is thin and there's a skinny rope going though your harness and nothing else keeping you from certain death except a grip that could choke a statue — but a grip I was losing. Where was my hold? Where was the damn crack to put my hands? Where, pray tell, were my brains? I was 500 feet above earth, the wind was blowing, and as I began to slip, my fingernails scratching down the surface, I heard, from somewhere deep inside me, the unmistakable sound of a whimper.

Mama! ...

All right. I'll catch you up. I had come to this magnificent structure, Devils Tower, to address an ancient yearning in my soul. Remember the movie "Close Encounters," when Richard Dreyfuss couldn't get that mountain out of his mind? This was the mountain.

It haunted me, too. Of course, I didn't expect to find aliens.

Then again, I was in Wyoming.

Which brings me to my guide, the man who would take me to new heights, the man I knew only as Petefish — Andy Petefish — the legendary owner of Tower Guides, who told me, over the phone, to come to the base, find his trailer by the river and knock. This I did.

Nobody answered.

M OUNTAINS ARE NOT MY normal line of work. Normally, I stick a pad under some basketball player's nose and ask a brilliant question about zone defense. But ever since the big shots at this newspaper mistakenly approved an expense account for a week's worth of adventure travel, I knew I had to challenge the Devil, America's first national monument. Reach the top. Conquer my fear. No sooner had I finished my first escapade, surfing the Great Lakes, than I was here, in the badlands, in the shadow of the beast.

I knocked again. It was a ragged, old trailer, and not far away I saw a pair of gravity boots on a pole. At least this Petefish guy knew how to hang upside down — which, come to think of it, wasn't really encouraging.

I wandered back to the park entrance. The Tower was huge. Foreboding. Mostly it was steep. I mean, like straight up? Like a wall? And I'm thinking, "This is crazy. Lemme out of here. I am not a human fly—"

"Excuse me."

I spun around. Here was a lean man, with chiseled cheekbones, piercing blue eyes, tousled blond hair and the easy stance of one used to heights and bored with earth. He slid out his hand. The grip was powerful.

"Andy Petefish, I presume?"

He nodded.

"We're not really going up that, are we?" I pointed to the summit.

He studied me. "Why not?"

"Because I'm a chicken?"

He stared blankly. So I guess humor hasn't found its way to Wyoming yet, either.

Now, normally, you don't just show up and climb Devils Tower. Once upon a time, it was considered one of the hardest climbs in the business. The ancient Indians, who prayed here, had a legend about this monolith: A long time ago, seven young girls were being chased by giant bears, and just as the bears were about to catch them, the girls jumped on a low rock and pleaded, "Take pity on us, rock! Save us!" The rock began to grow, pushing the girls higher, out of danger, up to the sky, even as the bears slashed their claws into its side, creating the famous columns that make the Tower unique.

Take pity on us, rock! Save us!

It was a line I planned to use.

WHAT YOU WEAR TO CLIMB A ROCK: Special shoes, with sticky soles, a harness that fits snugly under your butt, ropes, clips and a hard hat.

WHAT YOU LOOK LIKE: One of the Village People.

"See this knot?" Andy said, tying a monster through my harness hook on the morning we attempted the climb. "Never, ever untie this."

Gotcha.

"And never unhook from the rock until I yell down that you're on the rope."

Gotcha.

"Don't tense up. Tense muscles don't work well."

Gotcha.

"Any questions?"

"Can I send a substitute?"

He smirked. It was 5 a.m. The sun was just yawning through the darkness. Andy, who wanted to be first on the mountain — "Avoid rush hour traffic," he said, which I guess is funny, in Wyoming — worked methodically, sorting his ropes, clips, slings, loops, holds and other devices to keep me from dying. I honestly believe that Andy Petefish, had he been going alone, would have needed a pair of Reeboks and a T-shirt and he'd be at the top in 20 minutes. Some men give you that kind of performance.

And some don't. Like me. Andy — who likes his pupils to have a little more training — told me to get rid of my watch, my ring, anything that protrudes, and to empty my backpack of all but the essentials, like water and courage. As he ran through the checklist, I glanced at the Tower's silhouette. It was awesome. Scary. It seemed to eat half the sky. I can't be sure, but I thought I heard it say, "Your mama wears Army boots."

"Ready?" Andy said.

Up we go.

THERE'S MORE THAN ONE WAY to scale a rock. Naturally, I asked for the elevator method. Andy, however, chose the Durrance Route, named for one of the first men to tame the Tower. "It's an easier climb," he said.

I mumbled silent thanks to Mr. Durrance.

Until I saw it. This was easy? It looked like the side of the Empire State Building, without windows. You climb a rock like this in "pitches," where the guide shimmies up, attaches the rope to pre-nailed hooks, then yells down to the climber, "On belay!" which means, basically, "Go home, you idiot!"

No, actually, it means you're safe to try to climb. I emphasize the word "try." The first pitch, about 80 feet, nearly killed me. You find yourself flat against sheer stone, running your feet desperately up and down, searching for a foothold, panting like a tired dog and clinging to anything solid as if it's your last hope. Remember slow dancing in high school? That's nothing compared to how tight you hold a rock.

"Stick your hand in a crack, turn your forearm and use the leverage to lift yourself," Andy yelled.

This makes about as much sense as it sounds. By the time I reached the top of the pitch, I was more bruised than a British rugby team.

"Good job," Andy said, sorting through his clips and hooks.

"I ... bunh ... huhh ... ah ... " I said.

Second pitch. Another 80 feet. Here I knew I was in trouble, because when Andy went up, he disappeared from sight, meaning the rock actually jutted out, at a backward angle.

"ON BELAY!" he yelled.

"I'M A MORON!" I replied.

Again, I found myself midway through with nothing to grab onto, and no place to go. Never have the words "get a grip" held more meaning.

"I'm ... in ... trouble here!" I hollered.

"Wedge inside a crack," Andy answered, "then push against your back, while using your elbows and legs for leverage to lift."

Did this guy write VCR manuals?

I tried to do what he suggested, and nearly slipped altogether several times. My adrenaline was pumping like one of these self-serve gas hoses, and my knees were doing things they were never meant to do. When I finally reached the top of the pitch, throwing my hand over the tiny ledge, I was breathing so hard, I could have inflated a Goodyear blimp.

"OK, you made it," Andy said. "Relax. Take a drink of water."

Ha! I wasn't moving. My back was flat against the rock, my feet as far from the ledge as I could get. Andy hooked me in, and I was like a leashed dog waiting outside the supermarket.

Or in this case, above it.

I suddenly realized that the sun was strong. We'd been climbing several hours. "Look at that," Andy said.

"Not if it's down," I said.

"No, look."

We were already high as a skyscraper, and the Tower cast a huge shadow over the greens, browns and tans of the national park and the Belle Fourche River below. It was breathtaking. At least it would have been breathtaking if I had any breath left.

"This rope I'm attached to," I gasped, "it never breaks, does it?"

"Nah," Andy said. He fiddled with his equipment. "But you know, you got to be careful. Even car brakes fail once in awhile."

Up he went, smiling.

What did he say?

I HAVE NOTICED THIS ABOUT adventure guides. Most of them have a calmness that is so reassuring, you honestly believe if you were broken into a million pieces, they could put you back together. Andy, who has guided hundreds of people up the Tower during the last 12 years, had that kind of calm. He spoke of the tranquillity of the mountain. How he never got tired of finding new faces of the rock to climb, which he then got to name. I suppose he'd name mine "The Shut Your Eyes Route."

Of course, Andy had another adventure guide's trait: horror stories.

"You see that ledge," he said. "This guy they call Old Doc fell once, landed on that ledge, knocked his teeth out, bounced off and landed 40 feet below. He's OK, though. He's got money."

"Thanks," I said. "I feel much better now."

And yet, I must admit, the more pitches we made together, the more confident I grew. True, I was running out of flesh to rip. And Andy yanked me up a few inches when things got desperate. But, eventually, I felt cocky enough to try a technique he suggested, straddling one of the Tower's cracks and inching up, a step at a time. I pushed off one hold — and whoop!

I was falling.

"TAKE PITY ON ME, ROCK! SAVE ME!"

Isn't that what the girls said?

I fell for only a split-second. The belay rope caught me, I jerked and an icy shiver went through my body. I grabbed a crack. Then promptly began to sweat like a furnace. "Ohmigod, ohmigod, ohmigod, ohmigod," I stuttered.

"You OK?" Andy yelled down.

It was then I noticed the pigeons, flying below me. We were in the sky, above the birds' nests, lost in a tranquillity that would have been heavenly, had I not just wet my pants.

"I'm OK," I yelped. Inch at a time, I pushed, wedged, counter-forced and grabbed my way up. When I reached the ledge, Andy was singing.

"Cracklin' Rosie get on board … . "

Oh, God. Anything but Neil Diamond.

"How can you be singing?" I gasped. "I'm shaking here. I'm drenched. This is like, the hardest thing I've ever tried to do, I'm on a ledge that's as big as a shoe box, and even the pigeons are laughing at me. What's the deal? I mean, Neil Diamond?"

Andy looked at me the way adventurers look at their pathetic pupils, a look that seems to say, "You are a flea. Die." Then he squinted in the hot sun, and pointed to skinny bushes, about 30 feet up.

"See that?" he said.

"Yes?"

"That's the top."

I could have kissed him. But he might have pushed me off. And so it was. The top. I have never — and I am including every paycheck I've ever earned here — been so happy to see anything. I actually dashed the last few feet, and the surface flattened into low grass and rock.

"Where's the spaceship?" I said.

Andy was singing again.

I wandered in a circle, felt a rush of accomplishment, and began to leap like Rocky on the steps of the art museum. At the center of the summit, 1,200 feet above the river, there is a marker, and a metal canister that contains a register.

"Go ahead," Andy said, handing me the tube, "sign your name."

I believe he actually smiled.

I unrolled the paper, and noticed the cover, which had a sketch of the Tower and an arrow that said: "You are here." Very funny. I flipped through the pages, looking for a clean one, and I noticed one of the inscriptions.

"They'll never find me here (signed) O.J. Simpson."

I am not making this up.

Never mind. We had survived. We had scaled the Devil. I looked out over the vast Wyoming prairie and counted my blessings. I also figured Andy — who wasn't even breathing hard — must be half mountain goat. I took a deep breath, and soaked in the history of this place, the ancient Indians, and their charming legend of the seven girls on the rock. And then it hit me:

How did they get down?

Lord of the flies is hooked

July 28, 1994

L IVINGSTON, MONT. — A river ran through me. It ran through my shoes, my socks, my pants and my underwear. Cold Montana river water. Did I mind? Ha! I am rugged. I am tough. Besides, I was too busy having this stimulating discussion with my fishing guide:

"Look! I got something! Is it a fish?"

"It's a twig."

Reel, cast ...

"How about that? Is that a fish?"

"It's a branch."

Reel, cast ...

"Fish?"

"Tire."

"Fish?"

"That's my hat."

I have no skill for fishing. You probably can tell. We fished a little as kids in Philadelphia, but mostly we just sat around, throwing worms at each other. When a fish actually appeared on our lines, we were so shocked, we ran away. "How did THAT happen?" we'd say, racing down the hill in case the thing had a gun. Eventually, fish would get yanked out of the water, take one look at us, say, "God, not you again," and unhook themselves.

Which is pretty much all I knew about fishing — until I reached Montana. Suddenly, here I was, beneath the mighty Absaroka Mountains on the Yellowstone River, fly-casting in the same hallowed waters as the characters in "A River Runs Through It" — only with less music, less slow-motion camera work and certainly less luck. Actually, no luck. Unless you count catching the back of the boat as lucky.

Reel, cast ...

"Fish?"

"Log."

Nonetheless, I was happy to be here, simply because, compared to my previous experiences — surfing the Great Lakes, climbing Devils Tower — this was like a La-Z-Boy recliner. I was now halfway through my fantasy week of adventure travel. Soon, my boss would return to discover The Expense Account From Hell. I figured a nice big rainbow trout might soften the blow.

Not that I'd figured to catch one.

Reel, cast ...

"Is that a fish? HEY! IT'S MOVING!"

"That's my boot."

Why fly-fishing? Well. What adventure trip would be complete without a sport that used to be for old men in ugly hats and is now so trendy it makes Esquire magazine's cover? Fly-fishing. Everyone's doing it. They arrive in old campers or new Chevy Blazers, with aged wooden poles or yuppie graphite models. Fly-fishing is religion. Fly-fishing is Zen. Fly-fishing is … expensive.

"You'll need a rod," they said at the Montana Troutfitters Orvis Shop in Bozeman, where my adventure began.

"A rod," I said. "Hmm. Can I rent that?"

"And a reel."

"Naturally."

"And line."

"Line would be good."

"And boots."

"Well, sure."

"Waders."

"Waiters? They serve lunch?"

"Waders. These things."

They handed me a pair of what I thought were Dom DeLuise's pants. I shrugged and pulled them on, putting the straps over my shoulders. I looked liked part of a German oompah band.

"Uh, sir," the owner, Dave Kumlien, said, pointing at my feet, "you put your shoes on after the waders."

"Of course," I said, turning salmon.

Did I say salmon? Sorry. I meant trout. We were fishing for trout. That's what my guide said as we drove through the countryside. Like the guides who took me surfing and rock climbing, my fishing guide, a hearty, dark-haired fellow named Paul Tunkis, had this way of making the most complex things seem like common knowledge.

Common to everyone, that is, but me.

"I've got flies," he said.

"I'm sorry. Did you see a doctor?"

"Flies for fishing."

"Oh."

He opened a small case to reveal — and I say this with all due respect to fishermen like Ted Williams — some of the most disgusting synthetic creatures ever created. They had big tails and hairy wings. I'm telling you, if fish get hungry looking at these things, they deserve a hook in the mouth.

"You wanna try a nymph?" he said.

"I've got a girlfriend … "

"A nymph. One of these little flies. We can fish those first."

"Oh! Sure! Nymphs are good."

I SHOOK MY HEAD AS we bounced along. Nymphs? What's next? Hookers? We parked the trailer by the edge of the river. Paul pulled the boat off the hitch — by himself, naturally, as he is a member of the Guide Race, a superior form of human being — and handed me my rod and reel.

"Let's talk casting," he said.

"Great," I said. "I thought Robert Redford was all wrong in 'Indecent Proposal.' "

He stared at me. So I guess humor hasn't found its way to Montana yet, either.

"People say fly-casting is difficult," Paul continued, "but it isn't. It's a touch thing. Just pull the rod back, then flick it forward like this."

He snapped his pole quickly, and the line came flying off in a sweet little whoosh, landing gently on the river and floating downstream. He yanked it back, it flew up and over his head like a large lasso, then he snapped it forward again, midair, and it danced the other way, once more touching down gently on the current. Up. Down. Up. Down.

"See?" he said.

"Beautiful," I said.

"Try it."

I did what he did. I pulled the rod back, then snapped it forward. The line came shooting out, same as his. Right at my foot.

"Stop a little sooner," he said.

This time, I reached water — very shallow water. I tried again. A little farther. Again. A little farther.

"You'll get it," he said, pushing the boat out. "People tell you casting is some religious thing. It isn't. Knowing where to drop your fly is the trick."

Well. I've always said so.

It began to rain as we floated down the river. The dark clouds mixed like water paints in the huge Montana sky. Fortunately, rain doesn't hurt fishing. It doesn't make the fishermen very comfortable, but it doesn't hurt fishing.

"Let's cast from the banks," Paul said. "Maybe we'll have more luck."

"Do you carry an umbrella?" I asked.

He smirked. We walked along. The bank was dirt and stone.

"Step forward before you cast," Paul said.

"You mean — like, in the water?"

I squished ahead. My boots were submerged. A little farther. My shins were submerged. A little far— ooops.

Splash! I was soaked.

"Careful of the footing," Paul said.

"Thank you."

I stood up. I cast. I reeled. I cast.

I reeled. I rocked. I reeled. I rolled.

Nothing.

"Maybe it's the flies," Paul said.

He opened his little case — or, as fish like to call it, the munchie pack — and picked some weird colored insect, which might have been the Hemingway Caddis, or the Olive Elkhair Caddis. I cast that a few times. He tried another, which might have been the Gold-Robbed Hare ear, or the Tan Caddis Pupa.

I am not making these names up. These are real flies. Well. Real fake flies. Here is a list of some more, along with their distinguishing characteristics.

Yellow Humpy: Dry fly.

Mayfly: May not.

Brown Wooly: Likes Elvis.

Prince Nymph: Thinking of changing its name to symbol.

Hairwig Fly: Once dated Brooke Shields.

How do you know which fly to use?

Simple. You let your guide decide.

AFTER TWO HOURS, WE STILL hadn't caught anything. I didn't mind. Fly-fishing, I learned, is really about fooling the fish into thinking your fly is real, and not some ugly, hairy thing you bought in a shop. I never was much into fooling animals. Besides, the casting was hypnotic, and the scenery in Montana is so spectacular, you almost forget what you're there to do. I swear we floated past some of the prettiest real estate in America, mountains, green meadows, clear streams. Unfortunately, it was mostly owned by movie stars.

"That's Peter Fonda's place," Paul said. "I think Meg Ryan owns that ... the guy who started Mad magazine owns that ... "

Mad magazine?

Suddenly, there was a jerk on my line.

"Don't tell me," I said. "It's a sunken refrigerator."

"No," Paul said, slowly, as my line began shooting out, "you've actually ... got a fish."

"A FISH?"

I sprang to life. I squeezed the rod. Suddenly, I realized Paul had never shown me what to do if I caught something, probably because the idea was so comical.

"Work it!" he yelled. "Point the rod tip up!"

"Where's the tip?"

"Reel in the slack!"

"Which part's the reel?"

"It's swimming toward you!"

"Why? What'd I do?"

"Take up the slack! Take up the slack!"

For the next three minutes, I moved like a member of Devo, jerking every which way, fighting the fish. It ran left, right, out, in. Somehow — it probably got so dizzy — the thing did not escape. And there came a moment when I reeled and reeled and suddenly, at the end of my line, was a beautiful, live rainbow trout, 16 inches long, which looked at me as if to say, "You! That idiot from Philadelphia! I'm so ashamed!"

Paul threw a net over it.

"Congratulations," he said. "You want to unhook it?"

"What? Touch it? You must be crazy."

He laughed, mostly because he finally could go home, and we took a photo. He then released the fish, and it swam off in total embarrassment, unable to ever go home again.

As for me, well, I was exhilarated. The thrill of landing a fish is everything it's cracked up to be, and slimier. My breath was coming in nervous spurts, and I kept saying, "I caught something. I caught something." I didn't even ask what insect I used, although I am guessing, as a city kid, we went with Superfly.

"Well, what did you think?" Paul asked, as we floated back toward the trailer. I looked down the Yellowstone River, and up toward the mountains. The shower had stopped, and through the clouds a rainbow, an honest-to-goodness rainbow, shimmered in the sky like a gift. I felt a piercing emotion.

"I think," I said, wistfully, "I'm sitting on a hook."

More herd journalism

July 29, 1994

PRYOR, MONT. — These are grown men talking:
"HO, CATTLE! … yo, cattle, yo, cattle! … EEEEE YUTYUTYUT! … move, you no-goods … AGGAGAGAGAGA! … HO, CATTLE! YO, CATTLE!"

This is not normal conversation. Then again, we are talking to cows. Not we, exactly, because I am on a horse with my mouth open in utter disbelief. But the other people here at the Schively Ranch are instructing the cows to — in cowboy talk — git.

Git?

We are bringing in the herd. Or. As I said. They are bringing in the herd, and I am plopping along — actually, my horse is plopping, if you want to know the truth — wondering how I got here. I am not the type to bring in a herd. I might take a herd out for doughnuts. But moving it over the plains of southwestern Montana, on an Indian reservation, with mountains and valleys and streams, well, my approach would be to call Bekins and ask for its biggest truck.

"HO, CATTLE! YO, CATTLE … EEETEETEETEET!"

Now, before I explain how I wound up on this ranch, doing things such as branding calves and stepping in cow pies — "We'll teach you ridin', ropin' and wranglin'," the owner told me, to which I said, with great excitement, "Huh?" — I should confess my shameful history with horses.

As a city kid, I didn't spend much time around equine creatures. Now and then, my folks would drag me to a horse farm to try to learn to ride. Inevitably, the owner took one look at my knees, which were shaking like Ricky Ricardo's castanets, and fetched a horse named Pokey. They were always named Pokey! Every horse I got! How is that possible? And the owner would grin and say, "Pokey here's a nice horse. Yes, son. You and Pokey will get along jus' fine."

Then he'd lean in and whisper something in the horse's ear, which, looking back, I believe was, "Wake up, Pokey."

Here's my point: I still had trouble! I would kick Pokey to make him move, but Pokey would just lift his tail and make a disgusting noise. Then the owner rode past and clicked his tongue and instantly Pokey started going at a pace that a cowboy would call "napping" and I would call "Formula One."

Clumpity-clumpity-clump.

So coming to a ranch where nearly everything is done on, with or around a horse — which is still better than behind a horse, let me tell you — was a real stretch for me. But stretching was what this week was all about. I was on a mission, My Excellent Adventures, four fantasies to be completed before the return of my boss, who approved the idea, but not the budget.

"Face your fear," I told myself. "Face the smell … "

"Face the horse," the ranchers told me, "and step into the stirrup."

Unfortunately, the stirrup was chest-high. I tried to explain that if I could step into that, I could dunk a basketball, and I wouldn't need this job.

"Aw, here," they said, hoisting me up and flopping me over the saddle. The horse made a noise. I think it was snoring.

"What's his name?" I asked.

"Pecos," a cowboy said.

Hmm. I felt better. Until I realized Pecos is Spanish for Pokey.

DID YOU KNOW THE ORIGINAL "City Slickers" was to be filmed right here, on the Schively Ranch? That's right. The Bassitts, a delightful family that owns the place, had the land, the cows, the horses and the know-how. Unfortunately, the movie people waited too long and it got cold. The Bassitts had to get their herd to the winter ranch, in Lovell, Wyoming. As they say in the cattle biz, when you gotta mooove, you gotta mooove.

This brings us to cows. Cows are big, smelly and make funny noises, like NFL linemen, only cows can count higher.

"HO, CATTLE! YO, CATTLE … WHEEUPP, UPP, UPP OOEYYYY!"

They also eat grass, which is why we were here, moving the herd to a new food supply. Moving a herd is no easy task. They make a hell of a mess, kicking up dust as they clump their hooves, and make noises like Dick Vitale. Cows tend to follow one another closely, even jumping on each other's backs to try to get ahead. They remind me of investment bankers.

"Keep 'em in the group," Matt Bassitt, one of the cowboys, said, circling me on his horse. "Just ride towards 'em. Cattle are generally afraid of a horse."

Except if I'm on it.

"Go and get that one," Matt said, pointing to a steer that was wandering off to the side.

"Go get it?"

"Just ride around it, force it back in."

This meant getting Pecos, my horse, to go where I wanted him to go — as opposed to where he wanted to go. By now, Pecos had called all his cousins named Pokey and had learned I was a complete horse wimp. So when I kicked his sides, he looked back and rolled his eyes, as if to say, "Yeah, right."

But he moved, because, what else is there to do in Montana? We trotted around the steer — I think it was a steer, although, for all my experience, it could have been a zebra — and it looked up at me with these big steer eyes. I was supposed to yell something, so I listened to the other wranglers, including one guest — and I'm not kidding here — who actually barked like a dog.

I leaned over. "Move, please," I whispered.

And he moved! What do you know? He spoke English!

"We gotta brand some of them calves."

Everyone nodded. This was Joe Bassitt speaking, the 67-year-old owner of the ranch, a tight-lipped fellow who commanded such respect that I honestly think we would have nodded had he said, "All right, we're gonna round up the menfolk and poke 'em with a pitchfork."

Joe has one of those weathered faces that lets you know he is a man of the land. When he talks, his sons listen, his sons' sons listen, even the horses listen. Joe is the type to sigh and shake his head at stupidity, and you know he would come to New York City, take one look and throw up.

He has owned the ranch for 30 years, but in the early 1980s, the cattle business got really rough, and the family didn't know if it could make it. That's when the idea of taking in guests came about. At first, the locals laughed. Down at the feed shop, they'd shake their heads and say, "Wait a second. You're gonna get city folk to come out here and help you do your ranchin'? And they're gonna pay you?"

THIS SUGGESTED THAT CITY FOLK were even dumber than a barrel of hair, which is what most cowboys think anyhow. You have to admit, it does sound funny. I asked Joe whether he'd pay $700 to follow around a lawyer for a week. "Heck, no," Joe said.

Then again, ranchers are smarter than lawyers.

They must be because the guest business took off — especially after "City Slickers" — and now the Schively and ranches like it are booked months in advance, with groups coming from around the world to spend a week learning the Cowboy Way.

Which I can sum up.

City Way: walk.

Cowboy Way: squish.

City way: aftershave.

Cowboy way: manure.

City way: Yugo.

Cowboy way: Pokey.

City way: labeling machine.

Cowboy way: branding iron.

Branding iron?

"Hold 'em down now!" Joe yelled, as he aimed the hot poker at the side of the calf, to brand it in case it got lost. I was holding the back legs and someone else was holding the head, and here came Joe with the sizzling iron — sssssss — and he pulled back, leaving a nice, even half-crest, which is part of the Schively brand.

"You're quite an artist," I said.

"Ah," he said. "Here. You try."

The next calf was brought in, and, much as I was not crazy about this idea, I inched forward, shaking the poker nervously. I dabbed the hide like a kid touching a hot oven.

Sssss.

I pulled back. We all stared. I hadn't really made a crest as much as a, well, it was, kinda, I guess, I have no idea. I do know if this calf ever got lost, it would be returned to Beijing.

"Uh, you better lemme have that," Joe said, taking the poker.

No problem.

Answer the following question:

1. Smelling good is …

a. Very important

b. Overrated

c. Woman's work.

d. Hah! Jed! Did you hear that?

If you answered b, c or d, ranch life could be for you. There is no way to stay "morning fresh" on the range. As Matt said, "Out here, at the end of the day, you always know where you've been."

Or what you've stepped in.

Wait. It's time for ropin'! This is not the same as roping. Roping is what we did as kids, while jumping and singing silly songs. Ropin' is what you do to catch a horse, or a cow or a pickup truck.

"It's all in the wrist, see?"

I looked up. Actually, I looked down. My teacher was a boy who came up to my waist. He had red hair, a plaid shirt and far better roping technique than I could ever hope for.

Kids learn these kind of things on a ranch. They learn to rope, to ride, to clean the stalls, to shovel manure. It may sound trivial to you. Then again. It stacks up pretty well next to destroying the world on a video screen.

"Watch." The boy, named Tyler — one of Joe's many well-behaved grandsons — looped the rope overhead several times, once smacking me in the face. To his credit, he kept the lasso going, then released it at a plastic bull's head.

Gotcha! He yanked it in.

"Now, you try," he said. I took the rope, imitated his lasso technique, swung it over my head a few times and released. Voila! I caught my target. My target was the ground.

"It takes time," one of the cowboys said. I didn't mind. I would never rope a real animal anyhow because I'm sure it would just get ticked off, grab the rope and tie me to a fence.

Ding-a-ling-a-ling-a-ling.

Let's do lunch!

A man works up a hearty appetite on the range. Over meat, beans, cheese and chips, I spoke with Joe and his sons about the business. I asked important questions such as: Where do you keep the soap? Also, I asked, what made a real cowboy?

"Well, a lot of people just throw a rope on their pickup truck and call themselves a cowboy," Joe said, slowly. (He says everything kind of slowly.) "But to me, it's more than that. It's how you work, how you treat your animals, how you keep your ranch. To me, calling yourself a cowboy is something you have to earn, like an honor. That's the way I feel about it."

We all kind of nodded. Nobody said much.

THE LATE AFTERNOON WAS more chores, more riding, more looking at the mountains and listening to the stream. Life goes at a slower pace at places like the Schively, and the longer you stay, the more your butt hurts. No. The more your breathing slows down. One of the women told me that the first day city guests arrive, they're up at 6 a.m., looking for something to do, as if they've never left the office.

By the fifth day, they're sitting around, chewing on weeds.

And I believe it. As I rode around — beneath that huge Montana sky, my sneakers firmly in the stirrups, a cowboy hat around my neck — I realized something I was learning from these outdoor adventures: They humble you. They give you perspective. Your problems, instead of papers and reports, are things like gripping a rock, or finding a wave, one thing, one seemingly simple thing, and yet, you are overwhelmed, humbled by nature. You realize how big a world this is, and how small one person's complaining can be. I believe this is why people live here, on prairies and mountains and beaches. People in cities may think of them as amusing rustics, but the fact is, they enjoy a quality of life that can never be found in rush-hour traffic.

Of course, their laundry bills are astronomical.

The sun was setting. It was time to go. Joe and his wife, Iris, told me to come back anytime, and I believe they meant it, although I felt bad about that branded calf, which will suffer an identity crisis the rest of its life.

Still, I think I got the point of the cowboy/cattle/City Slickers thing. This is the point: There is more than one way to live your life. What a shame if you never get to see that.

The stars were out. The air was cool. As I drove into the Montana night, I felt tired, but good. I rolled down the window and heard the distant sound of laughter.

I think it was Pokey.

Good-bye, baseball
September 15, 1994

HERE GOES YOUR OLD FRIEND BASEBALL. You remember him from a happier time, when he walked with his head high, waving at children and swatting home runs. He is stooped over now, fat and bloated, drunk on his own greed. There is no saving him. No one even wants to try.

There goes your old friend baseball. The 1994 season is officially over, tossed away like leftovers, without a climax, without a winner, but with plenty of losers, a roomful of men who are so interested in getting the best sound bite on television they never even notice a grand tradition squashed beneath their feet.

"It is very hard to articulate the poignancy of this moment," sighed a puppet named Bud Selig, who, in canceling the season, lived up to his role as "acting" commissioner. "Baseball has changed like other industries. We cannot continue to do business as usual."

And minutes later, in New York, the players' mouthpiece, Donald Fehr, responded this way: "What do you expect from a cartel?"

Who are these men, you want to shout. Who are these navy blue suits and maroon ties and pasty skins that look as if they've never seen the warmth of an August afternoon, where baseball used to live? Who are these men? What right do they have to command something that was once such a part of the American quilt that sewed together children from Spokane to Providence on a single summer night, sitting by the radio, marking their blue-lined scorecards, listening to announcers bellow, "It's a long fly ball, deep to left!"

When there was nothing else to bring joy to the masses, there was baseball. When there was nothing else to unite father and son, there was baseball. When there was nothing for an old man or woman to fill the lonely night, there was baseball. It was, above all else, a metronome of American life, an unbroken ritual from April to October.

This has always been what makes it important. Not the latest pitching star, or the newest owner, but the assurance that life went on, that the seasons flowed, that players went from wiping sweat to wearing long sleeves to finally, on the last day, leaping into a happy pile. It was our nation's growth chart.

Who are these men? They have seized control, and it's like giving the car keys to a bunch of 7-year-olds. Canceled the season?

Do they know what they've done?

THERE GOES YOUR OLD FRIEND THE WORLD SERIES. There will be no annual visit this October. No letting the kids stay up late, no cutting out box scores and putting them in a scrapbook, no screaming fans, no crowded bars, no soldiers overseas huddled around a radio, eyes closed, fists clenched, whispering, "Get a hit ... get a hit." The Fall Classic has survived so much stronger adversity. It has filled rosters during two World Wars, when healthy young men were in low supply. It has filled stadiums during the Depression. It has endured scandals from the outside and the inside and has even endured midseason work stoppages, and yet, autumn after autumn, it was there, something you could count on: falling leaves, children in school clothes, a champion in baseball.

Now the leaves fall and kids are in school and the stadiums are empty. They have been since Aug. 12, when this strike began, when a union of players — not one of them being paid less than $109,000 a year, some being paid upward of $8 million — decided they simply can't live with what their bosses were suggesting, which was a limit on their salaries.

And so they left. And for weeks both sides postured and posed and swallowed network air time as if it were chocolate. They spoke passionately, but they were dedicated to themselves, not the game, and it is their own interests that they serve today.

"The problem is complex," they will tell you, and they'll prattle on about indexes and revenue sharing and small markets and cable. But it is all money, it is only money, and there is more than enough money to make all of them happy, owners and players, if they were the kind of people who could accept that no one doubles his income forever.

They are not. This is not even about right and wrong anymore. It's about respect for the game, the way fire fighters respect their job, the way police don't go on strike. That respect is gone. Anything is possible.

"This is not about greedy owners versus greedy players," Selig insisted. "This is about two sides trying to make adjustment to economic conditions. In the end, all will be better off, mainly the fans."

The fans, he said?

You don't know whether to cry or throw up.

THERE GOES YOUR OLD FRIEND HISTORY. More than any other sport, baseball keeps track of its efforts. There were strong men this year who threatened hallowed baseball records: Ken Griffey Jr. and Matt Williams, rattling the cage of Roger Maris and his 61 home runs. There was Tony Gwynn, out in San Diego, knocking on the door of a .400 batting average, something not achieved since Ted Williams hit .406 in 1941.

All that is gone now, wiped like chalk from a classroom board. You need a season to make a record. You need games to make a season.

Beginning in 1905, baseball has always ended in a city celebration. Some schoolkid had his favorite memory made with the last pitch. Some family went to the parade and took pictures. Who will remember 1994 that way? No one. It might as well have never existed.

There's a story about this sport that goes back to President Franklin Roosevelt, who is said to have telephoned Joseph Stalin one night. This was in the days when America and Russia got along. The call took awhile to place. Finally, when the connection was made, this is what the president said:

"Hello, Joe? It's Frank. Giants three, Dodgers nothing."

We don't tell stories like that anymore. We don't have them to tell. Baseball was a heartbeat, and a heartbeat will forgive you; it will let you speed it up, even skip it for a moment; it will keep on going and be there when you catch up, always, forever — unless you stop the heart.

They have stopped the heart of this sport. And in so doing, they set a precedent for all the money-grubbers that might own it in the future: If all else fails, it's all right to cancel the season. The hell with it. That's the history owners and players make today.

There goes your old friend baseball. You can't help him. You can't reach him. You can't even recognize him anymore.

It's all up Hill now
September 30, 1994

HE NEVER MENTIONED MONEY. He never gushed about some new car he was going to buy, or some new mansion with a hundred rooms. He made no joke about how "the ladies in Detroit better watch out," as one top draft choice had done years before him. He didn't preen or mug. He wore no earring. He didn't boast, "There's a new sheriff in town!"

You want to know the first thing Grant Hill did as a Piston? He listened to a question. And before he answered, he noticed the crowd in the back, and asked, politely, "Could you all hear that?"

That might strike you as trivial. Believe me, it is not. In this day and age, when sports are collapsing under the weight of their own greed and athletes seem able to speak only one word — it begins with "m" and ends with "e" — any sign of consideration, even asking whether the folks in the back heard the question, should be noted.

So take note. The Pistons got more than a player when they signed Grant Hill at the Palace. They got, as coach Don Chaney put it, "a package." That package contains: one brain, well-tended and developed; one heart, battle-ready; two hands that can score and defend; one torso that can twist until the basket is his; a set of eyes that have seen glory and defeat; a set of ears that have absorbed the best college coaching in America; a mouth that thinks before it speaks; and a memory that holds the life lessons of pro sports, as taught by a dad who lived them.

When you break it down that way, $45 million seems like a bargain. "I appreciate all that Mr. McKinney has done," Hill said moments after signing.

Vice president of basketball operations Billy McKinney smiled. "I appreciate the way he just got all that money and still calls me 'Mister.' "

Up Hill from here.

I KNOW PEOPLE HAVE HIGH EXPECTATIONS of me," said Hill, wearing a gray suit, white shirt and conservative tie, "but I have high expectations of myself."

The crowd seemed to swallow every word he said and beamed as if he were related to them. It has been awhile since the Pistons drafted a big-time, All-America college star. There were years when the team was so good, the top pick was cut before the season.

Of course, those years ended with championships. More recently they've ended with boos. So now they rebuild. Joe Dumars is the foundation. Lindsey Hunter and Allan Houston are important bricks. Oliver Miller and Mark West might be new walls. Hill is the cornerstone.

"Billy and I talked about the type of people we wanted around here," said Chaney, watching his new player smile and shake hands with well-wishers. "We got rid of some bad people, and we're going after people who know what it takes to win. ... I don't have to teach Grant how to be unselfish. It's there."

So are many other rarely seen qualities. For one thing, the kid graduated from college, an anomaly among top picks. He started a Detroit charity before he even saw a dime from the Pistons. He involved himself in the negotiating and financial elements of his career — rather than telling an agent "just send me the check."

And I can't remember the last time I heard a draft pick refer to his father's career as "a Renaissance."

Which is another thing. The parents. So many times you attend press conferences, and either the parents aren't there, or they sit and smile meekly and say, "Whatever he wants is OK by us."

Not Thursday. Here were parents who don't consider their job finished just because their child calls a press conference. Calvin Hill, the former NFL star, said his son must "keep his balance. Just because he's making money as a pro athlete, he isn't insulated from the real world. I remember thinking, when I first got into pro football, that the rules didn't apply to me. I want him to know they do."

Maybe some draft picks would be embarrassed by this, a father telling reporters that $45 million doesn't mean his son is all grown up.

I thought it was terrific.

AND LEST YOU THINK I'M over-impressed with education — what a sad world when thinking that would be wrong — note that the 6-foot-8 Hill also has the competitive fire of a typical sports superstar. He not only led his Duke team to two — and almost three — national championships, but when asked about Chris Webber, he quickly responded, "I've never lost to Chris Webber. Our teams played in the AAU as kids, and we won at 13, at 14, at 16, and then in college at Duke. I've never lost to him."

"You sure?" someone asked.

"Oh, yeah."

He smiled. And then, remembering his manners, he quickly added, "Chris will probably have something to say about that this year."

We have in this kid the etchings of something important: character. That has always been Dumars' trademark as well. And the thought of these two on the same team is reason enough to buy a ticket. I don't know how much the Pistons will win this season. But I know there won't be half-baked effort, sleepy defense and laughing after losses, as there has been in the past. Win or lose, the team led by Dumars and Hill will never shame itself.

And maybe that will be the kid's biggest contribution. At a time when you want to throw the sports section in the trash, Hill delivers the element we need most on the playing fields and hardwood courts of America:

Something to be proud of. Up Hill from here.

Bradley takes the high road
November 16, 1994

T O BE SO TALL AND never stumble? That is asking too much. And so
Shawn Bradley seems to accept the trips as part of his journey. He is high
as a window and narrow as a fax, and wherever he goes he gets stares and
questions and hoots and laughs and none of it is new. What could be new? He
was walking when he was 1 year old, and even then, instead of marveling at his
skill, people mistook him for a preschooler and said, "He doesn't talk. Is he
retarded?"

What could be new?

Only the money. They bark about money now because he is no longer in the
eye-bugging business, he is in the entertainment business. You buys your ticket,
you wants results. When Shawn Bradley left college, finished his Mormon
mission at age 21 and jumped straight from the churches of Australia into the
NBA draft, he was giving up the only leverage he had against a world that
expected miracles.

His right to say, "I'm not getting paid."

"I don't like it, to be honest," he says of the fact that "$44-million contract"
now follows his name in the thousands of articles written about him. "I wish they
wouldn't put that. But it's part of life.

"Maybe not part of life for everyone else. But for me."

He pulls off his shirt to reveal a long, pale torso that suggests a red-headed
boy ready to jump in the fishing hole. A country kid in a city game. A Mormon in
a sabbath-busting business. A 7-foot, 6-inch novice who is better-paid than 90
percent of NBA veterans.

What could be new?

H AVE YOU EVER MET everyone's expectations?" I ask Bradley. He thinks
before he answers — which separates him from half the league — and then,
as if watching a movie of his life, says, "I had a coach once who said he saw
something new from me every day."

That's pretty much the only way, isn't it? Something new every day? When
you have that height, that dexterity, you score 50, they expect 60, you block a
dozen, they say "tomorrow, two dozen."

So in some ways, Bradley's entire life has been a prep course for the rough
period he's enduring now, the boos from Philly fans, the snickers from
opponents, the attempts to thicken him with a 7,000-calorie-per day diet and the
growls about "a return on investment." After all, Bradley was the No. 2 selection
in the draft a year ago. The No. 1 selection, Chris Webber, won Rookie of the

Year. The No. 3 selection, Anfernee Hardaway, was the runner-up.

Bradley, meanwhile, got banged like a time clock, then suffered a knee injury and missed the second half of the season.

What did they expect? He hadn't played in 2½ years — and he looked it. After a recent vicious dunk by Shaquille O'Neal — which nearly took Bradley's head off — Orlando's Nick Anderson said, "That was child abuse."

"Child abuse?" What could be new?

W ITH ALL THIS, YOU EXPECT Bradley to be gun-shy, cynical. There is none of that. He proudly says he never slouched as a child, never tried to make himself shorter. "I had a family who loved me and told me to be proud of who I was."

And in a storm you wouldn't wish on your worst neighbor — even if he was making $44 million — Bradley keeps that attitude.

Last night, against the Pistons, he came off the bench — he doesn't start because of habitual foul trouble — and wasn't in for two minutes before the whistle blew. Foul No. 1. Then Mark West stole the ball from him, ran down, dunked, and Bradley swiped at the shot, missed like a cat trying to catch a fly and whacked West's head instead. Tweet! Foul No. 2.

He went to the bench.

It went this way all night. Come in, foul, sit down — he looked lost — until the final seconds, when he grabbed some boards and banked in his first basket. Still, the 76ers lost again, and somewhere in the streets of Philadelphia, the groans continued. Last season, Fred Carter, then the coach, said, "Shawn needs three seasons."

Carter was fired at the end of the year. He didn't finish the sentence: Three seasons is an eternity.

And yet, like a mountain climber looking up, the NBA has never been able to resist height. Reed-like giants such as Manute Bol, Chuck Nevitt, Swen Nater, Tom Burleson were always given chances because, hey, what if they found the horizontal to go with that vertical? The difference is, none of those men was paid franchise money. None had to live in the world's largest petri dish.

"I wouldn't do anything differently," says Bradley, who remains unfailingly polite, calm, drug- and alcohol-free. You wonder whether he'll ever have the meanness to challenge O'Neal or Patrick Ewing. You wonder whether his frame will ever hold the beef it needs.

Bradley might wonder, too. He doesn't show it. He keeps learning, patiently, and when he stumbles, he gets up. What could be new? He is married, with a baby daughter, Cheyenne, a name befitting a place where the only thing watching you is a great big sky. I ask if his next child were a boy, would he prefer him to be 7-feet-6 or 5-feet-11?

He thinks again. "What's the difference?"

And I believe he means it.

His death, their fall from Grace

December 18, 1994

A S THE YEAR FADES TO DUST, we mourn an old friend in sports. His name was Grace. He passed away in 1994. Cause of death was neglect. They found him wrapped in a blanket, frozen and forgotten, in an alley behind a TV studio. He left no survivors.

You may recall Grace from your youth — if you're old enough. He played for many teams. Many sports. Once upon a time, when his legs were strong, he was welcome on any playing field in America.

He was best known for tipping his cap in the baseball stadium, or speaking humbly with reporters in small towns. You saw him respecting a referee's decision in tennis, or handing the ball to the ref after a touchdown.

He could dunk a basketball — but gently, without yelling obscenities. He could grind for a hockey puck — but never pushed the stick into an opponent's throat. He even boxed a little, and after victories, he was humble. "I'm lucky tonight," he would say. "That man is a fine fighter."

This was long ago, before commercial endorsements, before ESPN highlights, before players practiced dance steps in front of the locker room mirror. Grace was a hero then. He never made a lot of money. In fact, he never took a paycheck for anything he did.

He died penniless. People laughed at his "lack of marketing."

T HESE ARE THE SAME PEOPLE who see sports as a star-making machine: shoe companies, agents, TV networks, media "pals."

The same people who bring you a new CD this Christmas, featuring rap songs by NBA players. One is called "Livin' Legal and Large" by Seattle's Gary Payton:

"I'm just a superstar, rolling down
the boulevard in my $50,000 car."

It doesn't matter that most of America doesn't know who Payton is — or that he's never won an NBA title, or that, as a point guard, he ranked 17th in assists last season. The NBA is about 'tude. Payton has 'tude.

Grace did not have 'tude.

He didn't even know what it meant.

Grace knew how to lose. He never would hire a hit man to whack an opponent, and he didn't blame reporters when he made a mistake. He wouldn't throw firecrackers at fans, like Vince Coleman, or desert his team to be with Madonna, like Dennis Rodman.

Remember Joe Louis, when he said, "Every man's got to get beat sometime"?

Grace taught him that.

He knew how to lose.

More important, he knew how to win. He knew that for every great play he made, many others were trying to do the same. He refused to rub their noses in his success. When he made an interception, he did not wiggle down the sideline, laughing at the opposing team, the way Deion Sanders does today.

And when he hit home runs, he did not flip the finger to opposing dugouts, as Ken Griffey Jr. did last season.

In June, during the NBA playoffs, Scottie Pippen dunked over Patrick Ewing. Ewing fell and Pippen stood over him, so Ewing had to stare up into his crotch. Pippen glared.

Later he said, "You wait your whole career for a moment like that."

Grace would never have understood that.

THROUGHOUT HIS SPORTS CAREER, Grace never wore his name on his uniform. He never held out of camp, or demanded that a contract be renegotiated. "A deal's a deal," he once said.

Later, when Grace retired from active sports, he coached. For a while, he worked with men like UCLA's John Wooden. Men who taught. Men who kept things in perspective.

But soon, Grace was driven out of coaching. He was squashed by obnoxious types like Buddy Ryan and greedy types like Rollie Massimino, who made a dirty deal with a university, then demanded they pay him off.

In the twilight of his career, Grace tried broadcasting. An understated voice, never intruding. Men like Ernie Harwell and Vin Scully shared the booth with Grace.

But soon, he went out of fashion, tossed aside for screamers like Dick Vitale, Chris Berman and John Madden. Grace never understood them. Never understood becoming bigger than the game itself. "They sure are loud," he would say, trying to be kind.

After that, Grace disappeared. No one seems to know exactly when, but those who loved him felt his absence like a cold wind.

Now he is gone.

Reaction to his death was mild. Only a few of today's athletes — Joe Dumars, Stefan Edberg, Barry Sanders — seemed to care about his tradition. Others were busy pulling off their helmets and pointing at TV cameras.

And so this is it, the obituary, the death of Grace. His last request concerned his funeral. For all he had done, he wanted only this: "Something small, something quiet, something dignified."

Hmm. Does anyone know how to do that anymore?

Christmas without the star
December 23, 1994

T HE BULLETS MISSED. SO IT was not his time to die. That is what his mother would say. Jamil Dowdell was leaning into the trunk of his 1977 Cutlass, getting a pair of gym shorts to play basketball. Suddenly, gunshots shattered the windows. Someone screamed. The kid they were shooting at ran past Jamil's car, and Jamil ducked behind the rear bumper. He waited until the firing ceased and the air was quiet. Then, still holding his shorts, he walked around to survey the damage.

"Are you OK, Jamil, are you OK?" yelled his brother-in-law, Tyrone Dozier, who came running when he heard the shots.

"Yeah, yeah, I'm OK," Jamil said.

"Let's get out of here."

"Nuh-uh. Not until somebody pays me for these windows."

"What?"

"Not until somebody pays me for these windows."

Maybe where you come from, you're not moving at this point. Maybe you're shaking with fear. Jamil Dowdell was not. He lived in the wilderness of Detroit, where breaking glass and sudden gunfire are part of the nightly concert, played over and over until you tune out the anguished melody and focus on the few notes you still control.

The bullets missed. Now there were windows to be dealt with.

"Somebody's gonna pay for these," Jamil said again, looking toward where the shots were fired. "I'm not leaving until they do."

He showed no fear.

He was 18 years old.

Tyrone Dozier shakes his head now. After that night, he thought, "Jamil is a man." He says this, looks over at his wife, Jamil's sister, India, who is wiping away tears. She sits next to Jamil's mother, Sheila, hands folded in her lap, and across from Bettye, Jamil's grandmother, who used to cook his favorite meal, hamburger soup. There are cousins and aunts and four young children running around the cramped living room here on Martindale Street. A plate of cookies sits on the table, and a Christmas tree is in the corner, sparsely decorated, without a star on top. It is late December. In the middle of the floor is a basket full of memories, a jersey, a prom photo, newspaper clippings.

"It's funny," says Bettye, the grandmother. "I keep waiting for him to come back from college. I keep saying that's where he is, and he'll be home one day."

She begins to cry. "That's how I deal with it."

This is a story about dreams sawed in half, about a city kid who crawled through the barbed wire and somehow emerged uncut, a handsome, athletic, honorable young man who was going to be the first in his family to attend a university. The scholarship was in his pocket. The basketball was under his arm.

The bullets missed.

But his time was almost up.

H E WAS GONNA make the pros." Tyrone Dozier — who helps coach basketball at Murray-Wright High — says this sincerely. Don't they all say it sincerely?

It is the dream that keeps inner-city athletes going, through the metal detectors at school, through the dope dealers on the playground, and some do make it, and maybe Jamil had a chance. He was a full-ride scholarship at Georgia, where his signing was statewide news. He averaged 17 points and nine rebounds at Northern High. He was second-team All-PSL. He had a sweet shot and quick moves that defied his 6-foot, 6-inch frame. India used to come to his games and yell, "Dunk one for your sister!" And Jamil would oblige with rim-rattling jams.

Still, you don't know a person from the shots he takes, but from the kindness he makes. Like the time at The Dancery, a Detroit teenage nightclub, when a stranger was shot in the middle of a crowd. Everybody ran — except Jamil, who carried the bleeding man until he reached a pay phone, then called 911.

Or the time, on Jamil's recruiting visit to Georgia, when he phoned from the airport and told his family he was going to help another recruit, a tall kid from the Caribbean, who was lost. A little while later, Jamil called back. The Caribbean kid made his plane. But Jamil, in helping, missed his.

On some nights, when other teens were out raising hell, Jamil, who had reassuring eyes and a thinly trimmed mustache, would stay home in the small house on Martindale, singing with his mother, matching her note-for-note on Al Jarreau songs:

"We're in this love together
We got the kind that lasts forever."

"He used to tease me, tell me his voice was better than mine," Sheila Dowdell says. She laughs, then exhales, folds her hands again.

Every clan has that one special member who lights up the room, who delights the children, who, when he's not there, has everybody saying, "When's he coming?"

This was Jamil Dowdell. The baby of his family, the tallest of the bunch. He did push-ups at night and shot hoops early in the morning, trying to get an edge. "Basketball is your way out of here," Tyrone had told him, and Jamil knew he was right. He played in all the summer programs, the hotbox church leagues, the AAU showdowns. College coaches started calling. And when Jamil committed to the Bulldogs, he stuck a "Georgia" decal on his bedroom door. He now had something half the kids in this city do not.

A place to go.

All he needed was the time to get there.

ONE WEEK AFTER THEY SHOT UP his car, the day before his high school graduation, Jamil got into an argument with Tyrone and India. Tyrone wanted him to get a cap and gown for the ceremony, said it would make his mother proud. Jamil, who had missed the cap-and-gown measurements, hated dressing up anyhow, wanted to get his diploma in regular clothes.

India, meanwhile, was angry that he still hadn't turned in his last English paper. "You're gonna blow the scholarship. You're gonna lose everything."

Jamil said, "No, I'm not."

He left. But that afternoon, he appeared at India's workplace, D'Mongo's Hair Salon. He was waving a paper.

"Look," he said, grinning.

It had been written the whole time. He had raced down to school with it that morning, and the teacher had marked it quickly. He got an A. Graduation was assured.

"See?"

"Well, all right then," his sister said, smiling despite herself.

That night, Jamil — who also got the cap and gown — talked about the haircut Tyrone would give him the next day. Then he went to pick up his mother at the Ford Plant where she worked. It was a routine trip for mother and son. But when she got into the car, she sensed something wrong. He asked her to drive while he sat in the back.

"He'd never done that before," Sheila Dowdell says now. "It was like he was afraid of something."

THERE ARE THOSE WHO BELIEVE in fate, even when it's horrible. They would not miss this: Jamil Dowdell walked his mother into the house. She offered him rice and beans for a late meal. He might have stayed, but his best friend, Michael Parker, who was living with them at the time, wanted McDonald's. So he and Jamil went for a ride.

It was the wee hours of Friday morning, the 10th of June.

On the same day, 10 years earlier, Jamil's father, Carl Matlock, had driven his car to a gas station on the east side. He was filling it up when a stranger appeared. The stranger had a gun.

And Jamil became another kid with a memory for a father.

Now, here, a decade later, Jamil was in the car, with 15-year-old Michael alongside him. They were heading southeast on Grand River, just west of Greenfield, when they noticed an oncoming vehicle — coincidentally, also a

1977 Oldsmobile — heading their way. It was swerving and going too fast.

"Look at that guy," Michael said, "he's driving crazy."

It happened in a heartbeat. The swerving car crossed the center line, made a turn and smash! The metal crunched and the engines died and the hood of Jamil's car bent clear over the passenger roof. In the terrible stillness that followed, Michael somehow kicked open the door and struggled around to Jamil's side. He was smacking his friend, pleading with him, grabbing his hand and saying, "Don't die! Don't die! Don't die!"

Then, dizzy, the world spinning, Michael lay down in the street, still whispering the words, "Don't die, Jamil."

But his time had come.

A T THE NORTHERN HIGH SCHOOL graduation that night, there was a moment of silence for the kid who almost made it. A prayer was offered. Students and teachers wept.

"There was nobody that didn't like Jamil," Parker says. "Nobody."

The diploma he wanted so much went unclaimed. The paper the family received instead was a police report, which showed that the cops smelled alcohol on the other driver's breath. But for some reason, that driver, a lawyer, was not given a Breathalyzer. He is charged today only with negligent homicide. He is yet to be tried.

"The police didn't do their job," Tyrone Dozier says, bitterly. "Why else would a man drive like that? ... In my heart, I know he was drinking."

At least the part of his heart that isn't broken, the part that doesn't sag like a heavy sack when he watches a Georgia basketball game on TV. Jamil's mother, Sheila, cannot bring herself to watch such things. Sometimes she looks at her son's red and blue No. 24 jersey, or the photos from his prom, or the English paper that he turned in that last day, the one with the "A" on the front. Ironically, the topic was "Teenage Pregnancy." Jamil knew all about it. He had had a baby son with his girlfriend last year, a boy named Kaheem Kafi.

Another child without his father.

On June 10th.

T HERE ARE A DOZEN WAYS to die in this city, and they find you quickly if you are young, black and male. You can spend a childhood here dodging bullets, drugs and abusive parents. So when a bright light like Jamil Dowdell scrapes past all that, gets to the finish line, scholarship in hand, only to be mowed down by a driver, well, you almost wonder if the game isn't fixed. When is it enough? How can anyone take a drink and drive? Isn't there a story like this every five minutes?

"The strangest thing," says India, the sister who spent the most time with Jamil, cooking for him, talking about girls, jobs, the future. "He wasn't himself the weeks before he died. He was almost sad. He told some friends, 'I'll never make it down to Georgia.'

"Then I heard he told some kids from the neighborhood, 'Y'all better wear suits when you come to my funeral. Don't be wearing no old clothes.' "

What does she think, that it was a premonition?

"Maybe that. Or maybe he had so much going right that, given everything that goes on around here, it was too good to be true."

In the end, it was. They buried Jamil Dowdell three days after graduation. Inside the True Faith Baptist Church, a friend sang "The End of the Road." A coach from Georgia came up to speak. A basketball opponent from a rival high school — who also wore No. 24 — laid his jersey in Jamil's casket, a salute.

And later, when Michael Parker — who survived the crash and lives with the nightmares — went up to Jamil's bedroom, he lifted the Bible that Jamil read every night. And there, underneath, was $240.

The money for the windows.

The shooters had raised it and given it back.

Remember that Al Jarreau song that Sheila and Jamil sang together? It has this lyric:

"We got the whole thing working out so right,
and it's just the way we planned it."

A nice song. But wrong. Sometimes you plan it, and it still doesn't work out right. In the small house on Martindale, there is noise now, but not as much, and laughter, but not as loud. They talk about presents and they remember how Jamil loved getting new basketball shoes, and soon they need Kleenex to wipe away tears. Someone was driving crazy, someone made a mistake, and now there is no star on the Christmas tree, and no star coming home for the holidays, and there is nothing they can do about it. Nothing at all.

Shooting, like it's their job
December 28, 1994

T HE PORCH LIGHT IS OFF. His mother says if you turn it on, "It just gives them something to shoot at." Same goes for the lamp in the den, which can be seen from the street. Off. They sit here — on an old couch, in front of bare walls and a TV set — in semi-darkness. Hiding in their homes.

"You'll want to move away from that window," the mother suggests.

"How many nights a week do you hear shooting?"

She blinks, as if surprised by the question.

"Every night. They shoot like it's their job or somethin'."

Every night. We are not in Beirut or Bosnia. We are on Faircrest Street in northeast Detroit, where half the houses are burned beyond repair, and the winter wind brushes the sidewalks with loose trash left by sanitation workers in a hurry. Nobody stays long in these parts. No one takes a stroll around the neighborhood. If you try to live a normal life here, you may not live long. Every night. Like it's their job.

Jemale Jackson, age 16, watches his mother, then glances at the TV. It flashes without sound. He flicks the channels. A sitcom. A car commercial. A football game — he holds there for a moment. Football. There was a time Jemale saw himself through football. He played at Denby High, played both ways, left guard, defensive tackle, he dreamed of a scholarship, maybe had a chance.

"I played baseball and got a trophy once in basketball," he says with teenage assurance, "but football was my life."

His old life. The one that ended June 22. Now his legs are limp and his feet don't move and he plays football only when he sleeps. In his dreams, he feels the air rush past his face, he feels motion, contact, speed. Once, he could run so fast. But he made a mistake, he behaved like a normal kid, he went outside after dark, Bullet Time. And he just couldn't run fast enough.

W HY DID I WALK UP THAT BLOCK? I ask myself that all the time. I knew it was past my curfew. But my cousin Mario was over, and I didn't want to be a sucker or nothing. …

"It was summer. Friday night, just before 11 o'clock. We went to the store, me, my cousin, some girls, about six of us. We didn't even have any money. So we didn't get nothing. We started walking back, and we were halfway home, we were on Glenwood, when it happened."

He pauses, shifts his neck. His face is soft and round, and his sweatshirt sags on his now-thin body. Jemale Jackson tells his story with the deadened tone of a prisoner already tortured. What can they do to him now? He assigns no blame. He does not cry. You asked, he tells.

"One guy in our group, Phil, he stopped to talk to these girls. We yelled, 'Come on, Phil.' Then we heard a gunshot, and nobody even looked, we just started running. Then I heard another shot. I tried to run, but I felt funny, and then I fell down on my face. My forehead hit the street."

Jackson had just become one of 277 kids under age 16 to be shot in Detroit this year. Thirty-three are dead. The others, like Jemale, are left alive to wonder why. The bullet, a .25 caliber, entered his back below his neck and lodged in his chest. No reason. No motive. The shooters — believed to be a local gang that wore red scarves — scattered quickly.

Jackson never saw them.

"When I went to move, I couldn't. … Then this kid, he came riding up on his bike. He saw what happened, and he rode away to get my stepfather."

And you?

"I just lay there."

People watched from windows. People watched from porches. Peeping eyes, awaiting the next round of horror. Jemale Jackson, a decent kid who was going to high school and wanted to go to college and whose big, tragic mistake was going to get some snacks at the store, lay paralyzed on Glenwood Street, in his Florida Panthers jersey and black denim shorts.

The future of this city nailed to the street.

THE POLICE NEVER SPOKE TO Patricia Jackson, Jemale's mother, or Robert Schell, his stepfather. Although there was a squad car at the site when the ambulance took Jemale away, no officers came to St. John hospital or Children's Hospital, where Jemale stayed for nearly two months. Eventually, Patricia, who was working two jobs to try to make ends meet, had to go to the 9th Precinct herself. She told them the story.

"It took about an hour," she says.

She has heard nothing since.

"As far as we know, there is not even an investigation into this," Schell says. He shakes his head. Who is he supposed to see? He works in a paint store in Sterling Heights, has been a father to Jemale since the kid was 7 years old. Jemale's natural father was never around. Spent a lot of time in jail. He is dead now. All Patricia knows is that "he died of natural causes."

He was 29. Natural causes?

"That's what I was told," she says.

If you find this incredible, you are lucky to live where you do. The truth is, young black men go down at an horrific rate in this city. There is not always a good explanation.

There is rarely justice.

So when Jemale, the ex-football player, came home from the hospital, paralyzed from his chest down, needing help to do even the simplest things — he had to wear a diaper, be bathed, have his limbs worked — he also had to suffer this indignity: to see his assailant, walking around, free as the breeze.

"Word got back around who did it, who shot me," Jemale says. "It was this guy, real dark skin, he's like one year older than me. He's in one of the gangs, maybe PPG, Pimps Players and Gangsters, or PDQ, Put 'em Down Quick, or CSC, Corner Street Crips.

"Anyhow, I seen him one day, by my street. I was in my wheelchair on the porch, and I saw him. My uncle was over, and he saw him, too."

Did he look at you?

"Yeah, he looked at me, and then he got in his van real quick and left."

What did you feel?

"Me? I wanted to shoot him. See how he liked it."

His eyes go thin and steely, for a moment he really means it, then he loosens and sighs. He is still not that cruel. He has never fired a gun. He has never been in a gang. He has been shot and he has seen others shot, and he once witnessed a man executed right across the street. Shot at close range, in the head, by two men who then ran away.

After all this, Jemale Jackson says, "Guns are stupid."

And he's the one with a bullet in his chest.

A LL I WANT TO DO IS move to someplace safe. Someplace where there's no shooting on your block or the next block over. That's all. That's good enough. Just two safe blocks."

Patricia Jackson exhales. "As soon as I can make the money, I want us to get out of here to a place like that."

She sits down next to her son, adjusts his Michigan cap. She works for the board of education but can only get part-time hours. She has held second jobs as a nurse's aide, a cashier, a cook. Maybe, between her and Robert, they make $20,000 in a good year. Patricia was once beaten by a man with a gun — there is almost no one in this neighborhood without a story — and she refuses to have a weapon in the house. She had taught this to Jemale and was proud he had learned it. Just as she was proud of his football and proud of his dream to attend Southern University one day. She remembers — on the day he was shot — his report card arrived in the mail. One A, two B's, three C's.

He'd been promoted to the 11th grade.

The next time she saw him, he was lying in the hospital.

"The only thing that helps me keep my faith is that Jemale is still here with me. He didn't die. He's still alive. A lot of mothers around here don't have that."

She slides a little closer to Jemale.

"At least he wasn't killed."

You want to scream.

IN CONGRESS THEY DEBATE a crime bill. In newspapers and on radio they debate "how to tackle the issue." Meanwhile, inside the decaying white frame house on Faircrest, Jemale Jackson squints to make out a brochure for a new wheelchair. He is due to get one sometime soon, hopefully before the money runs out. With improved movement in his arms and neck, he is planning to return to a new high school next month — most likely Osborn, one of the Detroit schools equipped with facilities for the physically disabled.

Still, there will be no sports. And none of the old dancing around. Jemale, once a popular, jovial teen, does not seem excited to leave his lonely routine of video games and TV.

"Are you worried people will look at you like 'the kid in the wheelchair'?" he is asked.

He shrugs, then looks at his mother, who is nodding sadly, and he nods, too.

Did you know that throughout this ordeal, Jemale Jackson cried just once? He did not cry when he was shot. He did not cry in the ambulance, nor at the hospital, nor when they poked him with tubes, or bathed him with a sponge, or wiped him like an infant. He did not cry then.

But when his mother came one day and he asked her, "Why did I get shot?" and she said no one knew, and the police, well, the police wouldn't do anything, Jemale thought to himself, "That's it. They threw my file away."

And he burst into tears.

He cried when he felt he didn't count.

The truth is they all count, every kid like Jemale, every last one of those 277 with a bullet wound and a story. They are the soil of our city. We have no future if they keep dying. How many more? This is only a few miles from all of us.

There's a story this week about a new bullet that is so destructive it rips through bulletproof vests and tears a hole in your body the size of a baseball. Some guy invented this for "the protection of our citizens." These maniacs, with their logic of more guns, more bullets. And for every one person who actually stops violence with a trigger, there are a hundred kids going down face-first. This is where we're headed, folks, right here, lights out on Faircrest Street, our own wild west, where Patricia Jackson says, "I'm at the point where I don't even jump when I hear a gunshot. We're so used to it, we expect it to happen."

Jemale misses this. He is still on the brochure of the Action-Pro Wheelchair. He studies the wheels, the shape of the seat.

"It's gonna be lighter," he says. "So I'm gonna be able to move faster, right?"

He stops on this word "faster," perhaps realizing it doesn't mean what it used to. He puts down the brochure, turns up the TV, and his mother and stepfather find a safe place to sit, away from the window, in case someone else wants target practice tonight. Lights out on Faircrest Street. How many more?

How many more?

1995

A small-town nightmare
January 13, 1995

THE BOY WAS WEARING HIS varsity letter jacket when the jury announced its verdict. "Guilty," the man said. Guilty? It was Wednesday afternoon. Late September. Back at Saline High School, the football team was getting ready for practice, awaiting his return. He had told them not to worry. He was confident. He would be there.

Guilty?

"How am I gonna graduate?" he remembers thinking.

They took his jacket and wallet.

"What about college?"

They took his keys.

"What about dad?"

His father stood helpless, a few feet away. All he could say was, "Call me. As soon as you can, call me."

The courtroom crowd mumbled in disbelief. The boy was put in a cell. They took his tie and shoelaces.

"What about my future?"

Guilty?

A few miles away, the girl was feeling nauseated. She had spoken on the stand, told them what happened that night, the guys, the sex, the crack about "let's use a bottle on her," all of it. Several times the lawyers had to stop because she was crying so hard. At one point she went into a rest room and vomited.

She didn't stay for the verdict, and neither did her family. But soon enough, they knew the town's reaction. A car full of students drove past the mother's store, spotted the girl, and yelled: "You bitch! You whore! We're gonna get you!"

Five high school boys, one high school girl. And when this story is told, you might not feel sorry for any of them. In the pre-sunrise hours of one cold Saturday morning, they had group sex in the basement of a condo. The boys took turns doing things with the girl. And the girl, depending on whom you believe, either encouraged the whole thing or cried her way through it, frozen with fear.

Two days later, the boys were finishing school, and some were heading home. "Did you hear?" one said.

"What?"

"——'s going to the police."

"The police? For what?"

"She's saying we raped her."

"Raped her?"

"The police?"

This is a story of a small town taking sides, as if some invisible line were drawn in the snow. You can stop anywhere today in Saline, by the red brick storefronts, or the Taco Bell, the Ford plant, the apartments in town, the custom homes out on the wide dirt roads, anywhere, doesn't matter, just ask the question: Whom do you believe? The football player? The girl? Fewer than 7,000 people live in this normally quiet town, and this morning, it might feel like all of them are squeezed inside Washtenaw County's Circuit Court No. 5, awaiting the word of Judge Melinda Morris.

Today, 18-year-old Bobby Shier Jr., the only one arrested, the only one tried and the only one found guilty that night of first-degree criminal sexual conduct — rape — learns his fate.

It could be a new trial.

It could be 20 years in prison.

He insists he's innocent. And much of the town agrees with him.

Meanwhile, the girl has switched schools, undergone counseling and, according to her family, is too afraid even to take a shower when she's alone in the house.

"She struggles with this every day," said her mother, fighting tears in speaking to the press for the first time.

"This has been a year from hell. I know Bobby is in prison. But my daughter's in a prison, too."

How did this happen? How can families that used to be friends not have spoken for more than a year? How can kids who used to trust each other now walk through hallways tensing up, glaring, yelling insults, clenching fists. Teenage boys with schoolbooks under their arms say, "She wanted it. She was a slut." And teenage girls with their hair in ponytails say, "They gang-banged her" — until it sounds like something out of a bad soap opera.

She says they did.

They say they didn't.

How, in one night, can the world change so fast?

From Bobby Shier's police interview:

Police: Did you get the impression that she didn't want to have sex?

Bobby: Sort of, yeah, I did.

Police: What made you think that?

Bobby: Just the way she was acting. … If you have sex with them before, you can tell they're different the next time. …

Police: You continued on?

Bobby: Yeah.

Police: Figuring, well, she'll be a little more responsive?

Bobby: Yeah.

Police: But that didn't happen?

Bobby: No, and I quit then.

WHEN THE JAIL DOOR OPENS, and he first steps out, your immediate impression is "teenage." He is kind of thin for a football player, with a gangly walk, dark hair that falls onto his forehead, a thick neck, crooked teeth, a few pimples. This is not Michael Douglas or some dashing character out of a made-for-TV movie about sexual harassment. Bobby Shier, a solid loaf of a kid, has surrendered his No. 70 Saline football jersey for a green cotton shirt that reads "Washtenaw County Jail."

On the day they brought him in, September 28, 1994, the first inmate he met was a guy nearly twice his age.

"You're so young, what are you in here for?"

"Breaking and entering," Bobby lied.

The next day the guy had a local newspaper.

"What'd you say your name was again?"

"Bobby."

"Bobby what?"

"Uh ... Shier."

The guy held out the paper with Bobby's picture on the front page. Jury convicts Saline student of rape. Bobby swallowed. The guy ripped out the story, crumpled it up.

"Flush this down the toilet before anyone sees it."

It is hard to believe that two days earlier, Bobby had been at football practice at Saline High, going through tackling drills and knocking back blockers from his defensive lineman position. There was a big game that Friday night, the team was undefeated, and Bobby, who actually went to trial in the morning and to practice in the afternoon, planned on being there.

The son of a Ford plant material handler, he had no previous record, and although he admits to drinking beer and smoking pot, he maintained a "B" average in school. "I always liked him," said Saline football coach Jack Crabtree. "You asked him a question, he was honest."

At one point, Bobby and the victim — whom we will call Linda, which is not her real name — were a couple, at least as much as high schoolers can be a couple. They went to movies, parties, even went skiing once. They had sex numerous times. After a few months, they broke up, he said, because she slept with someone else. No big deal. Bobby admits to having had three sexual partners himself. This might not sound like high school to you. But maybe it has been awhile since you have been in high school.

Linda is a smallish, blond-haired girl, the oldest of five children. Her father drives a truck and her mother owns a shop. Linda has a learning disability and was held back a grade. Because of this, her mother said, she is often compared to her next-younger sister, who is now in the same grade, but is a star student and a star athlete, whereas Linda is not. Linda was always being told, "You're so pretty, you're so pretty." Maybe, after awhile, that became her identity.

"I know about her promiscuity," her mother said.

At Saline High, it seems to be a favorite subject. But understand this is the only high school in town, so stories here are shared like a drinking fountain.

They met in science class, Bobby and Linda. They had sex a few times. That should have been the whole story — if not for that night.

"I wish I had just stayed home," Bobby said, leaning over the prison table. "People can say anything they want to, they can say you raped them when you didn't even touch them.

"It's them against you. It really is."

S HE WASN'T AT THE CONDO five minutes before one of them unbuttoned her pants, someone hit the lights, and they all said good-bye to childhood, right there on the beige carpet.

That much they agree on. What happened that night is told at least six different ways by the six people involved. None of it is pleasant. Most of it is shocking. About the only part not in dispute is that Linda, then 17, did go willingly to the home of schoolmate Paul Castellucci at around 4 a.m. Saturday, November 20, 1993. She had snuck out of her house, along with her sister, looking for a party, and now it was late. They never found the party, her sister was sleepy, but Linda still wanted to have fun.

Fun, she will tell you, not trauma.

She considered the five guys "my friends."

Until that night.

Bobby was one of the guys. He was staying at Castellucci's house, along with his football teammate Jeff Rathiewicz, then 17, and buddies Todd Mills, then 17, Chris Calhoun, then 16, Ryan Fox, then 18, and Castellucci, then 16. They had been drinking earlier in the evening, and how drunk they were is still in question. They had tickets to the Michigan-Ohio State football game later that day, which is why they were all sleeping over.

Some were half-asleep when Linda called.

"We shoulda just hung up," Bobby said.

Instead, he, Todd and Chris got in Todd's blue minivan and picked up Linda from her girlfriend's house. She wore a flannel shirt and baggy blue jeans. They offered her a beer on the ride over, and they entered the condo on Woodcreek Court through the back entrance and the sliding glass doors. It was a typical teenager's lower-level quarters — two bedrooms, a center den area, couch, table, couple of posters on the walls, a TV. Good place for a sleep-over. Good place for a party. Paul's mother and younger brother were asleep upstairs, which neither surprised nor worried any of the teens. Most, including Linda, had been there many times before.

"Me and her began to wrestle, playing around," Bobby said. "She was teasing me about football and I was teasing her about soccer, because she played soccer. It was frisky playing, you know? Then I got up off her, and she sat on Jeff's lap."

After numerous interviews with the subjects, the rest — which, we should point out, is not for the puritanical — must be told in separate voices, because the versions are different, and the difference is what this whole thing is about.

The boys' version:
   Jeff began to unbutton Linda's baggy blue jeans. Todd pulled them down from the bottom cuffs. Linda said: "If you keep doing that, they're going to come off," but she didn't seem to mind. Once her pants were off, Todd — who later said, "I couldn't believe she let us do that" — offered them back to her but she waved them away.

   Someone turned off the lights, and Todd, Jeff and Chris helped her down to the floor, out of her clothes, and along with Ryan took places around her. She was now naked and laughing, and feeling around her, saying, "Who's this? Who's this?" Bobby, who had gone into Paul's bedroom, re-entered the room and joined them. Paul stayed in his room.

   In the minutes that followed, she performed oral sex on one of the boys, while engaging in intercourse with another. The boys fondled her, moving around to different positions. They maintain she did everything with no coercion, and that she laughed and joked during the process.

   Todd: "Her arms were free and her legs were free, and if she wanted to get up and walk away at any time, she could have."

   Jeff: "I remember her giggling; she unzipped Chris' pants. … He made a remark about (her skills) and she said, "Oh, yeah, where did you hear that?"

   Bobby: "She wasn't saying no to anybody."

   Eventually — maybe a half-hour after this began — Bobby took Linda's hand and went to a back bedroom, which contained two bunk beds. The two of them had had sex in this bedroom a few weeks earlier. Now, Bobby said, "I asked for oral sex and she said no, she didn't want to do that. And I was like, well, you wanna have sex then? And she was like, yeah, I don't care."

   He put on a condom and there, on the bedroom floor, began to have sex with her. He noticed she was not acting "as into it" as he recalled and he asked why. She said she was tired. He continued, maybe for 10 minutes, until several of the other boys banged on the door. He then left the room. He admits she might have been crying at this point.

   Ryan entered, with whom she had oral sex.

   Todd followed, carrying a bottle the others had given him. They made jokes about "using a bottle on her." But he told her he would never do something like that. He asked if she wanted her clothes. She did.

She came out, dressed and sat and talked for a minute. She said she had to get home before her mother woke up and realized she was out. Todd drove her home.

Todd: "It was close to 6 a.m. We were laughing and joking the whole way to the van.

"On the way home ... I remember asking her, 'Why do you let guys use you like that?' She was like, 'Guys don't use me, I use them to get my pleasure.' ...

"A few minutes later, I dropped her off and she ran up to her house."

That was the last time any of the five boys talked to her.

That is their story.

The girl's version:

What Linda told the police was significantly different.

Yes, she had gone there willingly, and yes, she had wrestled with Bobby. But when Jeff began to unbutton her pants and Todd was pulling them off, she told him to stop. The lights were then shut off, and the boys began leaning over her, undressing her, holding her down. She admits saying, "Who is this?" and "Who is by me?" but in a confused and frightened way, not a playful one. She said whenever she expressed concern, the boys told her to shut up and not worry. She also said one of them joked, "This is like an orgy," to which she replied, "No, more like a gang bang."

She said she was forced into oral sex with the boys, that her arms and legs were held down, and that she was confused and scared and worried that if she didn't go along, they might become violent.

When Bobby led her to the back room, she says she was crying. Although she never yelled for help — "I thought they were my friends" — she says she told Bobby she wanted to stop and he didn't.

During the trial, she said, "My whole body was numb. It happened so fast. The situation was out of control. I couldn't handle it."

She also denied that Bobby, her ex-boyfriend, asked her if she wanted to have sex. "If he had asked I would have told him no."

She also told police the boys were drunk and, in addition to the talk about the bottle, made jokes about taking pictures.

When she got home, she was sore and confused. She worked that day at a nursing home, and the next morning, told her sister what had happened.

"They raped me," she said, crying.

Her sister later told police: "At first I was upset that she would let them do that to her. But then I asked for details and decided it was not her fault."

That night, Paul called her house, asked how she was doing. "I told him I was sore and he said, 'Well, all's good in fun,' and he said the guys were worried about something getting out."

It would get out.

And they were right to be worried.

S GT. BOB DIETRICH, WHOSE straw-colored hair matches his mustache, has been with the Saline police department 18 years. He said he knew from the start "this case would be a pain in the butt." Linda had left school Monday after telling her story to the school counselor and had gone to a hospital emergency room, explaining that she had been raped.

Under law, this requires a police report.

After taking her statement — "she was pretty shook up" — Dietrich sent officers out to pick up the five boys for questioning.

Four were not home.

Bobby Shier was the fifth.

He was in his father's apartment, and his father had just left. When the knock came, he thought about not answering the door. He answered it anyhow. He was not obligated to go with the officers, but he did, he said, because one of them barked, "Do you know what the word arrest means?"

At the station, he told them his version of what happened, all the graphic details, without a lawyer present, because, he said, "I didn't have anything to hide."

Had he not done this, even Dietrich admitted, "he might never have been charged."

But Bobby Shier was not the type to hold much back. He was cocky, vocal — his football teammates say, "You always knew where he was on the field" — and he knew some of the police because, after all, this is a small town, and so, on tape, he told the story of that night in his typical fashion, which some call "flippant" and others call "Bobby." There was no regret for what happened. He felt he had done nothing wrong.

"It was consensual," he said. "She never said 'no' or 'quit.' "

A few weeks later, he was picked up again to take a polygraph test. During that conversation with Dietrich — which once again, Bobby agreed to without a lawyer — he made the most damaging statement of all.

Dietrich: "Why don't we back up to the beginning of the night. Who was talking about what?"

Bobby: "Me, Chris, Todd, we planned on gang-banging her, all of us."

Dietrich: "Was that the exact word used, 'gang bang?' "

Bobby: "Ahhh ... I wasn't saying that we could all do her, it was Chris and Todd saying how we could all mess around with her and see how many guys she could do."

Dietrich: "What made them think that?"

Bobby: "She has a reputation of sleeping with a lot of guys. ... "

Dietrich: "What words did you use? It's OK. You're not going to tell me anything I haven't heard before."

Bobby: "OK, words like, maybe we can double-team her or triple-team, something like that. I already knew what she was like. ... "

When he was done talking, they didn't even administer a polygraph because, the police chief now says, "He wasn't denying anything. What would we polygraph him on?"

This is one of the points being challenged today.

Meanwhile, Jeff and Todd hadn't even made police statements, and the others had done so only with lawyers. None of them was charged.

But Bobby? Well. This was too much to ignore. Two full statements, in his own brazen words. The reports went to the Washtenaw County prosecutor's office, and prosecutor Brian Mackie, who had been elected on a tough stance on sexual-assault crimes, saw plenty to go on.

"To the untrained eye, he appeared to be the ringleader," Mackie said. "You bet we were gonna use those statements."

Bobby Shier, who said he had "nothing to hide," had just taken his first step toward jail.

IN THE SMALL, LOWER-LEVEL apartment where he and Bobby used to live, Robert Shier, Bobby's father, a beefy autoworker with a straightforward manner, sits with numerous friends, including the Mills family, whose son Todd was part of this whole mess. Todd admits to sexual encounters that night with Linda, but, like the others, has not been charged and probably never will be. Without a statement like Bobby's, it's too much "he said, she said." Too hard to prove.

Such an odd assembly, one family luckier than the other. They sip coffee together and do what the whole town has been doing for months. Talk about the case. There are some of Bobby's sports trophies on the shelves, and some photos of him on the table. Although he phones frequently from jail, the last time they all saw him free was at the trial.

"We didn't meet our lawyer until 15 minutes before it began," Robert Shier recalled. "That's my fault. I didn't know how it all worked. I said, 'Aren't the other boys gonna testify?' He said they weren't.

"Hindsight is 20/20. Bobby shouldn't have talked to the police without a lawyer. And then, at the trial, I couldn't afford private, so I had to go with the public defender. Our guy (Lorne Brown) did a good job, but (Linda) got up there and started crying ... "

Bobby never testified. The prosecution simply played the tapes of his two statements, and a police officer later admitted, "You could see it in the jury's eyes. When he said, 'We planned to gang-bang her' ... I knew it was over."

Brown, the defense attorney, argued that lewd circumstances don't mean rape. Nine women and three men were on the jury. The trial lasted two days. The deliberation lasted 2½ hours. During that time, Bobby read the sports section of the local paper, looking for news of his football team.

Then the jury came back.

And that was the end of football.

"It was rape," Mackie says now. "The jury said it was rape, and it was."

"I'm not surprised Bobby denies it," said Eric Gutenberg, the assistant prosecutor who argued the case. "He feels if he didn't tie her ankles to the table, he didn't rape her. He wasn't looking for the signs."

"He showed no remorse," said Phil King, the probation officer who, after a two-hour conversation with Bobby, labeled him "a threat to the community," recommended extensive psychotherapy and suggested a sentence of five to 20 years in jail. "He still denies doing anything wrong."

What if he believes he's innocent?

"Well, then, there's something wrong with him."

Here, in the Shier apartment — and elsewhere in Saline — they disagree. They talk about the preliminary hearing, where Judge John Collins asked the prosecution: "Are you sure you really want to try this case?" They question the way Bobby was interrogated, claiming he was led to say certain things.

And, as you might expect, they talk about Linda. How she had consensual sex with Bobby just a few weeks before that night, and did the same with Jeff the weekend prior. She admitted this in court.

Besides, they say, she hardly behaves like a victim. They claim she was out with a boy two days after the incident — the boy confirms this, although it was "just as friends" — and, after Bobby's conviction, she was seen at a party hoisting a beer and yelling: "I put that son of a bitch behind bars."

They argue that the rape charge was something Linda made up to stay out of trouble with her mother. They claim Linda is starved for attention and cite countless boys she has supposedly slept with. (Some, when contacted for this article, admitted sexual relations. Others denied it.)

Finally, they point to another party, just a few weeks after the incident. There, three witnesses confirm, Linda danced and flirted and got drunk on beer. She hung on different boys, kissed them, and at one point, a guest said, "was on the floor, laughing, letting boys flick their cigarette ashes on her head."

Photos substantiate this.

Robert Shier has the photos in front of him.

"How can somebody who was just raped be out there acting like that?" he asked, holding a picture. "Does that seem like someone who's traumatized?"

THE RAPE SHIELD LAW, WHICH Michigan adopted 20 years ago, forbids bringing an alleged rape victim's sexual history into a case. It was designed, partly, to reduce a victim's possible humiliation at trial. But it does nothing about small-town humiliation once the trial is over.

So it does not stop the passing shouts of "whore" or "slut" that have gone on for a year, nor does it stop certain football players from vowing revenge because

Bobby's arrest disrupted their perfect season. It does not stop people from driving up to the fast-food window where Linda now works, buying food and dropping the money on the pavement.

A few miles away from the Shiers' apartment, on a snowy weekday afternoon, Linda's mother sits inside the small country store she owns on one of Saline's main streets. Her daughter — who, when asked to be interviewed for this article, said, "Thank you for asking me. You're the first person who's wanted to hear my side of the story" — was later advised by her lawyer to wait.

But her mother, for the first time, has agreed to talk.

She is in tears.

This is the other side of the story.

"We have heard all the rumors, believe me, we have," she said. "And I know all about my daughter. I know what she does.

"But none of those people were with me in that emergency room. ... None of them saw the blood on her underwear. ... None of them saw the swelling which was so bad, she couldn't even urinate. ...

"Those people weren't with us when my daughter couldn't sleep, the nights she had to be sedated. These were her friends! Her friends did this to her! My daughter checks the locks every night, she's afraid all the time. ... She started to cry a few weeks ago and said, 'Mom, I'll never, ever have a normal life.' ...

"She's had to switch schools. ... She's lost her senior year, her chance to graduate with her sister. ...

"I've heard the people say she's making all this up. But they don't know my daughter. I know my daughter. She was so ashamed. She took great lengths not to tell me. There is no doubt in my mind she was raped. She doesn't have the stamina to maintain a lie for this long."

She stops talking, wipes her eyes, then says: "Why would she?"

Contrary to some of the popular theories, it was Linda's mother, not Linda, who pushed to file criminal charges. Linda reportedly begged her mother to keep quiet. She said she couldn't go through with it.

"I have to live with that," the mother says now. "I made her go to court. And I would never, ever, put a child of mine through something like this again. ... "

She said she sees the accused boys and their families all the time. They look down. They walk the other way. She cries again at the mention of Cindy Calhoun, Chris's mother, who before the incident was a good friend. Their kids played soccer together. They used to meet at a Big Boy restaurant for breakfast.

They have not spoken since that night.

"It was crushing," she said. "We're shut out from so many families we used to know. Every school event, every open house, the minute we're in the same room, the tension is so horrible. ... "

Linda's mother said she is aware of her daughter's promiscuity. She knows of the assorted parties, even after the incident. She said Linda went through intense emotional swings, first shutting herself in, then pushing herself out.

"If you talk to rape counselors, that is not unusual," she said. "And to be honest, I don't care what she does if it helps her get through this."

Nothing, she said, will change what happened on the lower level of the Woodcreek Court condo that Saturday morning.

"She was raped. She was … raped."

She begins to cry again.

W HAT IS REALLY ON TRIAL in this case is what is on trial is most cases of acquaintance rape — the believability of the people involved. One side will argue the victim's reputation should not be under attack, that even prostitutes can be raped. The other side will argue that making an accusation does not make it true, that people accuse for all kinds of reasons, and besides, what does a girl think she's doing joining two former sex partners and three of their friends at 4 a.m. at their place?

So when the sun rises on this winter day, the questions will float like paperweight snowflakes all the way down to Circuit Courtroom No. 5. If Linda truly felt violated, why didn't she yell for help — from Paul in the other room, or his family upstairs? Then again, if Bobby admits she was crying, why didn't he take that as a sign to stop?

Is it true that Sgt. Dietrich made a statement: "Bobby's a stupid kid. We can get him to say anything," as some of the parents claim? (He denies this.) And if this crime were so apparent, why weren't the other boys charged?

Do you believe a friend named Georgie Carlton, who said Linda has never been the same since that night? Or do you believe a former friend named Alison Cotellesse, who says: "It's all this big act."

Five high school boys, not one of whom remembers her saying no.

One high school girl, who can't understand how they don't.

Rape? A ruse? Maybe the only real answer is that they're all too young to be doing what they're doing. How do you lasso a speeding generation? As Nancy Mills, Todd's mother, says: "We never taught our children that sex was a spectator sport."

Or as Linda's mother says, between sobs, "Can you imagine the rage when you hear someone say they're going to 'gang-bang' your daughter?"

It's a case for our times, an athlete, a girl, sex, outrage, anger, accusations, all of it before they graduate.

And, this morning, Saline draws its daily line in the snow. Whom do you trust? Why did they do it? How, in one night, could the world change so fast? One kid's in jail. One's in a nightmare.

You wonder if anyone is ever young anymore.

Final Fabs run out of ticks
March 17, 1995

D AYTON, OHIO — The heads were shaved and the color of the socks matched the color of the shoes, a serious shade of black. Nostalgia? Of course. But for longtime fans of the Michigan era once known as Fabulous, the best news was this: When the game started, the seniors were playing like freshmen.

So no legends would die tonight, right? No way. This was the good old stuff, Jimmy King and Ray Jackson, who may not have been everything people hoped for during the season, but were a human scrapbook last night in the raucous Dayton Arena. Midway through the first half, they began to run the court like two greyhounds just let off the leash. Slam. Jam. Steal. Convert.

No way they lose, right?

No way … .

They lose?

They lose. In the bittersweet tradition of the Fab Five era, the Wolverines exited the tournament badly, weirdly, and in a way that will give their fans something to talk about for weeks. How did they blow this one? How did they go from a crushing 14-point lead to a tie game at the buzzer, to a nearly scoreless overtime and an 82-76 defeat? How did the best night of Jimmy King and Ray Jackson's senior year turn into the worst? Good God. Who's writing this script? Hannibal Lechter?

Must be someone with a sicko sense of tragedy. And someone with no heart for Texans.

"It just hasn't hit me yet, that I'll never be playing for Michigan again," Jackson said after Western Kentucky sent the Wolverines home after the opening round of the NCAA tournament. "I never thought about losing."

Who had time? Here were King and Jackson, who dedicated themselves to one last push, the two oldest Michigan players, grabbing rebounds, motoring downcourt, behind-the-back passes, slam! Stealing the ball, motoring downcourt, hanging until the defender falls, slam! The Fab old days? There was so much nostalgia in the middle 30 minutes of this contest, you almost expected to hear a disc jockey saying, "And now, let's go back to the year 1992. Remember this one. … "

R EMEMBER THIS ONE? King grabbing the ball off the glass and putting it back, as he once did to win a tournament game against UCLA? Jackson sneaking behind a back screen for an alley-oop jam, as he once did against Texas in the Big Dance.

At one point, Michigan went on a 19-3 run — and every point was scored by the seniors.

But the Fab group was always better at middles than endings. Their legacy includes a second half in the championship game against Duke, Chris Webber's time-out against North Carolina, and now this Thursday night against Western Kentucky: With 9.1 seconds left in the game, a blond-haired kid named Michael Fraliex launched a three-point shot that seemed to take all his strength just to reach the rim.

Unfortunately, it was also straight as a tightrope.

Tie game. And the good-bye song began.

"This is not how we scripted it," coach Steve Fisher said after the first, first-round tournament loss of his career. "Things don't always go the way you want them to."

You can say that again.

End of an era.

Of course, most people came to Dayton ready to say good-bye to the Fab Five story. It began with such a thunderous introduction, it could never go out quietly. Greatest class ever recruited, five freshman starters, first to ever reach an NCAA championship final, only to lose, come back, reach the final as five sophomore starters, only to lose it again, on Webber's time-out that wasn't. To some, they will always be the near-miss kids, too brash, too loose, too distracted to get over the final hurdle. For others they were bigger even than their record, a symbol of brash and brilliance. There is no right or wrong on this. There are simply a lot of other teams wearing long shorts these days.

"I'll be able to tell my kids one day that I was part of the Fab Five," King said. "That will always mean something."

Even the harshest critics have to see a little sad irony in last night's collapse. Jackson had 28 points. King had 23 and career highs in rebounds (17) and assists (eight). The Texas connection that came here four years ago and waited all this time to lead the team, finally had the joint performance of their careers.

And they lost.

"Maybe the best thing you can say about tonight is that Ray and Jimmy went down firing," Fisher said. "They may have gone down, but there weren't any bullets left in their guns. … "

True enough.

But they still lost.

When you look at this game you will see much of Michigan's season inside it. Spurts of brilliance, keeping it close, but as Fisher put it, "Lacking a sense of closure."

What you didn't see all year, but saw last night, was the unified excellence of King and Jackson. They played as though the last lights of their lives were hanging on the scoreboard.

WHAT A PARTICULARLY SAD ending for King, who had been fighting the demons of expectations his entire career. As Chris Webber, then Jalen Rose, then Juwan Howard all took their turns in leading this team, King lay back, languid in that Texas sprawl-on-the-couch way he has, waiting his turn, figuring it would come. "We'll be great one day," he would say. "My time is coming … "

But when it showed up, King didn't. His stats this year were pretty good, but pretty good was never what he was after. He averaged more points than ever, 14.5 per game, but he shot worse than ever, and his three-point range was nearly nonexistent.

But Thursday night, in the regulation, he turned back the clock and was simply brilliant. There was nothing he couldn't do, no part of the game he didn't own. Rebounds. Steals. Assists. Three-pointers. He had it all.

Except the finish. The Wolverines went nearly eight minutes without scoring a point. The defense collapsed, they made mistakes. And all the nostalgia in the world won't make up for that.

"How do you feel about the whole Fab Five era at this moment?" someone asked King.

He thought for a moment. "It didn't end on an up-tick, did it?"

The press conference ended, and King and Jackson walked off the stage for the last time in their yellow uniforms. There was no applause. There were no tears. Just the words "it didn't end on an up-tick" hanging in the midnight air.

Right team; wrong ending

March 18, 1995

TALLAHASSEE, FLA. — There were tears all over the locker room floor, mixing with the dirt and the soiled, wet towels. Jud Heathcote had cried, and Shawn Respert had cried. Eric Snow sat motionless in a chair as reporters moved through and camera lights blinded the already stunned Spartans players. Someone leaned down, patted Snow on the shoulder, mumbled "Sorry," and that was it, the floodgates opened, he began to sob, unable to catch his breath. He was every kid after every big game that didn't go right. This is what they don't show you on ESPN SportsCenter. How dreams turn liquid and fall from your eyes.

"It's not supposed to … it shouldn't … end like this," Snow whispered.

No, it shouldn't. Fewer than 30 minutes earlier, they had still been on the court, Snow and Respert and the rest of this finest Spartans team in some time, they were still the No. 3 seed, the heavily favored team, and they still thought they could get it done. But this team from Utah, these nobodies, these never-heard-of-'ems in the purple uniforms — Weber State? — they kept hitting their shots and making their free throws and grabbing the ball after it bopped off several players' hands. One of their killer three-pointers seemed to lead to another, and finally, even Respert, the miracle shooter who had made seven three-point baskets of his own, threw up an airball.

And next thing you knew, it was the final seconds, and a Weber State player named Ruben Nembhard was breaking away downcourt, all alone, as Snow, the fastest guy on the Spartans, was giving chase — catch him! catch him! — but all he could do was slap from behind as Nembhard lifted for a basket. The whistle blew. And Snow and the entire state of Michigan fell to Earth with a thud.

"We are devastated," Heathcote would say after the 79-72 first-round upset that ended the Spartans' brightest season in years. "Devastated."

And to think, this was St. Patrick's Day, when green is supposed to be a lucky color.

HOW DID THIS HAPPEN? How did a game in which the Spartans shot nearly 70 percent for the first half — and led by nine at the break — suddenly unravel into a mad dash for redemption in the final minutes, with Snow driving the lane, looking for contact and Respert throwing up one prayer after another, trying to win it by himself. He would finish with 28 points, and had the Spartans won, there would be jokes about the distance of his shots, some of which were launched from another continent.

But there are no memories of that now. Instead, this is what you remember: Respert, the polite and friendly All-America, the Big Ten player of the year, watching helplessly as his fellow senior and best friend, Snow, landed after that fifth foul and lay on the floor. Snow's boyish face was already weepy. Oh, on any other night, Respert would be right at his side. But now, he remained on the foul line, hands on his knees, looking at the floor, letting another teammate help Snow because if Respert went over to him, that would be it for him, too. He'd be crying like a kid, and there were still eight seconds left.

Only after Snow was helped to the bench did Respert sneak a glance in his direction, like an older brother, just making sure.

It was the saddest look I've ever seen in sports.

"There were no words," Respert said later. "No words. We both knew there was nothing to say."

"Can you remember what you were thinking?"

He bit his lip. "I was thinking ... that's it? It's finished? For four years we were together, and now we have to start all over again, with other people?"

Isn't that pretty much how all Spartans fans feel this morning? They, too, had been together with Respert and Snow for four years — and with the coach, Jud Heathcote, for 19 years. Nineteen years? What kind of retirement farewell is that? The all-time coaching leader in MSU basketball history? Doesn't he deserve better? Wasn't this first-round game, a No. 3 seed vs. a No. 14 seed, supposed to be the reward for his excellent final season?

The reward, not the punishment.

"You know, Jud said to me as soon as the second half started, 'I don't like the way this game is going,' " Tom Izzo, the assistant who will take over next season, related afterward. His voice was cracking, too. "The old man, he just knew. He just knew ... "

Oh, Jud tried to save it. He tried zone, man-to-man, substitutions. He tried screaming at the refs, who made some questionable calls. But in the end, all he could do was watch the turnovers mount and the missed shots take their toll until, when the buzzer sounded, he clumped off in that familiar walk, as though playing drums with his shoes.

But let me say this. When the game was over, Heathcote's thoughts were not about himself, or his legacy. They were about his players. Under the rules, the coach and the designated stars must attend a press conference immediately after the game. Heathcote, Snow and Respert came, but clearly the kids were not ready. Someone asked Respert what he felt "after a first-round knockout," and Respert sniffed once into the microphone, and his face began to twist and contort, and no words would come.

"Look, guys," Heathcote interrupted, "I've always said the players shouldn't have to come to these things. It's not right. I've been arguing it for years. But for now ... well, could you just ask me the questions. Let's leave the players alone for a minute."

And remarkably, the reporters did.

It was one of Heathcote's finest jobs of coaching.

S ADLY, IT CANNOT MAKE UP for the pain. Spartans fans will have a terrible emptiness these next few days, particularly when they turn on the games Sunday afternoon and do not see their team anywhere.

But let's be honest. There is only one team that goes home truly happy from this often sadistic tournament. The rest must take solace in the memories they made. And this Spartans team made plenty of memories — never mind that most came during the regular season.

Better to remember Respert in those games, like the first Michigan-Michigan State contest this year in which he went unconscious in the second half, scoring 30 points, throwing the basketball through the net as if tossing a pebble into a canyon.

And better to remember Snow for his jet-pack drives downcourt and his flypaper defense and the eight straight free throws he made to beat Wisconsin. Surely the NBA can find a place for this kid's skills.

And better to remember Jud from any of a thousand other moments, banging his head like Curly in The Three Stooges, waving instructions as his team ran a play, bouncing off the court on his players' shoulders after the Magic Johnson-led national championship. You may or may not have liked Heathcote's style. But in all his time here, he has never shamed the university, he has spoken with candor and intelligence, he has not cheated to get recruits, and, above all — the finest measure of a coach — he has put his kids first.

And so we saved them for last. There is always sadness in a losing locker room. Yet, I swear, I cannot recall one in which the sadness was so contagious. The reporters, the cameramen, the cheerleaders down the hall, everyone seemed to be moist in the eyes. When your seniors are crying, your juniors and sophomores and freshmen are right behind.

This was a wonderful team, gone too soon from a tournament that does that to wonderful teams. When heads are clearer, they will remember the bright spots.

But for now, the bright spots were covered with a layer of tears, an aching in the stomach and the distant sound of a small team from Utah, celebrating down the hall.

Leaping tall buildings, he's back
March 20, 1995

INDIANAPOLIS — It wasn't the way he chewed gum as he jogged out of the tunnel, nor the ease with which he carried the ball in his first lay-up drill, one-handed, effortless, as if putting a glass on a shelf. No. What convinced you the guy was back for real were those familiar beads of sweat glistening on his smoothly shaved head, exerting himself again, in basketball, after nearly two years away. His number already was retired and a statue erected in his honor. Now he stripped off his warm-ups to the familiar red-and-black uniform. The crowd exploded. It was like watching Superman burst out of a phone booth.

Look. Up in the sky. The world's truly big stars have one thing in common: You can't take your eyes off of them. And all day Sunday at Market Square Arena, whether he was shooting, passing, driving, hanging, grimacing, falling down — or even just sitting on the bench — that's where your eyes were, locked on Michael Jordan. Was he smiling? Was he breathing hard? Was that really him, ducking his head, then pulling up high for a jump shot, quick as he ever was? Forget what the Chicago Bulls will pay this guy; every team in the league should kick in a Brinks truck. Jordan, in a single afternoon, has lifted the NBA to another level of interest.

"I'm back for the love of the game," said arguably the greatest player to ever play it, 21 months after his last game, a hiatus spent mostly in the minor leagues of baseball. "It's not financial. I'm still under my old contract. There's nothing under the table … although I wish there was.

"I'm back because I missed it."

How long, Michael, they asked, how long?

"I'm back at least until the end of the season. Hopefully longer. I want to help my team win.

"This is not a cameo."

Well. Whatever it was, however long it lasts — and with Jordan, you never know — Sunday was a remarkable afternoon in the history of athlete-watching. Before a screaming sellout crowd, and some 400 media members — at least 300 of whom had no idea they'd be here the day before — we saw Jordan's skills re-focus inside his 32-year-old body, like a photograph in the tray of a developer. He began with awkward shots. He missed his first six. He was out of sync. Then slowly, the shots got closer. He hit one, then another. He outjumped his defenders. He stopped running into his teammates. The tongue began to flop loosely from his mouth.

Finally, at 8:55 of the third quarter, he snatched the ball cleanly from an unsuspecting Rik Smits and exploded downcourt. The crowd rose as Jordan lifted to the basket, over two Pacers players, and finger-rolled the ball through the hoop. He landed with the hint of a smile. After all these months away, this is how long it took him — exactly 27 minutes and five seconds off an NBA clock — to return to a level no one else can touch.

Which is his own.

"Were you surprised he lasted 43 minutes in his first game?" someone asked Phil Jackson, Jordan's coach, who, like the rest of the Chicago franchise, is now back in the big light.

"Yes," Jackson said, "I was surprised. I told him, 'Mike, I didn't expect you to give me an overtime.' "

Look. Up in the sky.

FOR THE RECORD, JORDAN played longer than any Bull except Scottie Pippen. He survived leg cramps and fatigue and scored 19 points. Rusty? Sure. He took a third of his team's shots (28), made just a quarter of them (seven), had six rebounds, six assists, three steals, missed all four of his three-point attempts and had no dunks. And his team lost to the Pacers.

So on a statistical level, it might not have been the greatest moment in sports. But it was certainly a Large One. From the army of media, to the Learjet that Jordan took to Indianapolis — for security — to the seven pages one Chicago newspaper devoted to his return, to the tickets for Sunday's otherwise insignificant mid-season game, which were scalped for up to $500 a pop, LARGE was the word.

How big is Jordan? The five corporations for which he is a major spokesman — including Nike and Quaker Oats — saw their stocks rise an aggregate $2 billion in equity last week, largely on speculation Jordan would return.

"So I guess I'm the CEO of those companies now, huh?" Jordan said. "I'll tell you, none of it is trickling down to me. … I mean, beyond what I'm already getting."

He laughed. In his black-and-white plaid suit, white shirt, black tie, gold watch, gold bracelet and trademark stud earring, he looked every bit the three-time NBA champion, league MVP, $30 million-a-year-in-endorsements legend he was when he left the game.

Which brings us to a key issue. Jordan might have answered the question of "Can he return?" on Sunday — and never mind the jump shot, which will come, doing what he did with no NBA competition in two seasons is nearly superhuman — but he still hasn't answered, "Why did he leave?"

In his startling 1993 farewell news conference, Jordan was somewhat annoyed and looking forward to the serenity of life away from the NBA. He promised to "watch the grass grow, maybe mow it once or twice," play with his kids, spend time with his wife. He said he had accomplished all that he could in basketball. He said he was serious.

Then what happened? Four months later, he signed a baseball contract, jumped right back into the limelight, the only grass he watched was the stuff in the outfield between pitches, and his family saw him less than ever. Now he returns to the biggest sideshow you could imagine.

Jordan is a lot of things; consistent verbally is not one of them.

"When I left the game, I probably needed a break from it," he said Sunday. "I meant what I said about my family. And they're behind my decision. They know I need to be happy. But I found that I missed the game. I missed my friends. I missed my teammates. So I came back."

Maybe. Rumors will persist that he was told to take a break by the league, before his habit of laying down gambling bets got him and the game in trouble.

Not that anybody cares at the moment.

JORDAN SEEMED HUMBLE AT his news conference. Relaxed. Self-effacing. He even joked that he left baseball and returned to basketball because "at least I know what I'm doing in this game."

"It's funny," he said, "down in the minor leagues, all the guys wanted to play me in basketball. In Arizona, we got a gym and played pickup games. And the more of them we played, the more my appetite got whetted. ...

"I'm coming back to put something positive in the game. There's been a lot of negative. Some of the younger players today are not taking the responsibility they have to the game, for the love of the game. They're in it for the money and the business. I'm more from the era of Magic Johnson, Larry Bird, Doctor J. Some of those guys aren't able to come back. I'm coming back because I can."

Well. From an NBA perspective, that's a grand slam. What could be better than this? Biggest star of the game returns to save it from itself.

Maybe it's true. Maybe it's just a cleverly calculated plan by a clever man and some clever agents. It was Jordan's main advisor, David Falk, who issued Jordan's press release Saturday, which read, rather arrogantly, "I'm back."

Whatever. Time will tell if he can make the Bulls a championship team (it says here he can get them to the NBA Finals). And time will tell about team jealousies, about his 32-year-old legs and whether the NBA can afford Jordan, who, under the current pay scale, should get at least $10 million a year.

But for now, you ask whether his return is good for the game? Ask yourself this. If you know he's playing, will you turn on the TV?

Next question?

The rap on Neon Deion
March 29, 1995

AND NOW, BECAUSE FOOTBALL IS over and baseball can't get started, we bring you Deion Sanders, a man who clearly has too much time on his hands. He has come to rap. Bust it.

"It's Deion, stepping on the pe-on,
tell me have you seen one?
No, we haven't Deion."

I'm not sure what that means, but Deion raps it on his new album, so it must mean something, right? The two-sport superstar — who obviously never sleeps — is in Motown tonight for a concert at the State Theatre.

He's not attending it, he's giving it. Deion Raps. Bust it.

"Being prime time is easy for me
but there's a big difference between you and me, see?"

True. Here's one difference: I don't wear sunglasses indoors.

But that's just me. I also don't refer to myself in the third person — although I would like to because then I could say, "Mitch is going to lunch," and it would sound like I was talking about someone else — nor am I surrounded by an entourage.

Deion has an entourage. He came for our interview Tuesday with 1) a tour manager, 2) a regular manager, 3) a record company guy, and 4) several other gentlemen who, near as I can tell, were there to shoo away anyone who might bother Deion. They stood against the wall, nodding when Deion spoke, scowling when I spoke. I assume they are paid for this. At one point, the record company guy had his arms crossed and his head tilted sideways and was staring at me so intently, I felt compelled to play more of Deion's CD, "Prime Time" — now available in stores! — before he hurt me. Bust it.

"Inquiring minds what to know, about the All Pro
so they often ask me, why am I so flashy?
They say I got an ego
but it ain't easy to be me."

Now, call me old-fashioned, but I don't consider that a great song lyric. I consider Billie Holiday's "God Bless the Child" a great song lyric:

"Mama may have, and Papa may have
But God bless the child who's got his own."

Billie Holiday didn't rap. But as Deion likes to point out, it's a new era. I ask him about all the celebrating he does on the football field, and he says, "This is a whole new breed of athlete. This isn't like the days of Dick Butkus."

True. Can you imagine Butkus doing a rap record?

"I whack your legs, I whack your feet
I whack your head — out comes your teeth."

Anyhow, Deion is just one in a long line of athletes-turned-rap artists. Shaquille O'Neal sold more than a million copies of his rap album — "Shaq Diesel" — in which he shouts about his fame and talent. I find this interesting, since every time I interview Shaq, I can barely hear him.

There's also a new CD, "B-Ball's Best Kept Secrets," full of NBA stars rapping, and this fall, the NFL plans a compilation called "NFL Jams."

Personally, I would like to hear someone really unusual on that, say, kicker Morten Andersen of the New Orleans Saints.

"I come from Denmark, I like Ingemar Stenmark ... "

But that won't happen. Mostly we'll hear guys rapping about their cars, their women, their status. And that's what I don't get: The point of rap is the lyrics, right? So wouldn't a record by Deion suggest he has something ... to say?

What? I have listened to the entire album. Twice. And near as I can tell, this is Deion's message: "I'm rich; you're not."

Consider:

The place is packed, nowhere to find a seat
but I don't worry cause I sit in VIP.

Or ...

"Now it's on, to my selection,
which one will it be from your Benzo collection?
My 300? My 420? My 560?"

It sounds like the Home Shopping Network.

Now, before Deion gets bent out of shape — or worse, he sends that record company guy after me — let me state I once made my living as a professional musician, back in the days when you played the notes, you didn't "sample" them on your computer.

And — surprise! — I like and own a lot of rap music, from artists such as Arrested Development and Queen Latifah, who don't just sing about themselves.

And I do salute Deion for avoiding gangsta rap.

"That's not Deion," he says.

But this is. Songs titled "Prime Time Keeps on Ticking," "House of Prime" and "2 B Me" — which suggest an artistic inspiration that comes from looking in the mirror.

The music world doesn't need it, anymore than the sports world needs to see Elton John return a kickoff. I like Deion as an athlete, and he's far more intelligent than he lets on.

But there's talent, and there's marketing. This whole rap-athlete business is being pushed as superstars returning to their roots. But it's really about money, selling albums the way they sell shoes — by associating them with famous people. As Sanders raps in one of his songs:

"Look deep into my eyes, so you can see
the man who you envy."

I would, Deion, but you'd have to take off the sunglasses.

Kevin Jones, all American

April 11, 1995

T HE LITTLE CHOCOLATE DOUGHNUTS were in a box, next to the coffee urn. Normally, high schools don't provide food for their assemblies, but today was special, all these TV crews, radio people, sports writers. A table was arranged near the front of the room, and a reporter set down a microphone, alongside a dozen others. "Testing 1-2 … … testing 1-2," he said.

Suddenly, the whole room seemed to shift. The guest of honor had arrived. He didn't enter first. He was preceded by an entourage of friends, coaches, his grandmother, his aunt, his baby brother, more friends, more coaches and his girlfriend, whom he identified later as "my girlfriend." She wore a black dress and jewelry and had her hair pinned up, as if going to the prom, even though it was mid-afternoon and math classes were in progress upstairs.

Her boyfriend took his seat. He wore a stud earring and a colorful jacket. Only 18 years old, he was the largest person in the room, 6-feet-9, 300 pounds. It was for his body — and what he could do with it — that these people had come.

"Good afternoon," Robert Traylor began, reading from a sheet of paper. His voice was deep as a businessman's, but his words were those of a nervous teen. "I'd like to welcome everyone. … My dream is to play in the NBA one day. …

"I've chosen the college that can best help me achieve my dream. … "

The crowd held its breath. For three years, a parade of grown men, employed by major universities, had been coming to Detroit to watch Robert Traylor play. They called him at home, they called his friends, they called his relatives. They showed him videos, promised him stardom. They wooed him like a golden child.

Now, the payoff.

"The school I will be attending," Traylor said, "will be the University of Michigan. … " The room erupted in applause.

D OWN THE HALL, SITTING ALONE by a computer, was another high school senior named Kevin Jones. Like Traylor, Jones is black, lives in Detroit, and is being raised with no father in the house. His mother supports the family by working as a janitor.

Like Traylor, Jones also will be attending Michigan next fall — on a full scholarship.

But unlike Traylor, Jones, a thin kid with a disarming smile, got his scholarship for studying three hours a day, getting the highest grades, keeping his attendance over 95 percent and never violating school conduct rules.

Kevin Jones is the most important currency in the city of Detroit, a kid with a brain. He did not announce his college decision at a press conference; he had to wait for Michigan to accept *him*. A letter finally arrived at the house his family shares with another family in northwest Detroit. He peeked through the envelope and saw the word "Congratulations." He smiled. His grandmother hugged him and said, "I'm so proud of you! I'm so proud of you. ... "

Back at the press conference, reporters were yelling questions:

"Robert, when did you decide on Michigan?"

"Robert, do you think you'll start?"

"Robert, what did the Michigan coaches say?"

Traylor smiled at the last one. "I don't know. I haven't told them yet."

Not that it mattered. At that moment, it was being announced all over the radio.

THIS IS CRAZY. A PRESS CONFERENCE for a high school ballplayer? What message are we sending the other students at Murray-Wright High School, who were peeking through the doors, wondering what the fuss was about?

Don't misunderstand. Robert Traylor is a bright young man with a special talent. But a press conference about where he will dribble and shoot? Isn't there enough spotlight on these kids already? Besides, encouraging inner-city teams to shoot for the NBA is like encouraging them to win the lottery. Most will be disappointed.

Several years ago, a high school star named Chris Webber had one of these press conferences — and two years later, he held another to say he was leaving school for the pros. Someone asked Traylor about that Monday.

"I hope (I can) leave college in two years," he said excitedly.

Later he tried to correct this, but everyone knew what he meant. In his dreams of swimming in NBA waters, college is the diving board.

It is more than a diving board to Kevin Jones. He has no plans of leaving early. "I want to study business and open my own one day," he said. He showed a resume he had done himself. It noted his awards in the Navy ROTC, and his computer literacy in IBM and Macintosh systems.

This is no nerd. This is a good-looking kid who hears bullets in his neighborhood and remembers what his grandmother said, "When there's trouble, just keep walking." He works hard because he was taught to work hard, and he doesn't read off a sheet when he says, "One day, after I get my business going, I'm gonna come back to this school and teach math."

Which is more important than coming back to sign autographs.

The doughnuts were mostly gone now. Traylor's aunt was being interviewed, so were his friends, who mugged for the cameras. Traylor himself posed, wearing a maize and blue Michigan cap.

Down the hall, the computer flipped on, and a young man began a new application for room and board money. He started with his name, "Kevin Jones."

No offense, but if there had to be a press conference Monday, it should have been his.

The gentleman goon
April 14, 1995

HALLELUJAH, HOCKEY FANS! I HAVE the answer to your prayers. First, you people in the high seats at Joe Louis Arena, who have been crying in your beer since the departure of Immortal Beloved, the toothless driving risk, Bob Probert.

"PROBIE, PROBIE, WHEREFORE ART THOU, PROBIE?" you lament.

No more. I have a new word for you.

STUUUUUUUUUUUUUU!

That's right. Stu. As in Stu Grimson, the rugged new enforcer for the Wings who is 6-feet-5, built like Dolph Lundgren, and as ready for confrontation as any O.J. Simpson lawyer.

How can you not like a guy whose nickname is "The Grim Reaper"?

STUUUUUUUUUUU!

Thursday night, in his first Wings home game, Grimson wasn't on the ice one minute before punching San Jose's Jayson More. How's that for service, dudes? You're not even back from the pizza stand and the man is already throwing a punch! All right! Motown is Black and Blue Town Again! Party on! Go on upstairs and have a beer! I'll be with you in a minute! …

"STUUUUUUUUUU!

OK. Now that they're gone, all you people who think goonish hockey is unseemly and unworthy, here's the surprise. This guy Grimson is — how can I put this? — a gentleman. Really. He is religious, speaks politely, and is studying for his degree in economics. He has a wife and two young daughters — "the pride of my life" — he loves "Seinfeld" and has been spotted, according to one reliable Red Wings witness, "reading a book, and stuff."

That Red Wing would be Shawn Burr, who also noted Grimson's keen sense of humor.

"He told me this morning, 'Shawn, you're built like prime rib.' Then he said, 'Actually, you're more like the stuff they cut off the prime rib.' "

He punches, he punchlines.

Can I get a STUUUUUUUU?

OH, HEY, DUDES. You're back. Still partying? Well, why not? Less than 10 minutes after that first swing Thursday night, Grimson grabbed another Shark and did the muscle dance again.

This time it was captain Jeff Odgers. Oh, yeah. They whaled on each other! Some wicked head shots, ace! And in the end, with his jersey pulled over his head, The Grim Reaper still took Odgers to the ice!

Awesome.

STUUUUUUUU!

Hey. Why don't we dudes go upstairs and watch some more of "Hockey's Greatest Brawls"? Go ahead, man! I'll be up in a minute! …

OK. Now that they're gone, you more erudite fans will be happy to know that Grimson does not fight in bars, refuses to drink and does not see his job as reflective of his personality.

"The label 'Goon,' " he says, "is not a pleasant word. I know people expect enforcers in the NHL to be pugnacious and belligerent, but the truth is, we are all different people."

Pugnacious and belligerent?

"It's true, I'm not afraid of a punch. But I have respect for a punch as well."

Pugnacious and belligerent?

"I've also found, through the years, the ability to overcome fear is one of the most exhilarating feelings you'll have in your lifetime."

Whoa. Is this hockey, or Zig Ziglar?

A fighter who works with teens? An enforcer who spends several weeks each year with the Christian Hockey Ministries? A punching machine who not only likes Bruce Springsteen but admits that one of his favorite albums is the brooding, acoustic "Nebraska"?

Somebody wake me up.

STUUUUUUUUUU!

DUDES! YOU'RE BACK! Done with the tapes? Oh, you're making new ones, from Thursday night. Well, sure. After seven penalty minutes in the first period, Grimson came roaring back. Less than 30 seconds into the second frame, he was roughing it up with defenseman Shawn Cronin. I'm telling you. Grimson should come with his own "Batman" soundtrack. Biff! Bam! Zowie!

And then, once he got out of the penalty box for that one, he found a Shark he hadn't attacked yet — this was getting harder to do — and, you guessed it, he went after him. Defenseman Jim Kyte. Bam! Biff! Pow! I counted nine straight punches, dudes! And when the nasty ref sent Big Stu to the box, he got a standing ovation!

Unbelievable, man! Is this great or what? Let's go home and kick in a wall!

I'm right behind you, boys. …

OK. Now that they're gone, a few final thoughts for you peaceable folks. Yes, it's true, Grimson has scored only four goals in his six-year NHL career — he was with Calgary, Chicago and Anaheim before Detroit. But it is also true that Grimson says things like, 'How come you drive on the parkway and park in the driveway?' "

It is true that Grimson long ago gave up on an unblemished complexion —

after Thursday's game, his left eye looked like month-old hamburger. Then again, Keith Primeau hasn't had to fight since Grimson got here. And, besides, how can you knock a fighter who says, "I'm not much for dirty jokes"?

The way I see it, we got a guy here who can throw a punch and keep the bloodhounds happy without winding up in jail, in a ditch, or in the headlines. I'd call that a pretty fair acquisition.

So altogether now, men and women, greasers and nerds, activists and pacifists, can I get one for practice?

STUUUUUUUUUU!

"I like when fans yell that. Stuuu! That way, if they ever start booing me, I'll never know the difference."

It's a weird sport, hockey, isn't it?

Dumars' transition game
April 17, 1995

T HIS WAS SCARY, HE THOUGHT. How high are we? He looked down
through the window at the people, the cars, the newspaper vendors, the
glint of steel reflecting in the glass skyscrapers. Whoa! Too big. He sat on
the bed in the Grand Hyatt Hotel and called his father and mother back in
Louisiana. They assured him New York City was survivable for one night, stay in
the room, be careful. He double-locked the doors, just in case.

The next day he sat at the 1985 NBA draft and waited nervously for his name
to be called. He expected Denver to take him, but they passed, then Dallas, but
they passed, too, and so he figured he was going to Houston, with the 19th pick.
Houston needed a guard.

Then, the strangest thing happened.

"WITH THE 18TH PICK," commissioner David Stern announced,
"DETROIT SELECTS ... JOE DUMARS, McNEESE STATE."

Detroit?

He stood up, shook a few hands, all the while thinking, *"Detroit? Why
Detroit?"* He pushed a smile onto his face and faced the TV cameras. Soon he
was back in his room, packing his stuff. *Detroit?* Over the phone, the Pistons had
asked if he would fly in for a press conference, but he was too shy for that. He
wanted to get back to dirt roads and bayou heat. Before he left, he pulled out a
map and tried to locate this new employer. He had no clue. *Detroit?*

"If you stripped away the names of the states and said, 'Pick Michigan,' " he
admits now, "I probably would have pointed to Wisconsin."

That was a long time ago. Dumars has overcome his shyness, his fear of
cities and his poor geography. He has blossomed into a shining star of American
sports, an All-Star, an NBA Finals MVP, a Dream Team II captain, a charity
spokesman, a husband, a father, a community leader, a great interview. But for all
that has happened, he never lost touch with the scared Louisiana kid in that hotel
room that night, and so he remembers the lessons he had packed with him then,
from family who taught over lemonade glasses and shaded porch chairs. One of
those lessons was this: "Don't be like a bucket of crabs."

It means, don't be the type who is so threatened by others getting ahead that
he has to pull them down.

Last summer, in another NBA draft, the commissioner's voice sounded again.

"WITH THE THIRD PICK, DETROIT SELECTS ... GRANT HILL,
DUKE."

And Dumars exhaled. He was 31 years old now.

And once again, he talked to himself.

"Well, Joe, you have just gone from being a star — to being a mentor."

He would not be a crab.

No one here will ever appreciate that enough.

JUNE 1994, Ginopolis restaurant. Dumars is having dinner with Grant Hill, Calvin Hill, Tom Wilson, Billy McKinney and Don Chaney. Hill is shopping for teams. The Pistons want him badly. After dinner, Dumars takes the kid aside.

"Listen," he says, "I'm the veteran on this team. And I promise you, you can come here and not have to put up with any ego or attitude. No one will say, 'Who does this kid think he is?' I will make sure of it.

"You can come here and be The Man — with my blessings."

When Hill leaves Detroit, he tells his father and his agent, "This is where I want to play."

The morning air is brisk, and so is the traffic. Joe Dumars is steering his four-wheel-drive along the Detroit highways. He is stiff, tired and, as is common this season, coming off a loss. The night before, he faced old nemesis Michael Jordan, who returned to the Bulls after almost two seasons away. Jordan, playing in only his 12th game of the season, had the bounce of a teenager heading to a rock concert.

Joe had to guard him. In the old days, he did this better than anyone, but he also had help — Dennis Rodman, Bill Laimbeer. This day, Dumars, suffering a double groin pull, is on his own. He did what he could. Jordan scored 29.

"How old do you feel this morning?" Dumars is asked.

"Oooold," he says.

The Pistons are finishing another terrible season. They will miss the playoffs again. Dumars has said he won't play beyond his contract, which ends in 1997. Some feel he won't go beyond next year.

How unfair, you find yourself saying. This is no way for a two-time NBA champion to close the show.

"At least this season I think of us as a team that isn't winning — not as losers. Last season, I remember coming out for the tap a few times and thinking, 'We have no chance of winning this game. None.' "

Dumars was at his peak when this franchise began to crumble. He could shoot like a rifle, and his defense was like flypaper. He was a perennial All-Star. Coaches loved him. He could have demanded a trade. Go to a contender. Win another title.

Instead, he chose to lay down his career like a cape over the muddy waters of mediocrity, so that Hill and Lindsey Hunter and Allen Houston might have a bridge to a golden era. He would be their teacher. That would be his final legacy. Laimbeer tried to do this last season with the big men, but he quit midway through. Isiah Thomas quickly retired to front office glamour; he wasn't going to stick around just to show younger guys the ropes.

But Dumars? Well, hadn't he always gravitated to older people himself? He used to sit on his bunk bed in Natchitoches, Louisiana, listening to his five older brothers talk about school, sports and life. When he got to college, he befriended the older players and hung around with them.

Even his wife, Debbie, a college sweetheart, was the second person in her family that Joe fell for. The first was her father, who used to sit on the porch telling stories. The guy was in his 50s. Joe thought he was great.

"I've always said that once I got to seniority status, I knew how I would treat the guys coming behind me," Dumars said.

So he met with Bill Davidson, the Pistons' owner, and said if Davidson wanted Joe Dumars here, Joe Dumars wanted to be here. For the rest of his career. Win or lose. No matter what.

Here he stays.

FALL 1994 — In a meeting in Tom Wilson's office, Dumars insists that Grant Hill be given the proper treatment.

"You have your star for the next 10 years," he says. "You have to build around this kid. Don't worry about hurting my feelings. Don't worry about not overdoing him because of me.

"I'll be the veteran guy. I'll make sure the rest of the team is in line. But give Grant the full treatment. Press conferences. Billboards. Marketing. Everything. He's your franchise now."

Do you know how many times Joe Dumars has dunked? Five. That's right. Five times in 10 seasons. The most recent one was a game against Atlanta this year. He was on a breakaway. He went up and slammed, then looked over at his bench. The players were whooping and high-fiving.

"I told them, 'Guys, you have just witnessed history.' "

This is the genius of Dumars. In a league in which the next star can't be too down, too def, too cool, Dumars is a hero for being … square. He doesn't believe in showing off. (Hence the no-dunking, which, by the way, he can do with his eyes closed.) He doesn't party. He cannot remember the last time he was in a nightclub on the road.

"Sometimes I'll hear the younger guys talk about where they're going that night. And just for laughs, I'll say, 'You know, tonight I'm gonna meet you guys. I really am. About 10:30? I'm gonna be there. Wait for me now, OK?' "

Do they ever believe you?

"Nah."

Nah. But they'd like to. Dumars would be welcome at just about anyone's table. He has held counsel with such jammers as Shaquille O'Neal and Shawn

Kemp, during Dream Team II last August — both thought the world of Dumars — and he has gained the friendship of even the most reclusive superstars, such as Jordan and Adrian Dantley. People simply like to be around Dumars. He is principled without passing judgment and as friendly as a country neighbor.

He also breaks the mold. Instead of parties or women, he reads on the road. He goes to movies. He watches CNN and ESPN and gets the Wall Street Journal.

And he is curious.

A few summers ago, Dumars ran into a newspaper reporter. They got to talking about the media. Dumars said he'd like to see how a newspaper worked. The reporter said, yeah, sure, someday. Dumars said, "How about tomorrow?"

The next day, Dumars was at the newspaper, sitting in on editorial meetings, visiting the printing presses, studying the vats of ink.

Most guys can't do enough to stay out of the papers. Dumars is the only one who ever asked to come in.

WINTER 1994 — In the locker room after practice, Hill sits with Dumars. He tells Joe about this guy he's going to hook up with.

"He's a friend of yours," Hill says.

"No, he isn't," Dumars says.

"But he told me he knows you really well."

Dumars smiles. "Listen. A lot of people will tell you they know me really well. Just as there are people out there right now telling people how well they know you. No matter how sincere people are, no matter what they say, it doesn't mean you can trust them, OK?

"Don't ever let people's words be what you base your opinion on."

Hill nods, taking it all in.

'Hey, Bean ... come here ... look out ... come here ... look out ... "

Dumars is playing with his baby daughter, Aren, in the kitchen of his airy Bloomfield Hills home. His children — on several visits — seem a lot like him — quiet, observing. You don't notice much crying when a stranger is in the house. Just big eyes looking at you.

Dumars found refuge in his family as a way of dealing with the Pistons' slide. In the championship years, there was barely time to breathe between media requests, appearances, and, of course, a two-month postseason.

These last few years, Dumars has been finished with basketball by the first week in May. The time was reinvested in his family. His first child, Jordan, was born not long after Dumars' father died, during the 1990 NBA Finals against Portland. It was the perfect catharsis for Dumars, who adored Joe Sr., his work ethic, his simple way of looking at life.

"I went from being a son to being a father in less than a year," he says. "That will make you grow up."

*WINTER 1995 — During a game, a little past halfway through the season,
Grant Hill goes to pass the ball inbounds to Dumars. Suddenly a worried look
comes over Hill's face.*

"Joe," he says, "my legs are just gone. I can barely feel 'em anymore."

Dumars takes the ball and walks alongside Hill upcourt.

"You ever hear of The Wall?" he says. "You just hit it.

"Another few games, and you'll come out of it."

Fate will not be as kind to Dumars' career. Barring a miracle, he will end his
Pistons tenure during the rebuilding process. The likelihood of another
championship is as slim as Oliver Miller is hefty.

"What makes it easier to deal with is that I've already won two
championships and a Finals MVP Award. I'll be honest, if I hadn't done that, it
would be tougher. Maybe I wouldn't like a young kid coming in and taking
things away."

Instead, Dumars teaches. He teaches Hill about the media, time usage, ego,
life, he teaches Hunter about the point guard position and Houston about the off-
guard position. He plays hurt and wounded so that he can teach the team, about
grace under fire, about work ethic.

He sets a tone. Think about it. How many other teams could be dead last in
their division and almost never spill venom into the media? No swiping at each
other? No finger-pointing?

It is Dumars who makes this possible. In some ways, this year, this dismal,
statistically smelly Pistons season, might be his greatest team contribution — if
only for what he sacrificed. He is that rarest of crabs, ready to help others out of
the bucket.

Funny, no? A kid who had no idea where Detroit was 10 years ago, now such
a proud part of his team and his city? On a recent visit to Children's Hospital,
Dumars was introduced to a young patient. The boy shook his hand.

"I never met a real player before," he said.

"Are you a Pistons fan?" Joe asked

"I am now," he said.

What better legacy than that?

What was achieved? Truth

April 24, 1995

H E DIED QUIETLY, WHICH WAS NOT like him, in New York City, before
sunrise, in the wee hours, when the ratings don't matter. His heart —
which many claimed he never had — failed him at last.

Meanwhile, just a few blocks away, ESPN was preparing for its second full
day of NFL draft coverage, over-hyped and over-announced insanity, with the
insufferable Mel Kiper Jr. set to prattle on about split times.

No wonder Howard Cosell left us. He probably couldn't stand it anymore.

Down goes a legend. From his booming, nasal "Tell it like it is" statements to
intros such as "Miiiiile High Stadium, Dennnvah, Colahhrado" to live action
calls such as "Down goes Frazier! Down goes Frazier!" there has never been a
more imitated sportscaster. Back in the '70s, every teen wearing bell-bottoms
could do a Cosell impersonation.

But looking at sports in the sudden blankness of Cosell's death, we see that,
after all these years, people have been imitating the wrong part.

Cosell was not just noise. He was journalism. He poked. He prodded. He
asked frank questions. He dared you to use a dictionary.

"Once again, Danderoo, you have proven to be neither loquacious nor
truculent," he would scold broadcast partner Don Meredith on "Monday Night
Football."

"Aw, Howard," Meredith would drawl, "there you go with them 20-dollar
words again."

Fans, of course, sided with Meredith. So did sportscasters who followed.
Madden, Bradshaw, George Foreman — the list is long — found fame playing
the bumpkin. The bumpkin's easy. You're no threat. You're welcome at the party.

C OSELL WAS A THREAT. He did not attend the party. He knew that the
microphone made your voice louder for a reason, not simply for a laugh, and
so he attacked when he saw something wrong. He was brash, rude, arrogant,
abrasive and condescending.

He was also necessary.

"Oh, this horizontal ladder of mediocrity," he once said of the broadcast
business. He swore he could never do play-by-play at a bowling or golf
tournament, that he would rather work as a ditchdigger. This was back in the late
'60s, when Cosell and his bad hair, long nose and frequent cigar made him a
sight sports fans had never before encountered.

Even then he knew he was better than the rest. For one thing, he was a lawyer. Had been for 10 years before getting into broadcasting.

For another thing, he didn't love the games. He did not swoon at the smell of a locker room. For a while, he did sports for ABC while also hosting a Sunday night radio program in which he grilled politicians and businessmen. He saw both roles as the same. He had to be clear and entertaining.

And he had to be right.

Cosell didn't get famous for yelling stupid things like "TIME OUT, BABEEE!" He got famous, quite frankly, for his guts, and he often had more than the athletes he covered. It was Cosell who had the nerve to take on white bigotry that wanted Jackie Robinson and Muhammad Ali squelched. It was Cosell who took on the labor issue hypocrisies in the NFL. It was Cosell who watched Larry Holmes pummel Randall (Tex) Cobb in an inexcusable bloodletting boxing match. Afterward, Cosell walked away. He quit boxing.

"The sport should be abolished," he said. Never mind that he was doing this, as critics point out, after he'd made a name for himself through the ring. So what? If you keep your eyes open, your opinions might change. He stood for something. Besides, tell me one other broadcaster who ever walked away from a gig.

On that autumn night in 1982, as he watched Cobb's face turn to jelly, Cosell half-whispered his analysis: "What is achieved by such as this?"

It's a question too few in his business ask. They don't ask "What is achieved?" when they make up stupid nicknames. They don't ask "What is achieved?" when they ramble on with statistics. They don't ask "What is achieved?" when they put any dweeb with a telephone on the airwaves to vent his spleen.

NOISE RULES THESE DAYS. Cosell was more than noise. He had a point. He stood for something. It is amazing when you see the old footage of fans throwing bricks through TV sets in protest of Howard. Nowadays, we sit mindlessly in front of brain-numbing programs, and we don't lift a finger.

Cosell did nearly 40 years at ABC, including 13 years on "Monday Night Football." Much of what you see in TV sports today — opinions, brashness — began with Cosell. By the end he was burned out, bitter because he was in a jealous business; his contemporaries quickly attacked.

He died lonely, with many bridges burned. In the hair-sprayed world of TV, you can see why Cosell once said, "My greatest accomplishment may be my mere survival."

That is gone now. In the end, he couldn't stop the big machine or lift the horizontal ladder of mediocrity.

Down goes a legend.

Those who follow should imitate his journalism, not his shtick, but as Cosell might put it, that would be asking too much even for a legend like himself.

Worship those who love baseball

April 26, 1995

"I believe in the church of baseball."

From the movie "Bull Durham"

ANAHEIM, CALIF. — We have a problem. We've had a fight. We have fallen out of love with the sport that used to define us, and now baseball has come back, holding flowers, asking for forgiveness. This will not come quickly. For some, it may not come at all. I begin to make my peace the way I knew I would once I arrived here, at the hotel, for tonight's Tigers opener against the Angels.

I call John Doherty's room. At 9 a.m. Sleeping. I call at 10. Still sleeping. I call at 11. Already, I'm weakening.

"Hel ... lo?" says the groggy voice.

"Nice of you to get up."

"Huh? ... Ummmzzmt. ... I'm up, I'm up."

You look for reasons to give baseball another chance? John Doherty is my reason. Here, under the covers of another road-trip hotel room, is a major league pitcher who still acts like a kid. He still looks like a kid. He still talks like a kid. Lord knows, he still *sleeps* like a kid. Sometimes I think John Doherty is part of a Disney movie that wandered off the set.

"Something to drink?" the waitress asks when he finally plops down at the table, just after noon.

"Chocolate milk," he says. Chocolate milk?

John Doherty is 27 years old, he pitches major league baseball — has a fastball that moves better than most — and this is how much he cares about money: He has never seen his bi-weekly paycheck. It gets sent home to his mother and father on Long Island, and he trusts they will take care of it.

He has no expensive habits, no house, no fleet of cars. He doesn't even have a bank card for cash. He lives pretty much off the envelopes they give him for per diem — $62.50 a day — and even that, he has left over.

"Look at me, I mean, whadda I need?" he says, in a Long Island accent as thick as the Hershey's syrup in his milk. "I wear sweatpants every day of my life. I don't own any $2,000 suits. If I'm running out of money, I tell my fiancee to bring some when she comes to visit me.

"I just wanna play baseball, you know?"

WE THOUGHT WE KNEW. We kidded ourselves into believing the game was the thing, that players were just happy to be there. We found out otherwise. We learned of unions, free agency, revenue sharing, lockouts. Baseball became a board room, contracts replaced the bat and ball, and in the most recent confrontation, the players walked out and took away the World Series.

John Doherty went home to Long Island, to his bedroom in his parents' house. And he slowly went nuts. At night he would go out with his old friends and play darts at a bar, and all the competitive juices would flow. "Take it easy," they would say, "it's just darts."

During the day he would drive his uncle, who lives upstairs, back and forth to work, or do some shopping for his mom. Day after day, he would go to his high school gym and throw pitches to his old coach, a former minor-leaguer named Dom Cecere. It was Cecere who used to parade among his players howling, "You gotta love this great American game of baseball!"

Now Doherty would throw to him, a major-leaguer just looking to break a sweat. One time he began to zone out, imagining himself back in The Show, ninth inning, 3-2 count … The ball began to hum. Then zip. Then hurt. "Yeoowch!" Cecere yelled, shaking his glove.

"What are you tryin' to do? Kill me?"

"Sorry," Doherty said. "For a second there, I thought I was back."

NOW, OF COURSE, THEY ARE BACK. The Tigers open tonight. The games count. But it still feels artificial. The anger remains. It takes some getting used to. So I concentrate on Doherty. I listen — as he gulps down eggs and toast, the breakfast menu, even though it is lunchtime — and he talks about how he flew to spring training early, because he was "pumped up," and how he asked whether he could ride to the airport to pick up Alan Trammell and Kirk Gibson, and how he has been wearing the same glove the last few years, a Cal Ripken model he bought at Herman's Sporting Goods for $45.

"John," his more savvy teammates told him, "companies will pay you money to wear their glove."

"Yeah," he said, "but I like this one."

Recently, he was told what the strike cost him in dollars. About $100,000. His reaction: "Whoa."

He has come back to play, he pitches Friday night in Seattle, and he freely admits, "I've always known how lucky I am." I ask whether he sympathized with the replacement players who tried to earn a moment in the sun.

"Yeah," he says, "but there's more to playing major league baseball than playing in a major league park."

Indeed there is. And some of his spoiled contemporaries had better learn it.

You gotta love this great American game. I think about that sentence. It's a new season, and for me, a new set of standards. I no longer care about the sneering Barry Bonds, the brooding Roger Clemens, or the wasted glory of Dwight Gooden and Darryl Strawberry. From this moment forward, my definition of a great ballplayer has nothing to do with talent.

My definition of a great ballplayer is now one who loves the game the way he should love it. That is my church. John Doherty is the first one in. The healing begins. Play ball.

Juwan Howard, promise-keeper
April 28, 1995

I WAS SUPPOSED TO HAVE TODAY OFF. And I could have used it. The red-eye flight from Los Angeles left me groggy and slow, tripping over my bags as I trudged through the airport. I had filled my weekly quota of columns. The cab dropped me off at home.

The sun was coming up. The bed looked mighty tempting.

Instead, I am filling this space because I owe it to the subject, because his story deserves an ending more than I deserve a nap. After all, he came back to finish what he started. The least I can do is follow suit.

Tomorrow in Ann Arbor, Juwan Howard, a millionaire, will walk down the aisle and get his college degree. On time. As promised. He is an NBA player, a budding star, he has corporations interested in him and agents drooling over him and enough money to get any luxury car he wants — without ever being asked for his educational credentials.

But on a cold November day five years ago, Juwan told the most important person in his life that he would graduate from college, be the first in his family to do so, and she kissed him a thank-you before saying good-bye.

That was the last time Juwan saw his grandmother alive. At the time, he was merely a high school player. He had no money, no guarantees, and when that day ended, he had no home — not if you define home as the place the person who raised you lives. Jannie Mae Howard died that afternoon, a heart attack, at the same hour her grandson was announcing he would play for Michigan.

It would have been easy, in the years that followed, to say, "My life has changed. I'm all alone. I have to take care of myself now. Forget what I said."

Juwan Howard doesn't forget. He doesn't forget his basketball fundamentals, he doesn't forget his manners.

And he doesn't forget his promises.

Would the candidates for graduation please rise? ...

I KNEW IF I KEPT PUSHING IT OFF, I'd never get it done," Howard said. "And I really wanted to do it. I know a lot of people doubted me. But — you're gonna think I'm crazy when I say this — the degree means more than the money I'm making. It's something I'll have and put on the wall and always be proud of."

When Howard announced he was leaving Michigan last April, after his junior year, some hearts were broken, other people were skeptical. They wondered whether his promise to graduate had any more weight than all the other promises before it — ones that were never kept. How many athletes have said "I'll be back" and never opened a book again?

Howard, in his own quiet way, said, "Watch me." He needed 32 credit hours and began to chip away by taking courses last summer, even before he was drafted by the Washington Bullets.

Signing a contract for $1.3 million this year didn't stop him. He studied communications on road trips and mailed in business papers from the nearest post office.

"We would see him on buses doing schoolwork, and we'd tease him about it," Bullets teammate Doug Overton said. "But we're very impressed."

They should be. A lot of athletes get to the NBA and feel compelled to fill the day with shopping, styling, making cellular phone calls about things that don't really matter — all the trappings of what they call "living large."

Howard lived large within himself. "It took me a few weeks to get used to NBA life, but after that, I saw that you have all this free time," he said. "Like after practice, you have the whole day to do what you want."

This is so true. Many pro athletes could do so much more with their lives. But they sit around watching ESPN, then act as though their days are stuffed.

Howard saw through this lie in a week.

So he took correspondence classes and independent study and on Saturday morning, his credits complete, he will stand beside his friends Jimmy King and Ray Jackson, the two Fab Fivers who never left, and he "will be so happy I might burst out crying."

Please come forward when your name is called. ...

THERE IS A LESSON HERE, of course. It has to do with commitment and priorities. It also has to do with not being a hypocrite.

"When I go out to speak," Howard said, "like at the NBA Stay in School Jam, what kind of message am I sending? I left after my junior year.

"But now I can say, 'Yes, I did leave school but I went back and got my degree.' And it didn't take any time at all. I'm not telling someone to be like me, but I think we're all role models out here."

All during his years at Michigan, Howard set the best example. He worked harder than most. He never got in trouble. He found time for charity work and hospital visits, and he befriended a young patient who lived two years longer than doctors predicted. His family thinks Juwan was the reason.

So Howard has a history of bending time. And now he bends it in his favor. The 6-foot-10 forward said the blue gown might be a little short — "The biggest they have is XXL, and that's for a guy 6-foot-6" — but he'll get by. He'll take pictures and toss his cap high into the air.

Juwan Howard, bachelor of arts, communications. ...

As for the most-asked question Saturday in Ann Arbor — "So, what are your future plans?" — Howard, already one of the most promising players in the NBA, has this response: "I'm coming back for my master's."

You can wake me for that story. Anytime.

Moeller: Spotlight, no illumination

May 5, 1995

O NE FALSE MOVE. THAT'S ALL you get now. One false move and they chop your head off, leave you hanging upside down in the spotlight. Too bad, see ya, thanks for joining us in The Public Life. A good man is without his job this morning. He might never coach again, all for a mistake that is made a thousand times every day all over this country. Gary Moeller's crime was not getting drunk and making a fool of himself — heck, they'd have to fire half the football people in America for that.

His crime was getting caught in the spotlight, and having his story dissected like a high school lab rat.

Shame on them, shame on every one at Michigan who let this hurricane of publicity blow them away from what they owed a good employee of 24 years: a chance to redeem himself.

And shame on us, every one in this business who grabbed those tapes of Moeller swearing at police, cursing at his wife, begging for forgiveness, and threw them right into the airwaves and headlines. What purpose did that serve? He never accused the police of harassment. He never denied being drunk. Yet we pasted him, lambasted him, then said how sorry we felt for him.

The American spotlight.

One false move.

"Doesn't Moeller deserve a second chance?" someone asked Joe Roberson, the U-M athletic director, once he had announced Moeller's "resignation." It followed the coach's recent arrest for disorderly conduct at a Southfield restaurant.

"Second chances are somewhat dependent on the circumstances that lost you your first chance," Roberson said. "In my view, given what has happened, it would have been quite difficult for Gary to have been an effective leader of the team."

Congratulations, Michigan. The law needed another week just to *arraign* Moeller; you have already sentenced him.

One false move.

N OW, IT'S TRUE, MICHIGAN was within its rights to do what it did. Moeller's contract clearly states that if he embarrasses the university in any way, it can terminate without pay. So agreeing to give him two-and-a-half years' worth of the remaining three years on his $130,000-per-year contract is more than generous, at least financially.

But bailing out on him because his incident became national news is only making the Media Beast bigger by surrendering to it.

Roberson's feeling was that, after the magnitude of this story, Moeller would have a hard time addressing future players about the dangers of bad habits. Roberson — and the school — felt that Moeller's drunken curses and pushing a cop cost him his credibility in the homes of future recruits, especially when the mothers ask, "Will you take care of my son?"

Well. Maybe, Joe. Don't be so quick to dismiss the healing power of time, and the short memory of the American public. We live in a country where the current mayor of Washington, D.C., was busted for drugs the *first* time he had that job. Teddy Kennedy is frequently parodied as a drunken windbag, yet is still one of the most powerful politicians in America. Here in Detroit, we have an admitted alcoholic anchorman back on TV — after yet another fall off the wagon — not only bringing us news, but shaping it.

And how many chances were college coaches from Jerry Tarkanian to Barry Switzer given before they finally were shown the door? More than one, I'll tell you that.

Sure, the news explodes these days, but it also fades quickly. It is quite possible that a year from now, this whole Moeller thing would be small in the rearview mirror. And perhaps Moeller would even be that much smarter, a symbol of someone who learned from his mistakes.

If so, Michigan made a terrible and hasty decision. If not, Roberson and President Jim Duderstadt could always have addressed it later. Why not try it? Are they so afraid in Ann Arbor of falling a step behind in the race for football supremacy that they forget about compassion and loyalty?

Are they so blinded by one-way dignity that they can't see the hypocrisy of a sport that accepts millions of dollars from beer companies, yet tosses a coach after one drunken incident?

And it was one drunken incident. Let's not forget that here. No one is suggesting that it wasn't a terrible thing for a head coach to do, or that he shouldn't have to pay a price — maybe go through a rehab or education program, even if he doesn't have a huge problem, just to show good faith.

But the feeding frenzy over Moeller makes it feel like he committed 30 crimes, when he didn't. One night. One incident. First offense. That's it. Moeller has no history of alcohol problems, no history of arrests, no history of bad behavior in public. He didn't kill anyone. Didn't hurt anyone. Didn't involve any of his players.

"I want to make it clear that my conduct last Friday is in no way indicative of an alcohol problem," Moeller said in a prepared text read by Roberson. "It does not reflect on any family difficulties between my wife, Ann, or any other member of my family.

"I have left my job as head football coach, but I still have my family and dignity."

What's left of it, after we got done chewing on it.

One false move.

A WORD HERE ABOUT THE "terrible" things Moeller said while intoxicated. How many *good* things have you heard from a drunken man's mouth? Once you accept that he was intoxicated — which he quickly admitted, even to the cops — you gain nothing from examining his statements. It's gibberish. Anyone who has ever had too much liquor at a New Year's Eve party can relate.

Would you have liked a tape on yourself then? Would you want a camera rolling in your bedroom when you and your spouse have a fight — and then see it on TV? This public gorging on Moeller's embarrassment was disgusting and completely unnecessary. What kind of society have we become when police automatically tape their arrests — to protect themselves from lawsuits — then release the tapes to the news media because of a Freedom of Information Act?

So many laws to protect our rights.

Then why does this feel so wrong?

And it is. Wrong. We all seem to know it. Yet no one seems able to do anything about it. Roberson is a good man, and he offered Moeller a good package, but he didn't save him. He seemed to feel he couldn't. And the rest of us? We shake our heads and cluck our tongues and say, "Too bad he didn't drink at home."

Shame on them, shame on us. Let every university board member who's never had too many martinis step forward. Let every provost and professor who's never yelled something vicious at his mate step forward, too. Let every reporter, anchor and talk-show host, every would-be hero and wannabe public figure who never did anything wrong, never argued with a cop, never got a little too loud in a bar, never did a single thing he'd like to have back, come forward right now, raise your hand.

And mark your time. We are all under the same gun now. We all have to play by the same spotlight rules that just sank Moeller. No mercy. No patience. One false move and everything you've done is washed away, you're on the dead pile, food for the vultures.

Some world we live in, huh?

Vernon goes underground
May 23, 1995

A S A MAN WHO WOULD LIKE to see a Stanley Cup come to Detroit before Bruce Willis makes *"Die Hard IV: My Hair Falls Out,"* I propose a deal with the city of Birmingham. That is the city in which the Red Wings' goalie, Mike Vernon, lives. Birmingham. Here is the deal:

If the Wings reach the Stanley Cup finals, you stop drilling your sewers until they capture the title, OK? Or better yet, how about stopping right now? Today? In the second round of the playoffs? This way, Vernon can get some sleep.

I'm not kidding. Every morning, around 7, the drills begin in Birmingham, rattling the quiet in Vernon's parkside neighborhood. "They're doing something with the septic systems," he says, rolling his eyes. "It's a racket."

This cannot be good for a goalie's nerves — as though a goalie had any left. Just think. You spend all night whacking pucks from your head, you take a long, hot shower, you drive home, settle into bed, close your eyes and …

Ratatatatatatatat!

I mean, come on, Birmingham, whose side are you on here? Sewers? Why not make something more indigenous to your area, like cappuccino?

No. Scratch that. Vernon doesn't need the caffeine. Already, the star of this team is a jumping jack. You watch him go through interviews, and you notice he talks quickly, he laughs, stops laughing, laughs again, sits forward, sits back. Maybe such darting motion is what makes him an ace in the net.

Then again, when I ask Vernon — who has won five of his six Wings playoff games — how he stays so calm on the ice, this is what he says: "I'm not as *not* nervous as you think."

And Birmingham wants to drill at 7 a.m.?

What is it trying to do, push him over the edge?

C LEARLY, SOMETHING MUST BE DONE. Vernon, when he allows a rare bad goal, already apologizes to his team by saying, "I fell asleep out there."

We don't want him to mean it.

I can just see the headlines: "WINGS LOSE; SEWERS BLAMED."

Or, "B'HAM CLOGGED; WINGS FLUSHED."

The saving grace in all this is that Vernon, a solidly built, wavy-haired, slightly cocky 32-year-old, was born to be a goaltender. Sleepy or not, even jackhammers couldn't shake him from his destiny.

This is a kid, raised in Calgary, the son of a hockey coach, who brought his pads to school and put them in the coatroom beside the other kids' boots. He says he never — *never* — played forward or defenseman.

"I wanted to play every minute, and goalies didn't sit the bench," he says.

When Vernon was 6, he was given a goalie mask. He took it home and spray-painted it green, the color of his team. (Of course, at 6, his team probably took naps between periods.)

The next day he wore the mask — even though it was still sticky — and when the game ended he took it off. The kids started laughing.

His face was covered in green paint.

You could say the job stained him right there. But it wasn't done testing his nerves. Vernon led the Calgary Flames to a Stanley Cup in 1989, then spent five years besieged by fans in his hometown. They wouldn't say hello in restaurants, in shops, in the street.

No. They would ask him questions. *"What about that goal last night? When are we going back to the finals? What about the other goal last night?"*

"It got to be that come the playoffs, I would only eat in places where I knew the owner and he could hide me in a back room," Vernon says.

It didn't help. After the glory of '89, Calgary, despite excellent regular seasons, never got past the first round of the playoffs. Things got so bad that, at one point, Vernon went to a local basketball game — to watch a team in which he was part investor — and the fans heckled him.

They heckled him — and he owned the team?

Whatever happened to executive privilege?

WAIT. WE'RE NOT THROUGH. Vernon decided to get married, and the week of the wedding, the Flames traded him to Detroit. Now. Anyone who has ever tied the knot knows the week of the wedding, you can blink and the bride and groom start screaming hysterically.

Yet here he was, traded half a continent away.

He remained calm. But somehow I think — despite his stellar performance so far — we don't need to push Vernon's nerves. True, he is the answer to last year's Detroit prayers (those prayers being "Get us some goaltending!"), and true, in his six Detroit playoff games he has a goals-against average of 1.67.

"The key is not being great," he says, "the key is being consistent."

Except in the playoffs, where, for goalies, the key is being consistently great. This is asking a lot. So we ask Birmingham a little.

Take June off, B-Town. Let Vernon get some sleep. Or drill at night. Or during road trips. The septic system isn't going anywhere. Besides, think of how happy your citizens will be if Vernon stays hot and the Wings win the Cup. There'll be loads of celebrations in Birmingham and people will drink lots of cappuccino — and maybe even feel kooky enough to run into a local store and pay $200 for a bathrobe.

I hope this works. I hope this makes Vernon sleep better. I am here to help. That is all that's bothering you, isn't it, Mike? "Actually, there's this bird that comes by every morning and makes a hell of a racket, too."

OK. Where's Ted Nugent?

Who needs a used Rodman?

May 26, 1995

W HEN PEOPLE HEAR THAT Dennis Rodman wants to blow his brains
out, sleep with men and play his last game in the nude, they say to
themselves, "Wow, that guy is crazy."

I say, "Must be another magazine article."

Rodman is a magazine publisher's dream. For one thing, he'll pose any way
you want. Because magazines sell mostly by their covers, getting Dennis to
photograph in hot pants and a dog collar — as he does on this week's Sports
Illustrated cover — is their idea of heaven.

Even better for magazines, Dennis will *say* anything you want. A few months
ago, he told GQ about Madonna's sexual technique. GQ reacted as if it had
unearthed the Dead Sea Scrolls. Now, this week, here comes Dennis again,
telling SI about his fantasies, and saying, "Madonna wanted to have my baby. ...
She has ways of making you feel like King Tut."

Of course, since King Tut is a mummy, I'm not sure this is a feeling you'd be
after. But that's beside the point. Sports Illustrated did the same thing GQ did, lit
the flares for its issue, sending out advance photos and advance quotes as if it had
this enormous scoop. *Run and read it! We get Dennis to open up! Death wishes!
Gay dreams! You won't believe what he told us!*

What SI, GQ and the rest *don't* admit is that they are using Rodman. Only
slightly less than he is using them.

A S SOMEONE WHO HAS KNOWN Rodman since the day he was drafted nine
years ago, I blink in awe of how far he has traveled, from a shy kid who
wheezed and coughed through his first interviews, to a publicity-starved
daredevil who isn't particularly smart, but has learned this much: Neither are the
people covering him.

So he runs across the board like a mouse on acid, and he sees in his rearview
mirror that people actually follow, trying to figure him out. He dresses a little
wilder, spits out a few crazy sentences, and the crowd behind him grows even
bigger. His bosses say, "You're trying our patience," but continue to show him
plenty. Meanwhile, the wilder he acts, the more people want to turn him into a
"genius."

This, by the way, was the pattern of Jim Morrison, Janis Joplin and John
Belushi. All of whom, not coincidentally, are dead from excess.

But never mind. America wants its celebrities, and we, the media, are only
too happy to create them. Rodman learned this from his dance with Madonna: To
steer your image, you steer the image-makers.

So Dennis takes a GQ writer to a tattoo parlor, and he takes an SI writer to a gay bar, and he mouths off and paints his body and markets himself into a perfect symbol of American Celebrity: nine parts noise, one part talent.

The shame is, in Dennis' case, he once was more than that. He was nine parts talent. But his survival hinged on separating that talent — basketball — from the Technicolor madness of his off-court life. When he played, he played like a demon. He focused on the game. He pursued the ball as if his life were inside it. I still remember him crying at halfcourt when the Celtics beat the Pistons in the playoffs. Crying?

No more. Rodman, 34, now says, "I'm not an athlete, I'm an entertainer." During Game 3 of the San Antonio Spurs' series against the Lakers, for no apparent reason, he made a scene, lying down during a time-out and covering his head in a towel. He wasn't used again until Game 5.

This week, in Game 1 of the Western Conference final against Houston, he zoned out in the closing minutes, blew an assignment, then took his shoes off rather than listen during the final time-out. His team lost.

This is a new low for Rodman — and maybe the one that, finally, his teammates do not forgive. You can monkey around, but not when you get within smelling distance of a championship. The playoffs used to mean everything to Rodman. Now he is hooked on hype and has brought his addiction into church.

It's the beginning of the end.

R ODMAN ALWAYS HAD AN ENTOURAGE, even here in Detroit, but it used to be kids, teenagers. He liked them. He trusted them. In San Antonio, the entourage is adults — models, businessmen, entertainers. This is significant. It means he has graduated to bloodsuckers.

It also means he has something bigger to worry about. Eddie Murphy and Mike Tyson are two of Rodman's contemporaries who did the Elvis Entourage bit. Both had rude awakenings.

Rodman's fall, when it comes, could be even worse. His talent — regardless of what his new friends claim — is basketball. That's it. He is not an actor. He is not a singer. He rebounds and plays defense. When that goes, the money goes.

And when the money goes, so do the "friends." With Dennis blowing $30,000 a pop at crap tables in Las Vegas, it won't take very long.

And at that sad point, Rodman will find himself staring at the man he was 12 years ago — an airport janitor with no idea what was about to happen to him. Rock stars won't find him cool anymore. Shoe companies will have other foils. The magazines that today so happily suck up his Crazy Juice will turn up their noses. Yesterday's news.

Can I tell you something? At that point, Dennis' saying "Sometimes I just want to blow my brains out" won't be amusing. It won't be hype. It will be a serious warning to the people who care about him.

If there's any of them left.

Keep octopi at arm's length

June 1, 1995

JOE LOUIS ARENA MIGHT NOT be the most modern facility in the world, but it's still the only place where any fan, no matter how much he paid for tickets, can get hit in the face with a fish.

I don't want to say there are too many octopi flying around the building. I will say the national anthem before Red Wings games now sounds like this:

"O'er the land ... of the ... (splat!) ... free ... (splat! splat!) ... and the home (splat-tat-tat-tat-tat!) of the ... (splat!) ... yuck."

Confess. What was once cute is now contagious. The octopus tradition has gotten out of hand-hand-hand-hand-hand-hand-hand-hand. (That is eight, isn't it?) The funny thing is, you never see anyone actually *walking in with them.* Which means fans hide these slimy critters in their purses, or their briefcases — or worse, under their shirts.

FAN: Hey, Fred! Long time, no see!

(Slaps Fred's stomach, hears squishy sound.)

FAN: Hmm. Still doing those sit-ups?

Now, based on my visit Wednesday to the local octopus outlet, a.k.a. Superior Fish in Royal Oak, tonight at the Joe could be Mollusk Mania. On an average playoff game day, Superior Fish sells — according to co-owner Kevin Dean, a wonderful man whose hand I refuse to shake — 25 octopi. *Twenty-five?*

We know these are for tossing at the Wings game because the customers used to ask, "How long do you cook it?" and now they say, "Do you have one with a really good grip?"

EMERGENCY PROCEDURE IF OCTOPUS LANDS ON SHOULDER

Step 1. Say quietly, "Honey, is that you?"

Step 2. If no answer, begin to shake violently.

Step 3. Hire lawyer from O.J. Simpson defense team.

Wait. Did you say you were from out of town? In that case, perhaps you don't know about the tradition of tossing an octopus on the Joe Louis ice, which used to happen once a year and now happens whenever the Red Wings complete a pass. OK. I know what you're thinking. "How did this strange tradition get started?" Frankly, this question has been asked so many times that we in Detroit are tired of answering it, but we will give the same explanation we have given everyone else, which is: "How the hell should we know?"

The most widely accepted theory, of course, is that former coach Jacques Demers, who used to throw his glasses after a big victory, once accidentally hit a fan, and that fan, who was a fish salesman, reached angrily into his bag and grabbed the first thing he could find and tossed it back, and that thing was, of course, a clock radio, which hit Jacques in the head and caused him to start speaking with a French accent, even though he was raised in Hoboken.

There is also this theory about eight legs and eight games to win the Stanley Cup. But, as you probably suspect, only fools go for that one.

COMMONLY HEARD EXPRESSIONS WHEN TOSSING OCTOPUS

1. "Incoming!"
2. "HERE ... WE ... GOOO ... oops, sorry, Ethel."
3. "Darn, I took the wrong purse."

Wait. Did I hear you ask for a solution?

Well, that would be appropriate, since clearly we have a problem. For one thing, the NHL is trying to build a national audience, and you can just imagine the family in Kansas trying to get into hockey, and they sit down one night and flip on ESPN just as Sergei Fedorov scores a goal and hey — here come the octopi! — and next thing you know, the kids are throwing up.

This would not be good for ratings.

Nor is it good for the Joe Louis ice. My extensive research has proven that, when an octopus is thrown from the lower-bowl seats, it lands as a small mess that vaguely resembles, to use the scientific term, vomit.

And no matter how hard they try to clean this up, there is always one little gunk stain left on the ice, and you spend the whole period watching to see whether famous NHL stars can skate through octopus guts.

ATTENTION: PROPER WAYS TO GRIP OCTOPUS

INCORRECT: By the head. This will feel like you sank your hand into a bowl of gray Jell-O. INCORRECT: By the leg. This will feel like you are shaking hands with the inside of a runny nose. INCORRECT: By the eyeball. This is ... ughh, yuck, I'm so disgusted, I can't speak.

By the way, fans are not the only ones to blame for Detroit's octopi epidemic. The Wings organization uses the slimy beast in many of its ads. And the team slogan for the Stanley Cup is "A Call to Arms," which, I suppose, is better than, "Hey! Let's Hit Someone in the Eye With a Tentacle!" — but still yields the same results.

Which is, of course, too many arms. And suckers. And single eyeballs. So, OK. We have, as they say in the military, a situation here. We don't want to make people stop buying octopi because that wouldn't be fair to merchants, some of whom might have tried to bribe journalists with some nice salmon steaks if they mentioned their name, which I wouldn't do for THE SUPERIOR FISH COMPANY or anyone else.

And we don't want to confiscate the octopi at the door because it already takes too long to get into Joe Louis Arena, and besides, how'd you like to be the guy who has to collect them? It's not like taking ticket stubs.

So the only solution I see for tonight's showdown against the Blackhawks is this: When the Wings score a goal, take out your octopus, swing it wildly over your head ... and throw it at someone from Chicago.

Tell 'em it's for Michael Jordan.

Limp in, moonwalk out
June 4, 1995

M Y PHILOSOPHY OF LIFE IS SIMPLE: Anything you can do lying down is OK by me. Which is how I came to be here, Joe Louis Arena, pulling a mask over my nose and mouth and sliding into the infamous hyperbaric chamber that now sits behind the Red Wings locker room. The chamber has made quite a stir as the latest techno edge in sports. As I understand it, you put injured or fatigued hockey players inside, they breathe pure oxygen for around half an hour, and they come out as Michael Jackson.

No. Actually, they are supposed to come out healthier. As Jim Flannery, the smiling technician with this OxyMed chamber, says, "Oxygen speeds up the healing process for injuries," so we should think of the chamber as "the ultimate ice pack" — the only difference being if you place the chamber on your head, you'll be crushed to death.

"Are you ready?" he says, closing the lid.

"Mmmphzt," I say.

You don't have to be naked or anything. But you do wear that mask, which makes it hard to speak. Eventually, you start acting like fighter pilot Chuck Yeager, smiling and giving the thumbs-up sign through the glass, even if what they're saying outside is, "Should we blow up the chamber now?"

"All set?" Jim asks.

Thumbs up.

"Here we go."

Thumbs up.

"I'm going to lower you one atmosphere."

Thumbs ... u ... what?

N OW, PERSONALLY, I DON'T EVEN like long car rides. So I definitely don't want to leave my atmosphere, especially without a change of underwear.

"It's just a term," Jim says through the exterior microphone, as my ears begin to pop. "We're pressurizing the chamber. That's how they measure pressure, by atmospheres. One atmosphere. Two atmospheres."

Hmm. A few more, I'll be able to visit Dennis Rodman.

I should mention here that I am breaking no rules. John Wharton, the excellent trainer for the Red Wings, agreed to let me try the chamber, in between Slava Fetisov and Slava Kozlov. Sort of a Slava sandwich.

Many Red Wings are now using the chamber, which is about the size of a coffin, if the person you're burying plays for the Dallas Cowboys. Perhaps Wings like it because there are no phones inside, and you get to watch TV. Also you can't hear the coach yelling at you.

Speaking of the coach, Scotty Bowman, who's normally rather secretive, escorted me right to the chamber, and said, "Let Mitch go in and try it."

Maybe he thought I'd come out as a foreign correspondent.

"The oxygen should start now," Jim says. "Breathe regularly."

I should mention that, before I got here, I kicked myself hard in the shin. Since the whole idea of these tanks is to heal quickly, I figured I should enter with an injury. Steve Yzerman is trying to recover from knee surgery by using this chamber. The Blackhawks' Gary Suter is using one for his bad hand.

Chambers work, experts say, because what you breathe inside is 100 percent oxygen, while the air we normally breathe is 20 percent oxygen, 70 percent nitrogen, and 10 percent exhaust fumes from Chinese restaurants.

"I heard Michael Jackson sleeps in one of these," I'd told Wharton.

"Nah. If you took in that much oxygen, you'd start acting really kooky."

Well. Like I said.

WHHHHHHHUUUU. WHHHHHHAAA. I breathe in. I breathe out. This is not my first encounter with a closed chamber. A few years back, I tried a flotation tank, which is supposed to relax you, so you can do more with your life. This, of course, is necessary if you spend two hours a day floating in the dark.

"You OK in there?" Wharton asks. There is a hissing sound, and some smoke from condensation.

"We're bringing you back up. Slava needs to get in."

A few minutes later, my ears pop again, and I hear the latch unbolt. I expect a flight attendant to say, "Ladies and gentlemen, welcome to Kennedy Airport … "

Instead, there's Jim, all smiles.

"How do you feel?" he asks.

"Billie Jean is not my lover."

"Huh?"

Just kidding. I feel fine. And my leg even stopped throbbing — although, to be honest, I didn't really kick myself very hard. Anyhow, the lesson is: Do not fear technology, no matter how weird. In fact, I heartily recommend the hyperbaric chamber for all the Wings.

The only drawback for me, personally, is that — and this is really small — when they shut the chamber lid, there was a fly in there with me, and now I have a fly's head.

Other than that, I feel great.

Guess who's coming for Stanley?

June 12, 1995

S O THIS IS HOW YOU MAKE HISTORY. You wait until after the midnight hour, double overtime, when the voices are gone and even the sweat glands are exhausted, then send a young Russian — whose last name is easier to pronounce than his first — charging down the ice, have him wind up and fire and … bingo! With a game so exhausting it took two days to play, the Detroit Red Wings finally jumped the moat and are outside the castle, banging on the door with an octopus.

Knock, knock, Stanley.

Guess who's coming for dinner?

For 29 years, the men who pulled on Detroit sweaters were always pulling them off before the championship finals. They were golfing, boating, fixing the house, while others skated in the Big Show. Last night — and this morning — the 1995 Wings made history by playing desperate, double-overtime hockey, dominating the ice, protecting their net and chopping relentlessly at the last obstacle in their way — a rock-solid Chicago goaltender named Ed Belfour — until finally, finally, after 82 minutes and 46 shots, the rock crumbled and fell, and the Promised Land was revealed.

Detroit 2, Chicago 1.

Knock, knock.

"What do you think making the finals will mean?" someone had asked Kris Draper before this game.

"Well, when I was a kid, there was this guy in my neighborhood, he won a Stanley Cup with the Islanders, and when he came back home, we went to his house for a party," he said. "And there was this big cake, shaped like the cup, and everybody was congratulating him, and I remember thinking, 'This is it. This is why I want to play hockey.' "

Knock, knock.

Wasn't this the answer to all those childhood dreams? A night Red Wings fans had waited for since their dads were teaching them how to *be* Red Wings fans. Overtime. Every shot sticking in the throat. Denis Savard leading a three-on-one break that surely spelled doom, then mysteriously losing control, and Nicklas Lidstrom getting in the middle and stealing the puck away. Doug Brown, wide open, taking a perfect feed from Sergei Fedorov, whacking the puck with everything he had, and Belfour — Mr. Magnificent — absorbing it like a bulletproof vest. Mike Vernon, doing the same on a point-blank shot from Joe

Murphy, with nobody between them, knocking it away, and in the second overtime, Murphy clanging one off the post. It was bodies flying. Oxygen disappearing.

And finally, Slava Kozlov, who hadn't scored a point this series, pulling up and firing through Belfour's legs, and the arena came unglued.

What a perfect fit! What a perfect finish, a Sunday night show in Detroit the way Ed Sullivan used to be a Sunday night show in America. Everyone was watching, you screamed when your neighbors screamed. And at 12:17 a.m., the whole town seemed to scream at once.

Knock, knock, Stanley.

Remember us?

WHAT A REMARKABLE PLAYOFF RUN — and an incredible conference final that will never be appreciated by the game count. Wings four, Hawks one? This was so much closer. All the Wings' wins were by one goal, three in extra periods. There were heroics in the net and heroics from the back of the chorus line, guys you'd never expect, a double-overtime winner from Vladimir Konstantinov, a tying goal from tough guy Stu Grimson, a game-winner from Draper — whom the Wings acquired for $1 from Winnipeg — even a 58-foot slap shot from Lidstrom, quietest guy on the team.

And the final game, with Kozlov continuing the string of unlikely stars.

No, this is not the end — the finals will start Saturday against New Jersey — but it is a foothold on the mountain, and a pause to take in the view. Finally, a chance for Steve Yzerman and Shawn Burr, Red Wings for more than a decade, to skate out before a national TV audience in June. Finally a chance for Mike Ilitch — who, no matter what you think of his ticket prices, has sunk more money into Detroit sports than any other man in history — to at least taste life in the big show.

Finally a chance for the national media to come to downtown Detroit for some other reason besides bashing it.

This is for all the "supposed to" years, when the Wings were supposed to beat San Jose, supposed to beat Chicago, supposed to beat Toronto. When Bryan Murray was supposed to have enough talent to get there. When Jacques Demers was supposed to inspire his young group over the rainbow.

And this is for all the years when nobody expected anything, that bleak period in the '70s when Detroit hockey was a sad joke, when "Dead Wings" was a more common — and sometimes more accurate — moniker for this team.

People outside Detroit may not understand why this town goes so crazy.

You know what?

Who cares?

Knock, knock.

Y OU CAN PICK A MOMENT from last night and wring the sweat from it. The overtime was choking — so were the final minutes of regulation — but to truly appreciate what the Wings were up against, you looked at the second period.

The Wings were a lightning storm. They peppered Belfour with shot after shot — 20 before the period was over, compared to two for the Blackhawks — and yet Belfour was a duck in a firing range, eluding every one. Fedorov had a point-blank chance on a perfect feed by Brown, he fired — and Belfour caught it falling down, like a shortstop snagging a liner up the middle. Keith Primeau had one close-range whack after another — all died in Belfour's body, his pads, his stick.

Finally, either the odds or exhaustion took hold, and on Detroit's 17th shot in a row — 17 in a row? — Yzerman, who hadn't scored a goal since May 23, yanked the puck off the boards, curled and fired, and suddenly the crowd was roaring and Yzerman was jumping off the ice, both arms raised, as if ready to hug the air.

Which, by the way, was raining octopi.

"That was amazing," Darren McCarty said between periods. "Steve is the heart and soul of this team."

Think then, what making these finals means for the captain, who for all these years has been the NHL's Best Player To Go Home Early. In the years when he, Gretzky and Lemieux were mentioned in the same sentence, it was always the other two winning and Yzerman waiting.

Not anymore. Let them watch for a change. Here was Yzerman finally holding up a trophy — the Clarence Campbell Bowl — and shaking it. Was that nice, or what?

And how about Paul Coffey, who has won four Stanley Cups and hungers for another like a vampire hungers for more blood? All the times his teammates asked him what it's like, and what could he say? "It's bleeping great," he would answer. Last night, they got to see just how bleeping great it was.

There's Mark Howe, 40, who was in the womb the last time the Wings won a Cup (1955), and Martin Lapointe, who gets to see the finals at age 21. There are Russians, such as Fedorov and Fetisov and Kozlov, who get to see how this thing they've always heard about — the Stanley Cup finals — really feels.

There's goaltender Mike Vernon, who was the golden boy of Calgary the last time he went to the finals — 1989 — and hasn't won a playoff round since. Can you spell redemption?

And, of course, there's the coach, Scotty Bowman, whose behavior is often enigmatic, except for one thing: His interest is in winning. Only winning. He has walked away with the NHL's prime rib six times before, and now, in his 60s, he dares to try it again. Say what you will about timing, players, authority, and the other excuses previous coaches used. Bowman is the guy to get them there.

A few days before this game, Dino Ciccarelli was having his morning coffee and talking about the only time he has been to a finals, 15 years ago with Minnesota. "The guys were asking me about it the other day, and they said, 'Aw, you don't even remember it.' And I said (bleep) I don't. I remember it like it was yesterday.

"It was 83 degrees outside, Sunday afternoon, we beat Calgary, and when we walked out the ramp, it looked like the biggest tailgate party in the world, there was a billboard that said "Way To Go Stars," there was music playing, people laughing and congratulating us."

That's the kind of crystal memory you get in moments like this. So years from now, the new boys of summer will remember this: a cool summer night that turned to early summer morning, with nearly every TV set in the city tuned to the same channel, and a final roar that shook the very girders of Joe Louis Arena, as a red-and-white rainbow began to form over the city.

Knock, knock, Stanley.

Daddy Octopus is coming.

Bowman defines staying power

June 16, 1995

SCOTTY BOWMAN LOSES IT. Not his temper, his ring. He had been playing with it, rolling it around, and it flew out of his hand and rolled under an orange seat in the Tiger Stadium mezzanine. Next thing you know, the 61-year-old coach of the Red Wings — the man some call a genius, others call a dictator, but none, absolutely none, calls warm and fuzzy — is poking under the seats like a kid, amid the peanut shells and hot dog wrappers, trying to get his ring back.

"It went over here," he tells some fans, who quickly join the search. "You see it? …"

The ring is from the Hockey Hall of Fame, where Bowman has his own plaque. Most people with that honor are retired, or dead. Bowman, the serious son of a Scottish blacksmith, is neither. He has won more games than any other coach in the history of hockey, six Stanley Cup championships, about to try for another, a virtual living legend — who, at the moment, bending over the seats in the fifth inning of a baseball game, hardly looks the part.

"You see it? … No? … How about over there? …"

Bowman has that short but powerful stature that goes well with tough coaches, a frank face, thin lips, jutting chin, straight brown hair that has vanished up front. He wears muted colors, even in casual dress, and on his barrel-chested body, clothes fit as if ordered to stand at attention.

Nothing sags on Bowman. He is a straight-line guy. He sees point B from point A and figures how to get there. He will not share his angst, nor spill his beans, he will not call a radio talk-show psychiatrist for advice. His dream relationship with the media is summed up by a coach he knew years ago, who used to write the press releases himself.

"He would write, 'So and so is hurt today,' or 'Such and such's father is visiting from out West, they're going fishing,' " Bowman recalls. "Then he handed the reporters the news, and he was done with it."

Oh, if it were only that easy! Then Scotty Bowman could control everything!

But it is never that easy. People talk about Bowman — especially this week, with the Red Wings in the Stanley Cup finals against New Jersey — and you hear the same old Bowman folklore, tales of rigid discipline, explosive temper, a devious mind that used to ask players for matches — even though he didn't smoke — so he could read the matchbook covers and see where the team was hanging out after hours.

And yet Bowman, like most serious, private people, has reasons for what he does, and incidents that provided those reasons. He is a paradox. This is a man who seeks maturity in his players, yet loves model trains and collects trading cards. A guy they call old-fashioned, who used videotape before other coaches knew what it was. A guy who takes heat for still living in Buffalo, yet who never talks about the handicapped son he doesn't want to uproot.

This is also the man, you might recall, who began his career in Detroit by benching popular forward Shawn Burr — and now Burr is one of Bowman's biggest supporters.

"Scotty gets your attention," Burr says.

That he does. As the search for the ring continues, a vendor slides over, points to Bowman's back, and whispers, "You think he can win the Cup? You think he can get it done?"

Bowman? He finishes what he starts — no matter how long it takes.

HE WAS LYING ON THE ICE at the Montreal Forum, a piece of his skull lying next to him. The crowd was pointing in hushed disbelief. A defenseman named Jean-Guy Talbot — who had already committed four penalties in this Junior A playoff game — now stood over young Scotty Bowman. Seconds earlier, Talbot, frustrated at his team's imminent defeat, had chased Bowman on a breakaway and clubbed him from behind, smacking him on the cranium, slicing his head open.

This was 1951. No one wore helmets. Bowman was unconscious. Talbot had blood on his stick.

"There were only 30 seconds left in the game," Bowman says now. "I think about that sometimes. What if the game had been 30 seconds shorter?"

Instead, Bowman was rushed to a hospital. They stitched his skull back together and inserted a metal plate that is still there. He spent three weeks in the hospital and the whole off-season fighting headaches. He tried a comeback. It didn't take.

He had been a promising forward, with a dream of making it big.

At 18, his playing career was over.

Yet it is the mark of Bowman's life that years later, as a coach, he hired Talbot to play for him in St. Louis. No grudges. No revenge. Finish that chapter. Close the book.

"Jean just lost control," Bowman says, shrugging. "He wrote me a long letter explaining it, pouring his heart out. I figure he just started me on my career 15 years earlier than planned."

Does this sound like a man who believes in fate? Well. Consider this: When he was a child, Bowman's mother took him and his siblings back to Scotland for a visit. They were supposed to stay a month, but, because of illnesses, wound up staying a year. Finally, they returned to Canada on a boat called the Athena.

On its return to England, the Athena was blown up by German torpedoes.

"I timed that out pretty well, eh?" Bowman says.

W ITH HIS PLAYING DAYS GONE, Bowman — whose father never missed a day of work in 31 years of pounding sheet metal — was training to be a paint salesman when his first real coaching chance came along with the Junior Canadiens. "I was learning all the numbers of paints, all the combinations. It wasn't bad, a steady job."

Instead, he began to dot the hockey canvas, moving up the ranks from kids to juniors to assistant in the NHL with the expansion Blues. Bowman had an eye for detail and a feel for the bench. One night, he suggested that St. Louis coach Lynn Patrick not use a certain defenseman on a shift. Patrick used him anyhow, and the opposing team scored.

The following morning, Patrick called Bowman and said, "I think this coaching business has passed me by."

Bowman took over the next game and led the previously dismal Blues to the Stanley Cup finals — not in five years, not in three years. *That* year. The finals? In his first try?

So began an amazing pro career in which Bowman soared to the top, making three straight finals appearances in St. Louis, winning five Stanley Cups as coach of the Montreal Canadiens — finishing what he started at the Forum all those years ago — winning another as coach of the Pittsburgh Penguins, and now, bringing the Wings to a place they haven't been in 29 years. It would take all day to list Bowman's accomplishments in the NHL — or the number of times he took himself out from behind the bench, only to return. Ironically, it was 10 years ago *this week* that Bowman stepped down as coach of the Buffalo Sabres and told the press corps: "As a coach, I've reached the level I wanted to reach."

Yet here he is, back again.

The most interesting part of Bowman's coaching career, however, isn't the statistics, or the five-year absence to be a TV analyst, or the unpredictable moves he has made during games, or the combative relationship he has had with the press. It's the touch. He seems to swing a hammer, yet the effects are very subtle. He took a Wings team known for high-powered offense and molded it into a defensive jewel. Like a serious potter, he doesn't stop until the clay is shaped.

He finishes what he starts.

"When I come in, I'm trying to get a team to believe in one another," he says. "That's what matters. It's OK if they don't like the coach. They can not like the coach or the general manager — but if they like one another, they got a chance."

Bowman doesn't seem worried whether they like the coach. Ken Dryden, the former Montreal goalie, once wrote of him: "He is not someone who is easy to like. He has no coach's con about him. He does not slap backs, punch arms or grab elbows. He is shy and not very friendly. … He is complex, confusing and unclear in every way but one. He is a brilliant coach, the best of his time."

Bowman probably liked that praise because it goes in several directions and then hits you with the point — much like his coaching.

For example, Bowman once thought his players were getting too self-bloated, so he scheduled practices around rush-hour traffic, "just to remind them what life is like for regular people." He frequently made forwards play defense in practice, and defensemen play forward, just to give them a better understanding of each other. Bowman had his guys keeping their own plus-minus statistics in little notebooks, long before the NHL did it on computers. And he admires the coach who once was so frustrated with his team's inability to score that he brought the net into the middle of the locker room and put a puck on top of it, to remind them of how small one was compared to the other.

Legend also has it that Bowman once got so mad at a player that he told him to go to the airport and then call him because "by that point I'll know who I traded you to."

He laughs at that, says he doesn't remember it at all.

A N EVENING BREEZE BLOWS THROUGH the stadium seats, where a couple of kids have joined the search for the ring. Bowman goes to Tiger Stadium now and then, on his own, just as he goes to his regular restaurants and coffee stops. He is a loner, but in typical complex fashion, he is a loner because he is a family man.

Many people don't know this. They see a gruff old coach whose family and house are in Buffalo and who commuted to his job in Pittsburgh and who now rents a home in Bloomfield Hills during the season. They see this and they say, "The guy is not committed. He's a mercenary."

Actually, it's quite the opposite. Bowman, who is married and has four healthy children, also has a 23-year-old handicapped son named David, who was born with hydrocephalus, better known as water on the brain.

"He was 7 weeks old when we found out," Bowman says. "Today, they'd pick it up while the baby was still in the womb."

Instead, the operation to relieve the pressure — "it was probably two days too late," Bowman said — also cost David his eyesight. His life has been a difficult series of treatments and special schools. Bowman remembers one night during the playoffs when David had to undergo an operation.

"Here I was, worried about this hockey game, and then I thought about what he had to go through. I said to myself right then, this game is not about life and death."

Over the years, with David in a special New York school for the blind, Bowman did not want to uproot the family. So he commuted during his years as a

TV analyst with "Hockey Night in Canada" and he commuted when he got the job in Pittsburgh and, yes, he goes home when he can with this job in Detroit.

But when he is here, he leads a somewhat nomadic life, often leaving his rented house in the morning and not returning until late at night. "I stay at the arena all day sometimes, eat there, watch the out-of-town games." At other times, he has a late dinner by himself at Big Daddy's Parthenon, a Greek restaurant in West Bloomfield, where the owners set him up with a private table near a TV set. He has a regular cup of coffee at Art Moran's car dealership, and he lunches every day with a Birmingham investment guy named Lenny — just out of habit. Bowman believes in streaks and omens and luck, so when he finds a restaurant — and company — that coincides with a winning streak, he keeps going back.

"Beau Jacks has worked for us, and so has this place called Boodles."

How about that? Six Stanley Cups, and he thinks a restaurant has something to do with it.

BOWMAN SAYS THIS IS HIS last coaching job. "No more after this. Mr. Ilitch told me when he hired me: 'When you're done coaching, I'd like to have you in the organization.' That would interest me."

So, of course, would one more Cup. When asked how a private man like himself would celebrate another championship, he shrugs. Says he plans to go to Scotland this summer, but then, he's doing that regardless.

Down on the field, the Tigers end an inning. The crowd rises to stretch. And finally, Bowman suddenly pops up, too, holding the missing ring.

"There it is," he says.

The kids lean in, and he shows it to them. They coo. As he slides it on, the man who, in 61 years, has left in his rearview mirror a doomed boat, a split head, six Stanley Cups and a litany of hockey influence from Guy Lafleur to Mario Lemieux to Jacques Lemaire, holds out his hand and smiles.

"This was a good omen," Bowman says, looking at the ring. "It means we're gonna get another one."

Uh-oh.

Nick at night: Big in Sweden
June 20, 1995

E ACH DAY, THE DOOR OPENS, and the reporters charge inside. They fan across the locker room and surround the biggest stars. Sergei Fedorov gets a big group. Paul Coffey gets a big group.

Steve Yzerman gets a big group.

Nicklas Lidstrom gets the two guys from Sweden. Day after day. Game after game. They sit by his locker and converse slowly, as if having a cup of coffee. They are there for one reason: to write about Nick. Nick at night. Nick in the morning. Just Nick.

"What about tonight's game, Nick?" they will ask today.

"What about last night's game, Nick?" they will ask tomorrow.

They speak in Swedish. They take notes and nod. No hurry, no rush. They are a foreign island in an ocean of American and Canadian media at the Stanley Cup finals. Their assignment is clear: Get Nick. Just Nick.

"How does it feel to be in the semifinals, Nick?" they asked last week. "How does it feel to be in the finals, Nick?" they asked this week.

Their stories go, every day, to several Swedish newspapers, including one in Vasteras, Nick's "hockey" hometown — which is not the same as his actual hometown, Avesta. But then, you would know this if you were Swedish. "What happened in Game 1, Nick?"

"What will happen in Game, 2, Nick? … "

To everyone else, Nicklas Lidstrom might be the quietest man in the Detroit locker room. If you are an American reporter, you know this: He is an excellent defenseman, he is the best-conditioned athlete on the team, he is thin, blond, extremely polite — and not exactly your first choice for a quote.

Unless you're Swedish. "We have only two players left," laments Jan Larsson, one of the two Swedish reporters who make a daily habit of Lidstrom. "It is either Tommy Albelin from New Jersey, or Nick from Detroit. That is all."

Just Nick.

W HAT DO YOU TALK TO them about?" I ask Lidstrom, after his countrymen have gone. "Oh, many things," he says, "what I think about the media, or what is the difference between this and the world championships."

Lidstrom could answer in English. But nobody asks. For some reason, in these media-soaked finals, most reporters ignore him. They go to Dino Ciccarelli, Shawn Burr, Mike Vernon. Never mind that Lidstrom, 25, is a key to the defense, a key to the power play, a wicked slap-shooter, and maybe the most admired player by his teammates.

Never mind. Most reporters figure he's Stefan Edberg on skates. All talent, no talk. What they don't know is that these Stanley Cup finals are broadcast live in Sweden at 2 a.m., and that Lidstrom's friends there leave thoughts on his answering machine.

And they don't know that Lidstrom was a New York Islanders fan growing up because the Islanders had Swedish players, or that the food he misses most is meatballs and mashed potatoes, or that he is the only son of a foreman and a cafeteria worker who live in a town that is famous for — and I am not making this up — a tree. A tree?

"You know the story of King Gustav in the 1600s?" he asks.

Sure. Great story. I was telling it at a party the other nigh—

"In the 1600s, Denmark tried to capture Sweden, and King Gustav hid inside a tree. It was a big tree, and he crawled inside, and they didn't find him."

And this tree is in your hometown? "Yes."

Is it a big tourist attraction? "No."

Is there a museum or a monument? Is there a plaque? Anything?

"No. Just the tree."

Those nutty Swedes. Can they party, or what? By the way, I ask the two Swedish reporters, Larsson and Bengt Eriksson, if they know about the tree.

"What tree?" they ask, looking at each other. "Maybe you mean the Dala horse." The Dala horse?

"It's a famous type of Swedish woodcarving. And the biggest one in the world is maybe 60 feet high, and painted red and yellow. It's in Avesta."

Wait a minute. Besides the tree, there's a 60-foot wooden horse in Nicklas Lidstrom's hometown?

"Right near the highway," Eriksson says, proudly. "You're surprised, yes? Usually, when you think biggest in the world, you think of America?"

Not when it comes to wooden horses.

A NYHOW, THIS IS WHAT YOU pick up in the quieter corners of the locker room. Lidstrom is a hero back in Sweden, even though he left when he was 21 and jumped straight to the NHL. Kids back home wear his jersey. Had he stayed a few more years, he might be as popular as Mats Sundin. Says Larsson, "This championship is very important for Nick's reputation in Sweden."

So this evening, when the Wings host the Devils, at least one foreign town has a rooting interest. And at least two reporters already know their angle. Nick at night. Nick in the morning.

Get Nick.

And, by the way, in case the Wings lose, and you're really upset, just remember: Somewhere, thousands of miles from here, there's a big wooden horse that wishes like hell it could get to a TV set.

From heaven to hell

June 26, 1995

E AST RUTHERFORD, N.J. — Down the hall you could hear the noise, the screams and cheers of a championship party. Bright lights beamed for TV reporters as champagne-soaked players hugged wives, parents, pretty much anyone who passed by. NHL officials raced back and forth, using walkie-talkies to monitor the location of the large silver cup, the Stanley Cup, which was bouncing happily from one New Jersey Devil to another. Security guards loosened their ties, wiped away the sweat and high-fived guests. "Unbelievable!" one of them yelled over the din. "Is this unbelievable, or what?"

Up the hall, Steve Yzerman, dressed in a gray suit, stepped out from behind a big steel door and stood there, all alone. He crossed his arms and looked down. Yzerman is not usually alone after a hockey game, not for long, so this was one of those accidental moments when he almost didn't know what to do. He listened to the party noise for a moment. As usual, it was someone else's party.

"You know what I was thinking tonight?" he said. "All during the third period, when the fans started their cheer and there was all that excitement in the building? I kept wishing I was in their shoes."

He sighed. "Right now, I don't feel much like a Stanley Cup finalist."

Six months of heaven, seven days of hell. This will be the last sad hockey column in a tornado of sad hockey columns lately, which is strange because Detroit didn't start writing sad hockey columns until last week. Until then, things were happy and fresh, full of miracle and wonder. The best team in the business. Home-ice advantage. Big bold predictions. The end of Lord Stanley's 40-year curse. Then came the puck drop, 8:20 p.m. June 17, and from that Saturday night until the next Saturday night, the bad news didn't stop. It was like a broken pipe in the basement.

Six months of heaven, seven days of hell.

"We were on the top of the world," Yzerman said wistfully, as if talking about high school. Someone asked whether what Paul Coffey had said was true: That losing in the finals hurts just as much as losing in the first round.

Yzerman nodded. "Maybe more."

Around the corner, standing by the bus, Coffey was dressed for the trip home. Someone asked his thoughts right after the sweep. "In American sports," he said, tapping his shoe on the concrete floor, "one day you're on top, the next day, you're a piece of bleep." He coughed. "Pardon my French."

S IX MONTHS OF HEAVEN, seven days of hell. It might be therapeutic to give a moment to the highs: The quick work made of the Dallas Stars. The splendid retribution against the San Jose Sharks. The nail-biting overtimes against the

Chicago Blackhawks. The feeling during those first three playoff rounds was invincibility, a bulletproof chest. The Wings could pile on the goals, but they could also bruise and bump. When they needed heroes, they just took turns, Nicklas Lidstrom whacking a 58-foot slap shot to win it, or Slava Kozlov poking in a breakaway in double overtime. Injuries didn't stop them. Enemy crowds didn't stop them. They were good *and* lucky.

And next thing you knew, Yzerman was shaking the Western Conference trophy over his head at Joe Louis Arena, and we had the wildest hockey moment ever in that building. Remember? This was when Mike Vernon was saying, "Aw, shucks, no big deal," instead of ducking reporters who questioned his big-game nerve in the finals. This was when Shawn Burr was laughing through his playoff goatee, instead of looking down, in tears, his face clean-shaven, having been benched for the first time in his playoff career.

Remember? This was when Coffey was the Socrates of the locker room, instead of the guy who didn't come up big, who was lying on the ice, in pain from a puck, when the winning goal was scored in Game 2. "What would you change if you could do this series over?" Coffey was asked.

"For starters," he said, "I wouldn't go down to block that shot."

What would they change? Vernon could have played much better. The defense could have played much better. The offensive stars, Yzerman, Kozlov, Ray Sheppard, Sergei Fedorov, could have played much better. The coaches could have done better.

You know what? It might not have mattered. Detroit fans forget there was another team here, and its players *also* wanted the Cup desperately. The Devils had talent. The Devils had motivation. They grabbed this series early, like a wrestler making a quick takedown. After that, it was just a question of the pin.

As THE BUS COUGHED OUT exhaust fumes, Keith Primeau made his way down the tunnel. The party noise grew more distant.

"I had wanted to watch them get the Cup," Primeau said. "I wanted it to hurt as long as it could. That way I never forget it."

"Why didn't you?" he was asked.

"Because my team went off the ice. We came on the ice as a team, we go off the ice as a team."

Credit them for that, for sticking together through this collapse, for not pointing fingers, not calling names. Credit them for beating first-round jinxes, for sacrificing stardom for team play, for going farther than the 28 Wings teams before them.

Six months of heaven, seven days of hell. This is the last sad hockey column. In a few weeks, the bitterness will be gone, and some of the Wings will begin to work out, break a sweat and think, as athletes must do — as good fans do, too — about a new season, when the end will be better than the beginning, and the final party will not be down the hall.

As American as Sampras
July 10, 1995

WIMBLEDON, ENGLAND — Boris Becker stood at the baseline and covered his eyes, like a child playing hide-and-seek. Later he would say, "I had the same chance of hitting his serve with my eyes closed as I did with them open." Perhaps, deep down, he was also hoping that when he lifted his hands, Pete Sampras would disappear.

No such luck. Boris peeked. And Sampras was still there, his expression the same, his machete — er, racket — rising to deliver the blow. Whump! Here came another ace. And whump! There goes another Wimbledon, stuffed into Sampras' pocket like the second ball he so rarely needs. Take your hands off your eyes, America. Pistol Pete isn't going anywhere.

And, to be honest, why should he? Here is a guy who, at age 23, has now won as many Wimbledons as John McEnroe and Jimmy Connors in their *entire careers.* He is the only American to ever take three straight. That's history, folks. Yet pockets of fans all over the world are already making like Becker, closing their eyes and hoping Sampras' bland persona and quick-death serves will somehow disappear.

Wait a second. Maybe the rest of the world can get away with this. Maybe Britain, which only gets excited when a player isn't wearing underwear, or Germany, or Australia, or other tabloid nations that prefer scandal to skill.

But America? The culture that complains about Dennis Rodman's attitude and Deion Sanders' showboating? What do we always say: Why can't athletes be better role models?

Consider this statement: "If there's one role model in the game of tennis, it's Pete Sampras. He's behaving perfectly on the court. He's a real nice fellow off the court. And he doesn't have a bad shot in his game."

You know who said that? Boris Becker less than an hour after Sampras broke his heart.

NOW IT'S TRUE, AFTER winning the title, Sampras pulled off his shirt, yanked on another one, and it was the same shirt. And this is pretty much Sampras; he's as consistent as a sunrise. And his serve is just a slam dunk. Your best hope against it? "Rain," Becker moaned.

In the four-set final, Sampras *never faced a break point.* All match! Not one! That's how accurate he was. Becker, one of the best returners in the game, could only watch ball after ball make like cruise missiles to the chalk line. "Pete had *second serves* that aced me," Becker groaned.

Yes, this made for short points — which are not as much fun as long ones.

But don't take it out on Sampras. He didn't make the rules. "It's grass-court tennis," he said. "People who understand the game know that."

Besides, anyone who watched Sampras saw more than mere cannon fire. They saw marvelous volleys, wicked passing shots and returns that defy physics. Yes, Sampras looks like Peter from "The Brady Bunch." And, yes, he tramps around the court with his head down, suggesting, as one Brit wrote, "a lawn-chair attendant in the off-season."

But come on. First we complain about guys giving fans the finger; then we complain that a guy's too quiet? I think we have to make up our minds.

You want a place to embrace Sampras? How about his heart? He dedicated this match to Tim Gullikson, his coach who is battling brain tumors back home. Sampras phoned him immediately after the win, and told him how Gullikson's brother Tom was in the stands yelling, "Go Pistol!" just like Tim would.

Not enough? How about Sampras' celebration plans? "I'm gonna go home and eat a good greasy hamburger, some fries, some Coke. Then lay around the pool, play some golf."

WHAT COULD BE MORE AMERICAN than that? And humility? How about Sampras encouraging Becker to take a lap Sunday with his runner-up trophy? Few champions would have stood for the loser waving to the crowd, blowing kisses. Sampras thought it was fine. This, after all, was the 10th anniversary of Becker's first win. Let him enjoy it. "He's a great champion," Sampras said.

I like that. Who cares if he's not dating Brooke Shields?

There's a story about Sampras flying first class last year. Barry Bonds, the baseball star, was sitting across from him. Sampras recognized Bonds, but Bonds had no idea who Sampras was. At one point, Bonds looked at him, then turned to a friend and said, "If that kid moves, you can have his seat."

Sampras thought it was funny. He got off the plane and went home, just as he does now, the three-time king of the biggest tennis tournament in the world. "Would you swap the title for the kind of cheer Boris got today?" someone asked. Sampras smiled. "No," he said. He's gonna be around a long time.

Thus ends a funky Wimbledon, which began with deflated balls to slow down big servers — yeah, real effective — and along the way featured the most dangerous backhand in Wimbledon history, that of Jeff Tarango's wife, Benedicte, who slapped an umpire after her hubby quit his match.

This was also the Wimbledon that saw Murphy Jensen miss the fish and his match, Martina Navratilova win another title, and Steffi Graf and Arantxa Sanchez Vicario give us a game for the ages.

It closes with Sampras, a kid, joining Bjorn Borg and Fred Perry among the men who have won Wimbledon three straight times. At 23? And people complain he doesn't throw tantrums? As Sampras once said, "The more I think about it, maybe I'm not the one with the problem."

There you go. Another ace.

So long, Sparky
October 2, 1995

BALTIMORE — He arrived for his last game hours before the first pitch yesterday as the fog was breaking up and most people were still in church. He removed his clothes in stages, hanging up his gray sports coat, followed by the tie and the shoes. He pulled his baseball shirt over his dark slacks and socks, and he sat down that way, half-man, half-manager, munching a doughnut and holding the omnipresent cup of black coffee, part of the reason his hands now tremble like a nervous safecracker. The other reason is that he is 61 years old.

"Here's something I don't get," he said, his voice almost as craggy as his leathered face. "We've been losing for years, and I get treated like a king. One night, we were leaving the park, and a guy yelled, 'Sparky, you're a legend!' And I said, 'Does a legend lose this many games?'

"And you know what? The guy didn't care."

Anderson shook his head. He cares. He is sick of losing. He is sick of going back to the hotel room and looking at his lineup and knowing that tomorrow he probably will lose again, and next year won't be any better than last year. He no longer loves the men he works for, and without that, Sparky Anderson, in his mind, owes you nothing. So this morning, he will announce his departure from the Tigers, after 17 years. It is not a retirement, not a firing. In typical Sparky fashion, everyone is a little confused.

And few people realize what they're about to lose.

There goes ol' Silver Hair. The best manager the Detroit Tigers ever had has danced around the subject of his departure all year, but he talked about it this day: "It's time to go. Let them get someone new in here, some new blood, give them a new kick, get them back in a war."

"And you?" he was asked.

He looked at his feet, still tucked inside the white rubber shower slippers that, for one more day, bore his No. 11. "I'll tell you this. I'm not calling no teams. I'm not contacting no teams. If nobody calls me, I will not be offended."

He leaned back in his chair. They'll call, and he knows it.

There goes ol' Silver Hair.

THE PHONE RANG. IT HAD BEEN RINGING all morning, friends wishing him luck, friends asking him questions, where will he go, what will he do? This time it was Jim Campbell, the man who brought Sparky to Detroit in 1979. After Sparky says good-bye to the current ownership today, he will have lunch with

Campbell and the longtime team physician, Clarence Livingood, before getting on a plane and flying away. Even now, his final loyalty is to the old regime, not the new one.

And why not? His best years were the early years, when the Tigers still developed young talent, and when they had a pitching staff that scared something besides birds.

That seems like a long time ago. Anderson, who always has been many things here — philosopher, historian, salesman, vaudeville act — has never had a year like this one. It began with him walking away from the game — over his refusal to manage replacement players — and ends with him walking away from the franchise, after 84 losses in 144 games. There was a night back in April when I interviewed Anderson as he waited for a call from the Tigers. The strike had ended, the players were headed to spring training, but Anderson still wasn't sure whether he had a job. This is a man who has won more games than all but two managers in the history of baseball. I listened to him say, "If they don't call me, they don't call me. I'm prepared."

Truth is, he was embarrassed. And that was the beginning of the end.

Now he finished getting dressed, leggings, pants, belt. I asked whether he planned on taking anything from this year, any souvenir or keepsake.

"The hat," he said.

"That's it?"

"That's it."

The hat?

OUTSIDE THE OFFICE, THE TIGERS PLAYERS were dressing for the final game of the season. There was a buzz in the room, like the last day of school. Players exchanged phone numbers and talked about tee times.

Against the far wall, Alan Trammell signed some baseballs. This would be his last game, too. He and Lou Whitaker had played nearly every moment of their major league careers for Anderson. "I'll be there for his press conference," Trammell said. "It'll be weird, it'll be emotional, but I can't miss it. I feel like I should be there."

Trammell was asked whether he thought the Tigers could have done anything to keep Anderson. He grinned sarcastically.

"I think," he said, "this is what Sparky wants."

Indeed it is. Anderson knows he still can manage. He also knows he can't spin gold from sawdust. It has been eight years since he has seen a postseason, 11 years since a World Series, he has maybe the worst pitching staff in baseball, few prospects on the horizon, and while he won't admit it, he is concerned that all this losing will cut into his historical glow. Maybe one day, they won't yell "You're a legend!" anymore.

And when you are one, that hurts.

So Anderson will check out. He even laid the ground rules for his next team — should there be one.

"I don't want to go to any rebuilding project. Oh, no. No more. I'd like to go back to winning some games. Having some victories would be nice. ...

"But I would only manage again under my conditions."

Which are?

"I have complete say in my coaches, that's No. 1. I keep who I want on my team, and I don't have to keep nobody I don't want. Nobody interferes with my clubhouse, and nobody—"

He points around his office.

"Nobody calls me here."

What he means is, no owner interference. Nobody telling him who to pitch, who to trade, what he thinks should be happening. In other words, Sparky won't be working for George Steinbrenner.

Why should he?

NOW GAME TIME WAS JUST 90 MINUTES AWAY. "I need to get my boys in here," he said. By this he meant Trammell, Whitaker, Cecil Fielder, Travis Fryman and John Doherty. Those players had been with him the longest. "They deserve a private meeting."

One by one they came in, Fielder, his arms thick as a longshoreman's, and Doherty, showing a pitcher's tan, and Trammell and Whitaker and Fryman, still in his underwear. And they shut the door, and they sat down one more time. A few minutes later they emerged. This, in part, is what Sparky had told them: "I haven't always said it ... but I want you to know how much I appreciate the way you've played and acted like professionals."

He also told them he was leaving.

There goes ol' Silver Hair.

How can we gauge what he did since 1979? He won a World Series and more games than any other Tigers manager. He took a ragtag team in 1987 and churned it into a division winner, giving Detroit arguably its best two weeks of baseball ever, seven games, all against Toronto, all decided by one run, the last being the clincher, when Frank Tanana got the last man to ground out and Sparky actually ran from the dugout and kissed his pitcher in celebration.

"That may be the sweetest moment I had here," he admitted.

There were other not-so-sweet moments, the time in 1989 that he left in the middle of the season — family concerns — and all the outlandish predictions he made for rookies that never came true (remember Chris Pittaro?). And the last seven years, as he said this day, were mostly dismal: 495 wins, 574 losses, never finishing higher than a second-place tie.

But remember, baseball is not football or basketball. You don't win because you have elaborate schemes or unbelievable motivation. You win when you have top pitching and solid defense and menacing hitting.

In other words, talent. He hasn't had a lot of it recently. He will now pursue a team that does.

WHEN THE GAME STARTED, ANDERSON was determined not to make a fuss. This, after all, was Camden Yards, not Tiger Stadium. He came out to deliver the lineup, and suddenly, in the stands behind home plate, fans began to clap. Anderson, with his back to the crowd, had no idea what was happening. Finally, he turned and ran back to the dugout, as the applause swelled into the upper deck, a standing ovation. Anderson glanced up before disappearing.

"Why didn't you walk back?" coach Dick Tracewski asked Sparky in the dugout.

"I didn't know they were clapping for me," he said.

He should have no such doubt today in Detroit. Love him or hate him, the man deserves a slap of appreciation. Sure, he was bloated with hot air, but he always took the game seriously, he fought for players he believed in, and was beloved by the ones who truly understood the sport. He was always kind to kids, was accessible to the media — heck, he was salvation to the media — and took criticism as part of the job. He never took a good team and made it bad, although he did the reverse more than once during his tenure.

In the locker room after yesterday's game — fittingly, another loss — he sat for the last time by his desk, his white hair now matted with sweat. His uniform was already in the laundry. Sparky had not asked for it.

Only the hat.

"Do you have any thoughts on your career at this moment?" a Baltimore TV man asked.

"Yeah," Anderson said. "I'd like to know where all the years went."

They went into a legacy that will not soon be repeated. The truth is, as long as the Tigers had Sparky, they had star power. Now they become one of the nobody pack, another young team with marketing execs.

There goes ol' Silver Hair. A few days ago, with the season long since dead, Sparky took a young pitcher into his office and chewed him out for his behavior on the mound. The next day, he pulled the kid aside and said, "I want you to know something. I did that because you needed it if you ever wanted to be great."

Maybe a few years from now, the kid will appreciate that kind of managing. Maybe, a few years from now, we will, too.

Nobody wins with O.J. verdict
October 4, 1995

A WOMAN WEPT. HER SOBS ECHOED through the courtroom, distracting you like someone coughing during a movie. Her voice, raw and broken, cried as the first "Not guilty" was read by the bailiff, and as the second "Not guilty" was read. On and on it went, this terrible sobbing, even as O.J. Simpson smiled and his lawyer, Johnnie Cochran, shook a fist as if his team had just scored a touchdown. The tears belonged to Kim Goldman. They streamed down her face and into her hair, matting it against her cheeks. She buried her head in her father's chest, but she couldn't stop. Her brother Ron is buried in the ground — same as Nicole Brown — and today there is no killer behind bars. In all likelihood, there never will be. She wept for her brother and Nicole Brown.

She could have wept for us all.

Who wins? Not the victims, not the families, not Simpson's children, who might always wonder whether Daddy killed Mommy. Not the police, who thought they were in charge when they were actually on trial. Not the jury, which rushed from its duty like kids who couldn't wait to go to the bathroom.

Who wins? Not blacks. The Boston woman who faxed a radio station with a note that read "Black Power Lives!" and the cheering crowds on the streets of LA are terribly misguided. O.J. is not free because he is black. He is free because he was rich and famous, and that is enough in this country to get an army of lawyers who will throw mud and smoke until the truth is simply a distraction.

This kind of purchased justice is nothing new. What's ironic is that it is practiced more by whites than by blacks in America. Any poor black man who thinks this case is a good sign if he gets in trouble better hope he wins the lottery. Otherwise, Cochran and Barry Scheck will not be rushing to his aid.

Who wins?

NOT COPS. THEY WERE THE ONES found guilty in this trial. Detective Mark Fuhrman, a snake of a man, was right when he said, "If I go down, the case goes down." He didn't know his racist words, not his evidence, would be what shook the verdict loose.

Who wins? Not Simpson. Yes, he is free this morning, but free to do what? He was addicted to fame, adulation, people believing a lie, that he was this sweetheart of a guy when he was nothing more than a punk who beat up his wife. Those pictures of Nicole Simpson looking like a bloody welt will never go away, neither will his voice on the 911 tape calling her a "bitch" and screaming, "I'll kill you!"

Simpson's old life is over. The corporate world that fed him will shun him now, and network sports won't touch him. Movies? I doubt it. The only non-family who will want him now are those who enjoy danger and those who want a slice of him for their own fame. Larry King will be his friend for a night. Barbara Walters, too. So? They are bloodsuckers (King went live after the verdict, shamelessly asking jurors to call him). As soon as Simpson cools off, he'll be spit out like bad food.

WHO WINS? NOT WOMEN. It might be open season on celebrity wives because the subtle message is if you're famous enough, you can get out of anything. The rise of sexual assault in the sports world is not discouraged by the outcome of this trial. The last words the jury heard were Nicole pleading "help me." The next thing they did was acquit her husband.

Who wins? Not the American people. Everywhere they look, they get depressed, from the fallen football hero, to the sloppy, racist police, to the lawyers who sank to new lows — even Robert Shapiro said he "would never work again" with Cochran or F. Lee Bailey — to the jurors. The jurors were the last disappointment. Four hours for a verdict? With all that evidence? In the end, they come across as selfish as the rest, painting themselves as victims ("We've been in there nine months," one juror snapped to explain the quick verdict. Another said, "Someone gotta win, someone gotta lose.").

The truth is, these jurors will spend more time on book deals than they did reviewing the case.

Who wins? Every expert worth a nickel says the evidence was enough to convict 10 people. In 16 months, no one has offered a whisper of another real suspect — and this is after Simpson himself offered $500,000 for information and a New York disc jockey offered $1 million. Not a peep?

And so it ends. The media made this a sideshow, the lawyers were only too happy to jump in, and all we can do is shut the damn thing off, do not give any more time to Cochran, Resnick or Kato as they dive into the pig slop of fame. And anyone who buys a pay-per-view interview with Simpson — which is surely coming — is as slimy as he is. You might as well pay a stranger to slug your wife.

In the time it took to hear this case, thousands of men and women were killed in equally brutal fashion. Their cases drew no headlines, no cameras. But this was never about the average American. It isn't now.

Who wins? Blacks still don't trust whites. Whites still don't trust blacks. Nobody trusts the police. Everyone hates lawyers. The victims are in the cemetery, nobody is in jail, and the final sounds of the Trial of the Century were the sobbing of a dead man's sister and the words "not guilty" being read for all the wrong reasons. Who wins?

The TV ratings, that's who wins.

Sometimes this country makes me so sad I want to fly away.

Secret Series

Has anyone here seen Kelly?
October 17, 1994

DATELINE UNKNOWN — This is how it began. They put their hands on a bat, one at a time, rising up the neck, a black hand, a white hand, a young man's hand, an aging second baseman's calloused fingers, up, up, until there was room for just one more. All eyes turned to, of all people, Michael Jordan, who smiled because it was his turn. He grabbed that handle like a climber grabbing a mountaintop.

"We're the home team," he declared.

"National League bats first," Ryne Sandberg said.

"OK," Don Mattingly said, standing up and looking over the group, "are we ready to do this?"

It is hard to describe the electricity that tickled the air at that very moment, the feeling that something heavenly was about to happen and only these lucky few knew it. Kirby Puckett lightly tapped Jordan's hand, as if to rub off some good luck. Roger Clemens smacked a fist into his glove. Young Mike Piazza seemed in awe of the event, so did a kid named Pokey Reese, and Matt Williams and Barry Bonds.

Ozzie Smith, the veteran shortstop, broke the silence.

"Ladies and gentlemen," he said, cupping hands around his mouth to mimic an announcer, "welcome to the Secret World Series!"

There were no fans, no TV cameras, no billboards. The sun was out. The breeze was warm.

They took the field.

WHAT THESE 21 BASEBALL PLAYERS are doing here — what I am doing here with them — will not be quickly explained, and let me apologize if things seem a little helter-skelter. I never intended to be writing dispatches this week from anywhere, much less an unofficial and highly secret series of baseball games that, unless I miss my guess, these ballplayers are hoping will count one day as the 1994 Fall Classic. The real one, of course, was crushed by the tidal wave of the baseball strike. October used to be a month for words like "Series hero" and "MVP." Now it's an endless economics lecture. Salary cap. Arbitration. Small-market revenues.

No one could stand it.

I couldn't. It was why I was on a plane, last Friday, headed for vacation in a destination that I must, for the moment, keep a secret (and will explain in due course).

Everything was normal until I caught sight of two familiar faces, Alan Trammell and Kirk Gibson, sitting side by side in first class. Odd, I thought. They're wearing sunglasses.

"Hey, Elvis?" I said.

"What's up? They settled the strike and nobody told me?"

They looked down to avoid me, which was also odd, since I've known these men for a decade. Finally, Gibson said, "We got a card show."

"All the way in ——?"

"They pay a lot of money."

I shrugged, moved back to my coach seat and didn't think twice about it until hours later, halfway through the flight, when I was nudged from a bumpy sleep. The two of them were leaning over me.

"What?" I said.

"We have a proposition," Trammell whispered.

They beckoned me to the back of the plane. And there, at 30,000 feet, in the din of the engines where no one could hear us, I was made an offer I won't forget: Give up my vacation for the next seven days, and they would let me join them on a story. "A real rare story," Gibson said, as if I'd be a fool to say no.

Here were the conditions: I was to tell no one where we were going — not even my newspaper. And I was to keep track of everything. That was crucial. They needed someone "to keep a record of all the things that happen."

"What things?" I asked.

Gibson shook his head. "Yes or no?" he demanded. I realize now he was testing me, and it's probably best he didn't say what they had in mind, for I might have blurted it out and the whole plane would have heard it, and then, who knows, they would have stuffed me in the lavatory toilet, I guess.

Instead, I looked at these two aging ballplayers, balding now, no longer the peppy kids I remembered from the 1984 World Series, when they were arguably the two best performers on the winning Tigers team. The strike might have ended their careers, and what a lousy finish for men who loved the game the way these two did. No good-bye parties. No night at the ballpark. Just fade away.

"Well?" Trammell said. "Yes or no?"

Gibson studied my face, then grinned, not even waiting for my reply.

"He'll do it," Gibson said.

Well. Heck. It was my vacation.

I SHOULD STOP HERE TO GIVE YOU a few facts of record because that is part of the agreement. The starting pitchers for Game 1 of the 1994 World Series — or at least the only World Series that we have — were Jim Abbott of the Yankees, for the American League, and Greg Maddux of the Braves, for the National League. The first pitch was thrown at 1:31 p.m., under a warm sun that glazed the field in fine light, and that pitch was a fastball from Abbott to Tony Gwynn of the Padres, which Gwynn smacked into centerfield for a clean single. It was the first of four hits on the day for Gwynn, who would later boast, "If this were still the season, I'd be up near .400 by now."

Of course they weren't playing the season. The season was destroyed, and players had scattered to their winter homes, sleeping in, getting soft, snacking on pizza and seeing more golf courses than Fred Couples.

Which explains my surprise when the Jeep we had rented Saturday pulled up to a small field in the shadow of a valley, where the grass was green and lush, and nearly a dozen familiar major league faces were already waiting, with bats, balls and gloves. They nodded at the Jeep, and Trammell rolled down his window.

"You didn't use your real name, right?" said a man whom I immediately recognized as Cal Ripken. And it was true, Trammell had gotten the Jeep at the airport using a phony identity, calling himself "Pio DiSalvo," the name of one of the Tigers' trainers. He also produced Pio's driver's license with a doctored photo, don't ask me how.

Now Ripken spotted me in the back.

"Who's this guy?" he said.

What followed was a heated discussion between the players that made me feel like a refugee at the border.

"We said no reporters!" one of them groaned.

"Once there's one, there's a million!"

In the end, it was Gibson, of all people, who talked them into it. Something about "trust" and "making it official." This was almost funny, since Gibson used to terrorize sports writers.

Things change, I guess. Ripken came back to the Jeep, opened the door, and welcomed me — under the same conditions that Gibson and Trammell had laid out. I shook hands with Puckett, Gwynn, Mattingly, Ozzie, Maddux, Abbott, Lenny Dykstra, Roger Clemens, and a tanned and weathered fellow who at first I thought was someone's father, but then I recognized as Nolan Ryan. He was chewing gum.

"You got a camera?" he drawled.

"In my suitcase," I said.

He nodded.

"Got film?"

IT WAS AN ODD COLLECTION OF players, and as of this writing I cannot tell you how they all came to be here. There has been talk about some fax that each of them received, but when I asked Ripken who sent it, he said he thought Puckett did, and when I asked Puckett, he said he thought Ripken did. Strange.

What's easier to figure is the motivation: Mattingly, for example, has never played in a World Series, and Jordan would do anything to get near one — and he has the money to make it happen — Williams, Gwynn and Ken Griffey Jr. were all on record paces when the '94 season was killed, so maybe this was a makeup for them. Gibson, Trammell, Puckett, Ripken, they love the game enough to try something this crazy.

"You know why I'm doing this?" Trammell had said on the plane. "Because it doesn't seem right that a year comes and goes and there's no World Series. Honest to God, if they had enough players without me, I'd say fine. Just as long as the thing is played."

So this was all I knew. As of yesterday morning, when we made the trip to the cemetery to dedicate this Series — more on that later — there were 15 major leaguers, one retired pitcher, one former NBA superstar-turned-minor-leaguer, and one complete stranger. The stranger's name is Kelly, Mike Kelly, a big, strapping guy with a mustache and a pet monkey. The record will show that Mike Kelly played catcher for the American League in Game 1 of the Series. The reason is simple.

He owns the field.

And it is a magnificent field, with emerald grass, tapered base paths, a gently sloping mound of dark dirt. The farthest fence is 409 feet to dead center, and on the other side is one of the prettiest views a person could hope to see.

"It's like God's ballpark," Mattingly said.

There are no lights — thus, all the games will be played during the day, "the way it should be," Ripken said. There are no billboards on the field, nothing commercial of any kind. There are a few small bleachers, made of plywood, and a spring-fed well not far from third base, complete with rope and bucket, for thirsty players.

There is only one road in.

"Can I help you gentlemen?" Kelly had yelled. We had been on his property for half an hour, marveling at the site, a few of the guys tossing the ball and playing pepper. Everyone thought it was a public field. Now Kelly stood there with his arms crossed, the monkey at his feet.

"This your place?" Ripken said.

"It is."

"How much would you charge to rent it for a week?"

"Well," he said, grinning, "that depends on what you plan on doing with it."

"We want to play baseball, dude," Dykstra chimed in, spitting a wad of tobacco juice.

Kelly looked at him and winked. "I'll thank you not to soil my field that way, Mister."

Dykstra swallowed.

"Now then," Kelly continued, "you want to play baseball. Well. I like a good game now and then. That's why I built this place. Matter of fact, I'm a bit of a collector."

Kelly invited everyone into his rather large farmhouse and down to the cellar, where he revealed an incredible collection of old-time outfits, pants, tops, leggings, the works.

"This stuff is worth a fortune," Roger Clemens marveled.

"Well, I'm not much interested in money," Kelly said. "These uniforms have been in my family for some time."

"What are you, Babe Ruth's grandson or something?" Gibson said.

Kelly laughed. "Not quite. Anyhow, here's my proposition. You can use the field, and the uniforms, you can even stay in the guest house across the way, free of charge, for one week, under one condition."

"What's that?" Mattingly asked.

"I get to play," Kelly said.

The major leaguers looked at one another and shrugged. The monkey jumped up and down and made a "kweeeee kweeeee" sound.

"What position you play?" Griffey asked.

"Catcher is my specialty."

Gwynn said to Griffey, "You guys need a catcher."

"Oh, thanks a lot," Griffey shot back. "Stick him with us."

"It ain't gonna make a difference, we're gonna kick your butt."

"In your dreams, old — "

Ripken interrupted. "Hold up! Look. We need a field more than anything. This place is perfect. It's private, and it's regulation size. Mr. Kelly here can play with us on the American League team."

"Yeah," Puckett laughed, "we're already letting Jordan play with us."

"Listen to you," Jordan said, smirking.

Ripken offered his hand, and Kelly shook it heartily.

The funny thing was, Kelly never asked who the players were.

OKAY. I AM IGNORING MY obligations to the game, which, after all, is why I was brought here. The rosters were increased about an hour before the first pitch, when a rented Mercedes pulled up to the field and out stepped Barry Bonds, Sandberg and an older fellow, in a suit. He smiled, and a happy mumble went through the squads.

Ernie Banks.

"Ryne called me and told me what y'all were doing," Banks said. "He said he was canceling his retirement just to play in one World Series, and I wanted to come just to watch, seeing as I never got to a Series myself.

"And when I asked if Barry was playing and Ryne said no, well, I had to call him up and tell him, 'Son, you cannot miss this. You never know if it will be your last chance.' "

Bonds, wearing sunglasses and jewelry, admitted he didn't want to come. He looked like a kid who'd been dragged to his aunt's house.

Two more cars pulled up. The first was a Cadillac with a Hertz sticker on the window. Out stepped Jose Rijo, the Cincinnati pitching star, along with a young man with a round face and sad, sleepy eyes. "Hey, man, this place is hard to find," Rijo said.

"Who's your buddy?" Smith asked.

"This is Calvin Reese, but everyone calls him Pokey. He's a heck of an infielder in our farm system. They say he's the next Ozzie."

Smith grinned. "Aim higher, kid."

Pokey smiled back. "Is it OK if I play?" Something about the way he asked it, or maybe because he looked like a good athlete, but everyone just sort of nodded. We would later learn that Pokey had lost the mother of his child just a year earlier and was still trying to deal with the grief. Maybe that's why Rijo brought him.

The last car was a jalopy, a Volkswagen with no muffler. It banged to a halt.

"Oh, cripes," Dykstra said.

Out stepped Mitch Williams, the pitcher. His hair was long and his beard unkempt. He had a tank top, baggy shorts and two new tattoos. The last time I had seen him was in the SkyDome in Toronto, when he threw a pitch to Joe Carter that Carter smacked over the wall to end the 1993 World Series. Because of that, Williams had been crucified in Philadelphia. Fans egged his house, cursed his name, he wound up in Houston, pitched badly there and was cut. You could easily see his reason for wanting to play another World Series — even a World Series like this.

He slipped on his glove.

"When do we start?" was all he said.

WHICH BRINGS US BACK TO the first pitch. Oh, I almost forgot. Nolan Ryan said they should sing the national anthem, even if they were in ——. He took his hat off and started singing, pretty badly, and the other guys joined in. It was kind of nice to hear all these off-key voices, wafting up into the turquoise sky. Never mind that Bonds forgot the words.

After that, Ripken said, "Someone should throw out the first ball, to make it official," and everyone looked to Ernie Banks.

"I'd be honored," he said.

Ernie tossed that ball in, and the game began, as I mentioned, with a clean shot by Gwynn up the middle. This was followed by another single, by Dykstra, and then Matt Williams sent the second pitch offered him over the fence for a home run, the first of the "unofficial" postseason.

National League 3, American 0.

"Take that, Griffey!" Bonds yelled from the bench. "Hoo! Big Matt's gonna beat you to the home run title here, too!"

When Abbott finally retired the side, he came back to the bench and went right to his catcher, the mysterious Mike Kelly.

"Hey," Abbott said, "what kind of signals are those?"

"Signals?" Kelly said.

"What you're doing with your hands."

"Oh, I was just swatting at a fly."

The next few innings saw the American League score its first run on an RBI double by Puckett. But the Nationals came back with two more, on Gwynn's second hit of the day, a two-run triple. It was 5-2 after four innings, and the AL was in trouble. Jordan had struck out twice, and Abbott looked tired.

"I guess now is when we'd go to a middle reliever," Trammell said.

"If we had a middle reliever," Gibson answered.

The fact was, each team had only three pitchers. So it was pretty much up to each starter to finish his game. Abbott settled down in the later innings, and Maddux seemed to tire.

In the eighth, Griffey hit a solo home run — "I'm right with you, Matt," he said as he passed Williams on third base — and Puckett, Ripken and Gibson came through with doubles, knocking in two more. The score was tied, 6-6, going into the ninth.

This is when the most remarkable occurrence of the day took place. Because there were no umpires, the catchers had been calling the balls and strikes. There were a few disputes, but, for the most part, things went OK.

Then Kelly came to bat in the ninth, and Mike Piazza got a little too competitive. A ball that was clearly low, Piazza called strike one. A pitch that seemed far outside, Piazza called strike two. Kelly stepped out of the box and looked at him.

"You care to take that last one back?" he said.

Piazza sneered.

"One more time," Kelly said. "You care to take that one back?"

Piazza said, "Hey, pal. It's strike two."

"Very well," Kelly said.

Now I should say that in his three previous at-bats, Kelly had struck out badly. I mean, not even close. Wild swing. No contact. The guys in the field hid their laughs behind their gloves. But now he dug his feet into the dirt, and he clenched his jaw, and he waited for the 0-2 from Maddux, a fastball, and uncorked the sweetest swing this side of Duke Ellington.

Pow! The ball flew — I mean flew — over the centerfield fence and out of sight. All we heard was a small splash. Kelly rounded the bases to the dropped jaws of the other players. He stepped on the plate, looked at Piazza and walked into the arms of his teammates.

And that is how the game was won.

"Who is this guy?" Ripken whispered to Puckett.

"Who cares?" Puckett said. "He's on our team — and we just won Game 1 of the World Series!"

They slapped hands in the dying sun and joined their teammates, who were mobbing this strange, mustached man. On the sidelines, Ernie Banks was smiling. "You know," he said, "if I didn't know better, I'd swear that Kelly guy was ... ."

"Who?" I said.

"Never mind," he said. "It's impossible."

At that moment, "impossible" seemed a somewhat outdated word.

Clemens on his last legs

October 18, 1994

DATELINE UNKNOWN — You could hear the groaning when the sun came up. The first game of the Secret World Series had been played — after two months without baseball — and while the smiles were still in place, the rest of the bodies were aching from the inactivity.

"Man, am I stiff," Alan Trammell, 36, said yesterday morning, limping into the kitchen of the Kelly farmhouse for some coffee.

"Tell me about it," said Ryne Sandberg, 35, already at the breakfast table. "I've been up since 4 a.m. trying to get this kink out of my shoulder."

Cal Ripken, 34, walked in, holding his back. "I need some Advil," he mumbled.

"Wake up Nolan Ryan," Sandberg said. "He should have a ton of it."

I was pretty fatigued myself, having been up most of the night writing and trying to transmit photographs. I've never been much with a camera. But as the only journalist allowed near this renegade World Series — staged by players who simply couldn't accept a strike canceling the Fall Classic — well, I didn't want to miss anything.

Sandberg asked me jokingly if this is as good a story as the hockey lockout.

"You know, it's weird," Ripken admitted. "We played a World Series game yesterday, and there were no replays on TV, no second-guessing on the radio. Nobody asking for tickets, nobody hounding us for interviews."

"It's like heaven, isn't it?" Trammell said.

"Yeah," Sandberg said, sighing. "It makes you wonder how things ever got so crazy."

Suddenly, a rap on the door. Everyone froze. Although the players are doing nothing wrong, there is definitely a fugitive atmosphere here.

"Should we answer it?" Trammell asked.

"Where's that Kelly guy? It's his house."

"I'll get it," Sandberg said. "I'm retired. Nobody recognizes me anymore."

He opened the door to see two women, one a squat blond wearing a two-toned baseball shirt, the other a taller brunette with a ponytail and a glove.

"Hello, Ryne," the tall one said.

"Nobody recognizes him," Trammell whispered in the kitchen.

"My name's Julie Croteau. This here's Lee Ann Ketcham. We play baseball for the Silver Bullets — you know, the women's professional team? We're playing winter league ball not far from here, and we heard a rumor about what you're doing."

"We're not doing anything," Sandberg said. "I'm just here on vaca—"

"Listen," said Ketcham, the shorter woman. "Your secret is safe. We won't tell anybody. We just want to be a part of it."

"What she means is," Croteau said, clearing her throat, "we want to play."

In the kitchen, Trammell dropped his coffee cup, and it smashed on the floor.

"Um," Sandberg said. "Could you wait here a second? ... "

A ND SO IT WAS, at 1:25 p.m., under another beautiful blue and cloudless sky, that two women were introduced, for the first time ever, as part of a Fall Classic, or at least the version that's being played here in ———. Of course, had the men not been so sore, I don't know if the women would have been so welcome. But Croteau plays first base for a living, and she committed only two errors all season for the Bullets.

"We'll take her," said Ozzie Smith of the National League squad, "as insurance in case Ryne's shoulder stiffens up."

Ketcham was a pitcher who accounted for five of the Bullets' six victories this year. Since each team in this Series has only three pitchers, there wasn't much grumbling when she was put on the American League squad. Well, actually, Kirk Gibson wasn't crazy about it.

"I thought we were playing a World Series here!" he yelled from the outfield during warm-ups. "Not 'The Dating Game.' "

Michael Jordan leaned over to Ketcham and whispered, "Don't let these guys intimidate you. They make fun of me, too."

Ketcham smiled. "Thanks, Michael."

Of course, Jordan did strike out four times in Game 1.

T HAT BRINGS US TO GAME 2, which differed from the opener in several regards. First, the facts: Jose Rijo from the Reds started on the hill for the National League; Roger Clemens of the Red Sox started for the American. Both men have pitched in the World Series before. Although Rijo has fond memories of 1990 and his MVP award, Clemens still stings from 1986, his Game 6 against the Mets, which was lost when that ball went through Bill Buckner's legs. You get the feeling that game, as much as anything, was the reason Clemens had flown all this way to pitch here yesterday afternoon.

Anyhow, the National League once again batted first. Clemens had to face Tony Gwynn as the leadoff man and, again, Gwynn began with a single, making him 6-for-6 in the Series. His hit was greeted with a round of applause.

Which brings me to another change: spectators. Unlike Game 1, several dozen people were watching Game 2, most of them children from the nearby town. They sat in the plywood stands and drank water from the well behind third base. They clapped and yelled and especially enjoyed Jordan, even though he struck out four more times.

At one point, a short man with jet-black hair set up a little grill and cooked chicken and pork dipped in paste made of, I think, taro root and herbs. At least that's what he said. It was good — you could smell it everywhere — and I saw Mitch Williams sneaking some between innings.

All of these fans seemed to know Mike Kelly, the mysterious, mustached owner of this spectacular playing field. At first, the players had said no spectators, but Kelly said it was his property, "I can let on whoever I want." The kids clapped and played with Kelly's pet monkey, which, to tell you the truth, gives most of the players the creeps. Still, it was fun hearing some cheers again.

(A word here about Kelly's home run in Game 1, which won the game in the ninth for the American League, 7-6. Most of the players agreed it was a fluke.

"The guy struck out like a Little Leaguer the first three times," Greg Maddux whispered afterward when some of the players gathered for a late-night snack. "How could he suddenly become Babe Ruth?"

Ernie Banks — who said Sunday that Kelly "reminds me of someone" — spent much of yesterday morning snooping around Kelly's basement, where Kelly keeps an incredible baseball memorabilia collection. I thought it was rude, myself, but who's going to argue with a legend?)

The second major change in Game 2 was an umpire. After the mini-fiasco at the plate Sunday, Gwynn said, "This is crazy. We can't call our own balls and strikes. We'll kill each other."

He made a call to Doug Harvey, the recently retired ump known for his no-nonsense style. Harvey got here yesterday morning. And a couple of Kelly's friends picked him up at the airport. They blindfolded him, just in case, and when he got here, he seemed a little disoriented.

"Hey, man, you sure you can see the plate?" Rijo said.

"Just get me some black coffee; I'll be fine," Harvey said.

They did. And he was.

SO. TO THE GAME. CLEMENS was strong for the first five innings, giving up two hits — both of them to Gwynn — and striking out seven of the first nine batters.

"Has Roger ptuuu been pumping iron during the strike ptuuu or what?" Lenny Dykstra, spitting tobacco juice into a cup, asked on the NL bench. "The guy's throwin' like ptuuu the Macho Man."

"The Macho Man?" Matt Williams said.

"Yeah, dude. Don't ptuuu you watch pro wrestling?"

Rijo, meanwhile, was good but not great. He walked several batters early. And in the third inning, after a bunt single by Trammell, Ken Griffey Jr. smacked a slider over the leftfield fence, his second homer of the series.

"Catch me if you can, Matty!" Griffey yelled to Williams, continuing their personal grudge match.

That 2-0 lead held up until the eighth inning, when things got really interesting. Before we get to that, two things of note.

THE SCOREBOARD: In Game 1, the score was kept by each team. But that night, Kelly got some wood and nails, and Don Mattingly, Jim Abbott, Kirby Puckett and Ryan stayed up late in the barn, building an old-fashioned scoreboard, the kind where you hang the numbers after each inning. "I haven't seen one of these since I was a kid," Mattingly said, grinning.

They posted it in the outfield, and during Monday's game, players took turns as scorekeepers. They were supposed to stay up there a half-inning at a time, when their team was at bat, but Mitch Williams seemed to enjoy it so much, he stayed for the last five innings.

"A birdbrain likes to be up in the air," Dykstra said.

THE ORIGIN OF THE SERIES: I continue to ask the players whose idea this Secret World Series was. They seem as puzzled as I am.

"I got a fax," Ripken said.

"Me, too," Mattingly said.

"Mine was signed by about six of the guys here, including you," Abbott said to Puckett.

"Well, I didn't send anything," Puckett replied, "and mine was signed by you."

The mysteries continue.

ALL RIGHT. THE FINISH. In top of the eighth, Gwynn, 3-for-3, drew a walk off Clemens. Mike Piazza singled and Matt Williams struck out, but not before Gwynn and Piazza pulled a dramatic double steal.

Kelly, the AL catcher, called time and went to the mound to talk to Clemens.

"You want to walk Bonds?" Kelly asked.

"No way," Clemens said, his face tightening.

Clemens hung tough and got Barry Bonds to pop to shallow center. But that took the best out of him. With two out, he walked Sandberg on five pitches.

Ozzie Smith came to the plate. Sandberg danced off first base — not that he was going anywhere with the bases loaded — but Clemens was so annoyed, he threw over. Sandberg dived back, landed and yelped in pain.

"Yeoww! Ah! Ah!" He rolled in the dirt. His shoulder. Out he came. As Ryan wrapped him with an Ace bandage — nobody thought about bringing team trainers — Sandberg looked down the bench.

"All right," he sighed, turning to Julie Croteau. "You wanted to play? Get in and run for me. Don't try anything funny."

And so, with the sun still brilliant in the afternoon sky, history was made. A woman entered the World Series. The small crowd of fans clapped loudly, and Croteau took her place at first. Clemens eyed her the way a cop eyes a suspect.

The pitch …

Smack! Smith sent a line drive to right-centerfield, and Griffey chased after it. Gwynn scored easily, and Piazza followed close behind. Griffey, with no play at the plate or second base, fired to third, where Croteau was headed, chugging like a small engine. The ball was a missile to Trammell's glove. Croteau went to slide, as Harvey, the umpire, raced down the third-base line for a better view. It happened so fast, and there are no replays, so I can only report what I saw: a cloud of dust as Trammell and Croteau collided.

"SAFE!" Harvey called.

For a moment, everyone was stunned. Trammell studied his glove, went to say something to Harvey, then instead tossed him the ball and reached over to help Croteau to her feet.

"Good slide," he said, and I thought I saw her smile.

I definitely saw her smile on the next pitch, when Rijo, the pitcher — no designated hitters in this Series — hit a sinking liner to Jordan in the outfield that he should have caught but instead misplayed and watched helplessly as the ball went — and I am not making this up — through his legs.

"No! NO! NOT AGAIN!" Clemens yelled. "BLEEEPING BLEEP! NOT AGAIN! THROUGH YOUR BLEEPING LEGS?"

Croteau scored, and that would be the final, 3-2. National League evens the Series. Suffice it to say, Clemens is not speaking to Jordan.

"I blew it, I blew it," a stunned Jordan kept saying.

"Forget it," Ripken said. "That's why we play seven games."

Evening was coming, and the small group of fans mingled with the other players, sharing some of that pasted chicken and pork — I think they call it poi. Kelly took his turn at the grill, laughing and playing host.

From the corner of my eye, I saw Banks walking to the field, looking as if he had seen a ghost.

"You missed the game?" I said.

"Look at this," he whispered.

In his hand was an old, crinkled cigarette trading card — it had to be from the late 19th Century — a picture of a ballplayer in a canvas uniform and a low-brimmed cap.

The caption said, "Kelly, catcher."

We both swallowed hard.

"It's him," he said.

Berra sends Bonds, collapses

October 19, 1994

D ATELINE UNKNOWN — The crack of the bat was sweet and true — a
solid hit, extra bases for sure — and as spectators rose in a collective
"oooh," Barry Bonds began to run.

He had not been much fun to that point, the only one of the 24 players at this
outlaw World Series who didn't seem to like the idea. Bonds stayed in a hotel
down the road, far from the other major leaguers, who were bunking at the Kelly
farmhouse. He ate by himself. He showed up 10 minutes before the games.

At one point yesterday, when he failed to chase a pop foul, Ozzie Smith
criticized him, and Bonds snorted, "Lighten up, old man. This whole thing is
bogus, anyhow."

Now, as he churned around first base, it looked anything but bogus. This was
the bottom of the 10th inning, Bonds' National League team was trailing, 11-8,
and two men already were racing around the bases ahead of him. The ball landed
in the gap in right-center. Ken Griffey and Michael Jordan gave chase.

"Back off! Back off!" Griffey yelled on the run, and Jordan tried, but as he
spun out of the way, his long legs got caught under Griffey and both men went
sprawling. The ball rolled to the fence, and now two runs were in and Bonds was
chugging from second to third, his cap flying off his head.

"GO, BOBBY! GO, BOBBY!" screamed his manager, Yogi Berra.

Go ... Bobby?

W ELL. OBVIOUSLY, A FEW THINGS have changed since my last dispatch.
For one, we now have managers at this Secret World Series: the
irrepressible, 69-year-old Berra for the National League, and the delightful, 82-
year-old Buck O'Neil for the Americans. Both men arrived yesterday morning,
apparently at the invitation of Ernie Banks, who met them at the airport, then
brought them here for a hastily called meeting.

"Men," Banks said, addressing the players, "I know this whole idea of
playing a World Series without TV cameras, no money, doing it for the tradition
was all your idea, and I'm not trying to tell you what to do. But there have been
managers nearly as long as there's been baseball.

"If you want to do things right, you oughta have a couple of skippers. Yogi
here, he's played in more World Series than anybody else, but he never won one
as a manager. And Buck here, well, things being what they were for a black man
when we were young, he never got the chance to manage in the majors — though
I'll swear to you men he's more than good enough."

Yogi chimed in: "Me and Buck think this is as good as the real World Series, only better."

"Besides," Banks said, lowering his voice, "I wanted these two old-timers here to back me up. There's something spooky about our host, Mr. Kelly."

"What do you mean, spooky?" Cal Ripken said.

"Well. Look at this."

Banks opened a box he had taken from the farmhouse and pulled out the trading card he had shown me the day before yesterday, plus an old glove, an even older bat, a dark uniform and some photos that looked like our Mike Kelly — but from 100 years ago.

"Does the name 'King Kelly' ring any bells?" Banks said.

Most of the younger stars were blank. But Alan Trammell rubbed his forehead. "Wait … King Kelly … I saw him in that Ken Burns PBS special. He was like the first controversial baseball star, right?"

"Not only that, King Kelly could play like the devil," O'Neil said. "I remember my daddy talking about him. Said nobody could stop the guy. He was fast — heck, he invented the hit-and-run — and he could hit the ball a ton. They even wrote a song about him, 'Slide, Kelly, Slide,' because of how he ran the bases."

"What happened to him?" Trammell asked.

"He died of pneumonia before his career was over — exactly 100 years ago."

"King Kelly. I remember hearing about him from the old guys in New York," Berra said. "He wore them fancy suits, like that Neon Sanders guy in basketball."

"Football," Trammell corrected.

"He plays football, too?"

"And," Banks said, "King Kelly — whose real name was Mike — was famous for traveling with a monkey."

Everyone froze. It was like an Agatha Christie novel. Our Kelly looked just like these photos. Our Kelly's first name was Mike. And our Kelly had a monkey.

"What are you saying?" Don Mattingly asked, slowly, "that this guy Kelly has been dead for years and … his ghost is letting us use his field?"

Just then, we heard the sound of laughter, a howling, cackling noise. It was Kelly, who had been eavesdropping and was now near hysterics.

"Gentlemen," he said, "I, ha ha, hate to disappoint you, but — ha ha — those pictures you have, they're of my great-grandfather. … Believe me — ha! — I'm not a ghost!"

Yogi stared at the picture, then at the man. "Holy cripes!" he said. "You're a dead ringer, and you're alive!"

S O IT WAS THAT WE DISCOVERED — or thought we discovered — the secret genes of Mr. Kelly. As to why he was living way out here in ——, with a major league ballpark on his lovely property, well, he wasn't so clear on that. Kelly had been taught the game by his father, who learned it from his father, who learned it from the legend himself. Our Kelly said he had played in high school and college — under a different name — and admitted he was gifted with special skills.

"Why didn't you go pro?" Kirk Gibson asked him.

"A question of pride," Kelly said. "My great-grandfather was an original. I could never surpass him.

"Besides, one baseball legend is enough per family, don't you think?"

"Not in Barry Bonds' family," Gibson quipped.

"Hey, has he shown up yet?" Ripken asked.

But it was only noon. Game time was 90 minutes away. Bonds was back at the hotel, watching ESPN.

IT WAS THROUGH BONDS, THOUGH, that we found out the world is catching wind of this Series. I figured the newspaper accounts and radio phone calls would arouse people's curiosity, but I've been careful to stick to my promise of not revealing where this is all taking place. Frankly, I'm amazed it hasn't leaked out because the crowd at Game 3 was nearly twice the size of Game 2. Again, there were lots of dark-haired children, and their parents, and they ate grilled pork and chicken, and one of Kelly's friends made lemonade and sold it for 25 cents a cup, just for kicks.

One of the kids asked if she could sing the national anthem, in her native tongue, and the kid was sensational, although Yogi later said: "I could only understand every other word."

Anyhow, back to the game, and Bonds' chugging around those bases, as Kirk Gibson raced over from leftfield and fired the ball in ...

Actually, wait, let's back up for a second. I forget sometimes this is the only official record of this World Series. The facts: Game 3 pitted Nolan Ryan for the American League against Mitch Williams for the National. Ryan had been retired for a year — but you never took the game's greatest arm lightly. And Williams? He wasn't really a starter, but with only three pitchers per team, the NL used whom it had.

"Go the distance, Mitch," Greg Maddux, the Game 1 starter, shouted.

And for a while, Williams had decent stuff. He retired the first 10 batters before tiring and allowing a walk and a two-run homer to Griffey — Griffey's third home run of the Series. That started a chain reaction that made World Series history.

Kirby Puckett sent Williams' next pitch over the leftfield fence.

Cal Ripken smacked the next pitch over the rightfield fence.

Kirk Gibson hit the next pitch halfway to Fiji.

Four straight home runs.

On four straight pitches. On the bench, Maddux whispered to Jose Rijo, "You got any other pitchers' home phone numbers on you?"

Kelly was next to bat, and the local crowd gave him a warm round of applause. Of course, the crowd was still only 164 people — hardly the roar we associate with today's game.

That's one of the nicest parts of this special World Series. You can hear that you're outdoors.

In quiet moments, as pitchers wait for batters, you can catch the sound of the wind through the palm trees, or the occasional squawking bird. When the shortstop chatters, "He's no hitter-he's no hitter-c'mon babe-humbabehumbabehumbabe" — well, you can hear that, even from the bleachers. And the smack of the wooden bat, or the thud when the ball meets the catcher's mitt, well, those sounds are here, as crisp and clear as childhood.

Most of us — including the players — have forgotten baseball's natural symphony — without the rock music, or ads on the electronic scoreboard.

"Batter up!" the ump yelled.

WHICH BRINGS ME TO ONE MORE deviation — and then I promise to finish the game account — and that is the visit we all made Sunday morning, before this Series began, to the grave site of a significant baseball man.

Kelly took us there. He knew the way. It's a fairly simple grave site, honoring a pioneer who died 102 years ago. Ripken, who knows the lore of the game as well as anyone here, tried to explain to the younger guys such as Griffey and Mike Piazza what holy ground this was for baseball's tradition.

"This man," he said, "was the real father of baseball. Abner Doubleday gets all the credit, but this guy did far more. Not only did he start the first real baseball team and play the first real game in Hoboken, N.J., and not only did he invent nine players to a side and nine innings to a game, but he was like a Johnny Appleseed for baseball.

"He traveled across the country, teaching kids how to play. He spread it as far as California, and then he set sail and wound up here. He never stopped teaching.

"I heard that he died with the ball from baseball's first real game. Nobody ever found it."

"It would have been neat to know him," Trammell said.

"Bet he could have settled the damn strike," Roger Clemens said.

Everyone was quiet for a while, until Ripken, I guess because he couldn't think of anything else, took off his O's cap and put it by the tombstone.

"This is why we should play the Series here," he said, "to honor him."

"I guess that's why you faxed us to meet you here, huh?" Griffey said.

"I didn't fax you."

"But I got a fax with your name on it," Griffey said.

"Me, too," Piazza said. The same went for Maddux, Rijo, Gibson, Ozzie.

"Hey, guys," Ripken said, "I hate to tell you, but I don't own a fax machine."

We all looked at each other, as a seagull flew overhead and squawked like the devil.

NYHOW, ALL THIS IS BACKDROP to Game 3, the first game in this Series
to go to extra innings, and the first time in history a batter has gotten 13 hits
in 13 World Series at-bats — Tony Gwynn, whose stroke is so amazing, the other
players are asking to touch his bat, hoping some magic rubs off.

Gwynn is batting 1.000. We thought .400 was a big deal.

Game 3, as mentioned, was also the first chance for Mitch Williams to atone
for the World Series pitch that has hounded him from his stardom in Philly to his
outcast status in the game today. But after the five-run, four-homer fourth inning,
he gave up a run in the sixth and two in the eighth.

Ryan alternated between fanning batters and fueling them. At the end of nine,
he had eight strikeouts and had allowed eight extra-base hits.

"Overtime!" Gwynn yelled to start the 10th.

"Great, I have to pitch to him again?" Ryan said.

Ryan did have to pitch to Gwynn, but only after the American League had
scored three runs in the top of the 10th — a Gibson double and a misplay by the
minor league second baseman, Pokey Reese, were the keys — and the score was
11-8, with the American League the likely winner.

Ten minutes later, Bonds threatened to tie it when he whacked that ball with
two on and two out, and he stormed around the bases, as Gibson fired to Puckett
— who was playing second base.

"GO, BOBBY! GO, BOBBY!" Berra yelled.

"Barry!" Bonds screamed at him as he rounded third and thundered toward
home. Here came the throw — Puckett has a rocket of an arm — Kelly caught it,
dived … .

"OUT!" screamed umpire Doug Harvey.

Game over. AL wins, 11-10.

"What a throw!" Puckett yelled at Mattingly, jumping into his arms.

"What a relay!" Mattingly yelled.

"We're halfway to the title!" their teammates croaked.

Bonds was up like a flash and charging, not at the ump but at Berra. "Why
did you send me, you dumb old man? What the bleep is wrong with you? And
you don't even know my name!"

Berra looked stunned. He mumbled. Then he grabbed his chest. His eyes
rolled back, and he fell over.

"Oh my God, you killed him!" Rijo yelled.

"What are you talking about?" Bonds said. He leaned over Berra.

As the players rushed to their manager — "He's breathing, call an
ambulance!" — a woman from the farmhouse came running out and beckoned to
Kelly. They whispered for a minute.

Kelly, somber, came to the teams.

"We've got more problems, guys. Someone named Steinbrenner has been
calling our local chamber of commerce. He's offering $10,000 to anyone who
can tell him whether Don Mattingly is playing. … "

Solo triple play upstaged
October 20, 1994

SOMEWHERE IN HAWAII — The party didn't last long — four days, to be exact. Four days of what baseball should be, a patient game played by graceful athletes who grab the sun and dip it in drama.

Party's over.

Game 4 of what America is calling the Secret World Series was barely completed — the National League players were still celebrating their incredible finish, an unassisted triple play by a 21-year-old rookie — when Barry Bonds and his ever-present portable TV gave us the news: "We bring you this special report. … "

Party's over.

"Listen!" Bonds had yelled, holding up the Sony Watchman. The others lowered their beers and fell silent at the newscast — "the Secret World Series is being played right here, in Hawaii" — and one by one, the happy faces drooped, the smiles disappeared. Suddenly, what had been a wage-less effort for the love of the game was transformed into a bunker mentality.

"How long till all those people get here?" Cal Ripken asked.

"Maybe they don't know exactly where we are," Roger Clemens said.

"Couldn't we just nuke 'em?" Lenny Dykstra said.

"Relax," Yogi Berra said, "they can't find us if we're a secret, right?"

I think Yogi's starting to lose it.

By the way, he's OK physically. There was some concern after Game 3, when Yogi fell over, holding his chest and appeared to suffer a heart attack at third base. Bonds had just hollered at Yogi for waving him home on a line drive.

"Oh my God, you killed him!" Jose Rijo screamed at Bonds.

Turns out Yogi just had, well, gas. In between innings he had been eating the grilled chicken and pork dipped in poi — a nice Hawaiian specialty served on the sidelines of this wonderful ballfield. The poi, combined with the heat and Bonds' screaming at him, caused Yogi to faint.

When he came to, Kirby Puckett was leaning over him.

"Yogi, man, we thought you were dead."

"No, somebody woulda told me."

Everybody cracked up.

Oh, if all of baseball could be like this.

Or THIS: GAME 4, A THICK loaf of a contest, heavy drama and tight pitching by the Braves' Cy Young winner, Greg Maddux, and the Yankees' Jim Abbott. Both were making their second starts of the Series, and both seemed to find a groove.

Maddux, at one point, struck out Ken Griffey, Puckett and Cal Ripken in order.

Abbott did not allow a baserunner for the first six innings — except Tony Gwynn, who doubled and drew a walk. Gwynn is weaving a miracle here, batting 1.000 for the Series and proving that the .394 season he was having — before the strike ruined it — was no fluke. He singles to left. He singles to right. He lines them up the middle. He smacks them to the fence.

"Man," he said, coming back to the bench after the first inning, "even I can't believe how hot I am."

By the way, he now locks his bat in a closet.

Still, the story of this day would be a 21-year-old, Double-A infielder from Chattanooga, who arrived here with Rijo and who hasn't said five words all week. His name is Calvin (Pokey) Reese. He is maybe 6-feet tall, with big, sad eyes and a slinky posture. One night, during the regular card game, Rijo told a few of the players, "Pokey's a good kid, but he had a tough break. Right after he got drafted, his fiance was killed in a car crash. Middle of the day. She was by herself. No real explanation.

"They had a little baby girl, 6 months old. Now, she's all Pokey has left."

Rijo sighed. "It broke his heart. He had some bad months in the minors. That's why I brought him here. Let him see what the game can be, you know? He's going to be in The Show one day. This kid can make plays."

He made one they'll never forget Wednesday afternoon, top of the ninth, with the bases loaded and Griffey at the plate.

Back TO THAT IN A MOMENT. But if this noble adventure comes to a sudden halt when the networks and agents and union people get here — American League catcher Mike Kelly already has guards stationed at the entrance to his property, which, fortunately, is pretty tough to find — well, I want this to be noted. Never have I seen such camaraderie among professional baseball players. It seems to deepen each day. When we arrived, some of them complained about sharing the bathrooms at the Kelly house, or walking the half-mile to the ballfield. Not anymore.

Same goes for their attitude toward fans. Initially, they didn't want even the locals from the village watching the games. "This World Series will be strictly baseball!" they insisted. But now fans and players mingle before and after the games. The athletes are in no hurry, they don't mind signing autographs, and none of the fans asks for more than one.

(To be honest, I've never seen sports fans like these. They're like something out of the 19th Century. They cheer even when a player makes an out. "Good try!" "Next time!" I'm telling you, there must be something funny in the mist.)

Speaking of which, I have yet to figure out whose idea this was. The players all say they got a fax signed by other players, but none of them admits sending the fax. How anyone had all their numbers — and why he or she didn't identify himself or herself — is a mystery.

But then, mysteries seem quite normal in this valley. Take our host, Kelly. He admitted a few days ago that he's the great-grandson of the legendary King Kelly, one of baseball's pioneers — which explains the uncanny resemblance. But Buck O'Neil, the 82-year-old American League manager, remains skeptical. He pulled me aside.

"You know, I'd swear old King Kelly was a bachelor," O'Neil said. "I don't remember hearing about a family."

"And another thing. I looked something up. You know when King Kelly died?"

"When?"

"One hundred years ago next month."

I kept that fact to myself. I figure with this whole thing about to blow up, the players have enough to think about.

MICHAEL JORDAN MIGHT BE THINKING more than any of them. He is putting together maybe the worst World Series in history — and I know it's killing him.

In the first three games, Jordan struck out eight times and hit only one ball out of the infield. He also committed six errors, including a ball through his legs that lost Game 2. Roger Clemens still isn't talking to him because of that. They pass each other at breakfast, and Jordan says, "Rog, man, look ... " and Clemens glares at him as if he wants him sliced up like lunch meat.

No wonder Bill Buckner moved out of Boston.

What's easy to forget is that while most of these players are taking pay cuts because of the strike, Jordan was never making much money to play minor league baseball. He did it for the love of the game.

Early yesterday, I heard a popping sound outside my window and discovered Jordan, at 7 a.m., out in a field, by himself, hitting balls, chasing them down, starting over again.

"You know what's the hardest part for me?" he admitted. "Not being excellent. At every level, I was always way ahead of my group. I could always lead.

"Here, it's like I can't even follow well."

He took another swing — and popped the ball up. I told Jordan that, for what it was worth, when he was Superman, I didn't always like him. I like him more now.

He thought for a second, said nothing and returned to his swings.

O F COURSE, A FEW BASEBALL supermen are here. And if outsiders ruin this series, well, shame on them for squashing the daily rivalry between Ken Griffey and Matt Williams for the home run bragging rights. Since Game 1, they have been circling each other like birds of prey.

When Griffey hits one out, he yells: "Did you see that, Matty? Whew! That went a long way!"

When Williams hits one, he says nothing. He just stares at Griffey as he rounds second base.

The battle reached a new level yesterday. In the top of the seventh, Griffey came to bat, and a fan yelled, "It's Babe Griffey!"

The Seattle star grinned, then seemed to get an idea. He looked at Williams, on third base, then pointed to the rightfield fence.

"He's calling his shot," I whispered to Yogi.

"Yeah, and he's pointing where he's going to hit a home run, too."

The pitch from Maddux came down the pipe — an emotional mistake by the hurler — and pow! It was headed for a volcano.

"Look out, Matty!" Griffey taunted as he jogged the base paths. "That one might bring lava!"

Williams looked straight ahead. But in the bottom of the seventh, when he came to bat — with Mike Piazza on base ahead of him — Williams broke his normal silence. He yelled: "Leftfield!"

And he pointed, too.

"I don't believe this," I whispered.

"It's deja vu all over again," Yogi said.

Jim Abbott, not wanting to be upstaged, threw Williams a low fastball, down and away. Not the kind of pitch you hit out. Not unless you're possessed.

Williams reached down, and beyond all reason, somehow got that ball and sent it exactly where he predicted — over the leftfield fence. The fans in attendance — all 193 of them — roared in delight as Griffey tried to look at the sky. It was a moment of one-upmanship that even the Babe would have been proud of.

S TILL, THE HIGHLIGHT, AS I NOTED, came in the ninth. With the Nationals clinging to their 2-1 lead, Maddux started Jordan with a fastball, and — surprise — Michael bunted.

"Run!" his teammates yelled.

They needn't have bothered. Jordan was off like a shot — and everyone was so stunned that he had made contact, there wasn't even a play.

The next batter, Don Mattingly, laced a shot down the leftfield line, which he legged into a double, with Jordan stopping at third. Maddux had little choice but to walk Alan Trammell intentionally, and who was next in line but Griffey.

The crowd stood up. Even the guy cooking poi put down his utensils.

"HIT IT OUT, BABE GRIFFEY!" someone yelled, but the kid was all business now. Maddux leaned in, clenched his jaw, went to the stretch and released. …

The sound alone suggested success. The "mmwhak!" was as pure as a tick of Big Ben, the ball shot toward centerfield, and the runners were in instant motion. And then — honestly, I still don't know how — second baseman Reese was flying across the airspace, snaring that ball like a jai alai scoop, landing on second base — two outs right there — then breaking into a sprint toward Trammell, who dug his cleats, kicked up dirt and nearly fell trying to reverse himself. Reese chased, Trammell ran, Reese was gaining, Trammell dug —

"THROW IT!" Ryne Sandberg yelled from first base — but Reese was obsessed, one more step, one more step, now, now! He dived, body stretching out, and just nipped Trammell's ankle a foot before Trammell reached the bag.

"OUT!" yelled the sole umpire, Doug Harvey.

Out? The game was over? An unassisted triple play? Only the second one in World Series history.

"PO-KEY! PO-KEY! PO-KEY!" the crowd yelled. Reese raised his head and wiped the dirt from his eyes. Before he could get up, he was mobbed by his National League teammates, who grabbed him and tossed him high in the air. "PO-KEY! PO-KEY!" It was the first time I had seen the kid smile since he had been here. It was as true a smile as you could ever paint. They carried him off in the warm Hawaiian sunshine as a school class sang a native song, something about "the loveliness of effort." …

That was five hours ago. We sit here now, late at night, awaiting the invasion of owners, lawyers, broadcasters, money-grubbers. Like the end of summer camp, I fear this whole thing is about to shut down, badly. And I'm not sure there's any way to stop it.

Rare Air: It's over and out
October 21, 1994

WAHIAWA, HAWAII — The coffee pot was nearly empty by the time the last players staggered down to breakfast. "Ohhhhh man," Lenny Dysktra moaned, rubbing his eyes.

Kirk Gibson sniffed as he filled his cup. "I hope I can see the ball this early."

It was 7:30 a.m., and already, half a mile away, a small crowd of spectators was gathered near the lush green playing field in the shadow of the Waianae mountains, where two dozen players — mostly major leaguers — soon would arrive, players who had vowed to finish their Secret World Series on their own terms.

They would play until a champion was crowned.

If it took all day and night.

It was the only way, they had decided.

"We can't let them ruin everything," Cal Ripken had said in a frantic group meeting after news leaked that the Series was being played here in Hawaii and the financial forces of baseball — owners, union officials, marketing people, TV networks — boarded planes for the island. Heck, they were probably here already, determined to shut down these games.

Donald Fehr had declared the Secret Series "treason to the brothers of baseball," claiming it weakened the strike. The owners called it a "violation of all contracts" because they weren't seeing a dime. ABC said "either we televise it, or we sue for damages." And the licensing people wanted all rights to sweatshirts, T-shirts and other souvenirs.

"Jeez, all we wanted to do was make sure there was a World Series this year," Jim Abbott said.

"Once they find us, we're history," Don Mattingly noted.

"We could keep moving," Ozzie Smith suggested. "Maybe get to another island."

"I don't think so," said Mike Kelly, the Hawaii native and great-grandson of King Kelly, the early baseball legend. "By tomorrow night, they'll be so many people offering so much money, no place will be remote enough."

"We could nuke 'em," Dykstra said.

"What is it with you and nuking people?" Ken Griffey asked.

"Hey, dude, we're history. If we're lucky, we have one day left before we lose control of this Series."

"That's right. And we're tied, two games apiece."

"You guys could forfeit."

"You forfeit!"

From the back of the room, a voice said, "I have an idea."

Everyone turned to Ernie Banks, who had been sitting quietly, listening to the wind. Banks — who had never gotten to play in a World Series — had become a sort of guru to this affair, watching the games from both benches, sharing stories, absorbing every minute. He gazed at ribbons of pink sunset in the darkening sky.

"Looks like a beautiful day tomorrow," he said, breaking into a familiar smile. "Let's play three."

A ND SO IT WAS on Oct. 20, 1994, Game 5 of the World Series began at 8:05 a.m., in the hazy morning sunshine, and before the day was done a champion would be crowned and victorious songs would echo through these canyons — but for now it was, "Good morning, batter up!" Tony Gwynn of the National League walked out, perhaps the first time in World Series history the leadoff man was yawning.

"Maybe he's too tired to hit," whispered Buck O'Neil, the 82-year-old American League manager.

Nope. Gwynn, blinking as he swung, laced the first pitch down the rightfield line for a long single. It should have been a double, but nobody runs very fast this early.

With that hit, by the way, Gwynn was 17-for-17, the best offensive World Series ever.

"Forget it, Rog!" Alan Trammell yelled to his pitcher, Roger Clemens. "Let's double up this next guy. Humbabe, humbabe, humbabe."

Clemens nodded, reached back, then stopped. He looked up at the sound of a distant engine that was growing louder in the sky. Gwynn looked up, too, and so did the others, Trammell, Griffey, Kirk Gibson, Barry Bonds, Mitch Williams, Julie Croteau, Yogi Berra, all of them.

O'Neil saw them first. He exhaled deeply.

"Helicopters," he whispered.

A S THIS WAS GOING ON, the baggage-claim area of Honolulu International Airport was like something out of baseball's central casting. Fehr, Richard Ravitch, 17 major league owners, including George Steinbrenner (of the Yankees, who employ Mattingly), and Jerry Reinsdorf (of the White Sox, who employ Michael Jordan), Dan Rather and Connie Chung from CBS, Tim McCarver and Jim Palmer from ABC, two dozen people from Major League Baseball Licensing, with cartons of souvenirs loaded behind them — all of these folks were throwing themselves into limousines and taxis and yelling directions across car roofs.

"Take us to the cemetery where that Alexander Cartwright is buried,"

Steinbrenner barked at the limo driver. "The field has to be near there. Hurry up, or I'll fire you!"

"But I don't work for you," the stunned driver said.

"Then I'll buy the company you work for and fire you! Now MOVE!"

B Y 10 A.M., GAME 5 WAS in the seventh inning, with the American League leading, 8-5, thanks to a two-run homer by Mattingly and a bases-loaded double by, of all people, Clemens.

The good news was, the helicopters had gone away. They came over the mountain and then abruptly turned around. "Lucky break," Ripken said, although we all were a little suspicious.

Not so lucky was Clemens' left knee. He had bruised it sliding into second on his double, and it was swelling beneath his uniform. He sat with ice between innings, but by the eighth he was limping with every pitch.

O'Neil, as manager, was faced with a tough decision. He had only Nolan Ryan, who was scheduled to pitch the next game — which would begin in an hour — or Abbott, who had pitched eight innings the day before, or Lee Anne Ketcham, the female walk-on from the Silver Bullets.

Logic would have dictated going with the major league guys, no matter what. But O'Neil took one look at Ketcham, whose eyes said, "I can do this," and he remembered all the days in his career when they said baseball wasn't ready for his type.

"Start warming up," he told Ketcham. "Just in case Roger can't make it."

In the top of the ninth, Clemens summoned everything he had. He was actually grunting between pitches. He got Dykstra to foul out on a change-up and got Mike Piazza on a fly to deep left. Matt Williams would have been the final out — had he not smoked a Clemens fastball over the rightfield fence.

"BLEEP IT!" Clemens yelled. "BLEEP! BLEEPIN' BLEEP!"

In the stands, mothers put their hands over their children's ears.

The score was 8-6. Bonds swaggered to the plate. "You got nothin' left, Roger," he taunted. "You got nothin' leffffft."

Clemens fumed. But Bonds was right. He sat on the first pitch — maybe an 80-m.p.h. fastball — and whacked it over Jordan's head in rightfield, about 50 feet over his head.

"Here we come, baby!" Bonds yelled, rounding the bases.

It was 8-7.

"Time!" O'Neil hollered. He rose from the bench, stepped over the white line, took a breath and nodded.

Out came Clemens, cursing.

And in went Lee Anne Ketcham.

N OW I WOULD LIKE TO TELL YOU that Ketcham mowed down the next batter, winning the game and scoring a blow for equal rights, women's sports and the free world.

But that would not be true.

What Ketcham did was throw four straight high balls to Ryne Sandberg, and four straight low balls to Ozzie Smith, and two straight outside pitches to Pokey Reese, followed by a foul ball, followed by two more outside pitches.

She loaded the bases on walks.

The crowd groaned.

"Damn it, Buck," Ryan mumbled on the bench, "put me in there before she blows the dang game."

The other American Leaguers were thinking the same thing. Gibson spit on the ground and shook his head. Griffey waved at O'Neil as if to say, "Come on, already!"

O'Neil walked out to the mound. He took the ball from Ketcham, and she looked down, exhaled and started to walk off.

"Where you going?" O'Neil asked.

She stopped. He stood there, rubbing the ball slowly.

"You know, when I was playing back in the old Negro leagues, we used to travel with nine players in one car. We had to sit with our arms reaching across one another just to make room. Four-hour drive, five-hour drive. We'd get out, stretch, then get back in with our arms the other way.

"We didn't do it for a cause, we didn't do it for race, politics or none of that stuff. We did it because we wanted to play. We were hungry.

"If you ask me, being hungry is the best quality a ballplayer can have. Don't you think?"

He half-smiled, then handed the ball back to her.

"I was just cleaning it off for you."

And so, at 11:28 a.m., under a partly cloudy Hawaiian sky, Lee Anne Ketcham threw this pitch to Jose Rijo: a low slider over the plate. Rijo pounded the ball high toward centerfield, and the runners took off, circling the bases. Two of them crossed the plate before Griffey reached the fence. The ball was coming down, fans were on their feet, Griffey bounded into the links, ricocheted up and caught the ball at the top of his trajectory.

He landed, feet first, like a kid jumping from a low tree. He held the ball over his head.

Game over. Americans win, 8-7. They were one win from the title.

"YEAH!"

Ketcham was mobbed by her teammates. They hoisted her in celebration.

"KETCHAM! KETCHAM!"

"Jesus, I'm lifting a woman pitcher!" Gibson yelled, half in jest. "This is the damnedest World Bleepin' Series!"

Ketcham looked across at O'Neil as a single teardrop fell.

His, not hers.

"C AN'T YOU GO ANY FASTER?" Steinbrenner was yelling. His limo was the first in a fleet that looked like a dozen presidential motorcades. They were winding their way from Nuuanu cemetery, up Highway 99, and across the Waikele River, as the white hotels of Honolulu faded into the landscape of these tropical islands. The sign read: "Wahiawa three miles."

"This is the only place I can think of where a guy could fit a ballfield on his property," the driver said. "But I gotta tell you, I never saw one."

"Just keep driving," Steinbrenner said. "When I get ahold of Mattingly, I'm gonna shake him upside down for every nickel I ever paid him."

Two cars back, Fehr was barking into his cellular phone. "That's right, operator, a Mike Kelly. ... Impossible! ... What are you talking about? ... Oh, for bleep's sake!"

He threw the phone across the seat. "She said there's no Mike Kelly listed on the entire island."

B ACK ON THE FIELD, THE PLAYERS took a 20-minute intermission before starting Game 6. Each night we had been getting together for a barbecue on Kelly's back patio, and the accomplishments of the Series were reviewed and debated. Since I was in charge of recording everything — that was how I got invited, remember? — and since time now was precious, I gave the teams a brief synopsis of where they stood after five of the best games ever to squeeze under the marquee "Fall Classic."

"Griffey and Matt Williams are leading the home-run battle ...

"Michael, unfortunately — "

"Don't even say it," Jordan said.

Everyone knew he was on a record pace for errors and strikeouts. But he managed to grin, and that made everyone feel better.

"Pokey Reese, your unassisted triple play was the second in World Series history. Congratulations."

The minor leaguer smiled shyly and looked down as Rijo slapped him on the back.

"And Tony Gwynn — you, Cowboy, are breaking every record known to man."

The players laughed and rolled their eyes. Gwynn was batting 1.000. What more could you say?

"Come on, Tony, let us touch your bat," Griffey, Mattingly, Trammell and Bonds said, getting on their knees.

"No way," said Gwynn, who had taken to sleeping with the tan Louisville Slugger model. "Nobody touches this baby."

"Uh, guys, I hate to rush you," Mike Kelly said. "But this ain't that big an island."

They nodded and grabbed their gloves and caps. The players took the field in businesslike fashion, and the crowd — I'm guessing 300, the biggest yet — applauded loudly. I looked at the big manual scoreboard the players had built the first day and the uniforms they wore with no names or numbers. They were playing during the day. They were not getting paid.

It struck me how far backward we had gone in five days. Or forward.

BY THE WAY, SPEAKING OF Kelly, I did some research. And Buck O'Neil was right. The original King Kelly died almost exactly 100 years ago. He was still a young man, but he had been fired from his baseball job for drinking too much. He was reduced to traveling around the country in burlesque shows, reciting "Casey at the Bat."

In 1894, he caught pneumonia and was taken to a Boston hospital. There, while being carried on a stretcher, the man who made sliding famous was somehow dropped by the orderlies. He rolled down the stairs. Injured and ill, he managed to make his last notable remark.

"That," he whispered, "was my last slide."

Three days later, he was dead.

Weird, huh? But true.

GAME 6 OF THE SECRET SERIES officially began at 12:01 p.m., Hawaiian time, with reliever Mitch Williams again starting for the National League and 47-year-old Nolan Ryan throwing for the American. After three innings, the score was 2-2, and after five innings, it was 5-5. Matt Williams had two home runs. Griffey had one. As the players came out for the sixth, nerves were tightening. The Series could be nearing the end.

Bonds pointed to the sky.

"Uh-oh," he said. "Check it out."

The Goodyear blimp.

ASK THIS GUY! ASK this guy!" ABC president Dennis Swanson yelled from the back of his limo. ABC, NBC, CBS and TNT were in a race of their own to get cameras set and begin broadcasting. Like the owners and union officials, they also were racing through the mountainous roads outside Wahiawa in search of the Kelly ballfield. The limo driver had no idea how close he was when he came upon a squat old man with a large nose sitting in a beach chair at the bottom of a road, a sombrero pulled over his eyes.

"Hey, buddy, does this road go to the Kelly place?"

"Never heard of him," the man said from under his hat.

"You know of any baseball fields around here?"

"Never heard of baseball."

"Baseball! You know, bats and balls, Mickey Mantle?"

"Never heard of Mickey Mantle."

Swanson leaned forward. "Forget this geezer. Let's drive up there and look for ourselves."

"Me no do that," the man said.

"Why not?"

"This a volcano."

"A volcano? What the hell are you doing here then?"

"Waiting for big explosion."

The man paused. "Me like explosions."

Swanson looked at his driver. "Turn around," he ordered.

The limo turned around, and so did the dozen vehicles behind it. As they pulled away, Swanson was yelling, "When we find these players, their little charade is over!"

Under the hat, Yogi Berra smiled.

"It ain't over till it's over," he whispered.

THIS IS HOW THE WORLD SERIES of 1994 ended. There might be some disputes, but I was there, and I'm telling you what I saw:

In the bottom of the ninth, the National League led, 6-5. It looked as if the Faux Classic would go to seven games — if it wasn't shut down first. The blimp was still overhead, and the approaching sound of helicopters was increasing every moment. The American League had the bottom of the order due up — catcher Mike Kelly, batting .050, pitcher Nolan Ryan, hitless in the Series, and Jordan, who was setting a record for strikeouts.

"Piece of cake, Mitchie," Ozzie Smith sang from his shortstop position. "Hum it, baby, hum it, baby, hum it."

Williams hummed it — and Kelly hummed it right back. A solid shot to the gap in rightfield — his first hit since the fluke home run in Game 1. Gwynn played it badly off the fence, and Kelly went to third with a stand-up triple.

"C'mon, Tony, gimme some defense," Williams implored. "I ain't losing another World Series, OK?"

Ryan came to the plate, and Williams smoked a fastball past him, strike one. He came back with the change-up, and Ryan was so fooled he swung wildly, spun around and fell on the plate. "Eeeyow!" he yelled. A groin pull. Bad one. His teammates helped him off.

"I'm getting too old for this," Ryan said.

With no reserve hitters, O'Neil had no choice.

"Abbott," he said. "Just get up there and ... whatever."

Abbott took a bat and went to the plate. I guess most people assume, since he was born with only one hand, that Abbott's hitting is nonexistent. That's not true; his senior year at Flint Central, he hit six homers and batted over .400. And when he came to the plate, he shot a glance down third base to Kelly. Wait. Did he smile?

The pitch came in — and Abbott wheeled and bunted, a perfect bunt down the third-base line. Kelly, who saw it coming, got a jump and was chugging home, a suicide squeeze. Williams yelled, "Ohhhh, bleep!" as he dashed for the ball, scooped it up barehanded and whipped it to Mike Piazza, who seemed to have the plate covered. Then Kelly — whose great-grandfather inspired the song, "Slide, Kelly, Slide" — did something I've never seen before. He whipped himself like a boomerang — as he slid — and curled around Piazza, who was so startled that he barely attempted a tag.

"Where'd he go?" Piazza said.

"SAFE!" the ump called.

The bench went nuts. Nobody had ever seen anything like that. Mattingly, Trammell, Griffey, Ripken high-fived and whooped as the crowd stood up to applaud the whirling dervish, Mike Kelly.

"You're the King!" Mattingly yelled. "King Kelly!"

The score was tied. I was sitting closest as Kelly walked back, dusting himself off. He looked to the sky and he mouthed something, and while most people thought he was giving thanks, I tell you, truly, this is what he said:

"Now that," he whispered to the heavens, "was my last slide."

A ND NOW JORDAN CAME TO BAT. He swung badly at the first pitch, took two more for balls, and then made about the worst swing I've ever seen, actually losing his grip on the bat. It flew toward the bleachers, barely missing the guy who sells grilled chicken and poi. It didn't miss his grill, however. It knocked the thing over. When Jordan retrieved the bat, it was not only chipped, it was covered in sauce.

"Uh, anybody got a spare?" he said.

What followed was either the nicest or dumbest thing a World Series player ever did. Gwynn, Mr. Perfection, called time from the outfield. He jogged in and got his special, tan, Louisville Slugger model.

He handed it to a startled Jordan.

"Why?" was all Jordan could say. "Why me?"

"Cause you stood by the game," Gwynn said. "We shoulda done the same."

Does it shock you, then, that Jordan dug his cleats and tightened his fingers around that bat and bent his knees and cocked his head and finally, finally got that look he always had when he was playing basketball and a last shot needed to be made? And Williams threw a pitch that was remarkably similar to one he threw last year about this time, to a fellow named Joe Carter, and Jordan stroked it on a clean shot up, up and away.

Home run. The final note.

"AAAAARRRGGGH!" Jordan yelled, dancing like a man sprung from a maximum-security prison. Final score: 8-6. Americans take the Series, four games to two.

Every game went down to the wire. Every game had a different hero. The 1994 season could go in the books. There was a world champion, after all.

"We did it, baby! We won!" the American players yelled, and they were quickly joined by the National Leaguers, who chanted, "We finished! We finished!" They waved up at the Goodyear blimp. "Nice try!" they yelled. Buck O'Neil was in tears. Yogi came running in, still wearing his sombrero, yelling, "That's the greatest thing I never saw!" The players, from Abbott to Ripken to

Julie Croteau to Pokey Reese to Bonds, Griffey, Williams, Dykstra, faces of today, tomorrow and yesterday formed a big line and bowed to the crowd, all 300 of them, which was clapping and whistling, the sound echoing into the valley.

"Hey, how about it for the man with the field!" Ripken yelled. "Give a hand, folks, to Mike Kelly!"

Everybody looked.

Kelly was gone.

W ELL, BY NOW YOU'VE PROBABLY seen the TV accounts. The owners, union officials, merchandisers and TV execs finally found their way up the road and came upon a ballfield, but it was empty and bare.

The Oahu authorities say the land in that area is a public park, and there is no record of a Kelly ever owning any of it.

The Goodyear blimp people tried desperately to air the few minutes of footage they shot, but apparently they were too far up. All you could see were the field and some bodies — or at least they looked like bodies. They might have been birds.

As for the players, well, they managed to get off the island without being mobbed. Don't ask me how. The last time I saw them, minutes after the game, they were jumping into three brown vans. Gibson and Trammell, who had invited me on this crazy experience, stopped me at the door.

"The deal's done," they said, smiling. "This is where we part company."

I stepped back, a little stunned, but I guess I understood. And then, because I couldn't think of anything else to say, I said, "Thank you."

"Just tell them what happened," they said.

And the van was gone.

In the hours that followed, nearly every inch of the area was examined. Only two significant things were discovered:

At the Nuuanu gravesite of Alexander Cartwright, the man who really invented baseball and who spread the joy of the game from the Atlantic to the Pacific — a tan bat, Louisville Slugger model, was found leaning against the tombstone.

And inside a large farmhouse near the mysterious ballfield, of all things, a fax machine.

Years from now, they'll debate whether this Series should count, whether it gets an asterisk, whether it is ignored as some sort of crazy stunt by deranged players. You know what? Talk doesn't matter. This might not have been the real World Series, but it was the only one we had. And for those of us who were there, it was every wonderful thing baseball is supposed to be.

You could look it up.

Well, maybe …

Comment

Small voice, big difference

November 1, 1992

I HEARD A KNOCK UPON MY DOOR
And opened it to see,
All the poor around the world
Looking back at me.
In tattered clothes and worn-out shoes
With families to feed,
They held their hands out, hopefully,
Could I address their need?
"Too many," I said, overwhelmed,
And shut the door in dread.
For I am just one person,
"There's a way," a small voice said.

NOT a moment passed before
I heard another knock,
And all the hungry, 'round the world
Were out there, to my shock.
Their bellies round and bloated
The eyes as blank as chalk,
They looked at me as if to speak
But fell, too weak to talk.
I shut the door in sorrow,
"There's too many to be fed!"
For I am just one person,
"There's a way," the small voice said.

WHO was this voice, I wondered?
When a knock drew my surprise.
Foreign armies 'round my house,
Blocking out the skies.
Their weapons spread for miles and miles
Their missiles at the fore,
They seemed to ask for my reply,
I quickly shut the door.
"There must be some mistake!" I cried
"These armies are misled,
"I have no power over them!"
"You do," this small voice said.

AND as I pondered for a while,
Another knock I heard.
This time the door revealed to me
A vision quite absurd.
All the nation's ill and sick
Were crowded on my lawn,
Wheelchairs, nurses, bandages,
Were stretched from dusk to dawn.
"What will you do?" they said as one,
"To pay for all these beds?"
"You're asking me?" I told them,
"They are," the small voice said.

AND then a knock, a rapping sound
And fire, like a torch,
I looked outside to see the
Nation's crime wave on my porch.
They seemed to stretch beyond the night
They branded guns and chains,
Stolen cars and stolen goods
Fell from my roof like rains.
"Go!" I shouted, "Go away!
"I won't call the police!"
I slammed the door, then heard that voice:
"You can make it cease."

AND so it went for all the day
The knocking never ending,
And every time a different cause,
Too big for comprehending.
And always came this foolish voice,
From where did this voice spring,
Assuring me I had power over everything?
"SHOW YOURSELF!" I hollered now,
"For this has gone too far.
"I'm busy, I've got work to do,
"I need to wash my car.
"This optical illusion
"Is fine for just a game,
"But thinking I can change the world
"Is really quite insane."

I waited then for some reply,
But quiet fell once more.
Finally, a faint and weakened
Knocking on my door.
I opened it to see a child there
Bending at the knee.
I gasped for breath and rubbed my eyes,
For this child looked like me

HIS face was hung in sadness,
His body thin and lone,
His eyes revealed a hopelessness
That chilled me to my bone.
I wanted to embrace him, but
He turned and walked away.
"You've left your child no future,"
I heard that small voice say.
"The power to create a change
"For hungry and for poor,
"Those armies, you ignored them
"Tho' just outside your door.
"Because you are one person,
"You gave nothing but your sighs.
"The sadness of this legacy
"Lies in your children's eyes"

NOW my heart was stirring,
My anger boiled and bubbled.
"Tell me, then!" I hollered,
"How I can save the troubled?
"Tell me how I can create
"This laughter from despair,
"Tell me where this magic cure
"Lies hidden in the air.
"Tell me how a person trying
"To work and sleep and eat,
"Can make a dent in problems
"Meant for armies, or Wall Street.
"Tell me how a simple soul
"Turns living from the dead"
And here it came, a single word,
"Vote," the small voice said.

Too late our applause

January 10, 1993

D IZZY IS DEAD. HE BLEW NOTES around the melody. He blew notes around the world. He was blowing them almost up till his death by cancer in a New Jersey hospital last week. And when he died, the music he made with his trumpet was replaced by another sound: applause. First from his friends, then his co-workers, then his country, then the world. It would turn, quickly, into a standing ovation, headlines, TV news stories, old footage, verbal tributes. It was the loudest the world had ever cheered him.

All he had to do was die.

For jazz artists and other non-pop stars of culture, death seems to be the only time that recognition comes close to achievement. On the same day that Gillespie, 75, passed to the angels, a brooding, starkly handsome Russian-born dancer named Rudolph Nureyev was dying too, in a hospital bed in Paris. Most believe he was smitten by AIDS. He said good-bye at age 54. The applause began the moment death claimed him. Nureyev! Such brilliance! Such artistry! What a terrible loss, we all lamented. He was truly the best.

And yet the saddest part of both their passings is this: How many of us know anything by either of these two geniuses? Try this test: Hum three songs made famous by Dizzy Gillespie. Hum one.

Now mimic the most outstanding movements of Nureyev in any of his ballet performances. Can you? Even one? The greatest of his time? Even one?

N OW TAKE A PARALLEL TEST: Name one Madonna song. Name any of her god-awful movies. Name who she was married to. You can answer these, I'm betting.

Now mimic the "Moonwalk" dance by Michael Jackson. Or name two parts of his face he's had altered by plastic surgery.

Don't tell me. You scored 100, right?

These facts we know. They jump to mind. Our high-gloss, fast-food, chew-and-spit culture is what most of us think of when we think "entertainment." Especially our children. And that is the saddest part.

What they don't know is that Quincy Jones, the man who produced Jackson's "Thriller" — the biggest-selling album of all time — was given one of his earliest breaks by, guess who? Dizzy Gillespie. What they don't know is that Dizzy helped father a form of music so revolutionary that people in the '40s screamed it had a bad influence on young people, the same tag rock 'n' roll suffered a decade later.

What they don't know is that Gillespie made dozens of records, wrote movie scores, created songs over the top of other songs. That his goatee, horn-rimmed glasses, bow tie and beret created a fashion fad of "hep" in the '40s that people rushed to imitate, although he never made a penny from it. Or that his musical legacy, bebop, is today what most non-music people think of when someone says "jazz." I remember Kirk Gibson, the baseball star, once teasing a visitor about liking jazz. He mimicked a trumpet sound and went "be-de-de-be-bop."

Gibson had no idea he was paying homage to Dizzy Gillespie.

He is not alone.

DANCE, MEANWHILE, HAS BECOME AN essential part of pop music. Bobby Brown, Hammer, Michael Jackson, to name a few, are as celebrated for their moves as for their music. The fact that they are can, in no small way, be traced to Nureyev. Ever since 1961, when he leapt over an airport railing in Paris and into the custody of French police, leaving communist Russia behind, the western concept of male dance has been altered.

Nureyev was muscular, powerful, his leaps were athletic as well as artistic. So dramatic was his talent that he once received 89 curtain calls at a single performance. He revolutionized his art and gave a rock-star persona to a field that previously had been best known for graceful women.

But what do our children know of him? Did they ever see him dance? Would they recognize "Swan Lake" or "Giselle"?

Probably not, because ballet is considered "culture" — a word that excites people overseas and somehow frightens them here. Say it to kids, they pinch their faces. "Oh, no," they groan, "we're gonna watch PBS?" So addicted have we become to movie-star, MTV, newspaper-tabloid bombardment that we are like those rats in scientific experiments, racing to the sugar, over and over, even though, without nutrition, we die.

Culture — jazz, ballet, fine art — is nutrition. It means fields where excellence — not how much noise you make — determines stardom. It lasts. It is honest. The night after two artistic giants left this earth, Americans stood in line at midnight — not to buy their records or dance tapes but to buy a stamp that featured Elvis Presley's face.

Gillespie and Nureyev deserved more. It's nice that we applaud them in death; applauding them in life would have been better.

"And the winner is … "

January 17, 1993

L OS ANGELES — Sinbad, the comedian, took the envelope, broke the seal, and read aloud: "And the winner, for best original song, is … " My hands were sweating. My heart raced. How embarrassing! A few months back, when someone called to say a song I had written had been nominated for a Cable Ace Award, my reaction was more noble: I laughed.

Cable? Awards? I kept thinking of this "Saturday Night Live" skit, in which a man bursts on stage to accept "Best Weather Map."

"I want to thank my mother!" he gushes. "People said this couldn't be done … "

Cable? They give awards for cable? But in the weeks that followed, people kept insisting what a big deal the Cable Ace was.

After all, cable includes HBO, MTV, CNN and ESPN.

"Larry King!" someone said.

Well, now. He's hard to top.

"LA!" someone said. "Spotlights! Limousines! Gorgeous models!"

Models?

Then a letter came from Dick Clark Productions, addressed to all nominees. It said, in bold: "If you win, please keep your acceptance speech to 30 seconds."

Acceptance speech? Dick Clark?

N OW, I WOULD LIKE TO SAY I tore up that letter and went back to my doctoral thesis, "Genetic Engineering: a Proposal to Save Mankind."

Instead, I booked a flight.

And before I knew it, I was getting the ticket ($475), the hotel room ($129), the car ($40), the tuxedo ($70) and the haircut ($25).

This was not the most embarrassing part.

The most embarrassing part was that my nomination got so much attention. It was written about. It was talked about on radio.

Then ABC News called, said they wanted to do a profile piece and send a camera to the ceremony to capture my winning moment.

"What if I lose?" I said.

"Don't worry. Also, we'd like to wire you."

"Wire me?"

"Yeah. Run a little microphone under your clothes. No one will notice."

And there I was, with an ABC cameraman sticking his hands up my shirt. I felt like "Serpico." I kept waiting for some thug to rip open my tux and yell, "He's wearing a wire! The rat! Get him, boys!"

I SHOULD MENTION HERE THAT the song I wrote was for a TV movie Arnold Schwarzenegger directed called "Christmas in Connecticut" — it's a long story — and that joining me at the ceremony, also paying way too much for their outfits, were the singer, Janine Sabino, the arranger, Johnny Sabino, the executive producer, Stan Brooks, and his wife, Tanya.

We found a row of seats. Larry King sat right behind us. And I'm thinking, "Wow! Larry King." Then someone came and escorted Larry away, saying, "We want the big stars up front."

That should have tipped us off.

Instead, like good little nominees, we sat there, the five of us — six, if you count the wire up my shirt — and we waited through such presenters as Alex Trebek and Leeza Gibbons. We waited through videos. We waited through 46 awards, including "Best Makeup." Finally, they came to our category. Sinbad took the envelope.

"And the winner is … "

I have always wondered what people are thinking during, "And the winner is … " Now I know. You are hanging on the very next word, trying to mind-meld with the presenter and make him say the first letter of your name — I'm thinking, "Mmmm … say Mmmm … " — and when you hear something else come out of his mouth, your first thought is, "No, dummy, that's not how you pronounce it." Then you hear a cheer from another part of the room, and you realize he's pronouncing it right, but it's someone else's name. You lost. And then you sit there, looking straight ahead. And then you wish a big rock would fall from the ceiling and bury you.

Which is pretty much what happened. Except for the rock.

I lost. Or didn't win. I would like to tell you who did, but within five seconds, the ABC producer was at my seat, saying, "Can I have the mike back?" And I had to pull this thing from under my shirt, in front of everyone, as if my car loan was up and she was the repo man.

I know all glory is fading. I didn't know they ripped it off your chest.

And when I got back to the hotel, there was a message: "ABC piece is delayed a week."

"Jeez," Janine said, "next they come for the tuxedo."

And that was that. My only consolation is that Larry King also lost, and he had better seats. Did I learn a lesson? You bet. Keep your head high. Be flattered by the nomination. And if you ever get asked to another awards show, take all the money you would have foolishly spent on airplanes, cars, hotels and tuxes and put it to a much better use:

Buy a weather map.

Margarito and the five miracles
April 18, 1993

H E WAS WALKING THROUGH THE FIELD to get to his father, and
suddenly, there it was. A big, black snake. "Were you scared?" the boy is
asked. "No," he says now.

The snake had a yellow belly. It was poisonous. The boy did what he was
taught to do in his Guatemalan mountain village: He did not run. He watched the
snake, saw it move toward him.

"Then what happened?"

"Bit me," he says.

The boy began to die. His mother, who had seen the whole thing happen, was
crying. She grabbed her poisoned son and rushed to her husband. They left their
crops and other kids and went down the mountain to the nearest hospital. The
doctors shook their heads: Such bites were usually fatal. The parents waited.
Days passed. Poor and saddled with responsibilities, they went home. Maybe
they prayed. Maybe they wept. But they left their son for dead. This was five
years ago.

Margarito Sils is now 11 years old and sitting in front of me, with jet-black
hair, olive skin and a smile that comes right out of the cookie jar. How he got
from that crop field in Guatemala to an ice rink at Joe Louis Arena is one of those
crazy miracle-dusted stories.

The kind we so desperately need to hear.

T HE FIRST LITTLE MIRACLE was Margarito himself. Left alone in that
hospital, his body fought the poison. He did not die. The snake bite robbed
him of growth between his ankle and foot, and he limped badly, but he lived.

The second little miracle is a group of U.S. surgeons, who came through San
Cristobal, Verapaz, in 1989 and noticed this cute kid with a bad limp who seemed
to live in the hospital, playing in the halls or throwing a ball outside. His parents,
they were told, could not be found. This is Guatemala, remember, not Henry Ford
Hospital.

The surgeons fell in love with the kid — he ate with them, played with them
— and while they couldn't take him to America without visas, they got
organizations to continue the search for his family. That led to the third little
miracle: The parents were found.

"Did you recognize your father after all those years?" Margarito is asked.

"Yes," he says. "And my mother."

The fourth little miracle is the humanitarian Michigan outfit called Healing

The Children, which brings in kids from Third World countries who need medical help unavailable in their homelands. It was under their wing that Margarito traveled to America last summer and began a treatment for his bum leg that can only be described as unbelievable. It is called Ilizarov. It was invented by a Russian surgeon. It involves pins and wires that are put through the bone and adjusted with pressure on an outside apparatus. That pressure eventually pulls the bone apart, allowing spontaneous new bone growth to fill the gap.

Make a short leg longer.

Make a dead leg grow.

I guess you'd call that the fifth miracle.

DURING HIS TIME HERE, MARGARITO has been living with a foster family, Doreen and Jon Lawrence of Sterling Heights. He had the same effect on them as he's had on nearly everyone: He melted them like wax. They held him. Kissed him. Sat with him as he marveled at TV. Once, they found him, sitting inside the car, hypnotized by the dashboard.

During his treatment, the Lawrences took Margarito to a Junior Red Wings game at Joe Louis. He was so excited by the action, he bounced in his seat. They went back. And back again. "When we found out Margarito would be going home soon, we called and asked if he could meet the players," Doreen says.

Next thing they knew, two of the players were at the house, teaching him how to hold a stick and how to take a slap shot. The following morning, Margarito was at the rink as a special guest. He sat in at team meetings. He went out when they skated. A Spanish-speaking kid from the hills of Guatemala, sliding around on center ice.

Margarito's "bad" leg is now two inches longer than his good one. "This way, he'll grow into his right size," Doreen says. When I ask how they know what his "right size" is, she says doctors "worked with a Polaroid of Margarito and his father. They estimated his adult height from that."

A Polaroid?

Margarito travels back to Guatemala in a few days. His parents will be waiting. If all goes well, this kid, left for dead with a snakebite, will jump back onto a life that tried to throw him. All because a handful of people, none of whom made a penny off this, saw the one thing left on this planet that nobody seems to argue over: a child who needs help.

You watch this kid kiss his foster mother. You watch him grab a hockey stick and try to swing it. You think about a village in Guatemala and an ice rink in Detroit. And you realize, if there's a way to connect those two places, there's a way to do just about anything.

Everyone is a childhood friend
November 21, 1993

T HERE'S A LINE FROM the Movie "Stand By Me," a line written by
Stephen King, which says, "I never had any friends like the ones I had
when I was 12 years old."

I have thought about that line a lot recently. It seems more true than ever.

Like most of you, I've made many friends as an adult. They are, in my eyes,
wonderful people. Great senses of humor. Admirable. Compassionate.

But I realize this: I have never wrestled them in the basement. I have never
locked their arms and rolled down a grassy hill. I have never grasped them from
behind on a bicycle seat, or lain on top of them on a sled. I have never really
touched them, except to shake hands or pat their backs. I am restrained. I am
polite. I am an adult. I keep my distance.

I think that has something to do with why the friends we make in our grown-
up years are never as close as the ones we make as kids. The things we share are
cerebral. We talk. We joke. But we don't play tag or buddy-up in a swimming
pool. We don't sneak into the fridge and scoop frosting with our fingers.

We are connected as adults, but not intertwined. It's the difference between
the insides of an organized closet and the insides of a high school locker. The
first is put together. The second is, by nature, all over itself.

We were all over ourselves as kids.

And then we grew up.

H OW MANY TIMES HAVE YOU heard this sentence? "Whenever I see (fill in
name), even if we haven't seen each other in years, it's like we haven't
missed a beat, we just pick up where we left off."

Childhood friends, right?

Isn't it strange? If you add up the total years you spend as a child, taking
away your baby years, it's what? Fourteen? Fifteen? Most of us have been
"adults" at least twice as long as that, some of us even 40 or 50 years. We can
drive from place to place. We can fly, we can use the phone freely, we can fax,
we can telegram — all these means of communication we never had as children.

And yet, something is lacking in our adult friends, as great as they are, that
certain closeness with the chums of our youth.

I have an idea what it is. For one thing, with adult friends, you talk about
money, cars, careers, who's making what; you talk about what a good deal you
got on this or that. We never talked about deals when we were kids. What kind of
deals? Someone got his Popsicle cheaper than we did?

Also, adults come in pairs. There are often wives to go with the husbands, and husbands to go with the wives. You can like one and not like the other, but chances are that friendship won't last.

And, of course, there's the time factor. Most adult friends have jobs and families. So plans must be made. Fun must be scheduled. The friendship is compartmentalized to evenings and weekends.

But that's still not the biggest reason.

THE BIGGEST REASON IS THIS: As children, we didn't know it all. Experiences were new. Emotions were fresh. And we discovered them with our friends.

We learned to fear the teacher with our friends right beside us. We learned the thrill of snowfall with our friends right beside us. Our first boy-girl kiss games, our first concerts, our first time driving the car without Mom or Dad — our friends were right beside us. We can look at them today and burst out laughing, or crying, or just shaking our heads at the simplest thing.

Because when we see them, we see ourselves.

We see ourselves in simpler times, when we didn't have a mortgage, a boss or a plane to catch. We like the image. We want to cherish it. So we cherish them.

It's funny. Growing up, my childhood gathering place was the curb near my house. In the heat of a restless summer afternoon, in the cool sunset of an after-school evening, my friends and I would sit on that curb, talking about the future.

And now that I'm older, doing all those things we talked about, you know what I miss the most?

The curb.

That's what I see when I see my old friends. I am embraced by memory. I am home. This week is Thanksgiving, a chance for many of us to reconnect with old pals. And for those who do, the conversations will be more emotional, the laughter will be more robust.

Stephen King wrote a follow-up sentence to that quote I mentioned, the one that reads, "I never had any friends like the ones I had when I was 12 years old." The sentence is this: "Jesus, does anyone?"

I know the answer. The answer is no.

Prom night: Dress for excess
May 1, 1994

W AIT A MINUTE, TEENAGERS. Not so fast. Come back here with that fashion article printed in this very newspaper just two days ago, the one with the headline "PROM-ising Alternatives" that dealt with new ways to dress for your high school prom without looking traditional, which is to say, a dweeb.

Gimme that paper!

Riiip … swiiip … shrshhh …

There now.

Have a seat. I'm afraid to say, teenagers, that while that article was very interesting and educational, it was, and we admit this with deep regret, A GIANT TYPO! That's right. One big mistake. It's quite embarrassing, really. Something must have gotten in our printing presses, I don't know, maybe one of the shop guy's tools, like a wrench or a bottle of Wild Turkey, and it wiggled around and, well, gosh, by some freak of nature, actually printed out an article that said, "When choosing your prom wardrobe, you should remain true to yourself. If you've never worn a tie in your life … don't dig one up just for the prom. … If it's stressful, don't do it."

Heh-heh.

You thought we meant that?

Kids. Come on. Do you believe Bart Simpson is a real person, too? Stress is the essence of a prom. Along with wearing bad ties, stupid dresses and a flower that costs as much as your CD collection. The truth is, proms were invented years ago by nuclear scientists to create a 24-hour period of total panic and misery, so as to simulate something you will face very shortly, namely, the rest of your life.

Can we talk about clothes?

I KNOW THAT IN THAT PREVIOUS article, you thought you read these words: "Forget about what's appropriate. Maybe the guys wear sequins and the girls wear combat boots. Think flowers, think love beads … "

Amazing what a little Wild Turkey will do, isn't it?

No, teenagers, I'm sorry to say, you can't think flowers or love beads when dressing or the prom. You can't think combat boots, or sequins for guys, unless you attend Elton John's old high school.

No. You must think — and please memorize these words — "miserable" and "uncomfortable" and "total dweebdom." You will dress this way, because WE had to dress this way, and our PARENTS had to dress this way, and that's ALL

THERE IS TO IT!

Men — and I call you men because, after prom night, you'll feel like men, once you finish throwing up — your dress is simple: a powder-blue tuxedo, powder-blue bow tie, ruffled white shirt and powder-blue shoes.

What's that? Not cool? HAHAHA! Did you hear that, Irv? Sid? Morty? The kid said it's ... not cool! AWWWWWWWWWW!

Shut up and put it on.

Now, women — and I call you women because, after prom night, you will feel like women, once you watch the guys throw up — your outfits are more varied. True, you must wear the traditional black velvet dress and a big corsage and high heels that make you walk like Pee-wee Herman doing his "Tequila" dance — but, hey, you get an option!

With straps, or without.

OK. Who's driving?

THIS IS A BIG PART OF the prom because, inevitably, there's the tender moment where you and your date wave good-bye to your parents as you screech out of the driveway, and your mother sobs, "There goes our baby" and your father sobs, "There goes my car."

Once you arrive at the prom, however, be prepared for nontraditional things, such as finding the punch bowl or trying to dance in a powder-blue tuxedo. (SAFETY NOTE: Men. Do not attempt any funky moves, no matter what the music. The only man alive who can dance funky in powder blue is James Brown, and he's not doing proms anymore.)

As the night progresses, you will feel sweaty beneath your tuxedo, your tie will fall off, plus your toes will be killing you. And you women who chose strapless, you see why that was a mistake.

This is part of the tradition. So is running to the bathroom every five minutes to stare in the mirror ("I can't believe it! I look like a dweeb!") and doing the slow dance at the end of the night, after which, you and your friends drive into the moonlight, someplace at least an hour away, and engage in the ancient prom ritual of throwing up and passing out.

Then you come home.

Cheer up. This is the best part. Because now you actually get to TAKE OFF THE CLOTHES, which feels slightly better than getting out of a Turkish prison. And you swear you will never dress like that again.

And — ta-da! — you can now relate to your parents. After you explain why their car is in a ditch. Also, you have learned this lesson: Never trust a prom article that contains the sentence, "Be proud of your nose ring."

And stay away from Wild Turkey.

What do you think they put in the punch?

Good, and dead

May 15, 1994

I CAME HOME THE OTHER DAY to find my garage strangely empty. The bicycles were gone, the golf clubs and tennis rackets were missing. It took a few hazy moments before it hit me: I'd been robbed.

This has happened before. And the initial reaction is always the same: anger. How could someone do this? How could someone have the gall to think that what I owned, what I'd worked for, was theirs for the taking?

This column is about that question — but not about that crime. I will get over the missing items.

Stella Sproule is not so lucky.

Sproule, by all accounts, was the most important currency of our city, a young black woman who put herself through college, found work and didn't feel the world owed her anything. She went to church regularly, had a spotless record and was well-liked by her colleagues.

It is the reason she is gone today, the reason her body was put in the ground with dressed-up bullet holes.

People die for all kinds of wrong things in this town.

Stella Sproule died for her name.

THE WOMAN WHO ALLEGEDLY had Sproule killed is Annie Cole, 32, a through-the-looking-glass version of the victim. Unlike Sproule, Cole had a criminal record — forged checks, fraud. She was wanted for violating parole.

Rather than pay for what she'd done, Cole allegedly came up with an idea: kill herself. Not by taking her own life. No. True to a forger's ways, she wanted someone else to pay her freight.

Enter Stella Sproule. For a brief period of time, at an auto supply company in Sterling Heights, Cole and Sproule had worked together. Cole noticed Sproule's spotless record and solid reputation, and allegedly decided to become Stella, take her name, her identification, as if someone else's life is something you can just pull on like a sweater.

One problem: The real Stella was still around. So Cole allegedly called some teens, including her 16-year-old nephew, and offered them $5,000 apiece to kill Sproule and leave the body where it could be found. Without even asking for the money up front, the nephew and his friend did this crime. They did it by forcing Sproule into a car and driving to an abandoned building. This comes from the police report.

So does this, in the nephew's own words:

"I told her to face the wall. I then put the gun to her head. ... I then shot. I then shot her again. Then I shot her again. Then we left.

"The next day, I went over to Ann's house. She asked if I thought Stella was dead. I told her that I didn't know. She told me that if Stella isn't dead, leave her there a few days and she will be."

They waited. Meanwhile, Cole allegedly got a jump on her new identity by using Stella's credit cards on a little shopping spree. After a few days, the impatient nephew called police and said he'd found a body, come quick.

When police arrived, Annie Cole was already at the building, claiming to be "Betty" Cole, a sister of Annie, whom she said she heard was dead. Believing her, police showed her the corpse and asked her to identify it.

What a moment. There was Cole, looking at the bullet-ridden body of a woman she had known, a good person, and someone she might well have had killed. This, apparently, was the sum of her guilt. She told the officers: "That's Annie."

POLICE TURNED THE CORPSE over to Cole, who made arrangements for cremation. The thought that Cole might not only have had Stella Sproule murdered but then was given her body is too disturbing to think about.

Fortunately, police smelled something rotten. They dug deeper, got confessions, and a few days later made arrests, including Cole, who had already fled to Mississippi. Stella Sproule's body was returned to her real family. She was buried 11 days after she was shot. Her loved ones still can't figure out what she did wrong.

The answer is nothing. All she did wrong was be everything right.

And another victim goes in the ground. We are reaching new lows in human behavior in our city, from children killed for sneakers to a war hero welcomed home with a murder for his insurance money. This is more than crime. It's an astounding decay in respect for life.

And please. Don't tell me about tough economic conditions. There have been tough economic conditions throughout history, and people still didn't kill their neighbors and slip into their skin. The unthinkable is now thinkable, and the only crimes not committed are the ones that haven't been thought up.

And meanwhile, someone must explain to Sproule's family how being good got her shot in the head.

You try to be wise. Understanding. But the anger boils. I look around an empty garage and feel fortunate to be robbed. It's out of control. Beyond belief. They can take anything now, your body, your name, anything they want.

Barbra, by Matt Michaels

May 22, 1994

H E ALMOST ALWAYS HAS A CIGARETTE in his mouth, if not that, a sucking candy, and he walks around the room blowing smoke or making tongue-clucking sounds and listening, always listening, because that is what a good teacher does. Listens. Now and then, he'll interrupt with a correction, or write something down, maybe show you how to play it. He makes it seem simple, and when you get frustrated, he'll blow a cloud of smoke, grin and say, "Relax. It takes two or three weeks to become a jazz musician."

Matt Michaels is a piano teacher, the best I've ever met, and I've met quite a few. He has a gray beard and glasses and he's lived here all of his 61 years and he plays in clubs and oversees classes in everything from combos to orchestras as director of Jazz Studies at Wayne State. But in the hours before and after, he does what he does best, he teaches, one on one, in his small, cramped office or a piano room of a suburban high school.

Weekdays. Saturday afternoons. Students coming in late, students going out. It is not glamorous.

It is not, say, Barbra Streisand.

But once it was.

B ACK WHEN STREISAND WAS a young, unknown nightclub singer, she came to Detroit to play the Caucus Club. Michaels was the house pianist.

He was a pro, so he didn't appreciate when the 18-year-old Streisand showed up late for gigs. The club owner kept booking her, however, and part of Michaels' job was to work with her. He didn't get paid for this. He did it anyhow. Week after week, month after month, giving her a repertoire, teaching her to sing in time. He got her work doing commercials. He wrote arrangements for songs. One of these she took to New York and used on "The Tonight Show," one of her early breaks.

Although Michaels wasn't fond of Streisand's aggressive manner — when someone offered to buy her a drink, she'd say, "No, but you can buy me a meal" — he recognized her talent and knew he was helping to develop something special. Maybe, in his heart, he felt when the world embraced her, he'd be embraced, too.

Instead, after nine months, Streisand left Detroit for Broadway, took all of Michaels' arrangements, music charts, imparted knowledge.

And never spoke to him again.

The years passed. Streisand became the biggest female star in the business.

Michaels stayed in Detroit, played the London Chop House, the now-defunct Playboy Club. He worked with artists such as Peggy Lee and Joe Williams, but they always left and he always stayed, playing, teaching. He came to Wayne State in 1979. Thousands of musicians have now been influenced by his guidance. Piano players swear by him. Maybe he could have been famous in his own right; instead, his passion comes in finding scholarship money for students.

And up to last week, if you asked him about Streisand, how she never even thanked him, he'd shrug and say, "That's the way she is."

STREISAND'S CURRENT TOUR IS the rage of the music business, with sellouts from London to LA. When Detroit was announced as a stop, I asked Michaels if he planned to see his ex-singer. He said no.

But last week, some guys in Streisand's orchestra dropped by Arriva restaurant in Warren, where Michaels works on Wednesday nights, and they said he should come. And the next day, Streisand's personal assistant called, and said Barbra would have invited him earlier, but he was "so hard to find."

Michaels laughs. "I'm in the phone book."

Tickets were left for Michaels and his wife of 35 years, Kaye. They got dressed up, and they went. Streisand announced Matt during the concert, and when the show ended, he and Kaye were taken backstage to see the star.

"She hugged me," Michaels says. "She said it was good to see me, and that she still uses some of my arrangements.

"We only talked for a few minutes. I wanted to talk more, but people kept interrupting, you know, introducing themselves."

Michaels, never much for that, quickly said good night and left. There is no jealousy, he says. "I couldn't deal with that kind of life. All I ever wanted was to make a living, play good music, pass on a few things … "

Streisand's concert features state-of-the-art production, film clips, Donna Karan dresses, a light show, $20 programs, tickets up to $1,000. It will gross millions of dollars, spawn an album, TV specials, you name it.

Yet as she left the Palace in her limousine Thursday night, and Matt Michaels went back to his cramped classroom, cigarettes and sucking candies, it is a toss-up as to who has done more for the honorable future of music.

Actually, it's no contest.

Freedom exits stage left

June 5, 1994

T HIS IS A GREAT COUNTRY, founded on great principles. But sometimes you wonder who's steering the ship. Take the case of Don Bondi, a 61-year-old teacher at Los Angeles' High School for the Arts.

Bondi was passionate about his job, was chairman of the dance department and was one of the working founders of the school.

Until six weeks ago.

At a student play, celebrating Mexican heritage, a young actor portrayed the governor of California, Pete Wilson, as a bumbling racist.

"I love Mexicans," the student playing the governor said. "Everyone should have one. … I even shop at K-Martinez, I mean Kmart. And I love Pick-N-Spick."

Bondi was in the audience, and he objected. He had this odd notion that high school students shouldn't use a play to defame the governor of the state. Call him crazy.

He booed when it was over.

He wasn't the only one. But he caught the eye of Maria Elena Gaitan, a Latino school board member whose son happened to be in the play. She got out of her seat and stormed over to Bondi.

"Control your racism!" she ordered.

Control your racism. Never mind that the show played the governor as a typically ignorant white buffoon. Gaitan's message was clear. You're in deep trouble, Bondi. You booed. You stepped over the line.

"If we've offended anyone … " a student on stage, sensing trouble, began to say.

"You have!" Bondi yelled.

"Then you needed it!" Gaitan shouted.

When the play ended, Gaitan escorted Bondi to the principal's office. Her son reportedly followed and threatened to physically harm Bondi, a student threatening to beat up a teacher.

Nonetheless, within hours, Bondi, the teacher, was given his papers and ordered off campus. He was reassigned to a desk job.

This is America in 1994.

P OLITICAL CORRECTNESS HAS RECEIVED enormous attention lately. There is a growing sense that tyranny of the majority has turned to tyranny of the minority. The slightest slip of the tongue can cost a person job, life-style and reputation. People complain they can't communicate anymore, that every word seems off-limits, and every group, from race to age to sexual preference, seems quick to scream prejudice for anything that doesn't go its way.

What gives, they ask? You can no longer call teams "Indians." The phrase "dutch treat" is culturally biased. In London, a school principal recently turned down tickets for her students to see "Romeo and Juliet" because she considered it — and we're not making this up — a "blatantly heterosexual love story."

Blatantly heterosexual?

Now, in general, I say grin and bear this stuff. It's the price we pay for being insensitive for so long, kind of like enduring a long tilt of an airplane that flew off course and needs to correct itself.

But in Bondi's case, I object, strongly, because one important principle is being used to squash another. And it's especially significant because it takes place at a school, a place of learning, where, supposedly, our young generation is being formed.

What are we teaching them here?

BONDI WAS PROBABLY RIGHT TO BOO. The play sounds awful, not to mention insulting. But more important, he had the right to boo. He didn't demand the play be stopped. He expressed opinion after it was over. "I booed," he told a Los Angeles Times reporter, "because I wanted to make a point. ... We are not here to defame people. ... Besides, booing is part of the theater."

Nonetheless, his principal, Bo Vitolo, reassigned Bondi to another school, saying: "Freedom of expression has limitations. Otherwise we would have anarchy."

Huh? This is a school whose students just portrayed the governor as a stumbling racist? She thinks a teacher booing will lead to anarchy?

And you wonder why people home-school their kids.

Listen. Freedom of expression is as integral to the fabric of this nation as equality of its citizens. In truth, they go hand in hand. Gaitan rushing up to Bondi and yelling, "Control your racism!" is merely an example of the very thing to which she's objecting. His answer, quite rightly, could have been, "Control your control!"

Instead, he is banished to a desk job while officials review the case. And Gaitan still sits on the school board.

What a strange world we have created. The funny thing is, the students should be thanking Bondi for some valuable lessons. Not only did he make a point about freedom of speech, he prepared them for their futures.

If that's the best play they can come up with, they'd better get used to boos.

Rosa Parks, twice a symbol

September 4, 1994

H EY, AREN'T YOU ROSA PARKS." It was a sentence she had heard a million times before, usually followed by a handshake, a hug and congratulations for her historic deeds.

Now she was in a red bathrobe, it was nighttime, and she had come downstairs to find this strange man in her home. Still, there had never been any evil — and it had been nearly 40 years — that followed when a fellow black American said, "Hey, aren't you Rosa Parks?"

So Rosa Parks answered, "Yes."

The man took her money, whacked her in the face, whacked her in the chest, and left.

Once a symbol, twice a symbol. When Parks refused to give her seat to a white passenger on an Alabama bus in 1955, she emblematized the civil rights movement: a simple quest for dignity by blacks in a white society.

Now, at 81, she emblematizes something else: a simple quest for dignity by blacks in their own community, by old people in a young world, by the nonviolent in a violent place.

Once a symbol, twice a symbol. There are those who wish that Parks' assailant had been white, some guy in a sheet and hood. That would have been easy. Draw the old lines. The oppressed vs. the oppressor.

But these are not the old lines. Rosa Parks' accused attacker was a 28-year-old black male who had the right to vote, the right to education, the right to work and to legal action against discrimination. Had he tried to make his life better, he'd have found scholarships available because of his race, and jobs designated for minority hires only. All these things exist largely because of the woman he whacked.

It didn't matter. He was hooked on drugs, he wanted money, and the only thing that might have stopped him was something he didn't have.

Respect.

Which, ironically, is what Rosa Parks has always been about.

L AST JANUARY, THE REV. JESSE JACKSON hosted a conference in Washington. The subject was crime. Black-on-black crime. The numbers on this are depressing, beginning with the fact that half the murder victims in this country are African American.

"Fratricide is no THREAT to the status quo!" Jackson bellowed. "If the oppressed descend into self-destruction, the oppressor will permit it. …

"The power will not come from the WHITE House or the COURTHOUSE, but from YOUR house and MY house!"

These houses, sadly, include many in cities such as Detroit, Washington and Atlanta, houses that are barred and double-locked, with handguns next to beds. The people inside do not fear rich white men banging down their door. They fear their own. Jackson was right about who's going to fix this. Not the status quo — meaning the comfortable majority. They can stay out of the deadly loop.

This is the loop. Crime is tied to poverty. Poverty is tied to education. Education to parents. Parents to values: staying in school, avoiding drugs, being there for your kids, and yes, respecting others enough not to harm them. Who is teaching these things?

As the attack on Parks made headlines in Detroit, in Chicago, an 11-year-old black youth killed a 14-year-old black girl as part of a gang initiation. Three days later, the boy was killed by his own gang members. Two shots. Back of the head. The suspects are ages 16 and 14. The gang's name: Black Disciples.

We are losing our most prized possessions. They are being gunned down by each other.

LET'S FACE IT. An 11-year-old is not inherently evil. He is what he is taught. The one in Chicago was taken from his mother at age 3, after police found cigarette burns and whip marks on his body. Where can that lead?

The Chicago murders — and the Parks case — show the depths to which people sink without alternatives. And it should make critics think twice about opposing parts of the new crime bill that spend money for community services and projects rather than jails. Think of that 11-year-old. If he could be taught something so incredible as cold-blooded murder, imagine the possibilities if steered in the right direction.

We are in this together. White citizens should feel no satisfaction here. Violence is violence; it will eat us all one day. Still, as Jackson said, black-on-black crime must ultimately be addressed by the black community. In a city where the mayor and police chief are both black, it is hard to blame crime on discrimination.

No. More and more, crime is about respect — or the lack of it — for life, for community, for the old and defenseless. For yourself. Rosa Parks was only seeking respect when she refused to move on that bus; that led to the most important social action of our time. Now, with puffy bruises on her aged body, we can only hope that her magic as a symbol is not gone. Another cause awaits.

Radio: All alike, all the time

March 19, 1995

T ALLAHASSEE, FLA. — Well, it's official. America is down to six radio stations. Six. Total. I say this because, having spent the last few days traveling though Detroit, Dayton, Atlanta, Charlotte, Orlando and Tallahassee, I have heard them all, the same six stations.

Over and over.

Half the fun of traveling used to be renting a car, starting the engine and flicking the knob to the local airwaves. Depending on which part of the country you were in, you might hear Murray the K, from New York City, screaming about the Beatles, or some laid-back, West Coast-type saying, "Can you dig it?" or some hillbilly named Chester Winchester spinning a country song with a title like "I'm So Lonely, The Dog Looks Good" and crowing "All-rahhhty-rooski, fo'ks, ah know y'all gonna like this one."

The thing was, Chester did know. Because he was from there. He broadcast from a tower on the outskirts of town, and if he played something people liked, they told him so the next morning at the coffee shop or the hardware store. Or they called him during his nine-hour shift.

"Hey, Chester? This here's Luke from over Stillwater County. Play that slow one by Hank Williams again, will ya? I'm trying to get Doris here to marry me … "

Nowadays, Chester doesn't pick the music. It comes down from some consulting firm that programs hundreds of stations just like it. The big, powerful record companies push the product they want sold. The playlist is faxed from headquarters. The disc jockeys — now called "radio personalities" — don't have accents, or input.

And Chester doesn't work there anymore.

H ERE ARE THE SIX RADIO STATIONS you will find no matter where you go in this country:

1) Morning Zoo/Top 40. This one features a couple of "crazy" guys with catchy names — Mike & Ike, Chip N' Dale, Jim & the Mad Man — who sound as if they're talking through their noses. They scream, do impersonations, ring buzzers and bells, and, most of all, in between Madonna songs, laugh at their own jokes. Because nobody else will.

2) Classic Rock. You'll know this station because it plays "Cold As Ice" by Foreigner once every 13 minutes. In between, you will hear Fleetwood Mac, Heart, Led Zeppelin and other groups we should have blown up in the '70s when

we had the chance. Classic Rock is the younger half of …

3) Oldies Rock. I remember one of the first oldies stations, down in Miami. It played doo-wop tunes from the Spaniels, the Del-Vikings, the Crests. It was unique and small. Nowadays there is an Oldies Station every traffic light, playing the same Beatles/Chubby Checker/Temptations records over and over, in a desperate attempt to convince those of us old enough to remember these songs that we are still hip.

Which we aren't.

4) Young Country. Once upon a time, country stations gave you the best feel for America. Small-time country artists could make a record in their garage and drive it to the stations themselves. And the disc jockeys were important to the isolated farmers who tuned them in.

"Ah'm gonna play a new one fuh ya from Tammy Wynette in jus' a second, but first, ah see there's a thundah-storm a-comin', so y'all better finish plantin' early this mo'nin' … "

Nowadays, country music is a giant, billion-dollar industry that has its own awards shows, theme parks and mega-stars. I saw Garth Brooks meeting with Newt Gingrich last week to discuss the arts. Garth Brooks and Newt Gingrich? What kind of charm can country radio have after that?

5) Easy Listening/Soft Rock. It doesn't really matter what music these stations play because you are asleep halfway through the song. The only human contact you get is a voice, which sounds like it just finished making love, crooning the phrase, "Less talk, more music." The polar opposite of this, of course, is …

6) All Talk/News/Information. These stations have the constant sound of typewriters in the background as a deep voice bellows, "All news, all the time." In between, they have a) Rush Limbaugh, b) Paul Harvey, c) updates by accent-less clones who sound like they're trying out for CNN.

YOU LISTEN TO ANY OF THESE stations in Louisiana or in Maine, it's the same thing. Radio has fallen into the Homogenization of America, as have airports, which now all feature TCBY Yogurt and Cinn-a-bon shops, and shopping malls, which all contain the same Gap and Athlete's Foot stores. Whatever happened to local identity? Regional flavor? Pretty soon five companies will own the whole country, and each will have 200 radio stations, sounding exactly the same, and there won't be a lot of point in traveling because wherever you go, you'll be home.

You know what? I miss Chester. I really do.

No one took advantage of Chung

May 28, 1995

WHEN CONNIE CHUNG WAS GIVEN ONE of the most powerful jobs in America, she didn't ask questions. She took it. She didn't care that she was made co-anchor of the "CBS Evening News" mostly because CBS wanted to beat NBC to the punch of hiring a woman. She never said, "That's the wrong reason to hire me."

Ratings were at stake. She took advantage.

When Chung chased a sleazy skater named Tonya Harding halfway around the world, desperate to be first to interview her, she made no apologies. She didn't say: "This isn't news. It's beneath someone of my position." She was right there, sucking up.

Ratings were at stake. She took advantage.

When Chung did specials such as "Life in the Fat Lane," when she went on her husband Maury Povich's tabloid TV show to promote herself, when she jackhammered her last shred of integrity by promising "just between you and me" to Newt Gingrich's mother, then airing her comments anyhow — she showed no hesitation. She thought it was hot stuff.

Ratings were at stake.

She took advantage.

So why on Earth should anyone feel sorry for Chung after CBS last week booted her off its news show and left Dan Rather to go solo? Chung cried foul. She said it was sexist.

But it was all about ratings.

Which got her the job in the first place.

WHAT A JOKE THIS NETWORK NEWS business has become. As Andy Rooney said, "It's four-and-a-half minutes' worth of reading."

I listen to Chung and Rather debate journalism, and I have the same reaction as most lesser-paid, harder-working members of this business: When was the last time those two got their hands dirty?

When was the last time Rather or Chung had to scrounge with the pack for an interview, or pore through phone books for sources, or badger police to get a quote?

The handful of times Rather and Chung leave the CBS building, it's with an armada of producers, previously arranged interviews and luxury hotels.

So the whole notion that any of this is hard work is ridiculous.

Still, within the framework of that, Chung takes the cake. Dan Rather — who reportedly is as egotistical as the best of them — at least once upon a time did some serious correspondent work. Chung, outside of a brief stint covering Washington in the '70s, made her ascent through anchoring local TV news — in LA and New York — and local TV news is the most cosmetic of media, always more concerned with the right blend of sex, race and age in its announcers. Chung was a jackpot. She moved up fast.

Sure, once she got to the top, she could have made an impact. But Chung seemed more interested in becoming one of the celebrities she profiled. She made People magazine's cover with her desire to have a baby, yet it's hard to think of a single important story she helped unearth at CBS, or a single probing interview — unless you count the time Marlon Brando jerked her around.

Sure, much of the fluff she chased was what her bosses wanted at CBS.

Fluff is ratings. It's ironic that the weekly "Eye to Eye" — her attempt at substance — failed miserably against "Seinfeld," a show that will do a half hour on chicken soup.

But such is American TV. Last week, Liz Smith, the gossip columnist, penned a heartfelt "open letter" to Chung. In it, she suggested, "Go back to being Connie Charm. Do your jokes, do your interviews … leave the serious stuff to Dan and the news division. … There is so much bad news these days. … You, Connie, could be the antidote."

Liz Smith advising Connie Chung. Perfect.

NOW, THIS WHOLE LITTLE DRAMA is hardly new. Remember Deborah Norville? NBC rushed her sexy looks into the "Today" show in place of Jane Pauley — Norville didn't object, by the way — then later dumped her.

Norville, who maintained that she was hired for her intelligence and reporting skills, soon tumbled into oblivion. She now hosts "Inside Edition."

Which she insists "is not a tabloid show."

Geez. You want them all to put a sock in it. In Britain, the people who read you the news each night are called "news readers." They are not famous. They are not celebrities. They read off a TelePrompTer, and that is all they're given credit for. No more, no less.

We lack that sensibility. And so Chung's story is some big deal. It shouldn't be. She didn't get where she was by being an expert in foreign affairs, nor by writing books, nor by grilling false icons the way Edward R. Murrow once did to Joseph McCarthy.

Chung got there because her ratings were good. And she is out because the ratings were bad.

The only mystery is why that is hard for her — of all people — to understand.

A famous love story
September 17, 1995

NEWS ITEM: After selling 10 million copies worldwide, "Bridges of Madison County" finally falls off the New York Times best-seller list, ending a near-record 162-week run.

MADISON COUNTY, IOWA — She looked at him long and hard, and he looked at her. From across the kitchen, they were locked into each other's souls, solidly, intimately. When she breathed, she could smell him, and her nostrils quivered with his manhood.

"I want to make love," she whispered.

He grinned. Through his blue work shirt his taut muscles rolled like thunder. He was the shaman. She was his muse. He grabbed the salt shaker from the wooden table.

"Want to try it … pretzel style?" he said.

Francesca blushed, the blush of a schoolgirl. For these blissful four days — it felt like 162 weeks — she had been filled by him, this handsome stranger, Robert Kincaid, photographer-writer from Bellingham, Wash., who drove an old truck named Harry. She bathed in his love, like soft oil from the hands of a god.

He was a god. How else could she explain it? He was the lion, and she was the cub. He was the eagle, she was the chick. He was the cow, she was the … well, you get the idea.

"Yes," she said softly. "Pretzel style. I've always wanted … but I never—"

"Shhh," he said, putting a finger to his lips. Since that fateful moment four days ago — it felt like 162 weeks — they had made love everywhere, in the den, in the barn, in his knapsack.

Now he stirred again, another slow tango, he moved toward her—

Rrrring.

She let it ring, not wanting the mood to end. "Oh, Robert Kincaid!" she wanted to cry out. "You are the moon, I am the stars, you are—"

Rrrring.

"Go ahead," he whispered, "answer it."

She lifted the phone. "Yes? … oh, God . …."

He stared at her. She dropped the phone.

"The … best-seller's list," she choked. "We're … off."

THE WORDS HIT HIM like an arrow through the heart. He stumbled backward and had to grab to keep from falling. His hand struck something and it fell and shattered.

"You klutz," Francesca said.

"What?"

"You can't move without knocking something over. That was my husband's favorite bowling trophy. Man, is he gonna be steamed!"

She inhaled, her nostrils filling with his manhood. "By the way," she said, "how about taking a shower?"

He blinked. Before him was no longer a goddess, but a middle-aged housewife in the same blue dress she'd been wearing since they met. "Don't you own any other clothes?" he asked. "Like something from this century?"

"Oh, listen to Mr. Fashion Plate."

"Hey, I'm not the one cheating on my husband."

"Well, thank God we used protection. Lord knows where you've been before me."

He sighed. She sighed. He was the bow, she was the quiver, but now they felt like an arrow stuck in mud. He went to the window. He looked out longingly, at the flat green landscape, the low branches, the Dairy Queen.

"My God," he said, "I'm in … Iowa."

S HE STARED AT HIM, hoping to see her shaman. But all she saw was a broken-down photographer with no health insurance.

He stared at her, longing for his angel. Instead, he remembered that her meat loaf gave him heartburn.

"Uh, I gotta be going," he said.

"So soon?" she said.

"I'll leave in the morning."

"Maybe this afternoon would be better. Less traffic."

"You're right. Less traffic."

"I'll go with you, to the edge of town."

They drove in silence to the bridge where they fell in love — and ran smack into 300 cars, all tourists from out of state. A police officer leaned in the window. "Sorry, folks. You'll have to detour. There's five weddings scheduled for this bridge today."

"Five weddings?"

"Ever since that dang book came out. You might want to grab some coffee at the Bridges of Madison County Cafe. I hear it's about to close. They got the Bridges of Madison County T-shirts there, reduced to half-price. And the Bridges of Madison County CD, they're selling that for a buck."

Francesca and Robert drove to the edge of town. She got out of the car.

"Well, see ya, adulteress," he said.

"Not if I see you first."

"Slut."

"Loser."

And off he drove, into the dying sunset. He was the oatmeal and she was the lump. It's funny, Francesca thought, how love changes when it isn't a best-seller, and she vowed that next time she would hold out for Mel Gibson.